CARNEGIE LIBRARY
LIVINGSTONE COLLEGE
SALISBURY, NC 28144

W9-AFF-595

Theoretical Criminology

Theoretical Criminology

Fourth Edition

by the late
George B. Vold,
Thomas J. Bernard,
and
Jeffrey B. Snipes

New York   Oxford
Oxford University Press
1998

Oxford University Press

Oxford New York Athens Aukland
Bangkok Bogota Bombay Buenos Aires
Calcutta Cape Town Dar es Salaam Delhi
Florence Hong Kong Istanbul Karachi
Kuala Lumpur Madras Madrid Melbourne
Mexico City Nairobi Paris Singapore
Taipei Tokyo Toronto

and associated companies in

Berlin Ibadan

Copyright © 1998 by Oxford University Press, Inc.

Published by Oxford University Press, Inc.,
198 Madison Avenue, New York, New York 10016
Oxford is a registered trademark of Oxford University Press

All rights reserved. No part of this publication
may be reproduced, stored in a retrieval system, or transmitted
in any form or by any means, electronic, mechanical,
photocopying, recording, or otherwise, without the prior
permission of Oxford University Press.

Library of Congress Cataloging-in-Publication Data
Vold, George B. (George Bryan), 1896–1967.
Theoretical criminology / by George B. Vold, Thomas J. Bernard,
and Jeffrey B. Snipes.—4th ed.
p. cm.
Includes index.
ISBN 0–19–507321–5
1. Criminal anthropology. 2. Criminology. 3. Deviant behavior.
4. Social conflict. I. Bernard, Thomas J. II. Snipes, Jeffrey B.
III. Title.
HV6035.V6   1998
364.2—dc20   96–38306

1 3 5 7 9 8 6 4 2

Printed in the United States of America
on acid-free paper

Contents

Chapter Sixteen: Critical Criminology   260

Marxism and Marxist Criminology—Postmodernism and Postmodernist Criminology—Feminism and Feminist Criminology—Assessments of Critical Theories

Chapter Seventeen: Developmental Criminology   284

The Great Debate: Criminal Careers, Longitudinal Research, and the Relationship Between Age and Crime—Criminal Propensity vs. Criminal Career—The Transition to Developmental Criminology—Thornberry's Interactional Theory—Sampson and Laub's Age-Graded Theory of Informal Social Control—Conclusion

Chapter Eighteen: Integrated Theories   300

Elliott et al.'s Integrated Theory—Braithwaite's Theory of Reintegrative Shaming—Tittle's Control Balance Theory—Vila's General Paradigm—Bernard and Snipes's Integrated Model—Conclusion

Chapter Nineteen: Assessing Criminology Theory   316

Science, Theory, Research, and Policy—Individual Difference Theories—Structure/Process Theories—Theories of the Behavior of Criminal Law—Conclusion

Foreword to the Fourth Edition

It now has been eleven years since the publication of the third edition of *Theoretical Criminology*. The reasons for the long delay in publishing a fourth edition are interesting from the point of view of what this edition seeks to accomplish.

I first started working on a fourth edition in 1990, but that effort ground to a halt when I was about one-third done. The increasingly complex and interrelated nature of criminology theory had made it difficult for me to divide the field into a sequence of neat little boxes (chapters), as is required in a textbook. I eventually became dissatisfied with my proposed organization of the material but was unable to reconceptualize it at that point. In addition, I had eliminated too much of the older material so that I could present recent work more completely while maintaining the approximate size of the book. I eventually realized that the very completeness of my presentations, as well as the loss of the older material, would make the book less accessible and less useful to its readers.

This book's major contribution to the field of criminology has been that it provides a coherent, accurate, and accessible overview of theories in their historic and social context. I had lost the thread of this major contribution, so I abandoned my attempted revision and decided to come back to it later when I had a better sense of what I was doing.

At that same time, I was working on two issues related to the role of theory in criminology. In the process of working on successive editions of this book, I became convinced that criminology was failing to make scientific progress. For example, in each successive edition, I threw out quite a bit of material because, in my opinion, no one would be interested in it any more. But I had not thrown out any material because I thought it had been falsified. This suggests an astounding lack of scientific progress over a forty-year period of increasingly vigorous and sophisticated empirical research.

I originally presented my concerns about this situation in a 1990 article entitled "Twenty Years of Testing Theories: What Have We Learned and Why?" In that article, I took a Popperian approach, with an emphasis on how to falsify theories in order to get rid of them. At the same time, I was working on integrating criminology theories. In my view, integration is an alternative to falsification as a way to reduce the number of theories in criminology. Where I believed that falsification had largely failed because research misspecified the theories, I also believed that if the theories were properly specified, then a much broader integration among them would become apparent.

All these issues came together in a 1996 article on theoretical integration written with Jeff Snipes. This article abandons the Popperian emphasis on falsification and takes a "risk factor" approach that deals in structured probabilities. This highly integrative approach maintains a focus on the empirical adequacy of theories but moves policy implications to the forefront. It also makes clear that there has been considerable scientific progress in criminology, but it is not in the form of falsifying theories.

Jeff has joined me as coauthor in writing this fourth edition of *Theoretical Criminology*, and our new concluding chapter interprets the field of criminology in these terms. As coauthor, Jeff brings strong abilities to accurately summarize and organize existing criminology theory and research. Ultimately, this involves having a good intuitive sense of theories and how they operate. Beyond that, he brings a fresh perspective on the field of criminology and its current overall organization. This was one of the stumbling blocks in my initial attempt to revise this book, and Jeff solved a number of my problems with alacrity and simplicity. Finally, Jeff brings much better quantitative skills than I possess. These skills are a great deal more important today than they were in the past, and they will be increasingly important as criminology develops in the future.

The goal of this fourth edition, as it was with the second and third, is to bring the text completely up to date in a way that provides continuity with the earlier edition while introducing a great deal of new material. But beyond that, I believe that this edition also structures the book to accommodate the increasing complexity of the field of criminology and rate of change within it. With this edition, I believe that *The-*

oretical Criminology is well positioned to move into the future of criminology for some time to come.

We wish to thank Diana Fishbein for making extensive comments and suggestions on the biology chapter. We also wish to thank Wayne Osgood and Lynne Goodstein for reading and commenting on various sections of the book, and Kim Menard and Mark Motivans for reading and making comments on the entire draft. Any errors or omissions are, of course, the sole responsibility of the authors.

T. J. B.

State College, Pa.
March 1997

Theoretical Criminology

CHAPTER ONE

Theory and Crime

Criminology as a field of study has been well documented by a long line of excellent and distinguished textbooks, both European and American, going back many decades.[1] Most of these texts concentrate on presenting *facts* known about the subject of crime. For example, they discuss the extent and distribution of criminal behaviors in society; the characteristics of criminal law and procedure; the characteristics of criminals; and the history, structure, and functioning of the criminal justice system. The theoretical material presented in these texts is usually somewhat limited. Almost all texts review the major theories about the causes of criminal behavior, and some texts present other theoretical material such as sociology of law, philosophy of punishment, or theories of correctional treatment.

As a text in theoretical criminology, this book does not concentrate on presenting the facts known about crime, although at least some of those facts are presented in the various chapters. Instead, this book concentrates on the *theories* used to explain those facts. The theories

1. Some of the textbooks in general criminology that have been published since 1992 can be mentioned: John Tierney, *Criminology*, Prentice Hall, Englewood Cliffs, N.J., 1996; Sue Titus Reid, *Crime and Criminology*, 8th ed., Brown and Benchmark, Madison, 1996; Stephen E. Brown, Finn-Aage Esbensen, and Gilbert Geis, *Criminology: Explaining Crime and Its Context*, 2nd ed., Anderson, Cincinnati, 1995; Hugh D. Barlow, *Introduction to Criminology*, 7th ed., Addison-Wesley Educational Publishers, Reading, 1995; Frank Smalleger, *Criminology Today*, Prentice Hall, Englewood Cliffs, N.J., 1995; John E. Conklin, *Criminology*, 5th ed., Prentice Hall, Englewood Cliffs, N.J., 1994; Frank Hagan, *Introduction to Criminology*, 3rd ed., Nelson-Hall, Chicago, 1994; Freda Adler, Gerhard O. W. Mueller, and William S. Laufer, *Criminology*, McGraw-Hill, New York, 1994; Piers Beirne and James Messerschmidt, *Criminology*, 2nd ed., Harcourt Brace Jovanovich, Orlando, 1994; Gennaro F. Vito, *Criminology*, Wadsworth, Belmont, Calif., 1994; Edwin H. Sutherland, Donald R. Cressey, and David F. Luckenbill, *Principles of Criminology*, General Hall, Dix Hills, N.Y., 1992; Larry J. Seigel, *Criminology*, West, St. Paul, 1992; Don C. Gibbons, *Society, Crime, and Criminal Behavior*, Prentice Hall, Englewood Cliffs, N.J., 1992; and Gresham Sykes and Francis T. Cullen, *Criminology*, Harcourt Brace Jovanovich, Fort Worth, 1992.

themselves, rather than the facts about criminality, are the focus of this book.[2]

A theory is a part of an *explanation*.[3] Basically, an explanation is a sensible way of relating some particular phenomenon to the whole world of information, beliefs, and attitudes that make up the intellectual atmosphere of a people at a particular time or place. For example, when modern people see a train move along the railroad tracks, they "explain" that phenomenon to themselves in terms of their knowledge of internal combustion engines. Primitive people also had explanations that enabled them to account for such phenomena, but they used primitive concepts such as the power of spirits or demons.

Scientific theories are one kind of explanation. In general, scientific theories make statements about *the relationships between observable phenomena*.[4] For example, some scientific theories in criminology make statements about the relationship between the certainty or severity of criminal punishments and the volume of criminal behaviors in society. Other scientific theories make statements about the relationship between biological, psychological, or social characteristics of individuals and the likelihood that those individuals will engage in criminal behaviors. Still other scientific theories make statements about the relationship between the social characteristics of individuals and the likelihood that those individuals will be defined and processed as criminals by the criminal justice system. All these characteristics can be observed, and so all these theories are scientific.

Because they make statements about the relationships among observable phenomena, a key characteristic of scientific theories is that they can be *falsified*.[5] The process of attempting to falsify a scientific theory involves systematically observing the relationships described in

2. Some recent texts that focus on theoretical material include Ronald Akers, *Criminological Theories*, 2nd ed., Roxbury, Los Angeles, 1996; Werner Einstader and Stuart Henry, *Criminological Theory: An Analysis of Its Underlying Assumptions*, Harcourt Brace College Publishers, Fort Worth, 1995; J. Robert Lilly, Francis T. Cullen, and Richard A. Ball, *Criminological Theory: Context and Consequences*, 2nd ed., Sage, Newbury Park, Calif., 1994; Franklin P. Williams III and Marilyn D. McShane, *Criminological Theory*, 2nd ed., Prentice Hall, Englewood Cliffs, N.J., 1994; Don C. Gibbons, *Talking about Crime and Criminals*, Prentice Hall General Reference, New York, 1993; Daniel J. Curran, *Theories of Crime*, Allyn & Bacon, Needham Heights, Mass., 1993; Larry Siegel, *Criminology: Theories, Patterns, and Typologies*, West, St. Paul, 1992; Randy Martin, Robert J. Mutchnick, and W. Timothy Austin, *Criminological Thought: Pioneers Past and Present*, Macmillan, New York, 1990; David Downes and Paul Rock, *Understanding Deviance*, 2nd ed., Oxford University Press, Oxford, 1988; and David A. Jones, *History of Criminology: A Philosophical Perspective*, Greenwood Press, Westport, Conn., 1986.

3. Arthur L. Stinchcombe, *Constructing Social Theories*, Harcourt, Brace & World, New York, 1968, pp. 3–5.

4. Ibid., pp. 15–17.

5. Ibid., pp. 5–6; Thomas J. Bernard, "Twenty Years of Testing Theories: What Have We Learned and Why," *Journal of Research in Crime and Delinquency* 27(4): 325–47 (Nov. 1990).

the theory and then comparing those observations to arguments of the theory itself. This process is called research: That is, the assertions of the theory are tested against the observed world of the facts.[6] If the observations are inconsistent with the assertions of the theory, then the theory is falsified. If the observations are consistent with the assertions of the theory, then the theory becomes more credible, but it is not proved; there are always alternative theories that might also explain the same observed relationships.

A theory can gain a great deal of credibility if all the reasonable alternative theories are shown to be inconsistent with the observed world of facts. At that point the theory might simply be accepted as true. However, it is always possible that some new facts will be discovered in the future that are inconsistent with the theory, so that a new theory will be required. For example, Newton's laws of physics were accepted as true for 200 years, but they were replaced by Einstein's theory of relativity at the beginning of the twentieth century due to the discovery of some new facts.[7]

Criminology has been blessed (or cursed, depending on one's point of view) with a very large number of scientific theories. The extent to which these theories are supported by the facts is another question entirely. Over sixty years ago Michael and Adler reviewed crime theories and concluded: "The assurance with which criminologists have advanced opinions regarding the causes of crime is in striking contrast to the worthlessness of the data upon which those opinions are based."[8] Michael and Adler's judgment was harsh even at the time, but their point should be kept in mind as the various theories are reviewed. Another point was raised more recently by Gould, who commented: "Some topics are invested with enormous social importance but blessed with very little reliable information. When the ratio of data to social impact is so low, a history of scientific attitudes may be little more than an oblique record of social change."[9] It may be that the history of criminology reflects more about the changing values of the larger society than it does about the changing scientific knowledge of crime.[10]

---

6. Thomas J. Bernard and R. Richard Ritti, "The Role of Theory in Scientific Research," in Kimberly L. Kempf, ed., *Measurement Issues in Criminology*, Springer-Verlag, New York, 1990, pp. 1–20.

7. Thomas S. Kuhn, *The Structure of Scientific Revolutions*, University of Chicago Press, Chicago, 1969.

8. Jerome Michael and Mortimer J. Adler, *Crime, Law and Social Science*, Patterson Smith, Montclair, N.J., 1971 (1933), p. 169.

9. Stephen Jay Gould, *The Mismeasure of Man*, Norton, New York, 1981, p. 22.

10. Cf. Ysabel Rennie, *The Search for Criminal Man*, Heath, Lexington, Mass., 1973.

In the broad scope of history, there are two basic types of theories of crime. One relies on spiritual, or other-world, explanations while the other relies on natural, or this-world, explanations. Both types of theories are ancient as well as modern, but only the natural theories can be called scientific since only they focus on observable phenomena. Spiritual explanations necessarily involve elements that cannot be observed, and therefore these theories cannot be falsified. Thus, even if one considers spiritual theories as the most adequate explanation of crime, they cannot be considered scientific.

SPIRITUAL EXPLANATIONS

Spiritual explanations of crime are part of a general view of life in which many events are believed to result from the influence of otherworldly powers. For example, primitive people regarded natural disasters such as famines, floods, and plagues as punishments for wrongs they had done to the spiritual powers.[11] They responded by performing sacred rites and rituals to appease those powers.

In the Middle Ages in Europe a spiritual view of the world was joined to the political and social organization of feudalism to produce the beginnings of the criminal justice system.[12] Originally, crime was a largely private affair in which the victim or the victim's family obtained revenge by inflicting a similar or greater harm on the offender or the offender's family. The problem was that private vengeance had a tendency to start blood feuds that could continue for many years until one or the other family was completely wiped out. The feudal lords therefore instituted methods by which God could indicate who was innocent and who was guilty. The first such method was trial by battle, in which the victim or a member of his or her family would fight the offender or a member of his or her family. Because God would give victory to the innocent party, the family of the loser would have no grounds for exacting vengeance on the winner, and the blood feuds were ended.

The problem with trial by battle was that great warriors could commit as many crimes as they wanted, secure in the knowledge that God would always give them victory. Thus, somewhat later in history, trial by ordeal was instituted. In this method the accused was subjected to difficult and painful tests, from which an innocent person (protected by God) would emerge unharmed while a guilty person would die a painful death. For example, a common method of determining whether a

11. Graeme Newman, *The Punishment Response*, Lippincott, Philadelphia, 1978, pp. 13–25.

12. Harry Elmer Barnes, *The Story of Punishment*, 2nd ed. revised, Patterson Smith, Montclair, N.J., 1972, pp. 7–10.

woman was a witch was to tie her up and throw her into the water.[13] If she floated she was considered innocent, but if she sank she was guilty. Other forms of ordeal included running the gauntlet and walking on fire. Trial by ordeal was condemned by the Pope in 1215 and was replaced by compurgation, in which the accused gathered together a group of twelve reputable people who would swear that he or she was innocent. The idea was that no one would lie under oath for fear of being punished by God. Compurgation ultimately evolved into testimony under oath and trial by jury.

Spiritual explanations of crime appeared in the New World in the Puritan colony on Massachusetts Bay. During the first sixty years of its existence, this colony experienced three serious "crime waves" thought to be caused by the devil. The most serious of these "crime waves" occurred in 1792, when the community was thought to have been invaded by a large number of witches.[14]

Our modern prison system also originated in association with a spiritual explanation of crime. Around 1790 a group of Quakers in Philadelphia conceived the idea of isolating criminals in cells and giving them only the Bible to read and some manual labor to perform. The Quakers thought criminals would then reflect on their past wrongdoings and repent.[15] They used the term *penitentiary* to describe their invention, a place for *penitents* who were sorry for their sins.

Today, some religious individuals and groups still attribute crime to the influence of the devil. For example, Charles Colson, who was special counsel to President Richard M. Nixon and who served seven months in prison for his part in the Watergate affair, attributes crime to sinful human nature.[16] He argues that religious conversion is the only "cure" for crime and spends much of his time bringing that Christian message to prisoners.

Spiritual explanations provide a way of understanding crime that is satisfactory to some people. The problem is that, because spiritual influences cannot be observed, these theories cannot be falsified. Thus these theories cannot be considered scientific, even if some thoughtful

13. Newman, op. cit., p. 97.

14. Kai T. Erikson, *Wayward Puritans*, John Wiley, New York, 1966.

15. Harry Elmer Barnes and Negley K. Teeters, *New Horizons in Criminology*, Prentice Hall, New York, 1945; Negley K. Teeters, *The Cradle of the Penitentiary: The Walnut Street Jail at Philadelphia, 1773–1835*, Temple University Press, Philadelphia, 1955.

16. Charles Colson, "Toward an Understanding of the Origins of Crime," in John Stott and Nick Miller, eds., *Crime and the Responsible Community*, Hodder and Stoughton, London, 1980. See also David R. Wilkerson, *The Cross and the Switchblade*, B. Geis, New York, 1963; Oral Roberts, *Twelve Greatest Miracles of My Ministry*, Pinoak, Tulsa, 1974, ch. 9; Gerald Austin McHugh, *Christian Faith and Criminal Justice: Toward a Christian Response to Crime and Punishment*, Paulist Press, New York, 1978.

and intelligent people believe that they represent the best explanation of crime.

NATURAL EXPLANATIONS

Spiritual explanations make use of otherworldly powers to account for what happens; natural explanations make use of objects and events in the material world to explain the same things. Like the spiritual approach, the natural approach to explanation is ancient as well as modern.

The early Phoenicians and Greeks developed naturalistic, this-world explanations far back in their history. For example, Hippocrates (460 B.C.) provided a physiological explanation of thinking by arguing that the brain is the organ of the mind. Democritus (420 B.C.) proposed the idea of an indestructible unit of matter called the atom as central to his explanation of the world around him. With Socrates, Plato, and Aristotle, the ideas of unity and continuity came to the fore, but the essential factors in all explanations remained physical and material.

By the first century B.C. Roman thought had become thoroughly infused with naturalism. For example, Roman law combined the spiritualism of the Hebrew tradition with the naturalism of the Greek tradition to provide a natural basis for penalties as well as for rights. The Hebrew doctrine of divine sanction for law and order merged with Greek naturalism and appeared in Roman law as a justification based on the "nature of things." Later, the rule of kings by divine right became a natural law looking to the "nature of things" for its principal justification.

In the sixteenth and seventeenth centuries writers such as Hobbes, Spinoza, Descartes, and Leibniz studied human affairs as physicists study matter, impersonally and quantitatively. Modern social science continues this naturalistic emphasis. The disagreements among social scientists are well known, but at least they have in common that they seek their explanations within observable phenomena found in the physical and material world.

In criminology, as in other social sciences, modern thought has abandoned the spiritual approach as a frame of reference and adopted a naturalist, scientific approach. Within the naturalist approach, however, one can distinguish different and in some ways contradictory frames of reference, based on different ways of thinking about crime. To give some sense of the breadth of the field of criminology, three such frames of reference are identified and briefly described in the paragraphs that follow.[17] The first frame of reference describes criminal behavior as freely

---

17. For a discussion of underlying assumptions in criminological theories, see Einstadter and Henry, op. cit. For a complex discussion of philosophical methods in criminology involving some of the same issues, see Bruce DiCristina, *Method in Criminology: A Philosophical Primer*, Harrow and Heston, Albany, N.Y., 1995.

chosen, while the second describes it as caused by forces beyond the control of the individual. The third frame of reference views crime primarily as a function of the way the criminal law is written and enforced. Thus, it focuses on the behavior of criminal law rather than the behavior of criminals.

CLASSICAL CRIMINOLOGY

First, there is the view that intelligence and rationality are fundamental human characteristics and are the basis for explaining human behavior. In this view humans are said to be capable of understanding themselves and of acting to promote their own best interests. Societies are formed because people rationally decide to make them according to patterns that seem "good" to them—either monarchies or republics, totalitarian dictatorships or democracies. The key to progress is said to be intelligent behavior brought about by careful training and education. Each person is said to be master of his or her fate, possessed of free will rather than driven by spirits or devils.

This is the frame of reference of classical criminology, as well as of classical thinking in other fields such as philosophy, political science, and economics. Within this frame of reference, the term "crime" is usually defined from a strictly legal point of view.[18] Crime may be defined as the commission of any act prohibited by criminal law, or the omission of any act required by it, and a criminal is defined as any person who commits a crime. Crime is seen as a product of the free choice of the individual, who first assesses the potential benefits of committing the crime against its potential costs. The rational response of society is to increase the costs and to decrease the benefits of crime to the point that individuals will not choose to commit crime. Within this frame of reference, then, the problem criminologists attempt to solve is to design and test a system of punishment that would result in a minimal occurrence of crime. That is, this frame of reference is concerned with theory and research on the question of deterrence.

POSITIVIST CRIMINOLOGY

Next is the view that behavior is determined by factors beyond the individual's control. This view implies that humans are not self-determining agents free to do as they wish and as their intelligence directs. Rather, it is more accurate to say that people can only behave as they have already been determined to behave. Thinking and reasoning are actually processes of rationalization in which individuals justify their

---

18. Clarence R. Jeffery, "The Structure of American Criminological Thinking," *Journal of Criminal Law, Criminology and Police Science* 46: 663–64 (Jan.–Feb. 1956).

predetermined courses of action, rather than processes by which individuals freely and intelligently choose what they want to do. Humans have changed and developed through a slow process of evolution, and not because intelligence has led to increasingly rational choices.

This is the frame of reference of positivist criminology, as well as of positivist thinking in other fields such as psychology, sociology, and philosophy. These theories arose in criminology after classical theories had dominated the field for about 100 years and repeated attempts to reduce crime by making punishments more prompt, certain, and severe had failed to succeed. In a sense, these new theories were offered as explanations of why classical theories had failed: If criminal behavior was determined by factors beyond the control of the individual, then punishing that individual would not have any effect.

Within this frame of reference, the problem criminologists attempt to solve is to identify the causes of criminal behavior. The original positivist criminologists looked mainly at biological factors, but later criminologists shifted their focus to psychological and then to social factors in their attempts to find these causes. At the present time, some criminologists hold that criminal behavior can be explained by one type of factor, while other criminologists take a multiple-factor approach, holding that there are many factors that increase or decrease the likelihood of a person engaging in criminal behavior.[19] Consequently, most of the chapters in this book are concerned with various explanations of those causes.

Criminologists who search for the causes of criminal behavior find it difficult to work within the framework of a strictly legal definition of the term "crime," such as used by the classical criminologists. That is because the law frequently distinguishes between legal and illegal actions on the basis of fine points ("technicalities") that have no bearing on the causes of the behavior. The law also groups behaviors into legal categories when those behaviors are not similar to each other from the point of view of their causes. Therefore, criminologists who search for the causes of crime tend to use "natural" definitions of crime, which focus on the "nature" of the behavior itself rather than on its legal definition. Once criminologists have defined the "nature" of criminal behavior, they then can analyze what causes that behavior.

For example, Gottfredson and Hirschi describe the "nature" of crime as acts that involve simple and immediate gratification but few long-term benefits, are exciting and risky but require little skill or planning,

---

19. Travis Hirschi and Michael Gottfredson, eds., *Understanding Crime: Current Theory and Research*, Sage, Beverly Hills, Calif., 1980, pp. 7–19.

and generally produce few benefits for the offender while imposing many costs on the victim.[20] Having proposed this "natural" definition of crime, they then analyze the causes of this type of behavior among humans. Many other examples can be cited.[21]

THE BEHAVIOR OF CRIMINAL LAW

Positivist theories of the causes of criminal behavior dominated criminology for over 100 years, much as classical theories dominated criminology for the 100 years before that. But like those earlier classical theories, the positivist theories do not seem to have produced the results they originally promised: to reduce and control crime. Since about 1970, some criminologists have abandoned the positivist point of view and returned to classical theories, taking the view that changes in criminal punishments can achieve the goal of crime control. But other criminologists have moved to an entirely new point of view.

These criminologists question positivist criminology's "natural" definition of crime, which assumes that there are essential differences between criminal behavior and legal behavior, so that they have essentially different causes. In contrast, these criminologists argue that many criminal behaviors are essentially similar to legal behaviors and that they involve essentially similar causal processes. The problem these criminologists attempt to solve, then, is to explain why some behaviors are officially defined as criminal while other essentially similar behaviors are not. This leads to a second and related problem: to explain why some people are officially defined as criminals while other people who act in

20. Michael R. Gottfredson and Travis Hirschi, *A General Theory of Crime*, Stanford University Press, Stanford, Calif., 1990, pp. 15–44, 89–91.

21. For example, Mannheim (*Comparative Criminology*, Houghton Mifflin, Boston, 1965, pp. 14–15) defends the view that criminology should study all antisocial behavior, whether it is legally a crime or not. E. H. Sutherland ("White Collar Criminality," *American Sociological Review* 5: 1–12 [Feb. 1940]) defined crime as behavior that is harmful to society and used this definition to pursue his studies on white-collar crime. Each edition of Sutherland's text contains the statement "Obviously, legal definitions should not confine the work of the criminologist; he should be completely free to push across the barriers of legal definitions whenever he sees noncriminal behavior which resembles criminal behavior" (e.g., E. H. Sutherland and D. R. Cressey, *Criminology*, 9th ed., Lippincott, Philadelphia, 1974, p. 21). In the 10th edition of the text, however (1978, p. 23), Donald R. Cressey qualified the statement by adding the following: "It is an error, however, to call such noncriminal behavior *crime*, no matter how repulsive it may be" (see also Sutherland, Cressey and Luckenbill, op. cit., p. 20). In his own work, Cressey (*Other People's Money*, The Free Press, Glencoe, Ill., 1953) replaced a variety of legal categories of financial crime with the concept of criminal violation of financial trust. He claimed that this definition included all forms of criminal behavior that were similar from an economic and sociological point of view, but excluded other forms of criminal behavior. He was then able to proceed with a causal analysis of this behavior. Thorsten Sellin (*Culture Conflict and Crime*, Social Science Research Council, New York, 1938) defined crime in terms of violations of group conduct norms, and Herman and Julia Schwendinger ("Defenders of Order or Guardians of Human Rights?" *Issues in Criminology* 5:123–57 [summer 1970]) defined it in terms of violations of basic human rights.

essentially similar ways are not. The theories that these criminologists propose have been described in a variety of ways but will be called "theories of the behavior of criminal law" in this book because they focus on how the criminal law itself is written and enforced.[22]

The criminologists who hold this view focus on the processes by which humans create the social world in which they live. They argue that the phenomenon of crime is socially constructed when a society defines certain people and actions as criminal, and that any of a wide variety of people and actions may, at one time or another, be the subject of these definitions. These criminologists therefore study the processes by which particular sets of people and actions are defined as criminal at particular times and places.

For example, consider the most serious of all crimes, murder. A classical criminologist might attempt to measure the effects of different types of enforcement and punishment policies on the incidence of murder in a society. A positivist criminologist might study the biological, psychological, or social characteristics of murderers to determine what caused their behavior. A criminologist who studies the behavior of criminal law, in contrast, might study the types of killings officially defined as murder, and attempt to determine why these killings are selected for definition as murders while other killings are not. They might also study the set of people defined as murderers by the police and courts and attempt to determine why this particular group had been selected out of all the people whose behaviors resulted in the deaths of other people.

These criminologists might study systematic differences in the enforcement of laws that result in certain groups being disproportionately processed by the criminal justice system. They might argue, for example, that wealthy and powerful groups tend to be weeded out of the criminal justice system at successive decision points, so that the end result is that poor and powerless groups are disproportionately convicted and imprisoned. Wealthy and powerful people who kill may be less likely

22. This term is derived from Donald Black, *The Behavior of Law*, Academic Press, New York, 1976. Black's term is broader in that it includes all "governmental social control." The present term includes only the criminal law and excludes other forms of governmental social control since those other forms do not influence the distribution of official crime rates. These theories have been described with a variety of terms. For example, Gresham Sykes ("The Rise of Critical Criminology," *Journal of Criminal Law and Criminology* 65: 206–13 [June 1974]) uses the term "critical criminology." The term "new criminology" has also been used to describe these theories. See Gibbons, op. cit., pp. 167–71; Charles E. Reasons, "Social Thought and Social Structure, *Criminology* 13 (3): 332–65 (Nov. 1975); Robert F. Meier, "The New Criminology," *Journal of Criminal Law and Criminology* 67: 461–69 (Dec. 1976); Eugene Doleschal and Nora Klapmuts, "Toward a New Criminology," *Crime and Delinquency Literature* 5(4): 607–26 (Dec. 1973). Both the terms *critical criminology* and *new criminology* may be misnomers (see Robert F. Bohm, "Radical Criminology: An Explication," *Criminology* 19[4]: 565–89 [Feb. 1982]), but there is as yet no commonly accepted term to describe this emerging perspective.

to be arrested, tried, or convicted at all, or they may be convicted of a less serious offense and given a more lenient sentence.

These criminologists may also examine differences in the types of deaths that are defined as murders by the law. For example, *felony murder* laws make an offender liable for first-degree murder if a death results from the commission of certain "dangerous" felonies such as forcible rape, robbery, arson, or burglary. No intent to kill is required, as the intent to commit the lesser offense is transferred to the greater one.[23] Under this law, if a shopkeeper has a heart attack and dies while being robbed, a person could be charged with first-degree murder if he or she was driving the getaway car, did not go inside the store, and had no weapon. If convicted, such an offender could then receive the death penalty.[24]

In contrast with the severity of this law are the extremely lenient laws associated with serious injuries and deaths resulting from the actions of corporate executives. Even the most outrageous examples of deliberate decisions resulting in numerous injuries and deaths may not be defined as crimes at all, or, if they are defined as crimes, the penalties may be limited to a minimal and symbolic level.[25] Many serious injuries and deaths associated with corporate decision making occur where there is the intent to commit a lesser offense (for example, to violate health or safety laws), combined with the full knowledge that the decision may result in serious injury and death to numbers of innocent people. If a law similar to the felony murder law were applied to corporate decision making, then many corporate executives might find themselves convicted of murder and sentenced to death.

Theories of the behavior of criminal law suggest that the volume of crime and the characteristics of criminals are determined primarily by how the law is written and enforced. Most people convicted of crimes are poor, but not because poverty causes crime. Rather, the actions typical of poor people are more likely to be legally defined as crimes, and the laws applying to such crimes are more likely to be strictly enforced. Burglary, larceny, armed robbery, and auto theft are all crimes typically committed by the poor, and the laws applying to these crimes are strictly defined and enforced. Fraud, embezzlement, corruption, and other kinds of white-collar crimes are typically committed by wealthier people. But the laws applying to these crimes are neither defined nor en-

23. Hazel B. Kerper, *Introduction to the Criminal Justice System*, West, St. Paul, 1972, pp. 111–12.

24. A similar case in which the offender did receive the death penalty is *Woodson v. North Carolina*, 96 S. Ct. 2978 (1976).

25. E.g., see Gerald M. Stern, *The Buffalo Creek Disaster*, Vintage, New York, 1976; Kai T. Erikson, *Everything in Its Path*, Simon & Schuster, New York, 1976.

forced as strictly, despite the fact that these crimes can cause many serious injuries and deaths and can result in large property losses. In general, both rich and poor persons can be vicious, brutal, greedy, and deceptive, but the poor person with these characteristics is more likely to be defined as a criminal than is the rich person. Thus differences in the crime rates between rich and poor persons may primarily reflect differences in the behavior of criminal law rather than differences in the behaviors of individuals.

THE RELATIONSHIP AMONG THE
VARIOUS FRAMES OF REFERENCE

Science with its naturalistic approach has abandoned the satisfying argument of spiritual explanations. To those who believe in spiritual influences, this does not invalidate their frame of reference; it only points out that scientists are unable to recognize the true sources of crime when they encounter them. Such individuals do not need, and have no interest in, the natural explanations of behavior. They are satisfied that they already have a more adequate explanation.

Something very similar also may happen with those who reject spiritual explanations and accept natural explanations but have different frames of reference. Classical criminologists may hold on to the view that crime can be judged in terms of deliberateness, intent, and understanding of right and wrong. These criminologists may view the search for the causes of crime as a fundamentally wrongheaded endeavor that produces no beneficial results. In contrast, positivist criminologists may reject both the spiritualism of some religious individuals and the free will of the classical criminologists. Within this frame of reference, however, some criminologists may focus on social factors and hold that there is little or no role for biological and psychological factors in the causes of criminal behavior. Others may argue that biological or psychological factors explain substantial amounts of criminal behavior, and social factors enter into the picture through their interaction with the biological or psychological factors. Finally, criminologists who propose theories of the behavior of criminal law may regard both classical and positivist theories as fundamentally misinterpreting the phenomenon of crime. In their view, the volume of crime in society and the characteristics of criminals are both reflections of the operations of the criminal justice system, not the behavior of individuals.

Within the naturalistic frame of reference, however, criminologists can do more than simply disagree with each other. All these theories are scientific, and so they all make assertions about relationships among observable phenomena. Criminologists therefore can systematically observe the world to see if the asserted relationships actually exist—i.e., they can conduct research. The results of research should indicate that some theories are consistent with observations in the real world, while other theories are inconsistent with them. This is the scientific process.

While this process probably works in the long run, in the short run it is often difficult to reach a conclusion about whether a particular theory is consistent with the observations. The research on a particular theory is rarely black or white—rather, there are innumerable shades of gray with some research providing support for the theory and other research tending to contradict it.[26] In that situation, different criminologists may reach very different conclusions about the same theories.

In the chapters that follow, the implications of some of these general propositions will be examined in much greater detail. The chapters have been organized primarily for the sake of convenience and clarity; no necessary separateness or mutual exclusiveness should be inferred. In general, the chapters are organized in the historical sequence in which the theories originated, so that the earliest theories are presented first. This is intended to provide the reader with a sense of how the field of criminology has evolved over time.

Chapters 2 and 3 focus on the classical and positive schools of criminology. These chapters present historical materials on how criminology emerged as a field of study during the eighteenth and nineteenth centuries. Chapters 4 through 17 present various specific types of criminology theories. These chapters are arranged in the order in which the types of theories emerged. For example, the earliest types of criminology theories focused on the biological and psychological characteristics of individual criminals, so the chapters covering these theories are presented first. Later types of theories tended to focus more strongly on social factors, so these are presented in later chapters. These chapters all contain modern as well as historical materials. That is, each chapter brings the work of the early theorists up to date by presenting more recent theories and research that take the same general point of view.

After presenting all the different types of theories, Chapter 18 discusses recent attempts to integrate those different types of theories into broader approaches. Finally, Chapter 19 offers some concluding thoughts on the current state of theorizing in criminology and how to advance criminology as a science.

---

26. As a practical matter, most criminology theories seem impossible to falsify. See Bernard, op. cit. As a result, the authors of the present text recommend that criminology abandon falsification itself as a criterion of scientific utility, and move to a risk factor approach (see Chapters 18 and 19).

CHAPTER TWO

Classical Criminology

The literature of criminology often refers to the classical and the neo-classical schools of criminological thought. These terms or labels are used to designate some important ideas in the long history of trying to understand, and trying to do something about, crime. The classical school is usually associated with the name of the Italian scholar Cesare Bonesana, Marchese de Beccaria (1738–1794). Its later modification, the so-called neoclassical school, is very similar as far as basic ideas and conceptions about the human nature are concerned. Both represent a sort of free-will, rationalistic hedonism that is part of a tradition going back many centuries.

THE SOCIAL AND INTELLECTUAL
BACKGROUND OF CLASSICAL CRIMINOLOGY

Classical criminology emerged at a time when the naturalistic approach of the social contract thinkers was challenging the spiritualistic approach that had dominated European thinking for over a thousand years. This broad spiritualistic approach included a spiritual explanation of crime that formed the basis for criminal justice policies in most of Europe. Classical criminology was a protest against those criminal justice policies and against the spiritual explanations of crime on which they were based.

One of the most important sources for these spiritual explanations of crime was found in the theology of St. Thomas Aquinas (1225–1274), who lived 500 years before Beccaria.[1] Aquinas argued that there was a God-given "natural law" that was revealed by observing, though the eyes of faith, people's natural tendency to do good rather than evil. The crim-

---

1. A brief review of Aquinas's ideas can be found in Thomas J. Bernard, *The Consensus-Conflict Debate*, Columbia University Press, New York, 1983, ch. 3.

inal law was based on and reflected this "natural law." People who commit crime (i.e., violate the criminal law) therefore also commit sin (i.e., violate the natural law). Aquinas held that crime not only harmed victims, but it also harmed criminals because it harmed their essential "humanness"—their natural tendency to do good.

This spiritual explanation of crime, and others like it, formed the basis for the criminal justice policies in Europe at the time. Because crime was identified with sin, the state had the moral authority to use many horrible and gruesome tortures on criminals. That was because the state claimed that it was acting in the place of God when it inflicted these horrible punishments on criminals. For example, Beirne quotes from the sentence that was imposed on Jean Calas in 1762, two years before Beccaria published his little book[2]:

. . .in a chemise, with head and feet bare, (Calas) will be taken in a cart from the palace prison to the Cathedral. There, kneeling in front of the main door, holding in his hands a torch of yellow wax weighing two pounds, he must . . . (ask) pardon of God, of the King, and of justice. Then the executioner should take him in the cart to the Place Saint Georges, where upon a scaffold his arms, legs, thighs, and loins will be broken and crushed. Finally, the prisoner should be place upon a wheel, with his face turned to the sky, alive and in pain, and repent for his said crimes and misdeeds, all the while imploring God for his life, thereby to serve as an example and to instil terror in the wicked.

The extensive religious symbolism in the manner of execution clearly suggests that crime is intertwined with sin, and that in punishing crime, the state is taking the part of God.

Beginning with Thomas Hobbes (1588–1678), "social contract" thinkers substituted naturalistic arguments for the spiritualistic arguments of people like Aquinas.[3] While Aquinas argued that people naturally do good rather than evil, Hobbes argued that people naturally pursue their own interests without caring about whether they hurt anyone else. This leads to a "war of each against all" in which no one is safe because all people only look out for themselves.

Hobbes then argued that people are rational enough to realize that this situation is not in anyone's interests. So people agree to give up their own selfish behavior as long as everyone else does the same thing

---

2. Piers Beirne, *Inventing Criminology*, State University of New York Press, Albany, 1993, pp. 11–12. Another widely quoted example from the same time period is the execution of Damiens, who had stabbed the king of France in 1757. See Michel Foucault, *Discipline and Punish*, Pantheon, New York, 1977, pp. 3–5.

3. A discussion of Hobbes and his relation to Aquinas can be found in Bernard, op. cit, ch. 4.

at the same time. This is what Hobbes called the "social contract"—something like a peace treaty that everyone signs because they are all exhausted from the war of each against all. But the social contract needs an enforcement mechanism in case some people cheat and begin to pursue their own interests without regard to whether other people get hurt. This is the job of the state. According to Hobbes, everyone who agrees to the social contract also agrees to grant the state the right to use force to maintain the contract.

Other social contract philosophers such as Locke (1632–1704), Montesquieu (1689–1755), Voltaire (1694–1778), and Rousseau (1712–1778) followed Hobbes in constructing philosophies that included a natural and rational basis for explaining crime and the state's response to it. These theories differed from each other in many ways, but all were rational and naturalistic approaches to explaining crime and punishment, as opposed to the dominant spiritualistic approach. By the middle of the 1700s, just before Beccaria wrote his book, these naturalistic ideas were well known and widely accepted by the intellectuals of the day, but they did not represent the thinking of the politically powerful groups that ruled the various states in Europe. Those ruling groups still held to the spiritual explanations of crime, so that crime was seen as manifesting the work of the devil. Consequently, the criminal justice systems of the time tended to impose excessive and cruel punishments on criminals.

Beccaria was a protest writer who sought to change these excessive and cruel punishments by applying the rationalist, social contract ideas to crime and criminal justice. His book was well received by intellectuals and some reform-minded rulers who had already accepted the general framework of social contract thinking.[4] Even more important for the book's acceptance, however, was the fact that the American Revolution of 1776 and the French Revolution of 1789 occurred soon after its publication in 1764.[5] These two revolutions were both guided by naturalistic ideas of the social contract philosophers. To these revolutionaries, Beccaria's book represented the latest and best thinking on the subject of crime and criminal justice. They therefore used his ideas as the basis for their new criminal justice systems. From America and France, Beccaria's ideas spread to the rest of the industrialized world.

---

4. Graeme Newman and Pietro Marongiu, "Penological Reform and the Myth of Beccaria," *Criminology* 28(2): 325–46 (May 1990).

5. Beccaria's work was extensively quoted by Thomas Jefferson, John Adams, and other American revolutionaries. See David A. Jones, *History of Criminology*, Greenwood, New York, 1986, pp. 43–46.

BECCARIA AND THE CLASSICAL SCHOOL

Cesare Bonesana, Marchese de Beccaria, was an indifferent student who had some interest in mathematics.[6] After completing his formal education, he joined Allessandro Verri, an official of the prison in Milan, and his brother Pietro Verri, an economist, in a group of young men who met regularly to discuss literary and philosophical topics. Beccaria was given an assignment in March 1763 to write an essay on penology, a subject about which he knew nothing. With help from the Verri brothers, the essay was completed in January 1764, and was published under the title *Dei deliti e delle pene (On Crimes and Punishments)* in the small town of Livorno in July of that year, when Beccaria was 26 years old.

In common with his contemporary intellectuals, Beccaria protested against the many inconsistencies in government and in the management of public affairs. He therefore proposed various reforms to make criminal justice practice more logical and rational. He objected especially to the capricious and purely personal justice the judges were dispensing and to the severe and barbaric punishments of the time. It is interesting to look at Beccaria's ideas as expressed in his own words in relation to some of the basic principles of his system of justice.

1. On the contractual society and the need for punishments[7]:

Laws are the conditions under which independent and isolated men united to form a society. Weary of living in a continual state of war, and of enjoying a liberty rendered useless by the uncertainty of preserving it, they sacrificed a part so that they might enjoy the rest of it in peace and safety. The sum of all these portions of liberty sacrificed by each for his own good constitutes the sovereignty of a nation, and their legitimate depositary and administrator is the sovereign. But merely to have established this deposit was not enough; it had to be defended against private usurpations by individuals each of whom always tries not only to withdraw his own share but also to usurp for himself that of others. Some tangible motives had to be introduced, therefore, to prevent the despotic spirit, which is in every man, from plunging the laws of society into

6. An account of the life and work of Beccaria may be found in Beirne, op. cit., ch. 2. See also Randy Martin, Robert J. Mutchnick, and W. Timothy Austin, *Criminological Thought: Pioneers Past and Present*, Macmillan, New York, 1990; and Elio D. Monachesi, "Pioneers in Criminology: Cesare Beccaria (1738–94)," *Journal of Criminal Law, Criminology and Police Science* 46(4): 439–49 (Nov.–Dec. 1955), reprinted in Hermann Mannheim, *Pioneers in Criminology*, Patterson Smith, Montclair, N.J., 1972, pp. 36–50.

7. Cesare Beccaria, *On Crimes and Punishments*, translated by Henry Paolucci, Bobbs-Merrill, Indianapolis, 1963, pp. 11–12. This and the following quotations are reprinted with permission of the publisher, Bobbs-Merrill Educational Publishing, Inc., © 1963.

its original chaos. These tangible motives are the punishments established against infractors of the laws.

2. On the function of legislatures[8]:

Only the laws can decree punishments for crimes; authority for this can reside only with the legislator who represents the entire society united by a social contract. . . . But a punishment that exceeds the limit fixed by the laws is just punishment plus another punishment; a magistrate cannot, therefore, under any pretext of zeal or concern for the public good, augment the punishment established for a delinquent citizen.

3. On the function of judges[9]:

Judges in criminal cases cannot have the authority to interpret laws, and the reason, again, is that they are not legislators. . . . For every crime that comes before him, a judge is required to complete a perfect syllogism in which the major premise must be the general law; the minor, the action that conforms or does not conform to the law; and the conclusion, acquittal or punishment. If the judge were not constrained, or if he desired to frame even a single additional syllogism, the door would thereby be opened to uncertainty.

Nothing can be more dangerous than the popular axiom that it is necessary to consult the spirit of the laws. It is a dam that has given way to a torrent of opinions. . . . Each man has his own point of view, and, at each different time, a different one. Thus, the "spirit" of the law would be the product of a judge's good or bad logic, of his good or bad digestion; it would depend on the violence of his passions, on the weakness of the accused, on the judge's connections with him, and on all those minute factors that alter the appearances of an object in the fluctuating mind of man. . . . The disorder that arises from rigorous observance of the letter of a penal law is hardly comparable to the disorders that arise from interpretations.

4. On the seriousness of crimes[10]:

The true measure of crimes is . . . the *harm done to society.* . . . They were in error who believed that the true measure of crimes is to be found in the intention of the person who commits them. Intention depends on the impression objects actually make and on the present disposition of the mind; these vary in all men and in each man, according to the swift succession of ideas, of passions, and of circumstances. It would be necessary, therefore, to form not only a particular code for each citizen, but a new law for every crime. Some-

8. Ibid., pp. 13–14.
9. Ibid., pp. 14–15.
10. Ibid., pp. 64–65.

times, with the best intentions, men do the greatest injury to society; at other times, intending the worst for it, they do the greatest good.

5. On proportionate punishments[11]:

It is to the common interest not only that crimes not be committed, but also that they be less frequent in proportion to the harm they cause society. Therefore, the obstacles that deter man from committing crime should be stronger in proportion as they are contrary to the public good, and as the inducements to commit them are stronger. There must, therefore, be a proper proportion between crimes and punishments.

6. On the severity of punishments[12]:

For punishment to attain its end, the evil which it inflicts has only to exceed the advantage derivable from the crime; in this excess of evil one should include the certainty of punishment and the loss of the good which the crime might have produced. All beyond this is superfluous and for that reason tyrannical. . . .

The severity of punishment of itself emboldens men to commit the very wrongs it is supposed to prevent; they are driven to commit additional crimes to avoid the punishment for a single one. The countries and times most notorious for severity of penalties have always been those in which the bloodiest and most inhumane of deeds were committed, for the same spirit of ferocity that guided the hand of the legislators also ruled that of the parricide and assassin.

7. On the promptness of punishments[13]:

The more promptly and the more closely punishment follows upon the commission of a crime, the more just and useful will it be. I say more just, because the criminal is thereby spared the useless and cruel torments of uncertainty . . . [and] because privation of liberty, being itself a punishment, should not precede the sentence except when necessity requires. . . . I have said that the promptness of punishment is more useful because when the length of time that passes between the punishment and the misdeed is less, so much the stronger and more lasting in the human mind is the association of these two ideas, *crime and punishment.*

8. On the certainty of punishments[14]:

11. Ibid., p. 62.
12. Ibid., pp. 43–44.
13. Ibid., pp. 55–56.
14. Ibid., pp. 58–59.

One of the greatest curbs on crime is not the cruelty of punishments, but their infallibility. . . . The certainty of a punishment, even if it be moderate, will always make a stronger impression than the fear of another which is more terrible but combined with the hope of impunity; even the least evils, when they are certain, always terrify men's minds. . . . Let the laws, therefore, be inexorable, and inexorable their executors in particular cases, but let the legislator be tender, indulgent, and humane.

9. On preventing crimes[15]:

It is better to prevent crimes than to punish them. That is the ultimate end of every good legislation. . . . Do you want to prevent crimes? See to it that the laws are clear and simple and that the entire force of a nation is united in their defense, and that no part of it is employed to destroy them. See to it that the laws favor not so much classes of men as men themselves. See to it that men fear the laws and fear nothing else. For fear of the laws is salutary, but fatal and fertile for crimes is one man's fear of another.

Beccaria also emphasized that the laws should be published so that the public may know what they are and support their intent and purpose; that torture and secret accusations should be abolished; that capital punishment should be abolished and replaced by imprisonment; that jails be made more humane institutions; that the law should not distinguish between wealthy and poor or between nobles and commoners; and that a person should be tried by a jury of his peers, and that when there were class differences between the offender and the victim, one half of the jury should be from the class of the offender, and the other half from the class of the victim. Beccaria summarized his ideas in a brief conclusion to his book[16]:

In order for punishment not to be, in every instance, an act of violence of one or of many against a private citizen, it must be essentially public, prompt, necessary, the least possible in the given circumstances, proportionate to the crimes, dictated by the laws.

Beccaria's ideas were quite radical for his time, so he published his book anonymously and defended himself in the introduction against charges that he was an unbeliever or a revolutionary. The book was condemned by the Catholic Church in 1766 for its rationalistic ideas.[17] But despite Beccaria's fears and some opposition, his book was extremely

15. Ibid., pp. 93–94.

16. Ibid., p. 99.

17. Ibid., p. xi.

well received by his contemporaries. The first French translation appeared in 1766, and Voltaire provided an elaborate commentary. The first English translation appeared in 1767 under the title *An Essay on Crimes and Punishments*. In the preface to that edition, the translator noted that the book had already gone through six editions in Italian and several in French, and commented that "perhaps no book, on any subject, was ever received with more avidity, more generally read, or more universally applauded."[18]

Following the French Revolution of 1789 Beccaria's principles were used as the basis for the French Code of 1791.[19] The great advantage of this code was that it set up a procedure that was easy to administer. It made the judge only an instrument to apply the law, and the law undertook to prescribe an exact penalty for every crime and every degree thereof. Puzzling questions about the reasons for or causes of behavior, the uncertainties of motive and intent, the unequal consequences of an arbitrary rule, these were all deliberately ignored for the sake of administrative uniformity. This was the classical conception of justice—an exact scale of punishments for equal acts without reference to the individual involved or the circumstances in which the crime was committed.

As a practical matter, however, the Code of 1791 was impossible to enforce in everyday situations, and modifications were introduced. These modifications, all in the interest of greater ease of administration, are the essence of the so-called neoclassical school.

THE NEOCLASSICAL SCHOOL

The greatest practical difficulty in applying the Code of 1791 came from ignoring differences in the circumstances of particular situations. The Code treated everyone exactly alike, in accordance with Beccaria's argument that only the act, and not the intent, should be considered in determining the punishment. Thus first offenders were treated the same as repeaters, minors were treated the same as adults, insane the same as sane, and so on. No society, of course, will permit its children and other helpless incompetents to be treated in the same manner as its professional criminals. The French were no exception. Modifications in practice began, and soon there were revisions of the Code itself.

The Code of 1810[20] tipped the lid just a little in permitting some discretion on the part of the judges. In the Revised French Code of 1819

18. Ibid., p. x.

19. John L. Gillin, *Criminology and Penology*, 3rd ed., Appleton-Century-Crofts, New York, 1945, p. 229.

20. In addition to the Revolutionary Code of 1791, other Napoleonic codes of the period often mentioned are Code de procédure civile, 1806; Code de commerce, 1807; Code d'instruction criminelle, 1808; the Code pénal, 1810; and the revised Code pénal, 1819.

there is definite provision for the exercise of discretion on the part of the judges in view of certain objective circumstances, but still no room for consideration of subjective intent. The set, impersonal features of even this revised *Code Napoléon* then became the point of attack for a new school of reformers whose cry was against the injustice of a rigorous code and for the need for individualization and for discriminating judgment to fit individual circumstances. These efforts at revision and refinement in application of the classical theory of free will and complete responsibility—considerations involving age, mental condition, and extenuating circumstances—constitute what is often called the neoclassical school.

Thus, the neoclassical school represented no particular break with the basic doctrine of human nature that made up the common tradition throughout Europe at the time. The doctrine continued to be that humans are creatures guided by reason, who have free will, and who therefore are responsible for their acts and can be controlled by fear of punishment. Hence the pain from punishment must exceed the pleasure obtained from the criminal act; then free will determines the desirability of noncriminal conduct. The neoclassical school therefore represented primarily the modifications necessary for the administration of the criminal law based on classical theory that resulted from practical experience.

ASSESSING BECCARIA'S THEORY

The neoclassical view is, with minor variations, "the major model of human behavior held to by agencies of social control in all advanced industrial societies (whether in the West or the East). . . ."[21] Its widespread acceptance in contemporary legal systems is probably a result of the fact that this view provides support for the most fundamental assumption on which those systems are based. Classical criminology provides a general justification for the use of punishment in the control of crime. Since punishment for that purpose has always been used in the legal system, it should not be surprising that this is the theory to which legal authorities adhere.

In addition, classical theory was attractive to legal authorities for a more general reason. It is based in social contract theory, which holds that all people have a stake in the continued existence of the authority structure, since without it society would degenerate into a "war of each against all." Since crime contributed to this degeneration, it was ulti-

21. Ian Taylor, Paul Walton, and Jock Young, *The New Criminology*, Harper & Row, New York, 1973, pp. 9–10.

mately in the best interests of all people, even criminals, to obey the law. Social contract theorists saw crime as a fundamentally irrational act, committed by people who, because of their shortsighted greed and passion were incapable of recognizing their own long-term best interests.[22] The fact that crime was concentrated in the lower classes was taken to be a symptom of the fact that these classes were filled with irrational, dangerous people.[23]

The ease with which the classical system of justice could be administered rested largely on this view. It supported the uniform enforcement of laws without questioning whether those laws were fair or just. Specifically, social contract theorists did not take into account the fact that some societies are unfair. For some groups, the costs of adhering to the social contract may be few and the benefits great; for other groups, the costs may be great and the benefits few. The latter group will probably have less allegiance to the social contract, a fact that may be expressed in the form of a higher crime rate.

That is a far different perspective than the view that high-crime groups are filled with irrational and dangerous people. Rather than relying solely on punishments, it would imply that an additional way to reduce crime is to increase the benefits of adhering to the social contract among the high crime groups in society.[24] This option was not attractive to the social contract theorists, who were themselves members of the propertied class. Thus they addressed the problem in such a way as to justify the existence of inequalities. Hobbes, for example, argued that lower-class persons could adhere to the social contract if they were taught to believe that the status quo was inevitable.[25] Locke maintained that all persons were obligated to obey the laws of society, since all gave their "tacit consent" to the social contract. But he also argued that only persons with property were capable of making the laws, since only they were capable of the fully rational life and only they would defend the "natural right" of the unlimited accumulation of property.[26]

Beccaria's position on defending the status quo was somewhat confusing. He argued that it was natural for all to seek their own advantage, even at the expense of the common good, and that this was the source of crime. Thus he did not share the view of the social contract

22. Ibid., p. 3.

23. See, for example, the discussion of Locke's view of the irrationality of the lower classes in C. B. MacPherson, *The Political Theory of Possessive Individualism*, Oxford University Press, New York, 1962, pp. 232–38.

24. E.g., James Q. Wilson, *Thinking about Crime*, Vintage, New York, 1983, pp. 117–44.

25. Macpherson, op. cit., p. 98.

26. Ibid., pp. 247–51.

theorists that criminals were essentially irrational. He was fully aware that the laws (which he said "have always favored the few and outraged the many") could impose massive injustices on the poor.[27] He went even further by arguing that the laws themselves could create crime:[28]

To prohibit a multitude of indifferent acts is not to prevent crimes that might arise from them, but is rather to create new ones. . . . For one motive that drives men to commit real crime there are a thousand that drive them to commit those indifferent acts which are called crimes by bad laws. . . . The majority of laws are nothing but privileges, that is, a tribute paid by all to the convenience of some few.

Thus Beccaria was not solely concerned with the establishment of a system of punishment. He recognized the problem of inequality in society, and implied that it was wrong to punish lawbreakers when the laws themselves were unjust. This aspect of Beccaria's writings is sometimes ignored, so that classical criminology is identified with the social contract position that crime is essentially irrational.[29] For example, Beccaria argued that the death penalty was ineffective because a thief would reason as follows:[30]

What are these laws that I am supposed to respect, that place such a great distance between me and the rich man? He refuses me the penny I ask of him and, as an excuse, tells me to sweat at work that he knows nothing about. Who made these laws? Rich and powerful men who have never deigned to visit the squalid huts of the poor, who have never had to share a crust of moldy bread amid the innocent cries of hungry children and the tears of a wife. Let us break these bonds, fatal to the majority and only useful to a few indolent tyrants; let us attack the injustice at its source. I will return to my natural state of independence; I shall at least for a little time live free and happy with the fruits of my courage and industry. The day will perhaps come for my sorrow and repentance, but will be brief, and for a single day of suffering I shall have many years of liberty and of pleasures.

The radical perspective of this passage is clear, as is the reason that Beccaria feared the official reaction to his book. On the other hand, the implication that Beccaria drew from this discussion was that the death penalty should be replaced by extended imprisonment at hard labor. His reasoning was that such a punishment was actually more terrible

27. Beccaria, op. cit., p. 43.
28. Ibid., p. 94.
29. Taylor, Walton, and Young, op. cit., pp. 1–10.
30. Beccaria, op. cit., p. 49.

than the death penalty, since the threat of "a great number of years, or even a whole lifetime to be spent in servitude and pain," would make a much stronger impression on a potential offender than would the threat of execution.[31]

Thus Beccaria seems to have implied that there are broader social causes behind the crime problem, but he did not make these arguments explicit. One of the effects of the neoclassical adaptation of Beccaria's theory was to prune carefully all of these radical elements from his work, leaving only the easily administered system of punishment as the response to crime.[32]

IMPLICATIONS AND CONCLUSIONS

Beccaria's theory is sometimes portrayed as an extension of the spiritualistic thinking that was dominant at the time, but this cannot be the case. Beccaria published his book anonymously because he feared the reaction to it, and the Catholic Church placed the book on the Index of Forbidden Books where it remained for 200 years. This was because Beccaria removed all spiritual elements from his explanation of crime, and the Catholic Church considered this to be heretical at the time.

In addition, Beirne argues that Beccaria's book actually constituted a fundamental break with the concept of free will.[33] Beccaria's primary argument was that human behavior was predictable and controllable. In particular, he argued that if punishments were public, prompt, minimal, and proportionate, then people would commit less crime. In the view of these who held spiritualistic explanations of crime, this was a highly deterministic argument that flew in the face of the theological assertions about human free will.

Beirne therefore argues that classical theories mark the beginning of the scientific search for the causes of criminal behavior.[34] In Beirne's view, Beccaria's intent was precisely to move away from that "free will" stance to a deterministic one. But Beccaria did so couched carefully in the language of the time because he feared retribution. Beccaria focused on the causal impact of criminal justice policies on criminal behavior, but also pointed to factors in the larger society that also had a causal impact on crime. These included factors that reduce crime, such

---

31. Ibid., pp. 49–50.

32. For a radical interpretation of Beccaria's theory, see Lynn McDonald, *The Sociology of Law and Order*, Faber and Faber, London, 1976, pp. 40–42. McDonald argues that Beccaria's is a "complete and recognizable conflict theory."

33. Beirne, op. cit., pp. 227–28.

34. Ibid., pp. 5–6. A similar but more tentative argument is found in Bob Roshier, *Controlling Crime*, Lyceum, Chicago, 1989.

as education, and those that increase it, such as poverty and economic inequality.

In that sense, Beccaria's theory really was the first step away from a pure free-will stance toward a deterministic behaviorism influenced primarily by criminal justice policies. From this point of view, there is no marked opposition between classical theories and the later positivist theories that searched for the causes of criminal behavior. Rather, this transition to positivism marks a continuing development in the direction in which Beccaria pointed.

CHAPTER 3

Positivist Criminology

Beccaria's theory changed criminal justice policies, especially in France, and led to the expectation that crime would soon decrease. But there was really no way to find out whether this occurred, since there were no annual crime statistics to measure whether crime was going up or down.

The first annual national crime statistics were published in France in 1827, about sixty years after Beccaria wrote his book.[1] It soon became clear that these crime statistics were astonishingly regular. The rates of crime in general and of particular crimes such as murder and rape remained relatively constant from year to year. In addition, some places in the nation had higher crime rates while others had lower, and these differences remained relatively constant from year to year.

Today, we take such regularity in crime statistics for granted, but at that time, those who held a "free will" theory of crime expected random changes in the number of crimes, especially in the number of unpremeditated crimes such as passion murders. The regularity of crime statistics suggested that Beccaria had been right in his argument that, rather than being entirely the product of free will, crime must be influenced by factors in the larger society. It also supported Beccaria's hope that, by changing those factors, crime might be reduced.

But the new crime statistics also made it clear that crime rates were going up, not down. Earlier local statistics had suggested the same thing. Even more distressing, these statistics suggested that recidivism was going up: People who had received the prompt, proportionate punishments provided by the new French code were committing more new

---

1. This introduction and the following discussion of Quetelet and Guerry rely heavily on the work of Piers Beirne, *Inventing Criminology*, State University of New York Press, Albany, N.Y., 1993, chps., 3, 4.

offenses rather than fewer. This suggested that Beccaria had been wrong to argue that changes in punishment policies alone could reduce crime.

The new crime statistics clearly revealed the failure of classical punishment policies, while at the same time suggesting that other social factors might influence the level of crime in society. This gave rise to a new brand of criminology, which eventually became known as positivism. Its goal was to study the causes of crime either in the larger society or in the individual.

GUERRY AND QUETELET

The development of national crime statistics in France was part of the larger development in Europe of relatively accurate official records, as part of the development of stable social and political organization. Systematic registries of births and deaths, for example, developed in European cities and states in the 1500s.[2] In the 1600s various items in the official records began to be counted and compared as part of an analysis of economic conditions and their consequences. In England such studies came to be called "political arithmetic,"[3] while in Germany they were called "moral statistik."[4] Edmund Halley (1656–1742), the astronomer for whom Halley's comet was named, compiled and published, in 1692–93, the first systematic "life expectancy tables."[5] Adam Smith used these same official data on social and economic conditions in his great work, *Inquiry into the Nature and Causes of the Wealth of Nations* (1776), as did Malthus in his controversial studies on population growth.[6]

Shortly after the publication of the first modern national crime statistics in France in 1827, Andre-Michel Guerry (1802–1866) published what is considered by many to be the first work in "scientific criminology."[7] Guerry was a French lawyer who, soon after he took an interest in these statistics, was appointed director of criminal statistics for the French Ministry of Justice. Guerry used shaded ecological maps to represent differing crime rates in relation to various social factors. After

2. Walter F. Wilcox, "History of Statistics," in *Encyclopedia of the Social Sciences*, vol. 14, Macmillan, New York, 1931, p. 356.

3. Bernard Lécuyer and Anthony R. Oberschall, "The Early History of Social Research," *International Encyclopedia of the Social Sciences*, vol. 15, pp. 36–37.

4. Yale Levin and Alfred Lindesmith, "English Ecology and Criminology of the Past Century," *Journal of Criminal Law and Criminology* 27: 801–16 (March–April 1937).

5. Lécuyer and Oberschall, op. cit., p. 37.

6. Cf. Thomas R. Malthus, *Essay on Principle of Population as It Affects the Future Improvement of Society*, London, 1798.

7. Terence Morris, *The Criminal Area*, Routledge and Kegan Paul, New York, 1957, pp. 42–53.

preliminary publication in 1829, his work appeared in expanded book form in 1833 under the title *Essai sur la statistique morale de la France.*

Guerry tested the commonly held belief that crime was associated with poverty, but he found instead that the wealthiest region of France had a higher rate of property crimes but only about half the rate of violent crime.[8] However, Guerry had measured wealth and poverty by the amount of direct taxation, and he pointed out that the wealthiest sections had a great deal of poverty in them. Although he did not directly measure the poverty in those wealthier provinces, he concluded that poverty itself did not cause property crime, but rather the main factor was opportunity: In the wealthier provinces there was more to steal.

Guerry also attacked the widely held view that lack of education was associated with crime.[9] New statistics were available on the reading and writing abilities of all young men subject to the military draft. Guerry used these statistics to determine the education levels of the various sections of France. The most educated sections were in northeast France, where almost 75 percent of young men could read and write, while the least educated sections were in western and central France, where only about 7 percent could. Guerry then showed that areas with the highest education levels had the highest rates of violent crime, while those with the lowest rates of such crime had the lowest education levels.

A second person to analyze these statistics was Adolphe Quetelet (1796–1874).[10] Quetelet was a Belgian mathematician and astronomer who had achieved considerable success in these fields while still quite young. In 1823, at the age of 27, the Belgian Royal Academy sent him to Paris as part of a project to build an astronomical observatory in Brussels. While there, he studied new statistical techniques that were being developed as part of "celestial mechanics." He also became familiar with the new social data that were first being collected in France at that time, such as the numbers of births and deaths in a year. On his return to Brussels the following year, he used his newly acquired statistical techniques to analyze some of the social data—e.g., he showed that there was considerable regularity in the rates of death each year. He then argued that the regularities in this social data were analogous to the regularities found in "celestial mechanics." He therefore used the term "social mechanics" to describe this type of analyses of social data.

---

8. Beirne, op. cit., pp. 119–23.

9. Ibid., pp. 124–27.

10. The following discussion is taken largely from Beirne, op. cit., pp. 65–110.

In 1828, he turned his attention to the newly published French crime statistics. He showed that there was considerable regularity throughout those statistics—e.g., in the number of people accused of crimes against property, in the number accused of crimes against persons, and in the ratio between these two numbers; in the number of those convicted, in the number acquitted, and in the ratio between those two numbers; in the ratio of males to females convicted of crimes, and in the distribution of convictions by age. He then suggested that it would be desirable to have similar statistics for other countries "to see if they follow a march as regular as the tables of mortality."[11] He went on to present his basic orientation toward these statistics:

. . . there must be an order to those things which, when they are reproduced with astonishing constancy, and always in the same way, do not change quickly and without cause. For the moment we are adopting the role of an observer. In the study of human affairs we rely on the same principles used to study other natural causes.

Quetelet then began to analyze this data more closely. He found that some people were more likely to commit crime than others, especially those who were young, male, poor, unemployed, and undereducated. Young males were more likely to commit crime under any circumstances, so that places with more young males tended to have more crime. But places with more poverty and more unemployment actually had less crime. As it turned out, the poor and unemployed tended to commit crimes in places where there were many wealthy and employed people. So crime was higher in places with *less* poverty and unemployment, but it tended to be committed by the poor and unemployed people who lived there.

Like Guerry, Quetelet suggested that opportunities might have something to do with explaining this pattern in that wealthier cities "might attract vagabonds who hope to find impunity by losing themselves in the crowd."[12] He also pointed to an additional factor: The great inequality between wealth and poverty in the same place excites passions and provokes temptations of all kinds.[13] This problem is especially severe in those places where rapidly changing economic conditions can result in a person suddenly passing from wealth to poverty while all around him still enjoy wealth. In contrast, provinces that were gener-

11. Quoted in Beirne, ibid., pp. 78–79.

12. Adolphe Quetelet, *Research on the Propensity for Crime at Different Ages*, translated by Sawyer F. Sylvester, Anderson, Cincinnati, 1984, p. 40.

13. Ibid., pp. 37–38.

ally poor and had little wealth had less crime as long as people were able to satisfy their basic needs.

Also like Guerry, Quetelet found that increased education did not reduce crime. People with more education tended to commit less crime on the whole, but they also tended to commit more violent crime. Those with less education committed more crime but it tended to be property crime. Quetelet therefore argued that increased education itself would not reduce crime.[14]

Quetelet concluded that the propensity to engage in crime was actually a reflection of moral character. Relying on Aristotle's views, he identified virtue with moderation: "rational and temperate habits, more regulated passions ... [and] foresight, as manifested by investment in savings banks, assurance societies, and the different institutions which encourage foresight."[15] Young males often did not have these very virtues, and so they committed high levels of crime. Similarly, these virtues tended to break down among poor and unemployed people who were surrounded by wealth. Thus, his main policy recommendations were to enhance "moral" education and to ameliorate social conditions to improve people's lives.[16]

Quetelet's most famous and controversial statement described crime as an inevitable feature of social organization[17]:

The crimes which are annually committed seem to be a necessary result of our social organization. . . *Society prepares the crime, and the guilty are only the instruments by which it is executed.*

This was an extraordinarily radical statement for the time, and Quetelet was forced to defend his theories against attacks by those who held free-will spiritual explanations of crime.[18] These critics saw his arguments as a deterministic heresy that necessarily implied atheism. Even worse, these critics claimed that Quetelet implied that nothing could be done to reduce crime. For example, Quetelet had argued that crime and punishment tended to be constants in a society[19]:

14. Beirne, op. cit., pp. 83–84.

15. Ibid., pp. 88–90. The idea of moderation as virtue is related to Quetelet's conception of the "average man," whose characteristics fall in the center of a normal distribution while "deviants" such as criminals are found at the tails. This in turn was an analogy from astronomy. See ibid., pp. 82–83.

16. Ibid., p. 92.

17. Quoted in Beirne, op. cit., p. 88.

18. Ibid., pp. 92–97.

19. Quoted in Beirne, op. cit., p. 82.

The share of prisons, chains, and the scaffold appears fixed with as much probability as the revenues of the state. We are able to enumerate in advance how many individuals will stain their hands with the blood of their fellow creatures, how many will be forgers, how many poisoners, pretty nearly as one can enumerate in advance the births and deaths which must take place.

In response to these criticisms, Quetelet repeatedly affirmed his belief in God and in the individual's ability to freely choose in the face of these causal factors. In addition, he argued that his theories really were very optimistic because they indicated that there were a limited number of causes of crime. He argued that governments should continue the types of punishment policies recommended by Beccaria, but he also argued that they should undertake a variety of social reforms that would improve the conditions of people's lives and would allow the moral and intellectual qualities of citizens to flourish. In that way, the causes of crime would be reduced, and a reduction in crime itself would follow.

Quetelet retained the view throughout his life that crime essentially was caused by moral defectiveness, but increasingly took the view that moral defectiveness was revealed in biological characteristics, particularly the appearance of the face and the head.[20] To that extent, his theories became increasingly like his critics had described them—i.e., deterministic and pessimistic in the sense that government policies could do little to reduce crime. This also made him a direct predecessor of Lombroso, whose major book was published only two years after Quetelet's death.

CESARE LOMBROSO

Cesare Lombroso (1835–1909) was a physician who became a specialist in psychiatry, and his principal career was as a professor of legal medicine at the University of Turin.[21] His name came into prominence with the publication of his book, *L'uomo delinquente (The Criminal Man)*, in 1876. In that book Lombroso proposed that criminals were biological throwbacks to an earlier evolutionary stage, people more primitive and less highly evolved than their noncriminal counterparts. Lombroso used the term *atavistic* to describe such people. The idea of evolution

---

20. Ibid., pp. 90–91.

21. Information about Lombroso's life and work can be found in ch. 2 of Randy Martin, Robert J. Mutchnick, and W. Timothy Austin, *Criminological Thought: Pioneers Past and Present*, Macmillan, New York, 1990; and in Marvin E. Wolfgang, "Cesare Lombroso," pp. 232–91 in Hermann Mannheim, ed., *Pioneers in Criminology*, 2nd ed., Patterson Smith, Montclair, N.J., 1972. For a more critical view, see ch. 4 of Stephen Jay Gould, *The Mismeasure of Man*, Norton, New York, 1981, where Lombroso's theory of atavism is presented in its historical and scientific context. Gould argues that scientists of the time, desiring to prove their own superiority and the inferiority of other racial and ethnic groups, cloaked their prejudices in the veil of objective science.

itself was relatively recent at the time, having first been proposed by Darwin in his book, *On the Origin of Species* (1859). That book had brought about the final break with the spiritualist, free-will thought of the past. Darwin presented evidence that humans were the same general kind of creatures as the rest of the animals, except that they were more highly evolved or developed. The ancestors of modern people were less highly evolved and were part of a continuous chain linking humans to the earliest and simplest forms of life. Even the idea that some individuals might be reversions to an earlier evolutionary stage had been originally suggested by Darwin, who had written: "With mankind some of the worst dispositions which occasionally without any assignable cause make their appearance in families, may perhaps be reversions to a savage state, from which we are not removed by many generations."[22]

Lombroso's theories will be presented in more detail in Chapter 4, but as a founder of the positive school of criminology he is something of an anomaly. Lombroso is known principally for the earliest formulation of his theory of the atavistic criminal. The real basis of the positive school, however, is the search for the causes of criminal behavior. That search is based on the conception of multiple factor causation, in which some of the factors may be biological, others psychological, and still others social.

Lombroso did much by way of documenting the effects of many of these factors. As his thinking changed over the years, he looked more and more to environmental rather than biological factors. This change and growth in his thinking was evidenced by the increases in the number of pages in successive editions of *L'uomo delinquente*. In its first edition in 1876, Lombroso required 252 pages to explain his theory of evolutionary atavism as the cause of crime. Twenty years later, in the fifth edition of his book, he needed over 1,900 pages to include all the items that appeared to be related to crime causation. Those included such things as climate, rainfall, the price of grain, sex and marriage customs, criminal laws, banking practices, national tariff policies, the structure of government, church organization, and the state of religious belief. Lombroso's last book, *Crime, Its Causes and Remedies*, was a summary of his life work specially prepared for American readers.[23] Published in 1911, two years after Lombroso's death, it includes discussions of many factors related to crime causation, of which by far the largest number are environmental rather than biological.

22. Charles Darwin, *Descent of Man*, John Murray, London, 1871, p. 137.

23. Cesare Lombroso, *Crime: Its Causes and Remedies*, 1912 edition reprinted by Patterson Smith, Montclair, N.J., 1972.

Lombroso's later, more mature thought therefore included many factors other than the physical or anthropological. He maintained that there are three major classes of criminals: (1) *born criminals*, to be understood as atavistic reversions to a lower or more primitive evolutionary form of development, and thought to constitute about one third of the total number of offenders; (2) *insane criminals*, i.e., idiots, imbeciles, paranoiacs, sufferers from melancholia, and those afflicted with general paralysis, dementia, alcoholism, epilepsy, or hysteria (strange bedfellows, to be sure); and (3) *criminaloids*, a large general class without special physical characteristics or recognizable mental disorders, but whose mental and emotional makeup are such that under certain circumstances they indulge in vicious and criminal behavior. Lombroso conceded that well over one half of all criminals were "criminaloids," so that they were not "born criminals" or "insane" in the sense that he used those terms.

By the time of Lombroso's death in 1909 it was evident that his theories were too simple and naive. Anthropology abandoned the conception of uniform, linear evolution with humans as the most highly evolved animal (and the English gentleman as the most highly evolved human), and then his notion of the atavistic criminal as a less highly evolved person became quite meaningless. Psychiatry and psychology were already marshaling evidence to show that the relationship between crime and epilepsy, or between crime and insanity, was much more complex and involved than Lombroso assumed.

Despite these criticisms, Lombroso's theory of the atavistic criminal received enormous public attention at the time. This gave it great prominence in criminology, while Guerry's and Quetelet's earlier work more or less dropped out of sight. As a result, for most of this century, Lombroso was described in criminology textbooks as the first criminologist to search for the causes of crime and therefore as the founder of positivist criminology.

Lindesmith and Levin, however, argued that Guerry's and Quetelet's earlier work had been "positivistic" in the sense that it involved a search for the causes of crime.[24] These criminologists noted that Guerry and Quetelet had emphasized social causes of crime, and speculated on why Lombroso's biological theory attracted so much more attention:[25]

It may be that the theory of the born criminal offered a convenient rationalization of the failure of preventive effort and an escape from the implication

---

24. Alfred Lindesmith and Yale Levin, "The Lombrosian Myth in Criminology," *American Journal of Sociology* 42: 653–71 (March 1937).

25. Ibid., p. 670.

of the dangerous doctrine that crime is an essential product of our social organization. It may well be that a public, which had been nagged for centuries by reformers, welcomed the opportunity to slough off its responsibilities for this vexing problem.

Radzinowicz made a similar comment[26]:

It served the interests and relieved the conscience of those at the top to look upon the dangerous classes as an independent category, detached from the prevailing social conditions. They were portrayed as a race apart, morally depraved and vicious, living by violating the fundamental law of orderly society, which was that a man should maintain himself by honest, steady work.

In spite of these criticisms, Lombroso's name is one that will long be remembered as important in the development of criminological thought. As Sellin has well said[27]: "Any scholar who succeeds in driving hundreds of fellow students to search for the truth, and whose ideas after half a century possess vitality, merits an honorable place in the history of thought."

MODERN CRIMINOLOGY AS THE SEARCH FOR THE CAUSES OF CRIME

Most criminology today is positivistic in the sense that it studies the causes of crime. But there are really two different methods of studying the causes of crime and therefore two different types of theories in positivist criminology. Lombroso studied the biological, psychological, and social characteristics of individuals to identify factors that increase or decrease the likelihood the individual will engage in crime. In contrast, Quetelet studied the social characteristics of different areas of France to identify factors that are associated with high or low crime rates in those areas. These two methods do not contradict each other, but they certainly are not the same thing. Lombroso's method of studying the causes of crime is associated with *individual-level* theories of crime, while Quetelet's method is associated with *societal-level* theories of crime.[28]

Consider, as an analogy, methods to study the causes of unem-

26. Leon Radzinowicz, *Ideology and Crime*, Columbia University Press, New York, 1966, pp. 38–39. See also Lindesmith and Levin, op. cit., p. 655.

27. Thorsten Sellin, "The Lombrosian Myth in Criminology," *American Journal of Sociology* 42: 896–97 (1937). This is a critical comment on the article by Lindesmith and Levin cited in n. 24.

28. See Thomas J. Bernard and Jeffrey Snipes, "Theoretical Integration in Criminology," in Michael Tonry, ed., *Crime and Justice: An Annual Review of Research*, vol. 20, University of Chicago Press, Chicago, 1996.

ployment. We could study why some people are unemployed while others are able to get and hold a job. If that is our purpose, then we would have to study the characteristics of unemployed people and compare them to the characteristics of employed people. A theory that emerges from our study probably would focus on factors associated with the individuals, such as education, motivation, and job skills. But we also could study why there are high unemployment rates at some times and places and low unemployment rates at other times and places. To do that, we would have to study the characteristics of times and places in which there was high unemployment, and compare them with the characteristics of times and places in which there was low unemployment. A theory that emerges from our study probably would focus on factors associated with societies, such as interest rates, budget and trade deficits, and currency exchange rates. Both would be theories of the causes of unemployment, but they would be very different types of theories because explaining why a particular person is unemployed is very different than explaining unemployment rates in a society.

A similar point can be made about theories of the causes of crime. Some individual characteristics are associated with an increased likelihood that the person will engage in criminal behavior. Much of contemporary positivist criminology, following Lombroso's lead, studies the biological, psychological, and social characteristics of individual criminals in the attempt to identify these characteristics. But some times and places have much higher crime rates than other times and places. These times and places do not simply have more people in them with the individual characteristics that are associated with criminal behavior. Rather, explaining rates of crime is different than explaining the likelihood that an individual will engage in it.

For example, in the original national crime statistics, Quetelet found what everyone already knew: that people who were poor were more likely to commit crime than people who were wealthy. But the interesting thing about Quetelet's research is that he found that regions in France with more poverty did not have more crime. In fact, places with more poverty had less crime. Places with more wealth had more crime, although the crime was predominantly committed by poor people in those places. Thus, while poverty may be a cause of crime at the individual level, it does not seem to be one at the societal level. Lombroso's method of studying individual criminals could never have found this information, since he would only find that poor individuals were more likely to commit crime.

THE RELATION BETWEEN POSITIVIST AND
CLASSICAL THEORIES

Positive criminology might seem opposed to the classical criminology presented in Chapter 2, but this is not necessarily the case. Rather, classical theories can be interpreted as implying a theory of human behavior that is quite consistent with positivism. In the past, classical criminologists have assumed that the certainty and severity of criminal punishments could affect criminal behavior, but that other variables in the environment could not. But in his defense of classical criminology, Roshier argues[29]:

In general, there was nothing inherent in Beccaria's intellectual position to preclude a consideration of the socio-economic context of crime, any more than there was to necessitate his sole concentration on deterrence... Indeed, it is an oddity that he seemed to see the criminal justice system as being the only aspect of the environment that influences individual decisions about whether it is worthwhile to commit crime or not.

Classical criminologists therefore could expand their theoretical frame of reference and examine how crime rates are influenced by a wide range of factors outside the criminal justice system, including biological, psychological, and social factors. All these factors could then be described as "causes" of crime. Reflecting this basic position, Beirne argues that the proper place for Beccaria's theory in the history of criminology lies "at the very beginning of the tradition to which it is commonly opposed, namely, positivist criminology."[30]

A similar point can be made about positive criminology. In the past, positivist criminologists have assumed that biological, psychological, and social factors can influence criminal behavior, but that the certainty and severity of criminal punishments could not. But in their defense of positive criminology, Gottfredson and Hirschi argue[31]:

No deterministic explanation of crime can reasonably exclude the variables of the classical model on deterministic grounds. These variables may account for some of the variation in crime. If so, they have as much claim to inclusion in a "positivistic" model as any other set of variables accounting for the same amount of variation.

29. Bob Roshier, *Controlling Crime*, Lyceum, Chicago, 1989.

30. Piers Beirne, "Inventing Criminology: The 'Science of Man' in Cesare Beccaria's *Dei Delitti e Delle Pene* (1764)," *Criminology* 29(4): 777–820 (Nov. 1991).

31. Michael R. Gottfredson and Travis Hirschi, "The Positive Tradition," pp. 9–22 in Gottfredson and Hirschi, eds., *Positive Criminology*, Sage, Newburg Park, CA, 1987.

Thus, positive criminologists can include the certainty and severity of criminal punishments among the many other factors that might influence criminal behavior.

Positivist and classical criminology therefore are really part of the same enterprise—they both seek to identify the factors that influence the incidence of criminal behavior. The basic controversy between them is empirical rather than theoretical: Which factors have more influence on criminal behavior and which have less?[32]

CONCLUSION

In the chapters that follow, the major theories on the causes of criminal behavior will be examined. Each of these theories suggests that certain factors, either at the individual or the societal level, might have a causal influence on crime. Research has disproven some of the earlier theories, in the sense of finding that the factors to which they point have no causal influence on crime whatsoever. Extensive research has been done on the more recent theories, but there is considerable disagreement about which factors have greater and which have lesser influence on crime.

The fact that there are no conclusive answers to the question of the causes of crime does not mean that criminology is unscientific. It is precisely because criminology theories are scientific, in the sense that they assert relationships between classes of observable phenomena, that they can be tested with research at all. Nonscientific explanations of crime, such as spiritual explanations, cannot be tested with research because they include phenomena that are not observable.

In general, the earlier chapters follow the lead of Lombroso in that they focus on the question of why one person engages in criminal behaviors while another does not. Thus, the earlier chapters emphasize factors associated with individuals, especially biological and psychological factors. Later chapters increasingly take Quetelet's approach, seeking to explain high or low crime rates by looking at factors associated with societies. But there is no absolute division between these two types of theories. Rather, it is a question of where their emphasis lies. This was true even for Lombroso and Quetelet. By the end of his life, Quetelet had included in his theory many biological factors that explained why some individuals are more likely to engage in crime, so that his theory ended up being quite similar to Lombroso's later one. And by the end of his life, Lombroso had included in his theory many soci-

---

32. See Bernard and Snipes, op. cit. This innocuous sounding statement contains major implications about the authors' view of the nature of scientific theories in criminology (see Chapter 19).

etal-level factors that seemed more appropriate for explaining rates of crime rather than the individual's propensity to engage in it. To some extent, Lombroso's theory had become like Quetelet's earlier one.

CHAPTER 4

Theories Related to Physical Appearance

One of the oldest scientific approaches in criminology theory emphasizes physical and biological abnormality as the distinguishing mark of the criminal. In this approach criminals are viewed as somehow different, abnormal, defective, and therefore inferior biologically. This biological inferiority is thought to produce certain physical characteristics that make the appearance of criminals different from that of noncriminals. Early criminologists studied the physical appearance of criminals in an attempt to identify these characteristics. The real explanation of criminal behavior, in this view, is biological defectiveness and inferiority—physical and other characteristics are only symptoms of that inferiority.

PHYSIOGNOMY AND PHRENOLOGY

The belief that criminals and evil people in general have unusual physical appearance goes back to ancient times. For example, in *The Iliad* (Pope's translation), Homer described the evil Thersites as follows:

One eye was blinking, and one leg was lame;
His mountain shoulders half his breast o'erspread,
Thin hairs bestrew'd his long misshapen head.

The venerable Socrates was examined by a Greek physiognomist, who found that his face revealed him as brutal, sensuous, and inclined to drunkenness. Socrates admitted that such was his natural disposition but said he had learned to overcome these tendencies.[1]

1. Havelock Ellis, *The Criminal*, 2nd ed., Scribner, New York, 1900, p. 27. A rather popular, psychoanalytically oriented discussion of the symbolic meanings of physical appearance, including the tendency to link beauty to goodness and ugliness to evil, can be found in Robin Tolmach Lakoff and Raquel L. Scherr, *Face Value: The Politics of Beauty*, Routledge & Kegan Paul, Boston, 1984.

Physiognomy—making judgments about people's character from the appearance of their faces—was a recognized study in the Europe of Cesare Beccaria. In 1775, Johan Caspar Lavater (1741–1801), a Swiss scholar and theologian, published a four-volume work on physiognomy entitled *Physiognomical Fragments*, which received nearly as favorable attention as the now much better-known work produced by Beccaria only eleven years earlier. In this work, Lavater systematized many popular observations and made many extravagant claims about the alleged relation between facial features and human conduct. For example, beardlessness in men and its opposite, the bearded woman, were both considered unfavorable trait indicators, as were a "shifty" eye, a "weak" chin, an "arrogant" nose, and so on. Details of these classifications are of little importance now.[2] The principal significance of physiognomy lies in the impetus it gave to the better-organized and logically more impressive view that came to be known as phrenology.

Phrenology focused on the external shape of the skull instead of the appearance of the face. Based originally on Aristotle's idea of the brain as the organ of the mind, phrenologists assumed that the exterior of the skull conformed to its interior and therefore to the shape of the brain. Different faculties or functions of the mind were assumed to be associated with different parts of the brain. Therefore, the exterior shape of the skull would indicate how the mind functioned.

The eminent European anatomist Franz Joseph Gall (1758–1828) is generally given credit for the systematic development of the doctrines of phrenology, though he did not originate or make much use of that term. In 1791 he started publishing materials on the relations between head conformations and the personal characteristics of individuals. Closely allied with Gall in the development of phrenology was his student and one-time collaborator, John Gaspar Spurzheim (1776–1832). It was Spurzheim rather than Gall who carried their doctrines to England and America, lecturing before scientific meetings and stimulating interest in their ideas.

Gall listed twenty-six special faculties of the brain; Spurzheim increased the number to thirty-five.[3] Their lists included faculties described as amativeness, conjugality, philoprogenitiveness (love of offspring), friendliness, combativeness, destructiveness, acquisitiveness, cautiousness, self-esteem, firmness, benevolence, constructiveness, ide-

2. Cf. Erik Nordenshiöld, *The History of Biology*, Knopf, New York, 1928.

3. For a history of phrenology, as well as a defense of its use in modern times, see Sybil Leek, *Phrenology*, Macmillan, New York, 1970. For a discussion of Gall and Spurzheim, see Leonard Savitz, Stanley H. Turner, and Toby Dickman, "The Origin of Scientific Criminology: Franz Joseph Gall as the First Criminologist," in Robert F. Meier, ed., *Theory in Criminology*, Sage, Beverly Hills, Calif., 1977, pp. 41–56.

ality, and imitativeness. These were said to be grouped into three regions or compartments, one the "lower" or active propensities, another the moral sentiments, and the third the intellectual faculties. Crime was said to involve the lower propensities, notably amativeness, philoprogenitiveness, combativeness, secretiveness, and acquisitiveness. These propensities, however, could be held in restraint by the moral sentiments or the intellectual faculties, in which case no crime would be committed. Character and human conduct were thus conceived as an equilibrium in the pull of these opposite forces. Animal propensities might impel the individual to crime, but they would be opposed by the higher sentiments and intelligence. Just as other organs were strengthened by exercise and enfeebled by disuse, so were the "organs" of the mind. Careful training of the child, and even of the adult, in right living would strengthen the "organs" of desirable faculties and inhibit through disuse the lower propensities with their concomitants of crime and vice.[4]

The obvious scientific criticism of the phrenological theory of crime was that no one was able to observe the physiological "organs" of the mind or their relation to particular types of behavior. The most serious obstacle to its acceptance by the public, however, was the deterministic nature of its analysis. If human conduct were the result of the organs of the mind, then people's fate was in the hands of their anatomy and physiology. This view was rejected and opposed by teachers, preachers, judges, and other leaders who influenced public opinion, because it contradicted one of their most cherished ideas, namely that humans are masters of their own conduct and capable of making of themselves what they will. It was the need to show that humans were still masters of their fate (as well as to respond to criticisms of the fatalistic position implied by his earlier work) that led Gall to publish his *Des Dispositions innées de l'âme et de l'esprit du matérialisme* (1811), in which he argued that phrenology was not fatalistic, that *will* and *spirit* were basic and supreme in the direction and control of human behavior.

CRIMINAL ANTHROPOLOGY: LOMBROSO TO GORING

Cesare Lombroso (1835–1909) extended the tradition of physiognomy and phrenology by studying all anatomical features of the human body, not merely the features of the face or the shape of the skull.[7] Lombroso was a doctor in the Italian army who was concerned about the problems, including crime, of soldiers who came from Southern Italy, in-

---

4. Arthur E. Fink, *The Causes of Crime: Biological Theories in the United States, 1800–1915*, University of Pennsylvania Press, Philadelphia, 1938, pp. 8–9.

cluding Sicily. At that time, the "Southern question" was a popular concern, with many allegations in the popular press and by conservative politicians that "the Southerners are inferior beings. . . lazy, incapable, criminal, and barbaric."[5]

Lombroso had a flash of insight while performing a postmortem on a thief who came from Southern Italy[6]:

> . . . on laying open the skull I found on the occipital part, exactly on the spot where a spine is found in the normal skull, a distinct depression which I named *median occipital fossa*, because of its situation precisely in the middle of the occiput as in inferior animals, expecially rodents. . . At the sight of that skull, I seemed to see all of a sudden, lighted up as a vast plain under a flaming sky, the problem of the nature of the criminal—an atavistic being who reproduces in his person the ferocious instincts of primitive humanity and the inferior animals.

Lombroso went on to perform autopsies on sixty-six male criminals, and he found that these had a significant number of characteristics that were similar to primitive humans. He also examined 832 living criminals, both male and female, 390 noncriminal Italian soldiers, and ninety "lunatics." These studies were presented in his book, *L'uomo delinquente (The Criminal Man)*, which appeared in 1876.

Some of the physical characteristics that Lombroso linked to crime included deviations in head size and shape, asymmetry of the face, large jaws and cheekbones, unusually large or small ears or ears that stand out from the head, fleshy lips, abnormal teeth, receding chin, abundant hair or wrinkles, long arms, extra fingers or toes, or an asymmetry of the brain.[7] Many of these characteristics were said to resemble lower animals, such as monkeys and chimpanzees.

Lombroso's theory generated strong reactions, both favorable and unfavorable, among his contemporaries. In response to criticisms of his theory, Lombroso offered to have an impartial committed study of 100 "born criminals," 100 persons with criminal tendencies, and 100 normal persons. Lombroso offered to retract his theories if the physical, mental, and psychological characteristics of the three groups were found to

5. Antonio Gramsci, "Some Aspects of the Southern Question," in Quintin Hoare, ed., *Gramsci: Selections from Political Writings*, International Publishers, New York, 1978, p. 444.

6. Cesare Lombroso, *L'uomo delinquente (The Criminal Man)*, 4th ed., Bocca, Torino, 1889, p. 273, as quoted by Enrico Ferri, *Criminal Sociology*, D. Appleton, New York, 1900, p. 12.

7. This is a partial listing adapted from the basic work by Gina Lombroso Ferrero, *Criminal Man According to the Classification of Cesare Lombroso*, Putnam, New York, 1911, pp. 10–24; reprinted by Patterson Smith, Montclair, N.J., 1972; and summarized by John Lewis Gillin, *Criminology and Penology*, 3rd ed., Appleton Century Crofts, New York, 1945, p. 79.

be identical. This challenge was never really met, since Lombroso's opponents said it was impossible to distinguish between the three groups accurately.

However, a study by Charles Goring, begun in England in 1901 and published in 1913, was to some extent a response to Lombroso's challenge.[8] Goring's study was strictly a comparison between a group of convicts—persons convicted of crimes and imprisoned—and a group of unconvicted persons who included university undergraduates, hospital patients, and the officers and men of units of the British army. Thus, no attempt was made to distinguish between "born criminals," persons with criminal tendencies, and normal persons. Also, Goring relied totally on objective measurements of physical and mental characteristics, where Lombroso had objected to such total reliance, maintaining that many anomalies were "so small as to defy all but the most minute research."[9] He argued that these could be detected by the eye of the trained observer, but could not be measured. Finally the study, as it evolved, went well beyond any attempt to prove or disprove Lombroso's theories, as Goring advanced his own theory of hereditary inferiority. Goring's theory will be presented in Chapter 6; in this chapter we will concentrate on his attempt to disprove Lombroso's theory that criminals had distinct physical characteristics.

Lombroso had asserted that criminals, compared with the general population, would show anomalies (i.e., differences or defects) of head height, head width, and degree of receding forehead, as well as differences in head circumference, head symmetry, and so on. Goring, in comparing prisoners with the officers and men of the Royal Engineers, found no such anomalies. There were no more protrusions or other peculiarities of the head among the prisoners than among the Royal Engineers. Goring also compared other characteristics, such as nasal contours, color of eyes, color of hair, and left-handedness, but found only insignificant differences. He compared groups of different kinds of criminals (burglars, forgers, thieves, etc.) on the basis of thirty-seven specific physical characteristics. He concluded that there were no significant differences between one kind of criminal and another that were not more properly related to the selective effects of environmental factors.[10]

---

8. Edwin D. Driver, Introductory Essay in Charles Goring, *The English Convict: A Statistical Study*, 1913 edition reprinted by Patterson Smith, Montclair, N.J., 1972, p. vii.

9. Cesare Lombroso, *The Female Offender*, Unwin, London, 1895; quoted in Goring, op. cit., p. 16.

10. Goring, op. cit., pp. 196–214.

The one general exception to his conclusion was a consistent "inferiority in stature and in body weight." The criminals were one to two inches shorter than noncriminals of the same occupational groups, and weighed from three to seven pounds less.[11] Goring was satisfied that these differences were real and significant, and he interpreted them as indicating a general inferiority of a hereditary nature. This interpretation agreed with his general thesis of hereditary inferiority (as measured by comparisons of mental ability and various other indices of hereditary influence) as the basis for criminal conduct.[12]

Goring has been criticized for being too anxious to disprove Lombroso's theories.[13] In general, this was because Goring considered Lombroso's work to be unscientific. Goring argued that "the whole of Lombroso's enterprise was conducted . . . with the unconscious intention of stamping a preconceived idea with the hall mark of science"[14] and that it could not be considered an impartial investigation of the theory itself. He also criticized Lombroso's willingness to declare that people who had never been involved with the law were criminals solely on the basis of their physical appearance.[15] Goring himself maintained that the use of the term *criminal* should reflect a legal reality—a person who has broken the law and been convicted—rather than any vague ethical or moral conception of "the kind of men who, whether they have or have not committed crime, we believe to be criminal at heart."[16] Finally, he argued that even if specific differences did exist between the criminal and the noncriminal, this would not indicate that the criminal was abnormal. Rather, the criminal was "a selected class of normal man" whose "qualities may present extreme degrees from the normal average."[17] Goring's point is similar to saying that professional basketball players are not tall because they are an

---

11. Ibid., p. 200.

12. Ibid., p. 287, especially Table 119.

13. Edwin D. Driver, "Charles Buckman Goring," in Hermann Mannheim, ed., *Pioneers in Criminology*, Patterson Smith, Montclair, N.J., 1973, p. 440.

14. Goring, op. cit., p. 16. For more on the unscientific nature of Lombroso's theory, see Stephen Jay Gould, *The Mismeasure of Man*, Norton, New York, 1981.

15. For example, Goring (ibid., p. 15) states that "on one occasion [Lombroso] pointed out, as an example of the criminal type, a youth who had never appeared in a court of justice: 'he may not be a legal criminal,' was the airy utterance, 'but he is a criminal anthropologically.' " This attitude arises from the search for the causes of crime, which tends to lead to "natural" rather than legal definitions of crime and criminals. See Chapter 1 for a discussion of this issue. See n. 22 for a discussion of a similar problem in the work of William Sheldon. For examples of modern criminologists who have a similar approach, see ch. 7 in Samuel Yochelson and Stanton E. Samenow, *The Criminal Personality*, vol. 1, Jason Aronson, New York, 1976; James Q. Wilson and Richard Herrnstein, *Crime and Human Nature*, Simon & Schuster, New York, 1985; and Michael Gottfredson and Travis Hirschi, *A General Theory of Crime*, Stanford University Press, Stanford, 1990.

16. Goring, op. cit., p. 21.

17. Ibid., p. 24.

abnormal anthropological type, but because they are selected at least partially on the basis of their height.

In contrast, supporters of Lombroso maintained that Goring had actually found significant differences between criminal and noncriminal groups for a variety of measures, but that he minimized these differences by "correcting" them for such variables as age and stature. When the differences were still significant after "corrections" had been made, Goring impugned the validity of the original data. Other assessments of Goring's work had generally found more support for Lombroso's theories than Goring admitted.[18]

In spite of numerous and extensive efforts to show that criminals were somehow physically different from noncriminals, the weight of expert opinion was against the proposition, and the general conclusions of Goring on the matter came to be accepted by most modern criminologists. Goring wrote[19]:

We have exhaustively compared, with regard to many physical characters, different kinds of criminals with each other, and criminals, as a class, with the law-abiding public. . . . Our results nowhere confirm the evidence [of a physical criminal type], nor justify the allegation of criminal anthropologists. They challenge their evidence at almost every point. In fact, both with regard to measurements and the presence of physical anomalies in criminals, our statistics present a startling conformity with similar statistics of the law-abiding class. Our inevitable conclusion must be that *there is no such thing as a physical criminal type.*

BODY TYPE THEORIES: SHELDON TO CORTÉS

Some of the more interesting attempts at relating criminal behavior to physical appearance are the so-called body type theories. The body type theorists argue that there is a high degree of correspondence between the physical appearance of the body and the temperament of the mind. It should be recalled that Lombroso had attempted to establish some relation between mental disorder and physical characteristics. Many others, before and after Lombroso, have made similar attempts.

The work of William Sheldon,[20] especially his book on delinquent youth, is a good example of a body type theory. Sheldon took his un-

---

18. Driver, Introductory Essay, op. cit., p. v.

19. Goring, op. cit., p. 173 (italics in the original).

20. William H. Sheldon (with various associates), *Psychology and the Promethean Will*, 1936; *Varieties of Human Physique*, 1940; *The Varieties of Temperament*, 1942; *Varieties of Delinquent Youth*, 1949; *Atlas of Man*, 1954. All published by Harper, New York and London. Information about the life and work of Sheldon can be found in ch. 2 of Randy Martin, Robert J. Mutchnick, and W. Timothy Austin, *Criminological Thought: Pioneers Past and Present*, Macmillan, New York, 1990. A thirty-year follow-up on Sheldon's work can be found in Emil Hartl, *Physique and Delinquent Behavior*, Academic Press, New York, 1982.

derlying ideas and terminology of types from the fact that a human begins life as an embryo that is essentially a tube made up of three different tissue layers, namely, an inner layer (or endoderm), a middle layer (or mesoderm), and an outer layer (or ectoderm). Sheldon then constructed a corresponding physical and mental typology consistent with the known facts from embryology and the physiology of development. The endoderm gives rise to the digestive viscera; the mesoderm, to bone, muscle, and tendons of the motor-organ system; the ectoderm, to connecting tissue of the nervous system, skin, and related appendages. Sheldon's basic type characteristics of physique and temperament are briefly summarized in the following scheme[21]:

Physique

Temperament

1. *Endomorphic:* relatively great development of digestive viscera; tendency to put on fat; soft roundness through various regions of the body; short tapering limbs; small bones; soft, smooth, velvety skin.

1. *Viscerotonic:* general relaxation of body; a comfortable person; loves soft luxury; a "softie" but still essentially an extrovert.

2. *Mesomorphic:* relative predominance of muscles, bone, and the motor organs of the body; large trunk; heavy chest; large wrists and hands; if "lean," a hard rectangularity of outline; if "not lean," they fill out heavily.

2. *Somotonic:* active, dynamic, person; walks, talks, gestures assertively; behaves aggressively.

3. *Ectomorphic:* relative predominance of skin and its appendages, which includes the nervous system; lean, fragile, delicate body; small, delicate bones; droopy shoulders; small face, sharp nose, fine hair; relatively little body mass and relatively great surface area.

3. *Cerebrotonic:* an introvert; full of functional complaints, allergies, skin troubles, chronic fatigue, insomnia; sensitive to noise and distractions; shrinks from crowds.

Each person possesses the characteristics of the three types to a greater or lesser degree. Sheldon therefore used three numbers, each between 1 and 7, to indicate the extent to which the characteristics of the three types were present in a given individual. For example, a person whose somatotype is 7-1-4 would possess many endomorphic characteristics, few mesomorphic characteristics, and an average number of ectomorphic characteristics.

Sheldon presented individual case histories, uniformly written according to a rigorous case outline, of 200 young males who had had a

---

21. The schematic arrangement of basic types has been constructed from the discussion in Sheldon, *Varieties of Delinquent Youth*, pp. 14–30.

period of contact, during the decade 1939–1949, with the Hayden Goodwill Inn, a small, somewhat specialized, rehabilitation home for boys in Boston. He found that these youths were decidedly high in mesomorphy and low in ectomorphy, with the average somatotype being 3.5-4.6-2.7. Sheldon had earlier studied 200 college students who were apparently nondelinquents, and had found that the average somatotype was 3.2-3.8-3.4. The difference between these two groups with respect to mesomorphy and ectomorphy is significant ($p = 001$).[22]

The association between mesomorphy and delinquency was also found in a study by the Gluecks, who compared 500 persistent delinquents with 500 proven nondelinquents.[23] The two groups were matched in terms of age, general intelligence, ethnic-racial derivation, and residence in underprivileged areas. Photographs of the boys were mixed together and then visually assessed for the predominant body type.[24] By this method 60.1 percent of the delinquents, but only 30.7 percent of the nondelinquents, were found to be mesomorphs.[25] The analysis included a study of sixty-seven personality traits and forty-two sociocultural factors to determine which of these were associated with delinquency.[26] The Gluecks found that mesomorphs, in general, were "more highly characterized by traits particularly suitable to the commission of acts of aggression (physical strength, energy, insensitivity, the tendency to express tensions and frustrations in action), together with a relative freedom from such inhibitions to antisocial adventures as feelings of inadequacy, marked submissiveness to authority, emotional instability, and the like."[27] They also found that those mesomorphs who became delinquent were characterized by a number of personality traits

---

22. Juan B. Cortés, *Delinquency and Crime*, Seminar Press, New York, 1972, p. 14. The definition of delinquency used in this study, however, had only a superficial resemblance to the customary use of the term in criminology. For example, Sheldon speaks of "biological delinquency," (*Varieties of Delinquent Youth*, pp. 782–819) and "mental delinquency," (pp. 820–83) not as criminal in the usual legal sense, but as factors to be rated in accordance with the extent to which observed behavior conforms to that which a particular constitutional type might be expected to produce. Subsequently E. H. Sutherland ("Critique of Sheldon's *Varieties of Delinquent Youth*," *American Sociological Review* 18: 142–48 [1951]) re-examined Sheldon's figures, classifying each youth according to the seriousness and consistency of his delinquent behavior, as reported in the case history. This classification showed that the most delinquent of the youths were significantly more mesomorphic than the least delinquent. See Cortés, p. 17.

23. S. Glueck and E. Glueck, *Physique and Delinquency*, Harper, New York, 1956.

24. This procedure is discussed in S. Glueck and E. Glueck, *Unraveling Juvenile Delinquency*, Harvard University Press, Cambridge, Mass., 1950, pp. 192–96.

25. Glueck and Glueck, *Physique and Delinquency*, p. 9.

26. For a complete list of these traits and factors, see Glueck and Glueck, *Physique and Delinquency*, pp. 27–31.

27. Ibid., p. 226.

not normally found in mesomorphs, including susceptibility to contagious diseases of childhood, destructiveness, feelings of inadequacy, emotional instability, and emotional conflicts.[28] In addition, three sociocultural factors—careless household routine, lack of family group recreations, and meagerness of recreational facilities in the home—were strongly associated with delinquency in mesomorphs.[29]

The Glueck study has been criticized because there was no control for the rapid body changes that occur in adolescence, because the method of somatotyping involved only visual assessment and not precise measurements, and because the delinquent population included only institutionalized youth.[30] In an attempt to overcome these problems Cortés used a precise measurement technique to somatotype 100 delinquents, of whom seventy were institutionalized and thirty were on probation or under suspended sentence. He also somatotyped 100 private high school seniors who had no record of any delinquency, and twenty institutionalized adult felons. He found that 57 percent of the delinquents were high in mesomorphy, as compared to only 19 percent of the nondelinquents.[31] The mean somatotype of the nondelinquents was 3.9-3.5-3.5, the mean somatotype of the delinquents was 3.5-4.4-3.1, and the mean somatotype of the criminals was 2.8-5.4-3.1.[32]

To determine whether body type was associated with temperament, Cortés had seventy-three boys who were clearly classified as to body type (i.e., whose predominant rating was at least 4.5 and exceeded the other two ratings by at least one-half unit) describe themselves in terms of a set of traits associated with the three temperaments. The results of this experiment show that there was a strong tendency for boys with mesomorphic physiques to describe their temperaments in terms that Sheldon had called "somotonic." Similarly, boys with endomorphic physiques used "viscerotonic" terms and those with ectomorphic physiques used "cerebrotonic" terms to describe their temperaments.[33] This is exactly the relationship predicted by Sheldon. This procedure was repeated with 100 college girls and with the twenty convicted adult felons, with similar results. Finally, using McClelland's Test for Need for Achievement, Cortés found that mesomorphy was associated with

28. Ibid., p. 221.
29. Ibid., p. 224.
30. These criticisms are reviewed in Cortés, op. cit., pp. 19–21.
31. Ibid., p. 28.
32. Ibid., p. 30.
33. Ibid., p. 53.

need for achievement (n Ach) and with need for power (n Power).[34] Cortés concluded[35]:

Delinquents and possibly criminals differ from nondelinquents and noncriminals in being *physically* more mesomorphic, more energetic and potentially aggressive *temperamentally*, and in showing higher need for achievement and power *motivationally*.

Cortés's conclusion may be criticized on several counts. The small number of subjects in the experiments makes such a broad generalization at least somewhat questionable. The differences in mesomorphy between the groups in this study may reflect differences in socioeconomic class rather than in criminality, since the nondelinquent group was from a private high school, and thus probably upper class, whereas most criminal and delinquent groups are predominantly lower class.[36] The experiments did not actually measure the temperament of the different body types, but measured self-perception of temperament, and no theoretical case is made that those who perceive themselves as energetic (mesomorphs) are more potentially aggressive than those who perceive themselves as tense and anxious (ectomorphs). The study does not directly relate delinquency and criminality to temperament and motivation. Rather, delinquency and criminality are shown to be related to mesomorphy, and mesomorphy is shown to be related to certain temperaments and motivations. The experiments linking mesomorphy to the "energetic" temperament included only seven delinquents and twenty adult criminals, an extremely small sample. It was found that mesomorphy was related to a higher need for achievement, but no significant differences between the delinquent and nondelinquent groups were observed.[37] Delinquents were significantly higher in need for power than nondelinquents, but no significant differences were found between body types of the nondelinquents.[38] This appears to be rather a mixed bag of results to support such a strong conclusion.

CONCLUSION

The tendency to believe that outward appearance reveals inner character is still with us today. For example, in the movies and on television, the good guys are usually played by attractive actors, while the bad guys

34. Ibid., pp. 88, 101.

35. Ibid., p. 348 (italics in original).

36. Ibid., p. 89. The author states that the nondelinquents "belong to higher social backgrounds, possess greater intelligence, and are more favored by many other variables. . . ."

37. Ibid., p. 89.

38. Ibid., p. 102.

are usually played by actors who are unattractive or even ugly. The tendency to believe that ugly people are bad may carry over into real life. Some studies have found a tendency in criminal courts for physically unattractive offenders to be treated as more serious criminals than average looking or attractive offenders.[39] Despite this tendency, there is no clear evidence that physical appearance, as such, has any consistent relation to legally defined crime.

On the other hand, theories that focus on physical appearance can be viewed more or less as a sophisticated form of shadowboxing with a more subtle and difficult problem, namely the extent to which biological differences explain differences in human behavior and particularly in criminal behavior. This more difficult problem will be explored in Chapter 6.

---

39. Michael Saladin, Zalman Saper, and Lawrence Breen, "Perceived Attractiveness and Attributions of Criminality: What Is Beautiful Is Not Criminal," *Canadian Journal of Criminology* 30(3): 251–59 (1988); and Victoria M. Esses and Christopher D. Webster, "Physical Attractiveness, Dangerousness, and the Canadian Criminal Code," *Journal of Applied Social Psychology* 18(12): 1017–31 (1988). In general, see Lakoff and Scherr, op. cit.

CHAPTER 5

Theories Related to Intelligence

Next to physical appearance, low intelligence probably has been the concept most often used to explain criminal behavior. As the simple but bold hypotheses of those who focused on physical appearance crumbled one by one (e.g., physiognomy, phrenology, atavism), the idea persisted that criminals were less intelligent than law-abiding people. The shift in emphasis from physical differences to mental differences was easy to make, for both portrayed the criminal as an inferior person. Thus the general logic of the theory remained unchanged.

Early testing of the intelligence of prisoners generally supported the hypothesis that criminals (or at least those who were incarcerated) were mentally inferior. Later studies found that most criminals had normal intelligence, and for a time the hypothesis that there was a relationship between criminality and low intelligence fell into disrepute. Since the 1970s, however, there has been renewed support for this hypothesis, particularly with respect to juvenile delinquents. The object of the present chapter is to explore these changing ideas about intelligence and crime.

BACKGROUND IDEAS AND CONCEPTS

The language and literature of all peoples have words to describe and stories to illustrate the conduct of "dull-witted" or "slow" individuals whose intelligence is no more than that of a young child. From a spiritualistic point of view, such mentally deficient or retarded people sometimes were thought to be possessed by the devil. They were sometimes banished as "unclean" and forced into exile and almost certain death.

With the transition from spiritual explanations to naturalistic ones, ideas about this affliction were modified. Instead of being explained as curses of God, they were explained as curses of nature. Inheritance and family line of descent became the naturalistic way of accounting for such misfortunes. This view was associated with the evolutionary theories of Charles Darwin and others in the late nineteenth century. Darwin argued that the evolution of a species proceeds through natural variations that occur among the offspring.[1] The weaker and the less capable offspring die off or fail to reproduce, while the stronger and more capable survive and flourish. Through this process of "natural selection" by "the survival of the fittest," the characteristics of the more capable offspring come to dominate the species, and the species itself evolves to a more advanced state.

These were the ideas of the time, and it was natural that they would be applied to the problems of crime. One person who did this was Lombroso, as discussed in Chapters 2 and 3. But Lombroso relied on a minor point in Darwin's theory: that certain individuals might be atavistic throwbacks to an earlier evolutionary stage. More important was the implication that, in addition to the development of superior strains of individuals who were destined to dominate the species, natural selection would result in the development of inferior strains of people who were destined to die out. While the superior strains of individuals would be characterized by many desirable traits, inferior strains would be characterized by many undesirable traits.

Richard Dugdale used this basic idea to explain the history of a family he called the "Jukes."[2] As part of his work for the Prison Association of New York, Dugdale found six members of this family in a county jail in 1874. He traced the genealogy of the family back over 200 years and found a history of "pauperism, prostitution, exhaustion, disease, fornication, and illegitimacy." He attributed this melancholy history to the "degenerate" nature of the family. His study had a striking impact on the thinking at the time, despite the fact that it was based on unreliable, incomplete, and obscure information and was filled with value judgments and unsupported conclusions. For example, Henderson, writing in 1899, cited the Jukes as typical of families of degenerates and argued that private charitable work to alleviate the suffering of these people was actually allowing them to reproduce in great numbers, resulting in "the rising tide of pauperism, insanity, and crime which threatens to overwhelm and engulf our civilization."[3] He argued that this "deterio-

---

1. Charles R. Darwin, *On the Origin of Species*, Penguin, New York, 1968 (originally published in 1859).

2. Richard L. Dugdale, *The Jukes: A Study in Crime, Pauperism and Heredity*, Putnam, New York, 1877; reprinted by Arno, New York, 1977.

3. C. R. Henderson, "The Relation of Philanthropy to Social Order and Progress," *Proceedings of the National Conference of Charities and Correction* 26: 1–15 (1899); partially reprinted in Frederic L. Faust and Paul J. Brantingham, eds., *Juvenile Justice Philosophy*, 2nd ed., West, St. Paul, 1979, pp. 48–57.

ration of the common stock" must be resisted by segregating such inferior people in institutions and not allowing them to reproduce.

These popular studies of degenerate families supported the popular opinion that criminals are what they are because they do not know enough to understand the hazardous nature of criminality or the satisfying rewards of a law-abiding life. But critical scientific judgment requires more exact and systematic procedures than were possible in such case studies before any considered conclusions can be drawn. Accurate comparisons call for exact measurements, and therefore the critical investigation of the relationship between crime and mental ability could come only after the development of intelligence tests and their applications to this problem.

INTELLIGENCE TESTING AND CRIME

The systematic observation and recording of individual differences has been a principal concern of experimental psychologists. The exact measurement of individual differences in "reaction time" has long been commonplace in the psychological laboratory. Other and often more subtle differences have also been studied, such as the ability to memorize, to complete or to straighten out sentences, to complete pictures, to recognize the meanings of words, and to do mental arithmetic. A variety of attempts have been made to measure these differences. For example, in 1880 a German psychologist, H. Ebbinghaus (1850–1909), devised a test of the ability to memorize so that the differences observed among individuals in this respect could be expressed on a numerical scale. This is the essential idea of an intelligence test, the object of which is to express numerically differences among persons in their ability to perform a variety of "mental" operations that, taken together, are considered "intelligence" or an indicator of intelligence.[4]

The distinguished French psychologist Alfred Binet (1857–1911) first took intelligence testing out of the laboratory and applied it to the persisting problem of retardation in the Paris schools. In 1892 he became assistant director of the then recently founded psychological laboratory

---

4. For a short factual account of the development of intelligence tests, see the article by Robert L. Thorndike, "Intelligence and Intelligence Testing," in *International Encyclopedia of the Social Sciences*, Macmillan and The Free Press, New York, 1968, vol. VII, pp. 421–29. Also see textbooks on psychological testing and chapters on this subject in general psychology texts, such as Lee J. Cronbach, *Essentials of Psychological Testing*, 3rd ed., Harper & Row, New York, 1970, pp. 197–226; Philip H. DuBois, *A History of Psychological Testing*, Allyn and Bacon, Boston, 1970; David A. Goshin, *The Search for Ability*, Russell Sage, New York, pp. 19–44; Frank S. Freeman, *Theory and Practice of Psychological Testing*, Holt, Rinehart, and Winston, New York, 1962, pp. 1–23; Gardner Lindzey, Calvin S. Hall, and Richard F. Thompson, *Psychology*, 2nd ed., Worth Publishers, New York, 1978, ch. 12, pp. 351–78.

at the Sorbonne (he became director in 1894, holding that position until his death) and began his lifelong quest for a way to measure intelligence, conceived of as native ability rather than learned behavior.[5] He first tried to assess intelligence by measuring the volume of the skull, following the method of his countryman Paul Broca, but quickly became convinced that such methods were useless. After writing a report on his findings, he abandoned the effort.

In 1904 Binet became a member of a commission to formulate policy for the administration of special classes in the public schools of Paris and returned to the effort to measure intelligence. This time, however, he decided to take a practical approach. He assembled a large number of small tasks related to everyday life but which involved the basic reasoning processes. These were then arranged in ascending difficulty so that the first tasks could be performed by very young children while the last could be performed only by adults. In this task he had the valuable assistance and collaboration of Theodore Simon, the medical officer of the Paris schools. Their first scale of tests appeared in 1905 and was called the *Binet-Simon Scale of Intelligence.*

This scale was revised in 1908, when the concept of *mental age* was added.[6] Binet decided to assign an age level to each task on the test. The typical 9-year-old, for example, would be able to perform the tasks graded for age 9 or younger but not for age 10 or older. The age level of the last tasks the child could perform would then be described as his or her mental age and could be compared with his or her chronological age. In 1912 the psychologist W. Stern suggested that mental age be divided by chronological age and the results multiplied by 100. This would then be called the *intelligence quotient*, or IQ (a quotient being the answer in a division problem). Thus the typical 9-year-old who had a mental age of 9 would have an IQ of 100, smarter 9-year-olds would have IQs above 100, while duller ones would have IQs below 100.

This test was revised again shortly before Binet's death in 1911. At that time Binet expressed his reservations about the ways in which his test might be used. The test had been designed to identify children who were doing poorly in school so that they could receive special help. Binet argued that the test should not be used to identify children of superior intelligence, since it was not designed for that purpose. He also warned against using the test to label slower students as unteachable so

5. The following account is derived principally from Stephen Jay Gould, *The Mismeasure of Man,* Norton, New York, 1981, pp. 146–58.

6. This method of determining IQ has now been discarded in favor of one employing means and standard deviations. For a discussion of the present method, as well as a discussion of the problems of the mental age method, see Cronbach, op. cit., pp. 215–18.

that, instead of being helped, they would be ejected from the schools. Binet was strongly committed to the view that these slower students could improve their performance if properly helped, and he set up special classes in the Paris schools for the children who did poorly on his tests. He wrote with pleasure of the success of these classes, arguing that the pupils increased not only their knowledge but their intelligence as well: "It is in this practical sense, the only one accessible to us, that we say that the intelligence of these children has been increased. We have increased the intelligence of a pupil: the capacity to learn and to assimilate instruction."[7] Thus Binet rejected the idea that intelligence is a fixed and inborn quantity that cannot be changed through instruction.

With the success of the Binet-Simon scale in Paris, numerous revisions, extensions, and adaptations were made in many lands. In the United States Binet's tests and articles were translated into English and popularized by H. H. Goddard of the New Jersey Training School for the Feeble Minded at Vineland. Somewhat later Lewis M. Terman of Stanford University published what became the best-known and most widely used form of the test, called the *Stanford Revision and Extension of the Binet-Simon Scale*. Binet's 1908 scale consisted of fifty-four individual tests arranged in order of difficulty so that the easiest test might be passed by a 3-year-old child, with the most difficult requiring the ability of an average adult. The Stanford Revision consisted of ninety tests, similarly arranged in order of difficulty from the 3-year-old level to that of the "superior adult."

Unlike Binet, the Americans were convinced that intelligence was a fixed and inborn quantity, so that their primary purpose in giving intelligence tests was to sort people into appropriate social roles.[8] Those with IQs above 115 or 120 were said to be appropriate for the professions, while IQ 75 to 85 was appropriate for semiskilled labor. Terman, for example, mentioned that "anything above 85 IQ in a barber probably represents dead waste."[9]

They were particularly concerned with identifying those whose intelligence was "subnormal." Their purpose, however, was the opposite of Binet's: They wished to institutionalize these people and prevent them from reproducing, much like Henderson had suggested earlier. This required that some IQ score be determined to be the dividing line between normal intelligence and feeblemindedness. Goddard gave intel-

---

7. Quoted in Gould, op. cit., p. 154.

8. Lewis M. Terman, *The Measurement of Intelligence*, Houghton Mifflin, Boston, 1916, p. 17; cited in Gould, op. cit., p. 181.

9. Terman, op. cit., p. 288; quoted in Gould, op. cit., p. 182.

ligence tests to all the inmates at his institution at Vineland and to all new inmates on admission. This testing program disclosed no inmate with a mental age over 13. Goddard therefore concluded that mental age 12 (IQ 75 on the then commonly held assumption that full mental ability is reached at chronological age 16) marked the upper limit of feeblemindedness, so that mental age 13 marked the lower limit of normal intelligence.

With that standard as the basis for comparison, Goddard and many other psychologists gave intelligence tests to the inmates of prisons, jails, hospitals, and various other public institutions. Goddard examined a large number of such studies on the intelligence of criminals.[10] The proportion of criminals diagnosed as feebleminded in these studies ranged from 28 to 89 percent, with the median study finding that 70 percent of criminals were feebleminded. Goddard therefore concluded that most criminals were feebleminded.

Goddard also discovered a large group of "defectives" living in the pine barrens of New Jersey and traced their heritage back to a man who had had an illegitimate child by a "feebleminded" barmaid.[11] Of 480 descendants of this union, Goddard claimed that 143 were feebleminded, 36 illegitimate, 33 sexually immoral, 24 confirmed alcoholics, 3 epileptics, 3 criminals, and 8 keepers of houses of prostitution. The man later married a righteous Quaker woman, a union ultimately resulting in 496 "normal" descendants who "married into the best families of their state."

Goddard mourned the "havoc that was wrought by one thoughtless act"[12] and concluded that criminality and feeblemindedness were two aspects of the same degenerate state, so that all feebleminded people were potential criminals. Feeblemindedness was said to be caused by a recessive gene that obeyed the normal rules of inheritance originally formulated by Gregor Mendel.[13] Thus Goddard argued that feeblemindedness could be eliminated through selective breeding. This led to his recommendation that the feebleminded be institutionalized and not allowed to reproduce.

10. H. H. Goddard, *Feeblemindedness: Its Causes and Consequences*, Macmillan, New York, 1914; reprinted by Arno, New York, 1972.

11. H. H. Goddard, *The Kallikak Family, A Study in the Heredity of Feeble-Mindedness*, Macmillan, New York, 1912. Goddard called this family the "Kallikaks" because the name combined the Greek words for "beauty" (*kallos*) and "bad" (*kakos*). Gould, op. cit., pp. 168–71, points out that Goddard had diagnosed feeblemindedness among this family by sight and did not administer any intelligence tests to them. Goddard also included pictures of them in his book that had been retouched to make them appear evil and retarded.

12. Goddard, *The Kallikaks*, p. 103.

13. Goddard, *Feeblemindedness*, p. 539. See the discussion in Gould, op. cit., pp. 158–64.

These ideas dominated the thinking of mental testers for a time but were directly challenged by the results of intelligence testing administered to draftees during World War I. Following Goddard, the Army Psychological Corps at first made the conventional assumption that those of mental age 12 or below were feebleminded and therefore not fit for military service. This procedure led to a diagnosis of feeblemindedness for 37 percent of the whites and 89 percent of the blacks tested.[14] The patent fallacy of assuming that nearly one half of the population was feebleminded was generally recognized. Thus Goddard wrote, soon after the war, "The most extreme limit that anyone has dared to suggest is that one percent of the population is feebleminded."[15] He later concluded that feeblemindedness might be remedied by education and that it was not necessary to segregate the feebleminded in institutions and to prevent them from reproducing.[16] Goddard was frank about his own change of mind: "As for myself, I think I have gone over to the enemy."[17]

Publication of the results of World War I testing also provided a new perspective on the relationship between intelligence and crime. A number of studies were done comparing the performance of prisoners with that of draftees on intelligence tests. These studies generally found insignificant differences between the two groups,[18] and several studies found that prisoners actually scored higher than draftees.[19] As a result of such studies feeblemindedness largely disappeared as a basis for explaining criminal behavior.

CURRENT CONTROVERSIES: DELINQUENCY, RACE, AND IQ

Although it is no longer believed that large numbers of criminals are feebleminded, the IQ of criminals and delinquents has become embroiled in a more recent controversy concerning the relationship between intelligence and race. African Americans, on average, score about 15 points lower than European Americans on IQ tests. Some scholars

14. Robert M. Yerkes, ed., "Psychological Examining in the United States Army," *Memoirs of the National Academy of Sciences*, U.S. Government Printing Office, Washington, D.C., 1921, vol. 15, p. 791.

15. H. H. Goddard, "Feeblemindedness and Delinquency," *Journal of Psycho-Asthenics* 25: 173 (1921).

16. H. H. Goddard, "Feeblemindedness: A Question of Definition," *Journal of Psycho-Asthenics* 33: 225 (1928).

17. Ibid., p. 224.

18. For example, see Simon H. Tulchin, *Intelligence and Crime*, University of Chicago Press, Chicago, 1939; reprinted 1974.

19. For example, see Carl Murchison, *Criminal Intelligence*, Clark University Press, Worcester, Mass., 1926, ch. 4.

have used the difference in IQ scores to explain the difference in crime and delinquency rates between the races. Their arguments have generally focused on the issue of delinquency rather than crime in general, and it is there that the stronger case has been made.

However, these arguments must be considered in the context of the overall controversy about the meaning of IQ scores. First, there is a controversy about whether IQ measures intelligence or whether it measures such other factors as academic achievement, reading ability, or "test-wiseness." If one assumes that IQ actually does measure intelligence, then there is a controversy about whether the tests are "culturally biased" so that the intelligence of minority groups is underreported. Finally, if there is a real difference between the intelligence of African Americans and European Americans, then there is a controversy about whether this difference is the result of genetic or environmental influence.[20]

The seeds of this controversy are found in a 1967 speech before the National Academy of Sciences by William Shockley, a winner of the Nobel Prize for physics for his role in the invention of the transistor.[21] Shockley speculated that the differences in IQ between African Americans and European Americans might be solely the result of genetic differences and that these genetic differences might also explain the differences in poverty and crime rates between these groups. He also suggested that "IQ test results may actually be a deeper measure, at least on a statistical basis, of a distribution of some more fundamental social capacity." He did not actually argue that the all-genetic model was correct, but urged that a National Study Group be set up to research the problem and to make recommendations if the IQ-Poverty-Crime problem was found to be related to genetic differences.[22]

In 1969 Arthur Jensen published a lengthy article in which he positively argued many of the points on which Shockley had only specu-

---

20. A review discussing this controversy can be found in R. A. Weinberg, "Intelligence and IQ: Landmark Issues and Great Debates," *American Psychologist* 44: 98–104 (1989).

21. W. Shockley, "A 'Try Simplest Cases' Approach to the Heredity-Poverty-Crime Problem," *Proceedings of the National Academy of Sciences* 57(6): 1767–74 (June 1967). Shockley founded a sperm bank for geniuses, with himself as the first donor, as part of his efforts to increase the genetic endowment of the human race.

22. Several such committees were set up. They concluded that this problem merited study, but denied that it was especially urgent. See "Recommendations with Respect to the Behavioral and Social Aspects of Human Genetics," *Proceedings of the National Academy of Sciences* 69: 1–3 (1972). By 1977, however, the question had become so volatile that one scholar, Herbert C. Kelman of Harvard, argued that it would seem advisable "to forgo research at this time on genetic differences in intelligence among racial groups." See Herbert C. Kelman, "Privacy and Research with Human Beings," *Journal of Social Issues* 33(3): 169–95 (1977).

lated.[23] Specifically, he contended that IQ tests do measure a factor that is important for performance in Western industrialized societies, and that about 80 percent of the individual differences on this score are determined by genetic rather than environmental differences. He concluded that remedial education programs had failed for precisely this reason. This article set off the large IQ controversy just mentioned.

Jensen's article was used by Gordon to argue that variations in delinquency rates are best explained by variations in IQ.[24] Gordon cited Jensen to the effect that IQ is largely a biological factor, and quoted several studies that support the hypothesis that delinquency is related to the biology of the individual. He pointed to the similarity between the distribution of IQ scores and the distribution of delinquency, and demonstrated that court record data from Philadelphia and national rates for commitment to training schools could be duplicated merely by assuming that all youths (both African American and European American) with IQs below a certain level, and no youths above it, became delinquent. He did not argue that such a relationship between IQ and delinquency actually exists, but that this coincidence "virtually necessitate(s) that there be some more reasonable functional relationship within sex between IQ and delinquency that is common or nearly common to both races." He went on to argue, without supporting data, that the delinquency rates of several other racial groups are also related to IQ. Japanese-, Chinese-, and Jewish-Americans have maintained low delinquency rates despite their minority group status and generally low economic position, and these groups are said to have somewhat higher IQs than European Americans. Mexican Americans are said to have both delinquency rates and average IQs somewhere in between those of African Americans and European Americans.

In a later article, Gordon responded to the frequent criticism that his results reflect differences in social class between African-American and European-American youth, and that they do not prove anything about a relationship between delinquency and intelligence.[25] If that were the case, Gordon reasoned, then direct measures of social class would predict delinquency better than indirect measures such as IQ. Gorden identified several measures of social class, including male income, family in-

23. A. R. Jensen, "How Much Can We Boost IQ and Scholastic Achievement?" *Harvard Educational Review* 39: 1–123 (1969).

24. Robert Gordon, "Prevalence: The Rare Datum in Delinquency Measurement and Its Implications for the Theory of Delinquency," in Malcolm W. Klein, ed., *The Juvenile Justice System*, Sage Publications, Beverly Hills, Calif., 1976, pp. 201–84.

25. Robert A. Gordon, "SES versus IQ in the Race-IQ-Delinquency Model," *International Journal of Sociology and Social Policy* 7(3): 30–96 (1987).

come, educational attainment, and occupational status. He then demonstrated that these direct measures of social class could not do what the IQ data had done: duplicate the Philadelphia juvenile court record data and the national training school commitment rates merely by assuming that all youths below a certain "class," and no youths above it, became delinquent. The social class measures that came closest to duplicating those rates were those that, according to Gordon, most closely approximated intelligence.

Additional support for the association between IQ and delinquency was presented by Travis Hirschi and Michael Hindelang, who reviewed a number of studies on the subject.[26] They found that low IQ was at least as important as social class or race in predicting official delinquency and that it was more important in predicting self-reported delinquency;[27] that delinquency is consistently related to low IQ within races and within social classes so that, for example, lower-class delinquents are more likely to have low IQs than lower-class nondelinquents;[28] and that the principal sociological theories of delinquency "have been saying for some time that IQ should be related to delinquency for the same reason social class is, or should be, related to it."[29] They argue that IQ as an explanation of crime and delinquency has been ignored in criminology because a strong bias against it arose in the early part of this century. At that time IQ as an explanation of crime and delinquency was strongly associated with the physicians (such as Goring and Goddard)

26. Travis Hirschi and Michael J. Hindelang, "Intelligence and Delinquency: A Revisionist Review," *American Sociological Review* 42: 572–87 (1977).

27. The term *official delinquency* refers to delinquent behaviors that have been recorded in the official records of criminal justice agencies and thus have become part of official delinquency statistics. *Self-reported delinquency* refers to delinquent behaviors reported by juveniles anonymously on questionnaires, and includes much behavior that is not known to criminal justice agencies.

28. The studies cited with respect to delinquency within social classes are A. J. Reiss, Jr. and A. L. Rhodes, "The Distribution of Juvenile Delinquency in the Social Structure, *American Sociological Review* 26: 720–32 (Oct. 1961). Travis Hirschi, *Causes of Delinquency*, University of California Press, Berkeley, 1969. Marvin Wolfgang, Robert M. Figlio, and Thorsten Sellin, *Delinquency in a Birth Cohort*, University of Chicago Press, Chicago, 1972; and D. J. West, *Who Becomes Delinquent?*, Heinemann, London, 1972. The studies cited for delinquency within races are Wolfgang et al., op. cit.; Hirschi, *Causes of Delinquency*; James F. Short, Jr., and Fred L. Strodtbeck, *Group Process and Gang Delinquency*, University of Chicago Press, Chicago, 1965; and Jackson Toby and Marcia L. Toby, "Low School Status as a Predisposing Factor in Subcultural Delinquency," Mimeo, Rutgers University, New Brunswick, N.J., 1961.

29. Hirschi and Hindelang, op. cit, p. 579. Support for this statement is derived largely from a review of Albert Cohen's *Delinquent Boys*, The Free Press, New York, 1955. Cloward and Ohlin's theory (*Delinquency and Opportunity*, The Free Press, New York, 1960) is said to predict that higher-IQ youths are more likely to become delinquent; labeling and conflict theories are said to be consistent with the low-IQ argument, since the system is seen as discriminating against these youth; Sutherland's "differential association" theory (Edwin H. Sutherland and Donald R. Cressey, *Criminology*, Lippincott, Philadelphia, 1978, pp. 80–83) is "strictly silent" on the matter; and "social control" theories are consistent with this view, although they have not emphasized it in the past.

who had dominated the field of criminology since the time of Lombroso. The sociologists who were beginning to take over the field were eager to focus attention on the effects of social conditions and away from the characteristics of the individual. Over the previous twenty years decreasing proportions of criminals and delinquents had been reported as feebleminded because of the repeated lowering of the "normal" mental age. Hirschi and Hindelang state that Sutherland "called attention to this twenty-year trend—which, in fact, continued for another 30 years—and allowed his readers to conclude that it would continue until the initial claims of difference between delinquents and nondelinquents had no foundation in fact."[30] But Hirschi and Hindelang point out that the difference between these two groups never entirely disappeared and seemed to stabilize at about eight IQ points.[31] Later studies have also found that more serious offenders have even lower IQ scores than minor offenders,[32] and that low IQ scores among small children are associated with later offending when these children become adolescents and adults.[33]

More recently, attention has focused on the verbal abilities of delinquents, as measured by IQ tests, and on the difference between the "verbal IQ" and the so-called "performance IQ". The verbal IQ measures the person's comprehension of language while the performance IQ measures the degree of nonverbal contact with environment and the capacity to work in concrete situations. For most people, the verbal and performance IQ scores are quite close to each other. But delinquents consistently show a large gap between the two scores, with lower verbal IQ scores but basically normal performance IQ scores.[34]

Quay suggests several reasons why low verbal IQ may be associated with delinquency.[35] First, low verbal ability may lead to school prob-

30. Hirschi and Hindelang, op. cit., p. 580. The reference is to Edwin H. Sutherland, "Mental Deficiency and Crime," pp. 357–75 in Kimball Young, ed., *Social Attitudes*, Henry Holt, New York, 1931; partially reprinted in Stephen Schafer and Richard D. Knudten, eds., *Criminological Theory*, D. C. Heath, Lexington, Mass., 1977, pp. 157–60.

31. This difference does not seem to be caused by problems in the administration of the tests. See Ronald Blackburn, *The Psychology of Criminal Conduct*, John Wiley, Chichester, England, 1993, pp. 186–89.

32. Alfred Blumstein, David P. Farrington, and Soumyo Moitra, "Delinquency Careers," pp. 187–219, in Michael H. Tonry and Norval Morris, eds., *Crime and Justice: An Annual Review of Research*, University of Chicago Press, Chicago, 1985; Deborah W. Denno, *Biology and Violence*, Cambridge University Press, New York, 1990.

33. Paul D. Lipsitt, Stephen L. Buka, and Lewis P. Lipsitt, "Early Intelligence Scores and Subsequent Delinquency," *American Journal of Family Therapy* 18: 197–208 (1990); Farrington, 1989.

34. R. J. Herrnstein, "Criminogenic Traits," in James Q. Wilson and Joan Petersilia, eds., *Crime*, Institute for Contemporary Studies Press, San Francisco, 1995, pp. 49–53.

35. Herbert C. Quay, "Intelligence," pp. 106–17 in Quay, ed., *Handbook of Juvenile Delinquency*, Wiley, New York, 1987.

lems, and the school problems may then lead to delinquency. Second, low verbal abilities may be associated with a variety of other psychosocial problems, and those other problems may then lead to delinquency. Finally, low verbal abilities may lead to a failure to develop higher-order cognitive processing such as moral reasoning, empathy, and problem solving. The lack of these cognitive processes may then lead to delinquency.

Other theorists, however, point out that verbal IQ is affected by educational achievement while performance IQ is not.[36] This suggests that the pattern of low verbal but normal performance IQ among delinquents may simply reflect the fact that they tend to underachieve in schools, particularly if they are from the lower socioeconomic class.

INTERPRETING THE ASSOCIATION BETWEEN DELINQUENCY AND IQ

It seems clear that, whatever it measures, low IQ scores are associated with crime and delinquency. But it is still necessary to explain why people with low IQ scores commit crimes more frequently than those with high scores. The explanation one accepts will depend to a large degree on one's view of what IQ measures.

The most common approach among those who study the IQ-delinquency relation is to assume that *IQ measures some form of abstract reasoning or problem-solving ability and that this ability is largely inherited.* Gordon, for example, assumes this perspective and suggests that ineffective child-rearing practices by low-IQ parents might be the cause of delinquency among their low-IQ children.[37] Hirschi and Hindelang also believe that IQ measures innate ability, but argue that IQ influences delinquency through its effect on school performance: Low IQ youths do poorly in school, which leads to anger at the school and to truancy, which then leads to delinquency.[38] This argument is consistent with research that shows that the school characteristics associated with educational failure are the same school characteristics associated with delinquency: high student-teacher ratios, low student attendance, high student turnover, and poor academic quality.[39] More recently, Got-

---

36. Gary Groth-Marnat, *Handbook of Psychological Assessment*, Van Nostrand Reinhold, New York, 1984, p. 76.

37. Gordon, op. cit., p. 269.

38. Hirschi and Hindelang, op. cit.

39. D. A. Hellman and S. Beaton, "The Pattern of Violence in Urban Public Schools," *Journal of Research in Crime and Delinquency* 23: 102–27 (1986). See also Kenneth Polk, "The New Marginal Youth," *Crime and Delinquency* 30: 648–59 (1984); and W. T. Pink, "Schools, Youth, and Justice," *Crime and Delinquency* 30: 439–61 (1984).

tfredson and Hirschi have suggested that youths with low intelligence tend to seek short-term immediate gratifications, where these actions often turn out to be criminal.[40] A similar argument was made by Wilson and Herrnstein, who suggest that those with low IQ are inclined to commit "impulsive crimes with immediate rewards."[41] All of these interpretations assume that IQ scores measure some form of innate ability.

In a second approach, it could be argued that *IQ does not measure innate ability, but instead measures qualities that are related to the dominant culture*. Jane Mercer illustrated the meaning of cultural bias by constructing a test of simple behavioral tasks related to intelligence, such as being able to tie one's own shoes by the age of 7.[42] The test was given to samples of lower-class African Americans and Mexican Americans, and middle-class European Americans, all of whom had IQs below 70. Of the African Americans, 91 percent were able to pass the test, of the Mexican Americans, 61 percent passed, whereas none of the European Americans did. This would indicate that many African Americans and Mexican Americans may be more intelligent than would appear from their IQ scores.

A third approach would be to argue that *IQ measures general abilities, but that those abilities are largely determined by the person's environment*. Simons criticized Hirschi and Hindelang's interpretation of the relationship between IQ and delinquency by citing this literature.[43] He cited a number of studies that reported IQ gains averaging about 15 points when low-IQ, lower-class children were placed in special classes, where most of those gains were produced in about one year's time. Hirschi and Hindelang had reported an average gap of only 8 points between delinquents and nondelinquents. Simons concluded that IQ is best viewed as "a broad set of verbal and problem-solving skills which are better labeled academic aptitude or scholastic readiness." He pointed out that the questions on standard verbal intelligence tests are

40. Michael R. Gottfredson and Travis Hirschi, *A General Theory of Crime*, Stanford University Press, Stanford, 1990.

41. James Q. Wilson and Richard J. Herrnstein, *Crime and Human Nature*, Simon & Schuster, New York, 1985.

42. Jane Mercer, "IQ: The Lethal Label," *Psychology Today*, Sept. 1972, pp. 44–47ff. For a critique of Mercer, see Robert A. Gordon, "Examining Labelling Theory: The Case of Mental Retardation," in Walter R. Gove, ed., *The Labelling of Deviance: Evaluating a Perspective*, Halsted-Wiley, New York, 1975, pp. 35–81.

43. Ronald L. Simons, "The Meaning of the IQ-Delinquency Relationship," *American Sociological Review* 43: 268–70 (April 1978). See also Scott Menard and Barbara J. Morse, "A Structuralist Critique of the IQ-Delinquency Hypothesis: Theory and Evidence," *American Journal of Sociology* 89(6): 1347–78 (May 1984). They argue that IQ exerts no causal influence on delinquent behavior but is a criterion used for differential treatment in certain institutional settings.

virtually indistinguishable from those on reading comprehension tests, and that the score distributions from the two types of tests are virtually identical. He also cited a study that showed that children in the early grades of lower-class African-American schools and of middle-class African-American schools had similar reading comprehension test scores, but by the eighth grade there were large differences between the two groups. That suggests that the lower-class children's interactions with their schools stagnated their growth, and that they were not mentally inferior to begin with. Finally, Simons pointed out that delinquents are almost always described as unmotivated students, and asked why anyone would think that these students would be motivated to perform to the best of their ability on the day the IQ tests are administered when they are not motivated to do so on any other school day.

THE BELL CURVE

The IQ controversy was reignited recently by the publication of *The Bell Curve* by Herrnstein and Murray.[44] These authors argue that intelligence as measured by IQ tests is quite important for functioning in the modern world, that there are large differences in intelligence among individuals, that those differences are largely inherited, and that attempts to raise the IQ of low-IQ persons through education have largely failed. They go on to argue that forces are operating to reduce the collective IQ of the American people. High-IQ people control the economy and the larger society, but they tend to have fewer children and to have them at older ages, so that they are shrinking as a proportion of the population. At the same time, low-IQ people have more children and have them at younger ages, so that their proportion of the population is increasing. The result is American society that is both "dumbing down" and becoming polarized into two very different groups. Herrnstein and Murray's argument was primarily directed at the class polarization of intelligence, but they included a lengthy discussion of the biological basis of racial differences in IQ scores and also argued that low IQ is linked to crime and delinquency.

The American Psychological Association appointed a task force to examine these assertions. The task force concluded that Herrnstein and Murray's book was the most comprehensive review and discussion of the subject to date, but that its major conclusions were wrong.[45] In par-

---

44. Richard J. Herrnstein and Charles Murray, *The Bell Curve: Intelligence and Class Structure in American Life*, Free Press, New York, 1994.

45. For an overview of the findings, see Tori DeAngelis, "Psychologists Question Findings of *Bell Curve*," *The APA Monitor* 26(10): 7 (1995). For the full report, see Ulrich Neisser et al., "Intelligence: Known and Unknowns," *The American Psychologist* 51(2): 77–101 (Feb. 1996).

ticular, they pointed out that if Herrnstein and Murray were right, then average IQ scores in the entire society should be declining over time (i.e., the "dumbing down" hypothesis), while race and class differences in IQ scores should be increasing (i.e., the "increasing polarization" hypothesis). But average IQ scores in the United States have increased slightly since the 1930s, which is the opposite of Herrnstein and Murray's "dumbing down" hypothesis. Also in the 1930s, there was an average 12.5 point gap in IQ scores between those with high status jobs and those with the low status jobs, but the most recent data show that this gap has shrunk to 8.5 points. In addition, the difference between African-American and European-American IQ scores has shrunk, although the data on racial IQ scores only goes back to the 1970s. This shrinking difference is particularly apparent in verbal IQ scores, which probably reflects changes in education associated with desegregation of schools and increased African-American attendance in colleges.

CONCLUSION

All this suggests that the overall differences in IQ scores between delinquents and nondelinquents probably reflect environmental rather than genetic factors. In particular, it suggests that the differences in verbal IQ scores reflect the underachievement of delinquents in schools rather than any genetic inferiority.

It is interesting to note that other attempts have been made to identify as racially inferior those ethnic groups whose children had high delinquency rates.[46] This practice goes back at least as far as the 1820s, when delinquency in New York was seen primarily as the result of inferior racial stock of the Irish.[47] After IQ tests were developed at the beginning of this century, they were used in an attempt to demonstrate the racial inferiority of the Southern and Eastern European peoples who at that time were immigrating in large numbers to the United States. For example, in six separate studies Italian-American children were found to have a median IQ of 84, or 16 points below the U.S. average; this is almost identical to the median IQ of African-American children today.[48] As a result of these and other similar studies the Johnson-Lodge

---

46. For a description of the succession of dominant delinquent groups in Chicago, see Clifford R. Shaw and Henry D. McKay, *Juvenile Delinquency and Urban Areas*, University of Chicago Press, Chicago, 1969, pp. 374–75.

47. Harold Finestone, *Victims of Change*, Greenwood Press, Westport, Conn., 1976, pp. 17–36.

48. R. Pinter, *Intelligence Testing: Methods and Results*, Holt, New York, 1923, cited in Paul R. Ehrlich and S. Shirley Feldman, *The Race Bomb*, Quadrangle, New York, 1977. Of course, in 1923 mental age was still being used in IQ testing, and the various newer and more sophisticated testing techniques had not yet been developed, but this does not affect the point made above, that IQ has long been used in the United States to demonstrate racial inferiority.

Immigration Act of 1924 was passed, with the explicit intention of limiting the immigration of these "biologically inferior" people.[49]

Thus the use of IQ tests in the attempt to demonstrate the genetic inferiority of certain groups is nothing new. Current assertions about an IQ-race-delinquency link will require reinterpretation if African- and Hispanic-American peoples, like their immigrant predecessors, are eventually assimilated into the nation's population and their children are no longer overrepresented in the juvenile courts. The most that can be said at present is that IQ tests have functioned, since their development, as a good predictor of delinquency. Youths with low scores on these tests have a higher likelihood of becoming delinquent than youths with high scores. But it is not at all clear that delinquents are less intelligent than nondelinquents.

49. Leo J. Kamin, "The Politics of IQ," in Houts, op. cit., p. 60. This article contains a good discussion of this way of thinking.

CHAPTER 6

Biological Factors and Criminal Behavior

This chapter focuses directly on the role that biological characteristics play in the origins of criminal behavior, independent of any association with physical appearance or mental deficiency. Some of these biological characteristics are genetic and inherited—i.e., they are the result of the genes individuals receive from their parents at the time of conception. Others result from genetic mutations that occur at the time of conception or develop while the fetus is in the uterus. These biological characteristics are genetic but not inherited. Still others may develop as the result of the person's environment, such as from injury or inadequate diet. These biological characteristics are neither genetic nor inherited.[1]

Early biological theories in criminology took the view that structure determines function—that is, individuals behave differently because of the fundamental fact that they are somehow structurally different. These theories tended to focus strongly on inherited characteristics. Modern biological theories in criminology, in contrast, examine the entire range of biological characteristics, including those that result from genetic defects (and thus are not inherited) and those that are environmentally induced. In addition, modern theories do not suggest that biological characteristics directly "cause" crime. Instead, they argue that certain biological conditions increase the likelihood that an individual will engage in maladaptive behavior patterns (e.g., violent or antisocial behavior), and that those behavior patterns can include actions that are legally defined as criminal.[2] Finally, modern theories increasingly focus on the

1. Saleem A. Shah and Loren H. Roth, "Biological and Psychophysiological Factors in Criminality," in Daniel Glaser, ed., *Handbook of Criminology*, Rand McNally, Chicago, 1974, pp. 103–6.

2. Diana H. Fishbein, "Biological Perspectives in Criminology," *Criminology* 28(1): 27–72 (1990).

interaction between biological characteristics and the social environment, rather than looking solely at the effects of biology itself. These are called *biosocial* theories of crime, and most biological criminologists recognize that this is where the field must go in the future.

This chapter is organized in the following way. First, research and theory about strictly hereditary factors will be presented. Next we discuss research on factors that may be hereditary and genetic but which may change during the life course in response to environmental conditions. Finally, the chapter will examine biological factors that are most likely caused by the environment.

FAMILY STUDIES

Explanations of human behavior in terms of heredity go far back in antiquity and are based on the common sense observation that children tend to resemble their parents in appearance, mannerisms, and disposition. Scientific theories of heredity originated around 1850 and were more extensively worked out over the next fifty or seventy-five years.[3] In connection with the development of the theory of heredity, new statistical methods were devised by Francis Galton and his students (notably Karl Pearson) to measure degrees of resemblance or correlation. Charles Goring[4] used these new statistical techniques in the analysis of criminality, arriving at the conclusion that crime is inherited in much the same way as are ordinary physical traits and features.

Goring assumed that the seriousness of criminality could be measured by the frequency and length of imprisonments.[5] He therefore attempted to find out what physical, mental, and moral factors were correlated with that measure. Goring found that those with frequent and lengthy imprisonments were physically smaller than other people and were mentally inferior.[6] Although there could be an environmental component to these factors, Goring believed that they both were primarily inherited characteristics.

Goring also found that there were high correlations between the frequency and length of imprisonment of one parent and that of the other,

---

3. A review of the development of theories of heredity can be found in most textbooks on genetics. See, for example, Eldon J. Gardner and D. Peter Snustad, *Principles of Genetics*, 7th ed., John Wiley, New York, 1984.

4. Charles Goring, *The English Convict*, His Majesty's Stationery Office, London, 1913; reprinted by Patterson Smith, Montclair, N.J., 1972. For discussions of Goring's work, see Thorsten Sellin, "Charles Buckman Goring," *Encyclopedia of the Social Sciences*, Macmillan, New York, 1931, vol. 6, p. 703; Edwin D. Driver, "Charles Buckman Goring," in Hermann Mannheim, ed., *Pioneers in Criminology*, Patterson Smith, Montclair, N.J., 1972, pp. 429–42; and Driver, Introductory Essay in Goring, *The English Convict*, reprint edition, pp. v–xx.

5. Goring treated crime as a strictly legal category, and thus preferred the term *convict* to *criminal*. See Driver, "Charles Buckman Goring," pp. 431–33, and Introductory Essay, pp. ix-x.

between the imprisonment of parents and that of their children, and between the imprisonment of brothers. Goring argued that these findings could not be explained by the effect of social and environmental conditions, since he found little or no relationship between the frequency and length of imprisonment and such factors as poverty, nationality, education, birth order, and broken homes. He also argued that these findings could not be explained by the effect of example among people who were closely associated with each other. For example, the imprisonment of one spouse could not be explained by the example of the other spouse, since most of them were already engaged in crime at the time they got married. Goring therefore concluded that criminality (i.e., frequent or lengthy imprisonment) was associated with inherited, but not with environmental, characteristics and recommended that to reduce crime, people with those inherited characteristics not be allowed to reproduce.[7]

There are serious problems with each of Goring's arguments.[8] The most important problem concerns the fact that Goring attempted to establish the effect of heredity by controlling for and eliminating the effect of environment. To accomplish that, it is necessary to have accurate measurements of all the environmental factors involved, which he obviously did not have. Goring dealt with only a few environmental factors, quite imperfectly, and these were roughly measured. Though these particular ones may have shown low correlation with his measure of criminality, other environmental factors might still be very important. By his method of reasoning, the failure to measure environmental influence adequately has the result of overemphasizing the significance of the influence of heredity.

Later studies of the families of criminals have been faced with a similar problem. Ellis reviewed these studies and found remarkably little evidence for the widespread belief that crime tends to "run in the family."[9] The evidence that does exist suggests that it is less rampant than is commonly believed.

In spite of these shortcomings, the significance of Goring's work should not be underestimated. Whereas others had argued that crime was caused either by environment or by heredity, Goring was the first to postulate that it might be the result of the interaction between the

---

6. The fact that no other physical characteristics were associated with criminality was taken as a refutation of Lombroso's theory. See the discussion of Lombroso and Goring in Chapter 4.

7. Driver, "Charles Buckman Goring," pp. 439–40.

8. See Edwin H. Sutherland and Donald R. Cressey, *Criminology*, 10th ed., Lippincott, Philadelphia, 1978, p. 120.

9. Lee Ellis, "Genetics and Criminal Behavior," *Criminology* 20(1): 43–66 (May 1982).

two, a view that is held by many criminologists today. Although his findings emphasized hereditary factors, Goring did not reject the influence of the environment as a cause of crime. He maintained only that empirical evidence was required to support this view, and that such evidence was not found in his study.[10] His major contribution, however, was his use of statistical methods in a comparative study of criminals and noncriminals. Karl Pearson correctly pointed out that anyone who wished to refute Goring's arguments would have to adopt Goring's methods to do so.[11] Pearson concluded: "Strange as it may seem, the contradiction of his conclusions would be a small matter compared with the fundamental fact that Goring's methods have ploughed deeply the ground, and traced firmly the lines on which the scientific criminologist of the future will be compelled to work."

TWIN AND ADOPTION STUDIES
Studies attempting to address the hereditary bases of criminality by examining traditional families have largely been abandoned, since it is essentially impossible to disentangle the effects of nature (such as genes) from those of nurture (environment). This prompted researchers to study twins and adoptees. Instead of attempting to eliminate environmental factors, one may control the hereditary factor. The study of the relative criminality of twins suggests this possibility, since in genetics there is a clear-cut distinction between identical and fraternal twins. Identical twins (monozygotic) are the product of a single fertilized egg and have identical heredity; fraternal twins (dizygotic) are the product of two eggs simultaneously fertilized by two sperms, and therefore have the same relation as ordinary siblings.[12] Differences in the behavior of identical twins therefore may not be attributed to differences in heredity, and presumably similarities of behavior could be attributed to their identical inheritance. Obviously this need not be true, since the similarities could be due to similarities in training. But any general tendency to greater similarity of behavior when heredity is identical sets up a strong presumption that the similarity is due to the influence of heredity.

A number of investigators have used this approach in trying to determine the role of heredity in criminality. One of the earlier and more

10. Driver, Introductory Essay, p. xiii.

11. Karl Pearson, Introduction to the Abridged Edition of 1919, in Goring, op. cit., p. xix.

12. Most humans share 99 percent of their genes with other humans. Dizygotic twins share 50 percent of the remaining 1 percent, whereas monozygotic twins share all of the remaining 1 percent. See Adrian Raine, *The Psychopathology of Crime*, Academic Press, Inc., San Diego, 1993, p. 54.

dramatic of these studies was that of the German physiologist Johannes Lange, published in 1929.[13] He found that, in a group of thirteen pairs of adult male identical twins, when one twin had a record of imprisonment, the other similarly had been imprisoned in 77 percent of the cases; whereas in a comparable group of seventeen pairs of fraternal twins, when one twin had been imprisoned, the other had a prison record in only 12 percent of the cases. In a matched control group of 214 pairs of ordinary brothers of nearest age, when one brother had a prison record, the other brother of the matched pair had a prison record in only 8 percent of the cases. Lange's conclusion is seen in the dramatic title he gave his book, which translates as "crime as destiny."

In similar studies a variety of results have been reported but all tend to show greater similarity of criminal behavior among identical than among fraternal twins.[14] Each of these studies begins with criminals who are known to have twins and determines whether the twins are also criminals. Such a procedure is open to subtle bias, however, since the investigator may attribute criminality in borderline cases only when it is convenient to do so.[15] To avoid the possibility of bias Christiansen used the official *Twins Register* of Denmark to study all twins born in the Danish Islands between 1881 and 1910 when both twins lived at least until the age of 15.[16] They totaled about 6,000 pairs. He then used the official *Penal Register* to determine whether either twin, or both, had been found criminal or delinquent. He found sixty-seven cases in which at least one of a pair of male identical twins was registered as a criminal, and in twenty-four of these cases (35.8 percent) the other twin was also registered. For male fraternal twins he found this to be true in only fourteen out of 114 cases (12.3 percent). For females he found "criminal concordance" in three out of fourteen cases of identical twins (21.4 percent) and in one out of twenty-three cases of fraternal twins (4.3 percent). Christiansen later demonstrated that concordance was higher for more serious criminality than for less serious.[17]

13. Johannes Lange, *Verbrechen als shicksal: Studien an Kriminellen Zwillingen*, Georg Thieme, Leipzig, 1929. English translation by Charlotte Haldane, as *Crime and Destiny*, Charles Boni, New York, 1930.

14. See a summary of such studies in Juan B. Cortes, *Delinquency and Crime*, Seminar Press, New York, 1972, pp. 31–35; David Rosenthal, *Genetic Theory and Abnormal Behavior*, McGraw-Hill, New York, 1970, pp. 225–36; and Karl O. Christiansen, "A Review of Studies of Criminality among Twins," in Sarnoff Mednick and Karl O. Christiansen, eds., *Biosocial Bases of Criminal Behavior*, Gardner Press, New York, 1977, pp. 45–88.

15. Cf. Sutherland and Cressey, op. cit., p. 116.

16. K. O. Christiansen, "Threshold of Tolerance in Various Population Groups Illustrated by Results from the Danish Criminologic Twin Study," in A. V. S. de Reuck and R. Porter, eds., *The Mentally Abnormal Offender*, Little, Brown, Boston, 1968.

17. K. O. Christiansen, "Seriousness of Criminality and Concordance among Danish Twins," in Roger Hood, ed., *Crime, Criminology, and Public Policy*, The Free Press, New York, 1974.

The principal difficulty with this method is that the greater similarity of behavior noted in the case of the identical twins may be due to the greater similarity of training and environmental experience just as well as to their identical hereditary makeup.[18] There is no certain way of separating environment and heredity as contributing factors in this situation. Referring to his own study, Christiansen pointed out:[19]

Nothing in these results, however, can be interpreted as indicating that a higher twin coefficient in [identical] than in [fraternal] twins, or in pairs with more serious than in pairs with less serious forms of criminality, is due to what Lange called the quite preponderant part played by heredity in the causation of crime.

One way to control for the possibility that identical twins share a more common environment than fraternal twins would be to study twins who were reared apart. Grove and his colleagues looked at thirty-two sets of identical twins who were separated shortly after birth,[20] and Christiansen looked at eight pairs of identical twins raised apart.[21] Although these studies were based on a small sample of twins, they both found evidence that antisocial behavior can be inherited. Finally, Walters performed a meta-analysis of fourteen twin studies published from 1930 to 1984, attempting to assess whether these studies on the whole find evidence of a gene-crime relationship.[22] He took into account such factors as the sample sizes of the studies, the quality of the research designs, the gender and nationality of the twins, and the year of the studies. Walters concluded that on the average these studies show evidence of a hereditary basis of criminality.

Another method for determining the effects of heredity on criminality is to study the records of adoptees. One of the first such studies was

18. As Raine (op. cit.) points out (p. 58), there are also problems in the accuracy of labeling twins as monozygotic or dizygotic. The most accurate method is DNA fingerprinting, which is not usually employed. Other methods have varying degrees of reliability.

19. Ibid., p. 77. For a similar conclusion, see also Steffen Odd Dalgaard and Einar Kringlen, "A Norwegian Twin Study of Criminality," *British Journal of Criminology* 16: 213–32 (1976). They found that when twins were grouped according to their mutual closeness, all differences between identical and fraternal twins disappeared. They concluded that "the significance of hereditary factors in registered crime is non-existent." For a criticism of this study, see R. A. Forde, "Twin Studies, Inheritance and Criminality," *British Journal of Criminology* 18(1): 71–74 (Jan. 1978). See also Shah and Roth, op. cit., pp. 133–34.

20. W. M Grove, E. D. Eckert, L. Heston, T. J. Bouchard, N. Segal, and D. T. Lyken, "Heritability of Substance Abuse and Antisocial Behavior: A Study of Monozygotic Twins Reared Apart," *Biological Psychiatry* 27: 1293–1304 (1990).

21. Christiansen, "A Review of Criminality Among Twins," in S.A. Mednick and K.O. Christiansen, eds., *Biosocial Bases of Criminal Behavior*, Gardner Press, New York, 1977, pp. 89–108.

22. Glenn D. Walters, "A Meta-Analysis of the Gene-Crime Relationship," *Criminology* 30(4): 595–613 (1992).

carried out by Schulsinger[23] in a study of psychopathy, which he defined as a consistent pattern of impulse-ridden or acting-out behavior lasting beyond the age of 19 years. He selected fifty-seven psychopathic adoptees and matched them with fifty-seven nonpsychopathic adoptees on the basis of age, sex, age at transfer to adoptive homes, and social class of adoptive parents. He then searched hospital records and found that 14.4 percent of the biological relatives of the psychopathic adoptees had suffered from disorders related to psychopathy, such as alcoholism, drug abuse, or criminality, compared to only 6.7 percent of the biological relatives of the nonpsychopathic adoptees.

A much broader study was done by Hutchings and Mednick, who examined the records of all nonfamily male adoptions in Copenhagen in which the adoptee had been born between 1927 and 1941.[24] First, the authors grouped the boys according to whether they had criminal records, and then looked at the criminal records of the biological fathers. A total of 31.1 percent of the boys who had no criminal record had biological fathers with criminal records, but 37.7 percent of the boys who had committed only minor offenses and 48.8 percent of the boys who themselves had criminal records had biological fathers with criminal records.[25] These figures indicate adopted boys are more likely to commit crime when their biological fathers have a criminal record.

Next, the researchers grouped the biological and adoptive fathers according to whether they had criminal records, and then looked at the criminal records of the boys. They found an interactive effect between the criminality of the biological and the adoptive fathers.[26] When only one was criminal, the effect was not as significant as when both were criminal. In addition, the effect of the criminality of the adoptive father was not as great as the effect of criminality of the biological father.

Hutchings and Mednick then selected all the criminal adoptees whose fathers (both biological and adoptive) had been born after 1889 to maximize the reliability of police records. The 143 adoptees who met this criterion were matched with 143 noncriminal adoptees on the basis of age and occupational status of adoptive fathers. The criminal adoptees were found to have a higher percentage of criminal adoptive fathers (23 percent vs. 9.8 percent), of criminal biological fathers (49 percent vs. 28 percent), and of criminal biological mothers (18 percent vs. 7 percent).[27]

23. Fini Schulsinger, "Psychopathy: Heredity and Environment," *International Journal of Mental Health* 1: 190–206 (1972); reprinted in Mednick and Christiansen, op. cit., pp. 109–25.

24. Barry Hutchings and Sarnoff A. Mednick, "Criminality in Adoptees and Their Adoptive and Biological Parents: A Pilot Study," in Mednick and Christiansen, op. cit., pp. 127–41.

25. Ibid., p. 131, Table 4.

26. Hutchings and Mednick, op. cit., p. 132, Table 6. See also ibid., p. 137, Table 8.

27. Hutchings and Mednick, op. cit., p. 134.

This sample of Danish adoptees was expanded to females and the entire country of Denmark, and re-analyzed by Mednick and his colleagues.[28] These researchers found that the adoptee's probability of being convicted of a crime was influenced by the number of court convictions of their biological parents, but not their adoptive parents. This was true for property offenses but not for violent offenses. Later re-analyses of the same data found that the socioeconomic status of adoptive and biological parents, personality disorders of the biological parents, and the number of placements before final adoption all influenced adoptee convictions.[29] Again, these relationships held mostly for property offenses but not for violent offenses.

Somewhat similar results were found in another large study of adoptees born in Stockholm between 1930 and 1949.[30] Initial analyses indicated that the adoptees were no more apt to be criminals than the general population,[31] but later analysis found some evidence of the heritability of petty crime and alcohol abuse, especially among males.[32]

Walters performed a meta-analysis of thirteen adoption studies published between 1972 and 1989, finding significant evidence for heritability of crime and antisocial behavior.[33] However, two limitations of adoption studies might be mentioned. First, in several of the studies, adoptive parents engaged in criminal behavior at much lower rates than

28. Mednick, W. H. Gabrielli, and Hutchings, "Genetic Influences in Criminal Convictions: Evidence from an Adoption Cohort," *Science* 224: 891–94 (1984). For a review of all adoption analyses see Gregory Carey, "Genetics and Violence," in Albert Reiss, Klaus Miczek, and Jeffrey Roth, eds., *Understanding and Preventing Violence*, vol. 2, National Academy Press, Washington, D.C., 1994, pp. 34–39.

29. K. T. VanDusen, Mednick, Gabrielli, and Hutchings, "Social Class and Crime in an Adoption Cohort," *Journal of Criminal Law and Criminology* 74: 249–69 (1983); L. A. Baker, "Estimating Genetic Correlations among Disconcordant Phenotypes: An Analysis of Criminal Convictions and Psychiatric Hospital Diagnoses in Danish Adoptees," *Behavior Genetics* 16: 127–42 (1986); Baker, W. Mack, T. E. Moffitt, and Mednick, "Etiology of Sex Differences in Criminal Convictions in a Danish Adoption Cohort," *Behavioral Genetics* 19: 355–70 (1989); Moffitt, "Parental Mental Disorder and Offspring Criminal Behavior: An Adoption Study," *Psychiatry: Interpersonal and Biological Processes* 50: 346–60 (1987).

30. M. Bohman, "Some Genetic Aspects of Alcoholism and Criminality: A Population of Adoptees," *Archives of General Psychiatry* 35: 269–76 (1978); Bohman, C. R. Cloninger, S. Sigvardsson, and A. L. vonKnorring, "Predisposition to Petty Criminality in Swedish Adoptees. I. Genetic and Environmental Heterogeneity," *Archives of General Psychiatry* 39: 1233–41 (1982).

31. Carey, op. cit., p. 36.

32. Bohman et al., op. cit.; Cloninger, Sigvardsson, Bohman, and vonKnorring, "Predisposition to Petty Criminality in Swedish Adoptees. II. Cross-fostering Analysis of Gene-Environment Interaction," *Archives of General Psychiatry* 39: 1242–47 (1982); Sigvardsson, Cloninger, Bohman, and vonKnorring, "Predisposition to Petty Criminality in Swedish Adoptees. III. Sex Differences and Validation of the Male Typology," *Archives of General Psychiatry* 39: 1248–53 (1982).

33. Walters, op. cit., pp. 604–5. The overall effect in the adoption studies was somewhat stronger than that in the twin studies, but this is probably because the adoption studies had larger samples than the twin studies, making it easier to achieve statistical significance.

the normal population.[34] This makes it difficult to generalize about the effects of family environment, and to examine the interaction between environment and genetics in its potential joint influence on behavior. Second, several studies found hereditary effects for petty and property offenses, but not for more serious and violent offenses. But this result may reflect the fact that petty and property offenders are more likely to be frequent offenders. Thus, hereditary effects would be much easier to find with those offenders than with serious and violent offenders, who commit crimes very infrequently.

NEUROTRANSMITTERS

Neurotransmitters are chemicals that allow for the transmission of electrical impulses within the brain and are the basis for the brain's processing of information. As such, they underlie all types of behavior, including antisocial behavior.[35] About thirty studies have examined the linkage between neurotransmitters and antisocial behavior. These studies at least tentatively suggest that the levels of three different neurotransmitters may be associated with antisocial behavior: serotonin, dopamine, and norepinephrine. Most of these studies have been published since the late 1980s, so that this area is on the cutting edge of research on biology and crime.[36]

Scerbo and Raine performed a meta-analysis of studies on the relationship between neurotransmitter levels and antisocial behavior.[37] They reported that twenty-eight studies, on average, found that antisocial people have significantly lower levels of serotonin than normal people. Studies of norepinephrine and dopamine did not show any overall differences in these transmitter levels across the groups of subjects,[38] but when only studies using a direct measure of neurotransmitter functioning were considered, an effect of norepinephrine on antisocial behavior was also found.[39] The authors concluded that it is important to control for alcohol abuse when examining the effects of neurotransmitters, since alcoholism itself is associated with differences in neurotransmitter levels.[40]

34. Carey, op. cit., p. 43.

35. P. A. Brennan, S. A. Mednick, and J. Volavka, "Biomedical Factors in Crime," in James Q. Wilson and Joan Petersilia, eds., *Crime*, ICS Press, San Francisco, 1995, p. 82. For an introduction to neurotransmitters see also Raine, op. cit., pp. 83–84.

36. Raine, op. cit., p. 82.

37. A. Scerbo and A. Raine, "Neurotransmitters and Antisocial Behavior: A Meta-analysis," reported in Raine, op. cit., p. 87.

38. Ibid.

39. Ibid., p. 91.

40. Ibid., pp. 92, 98–99.

Investigators also have isolated DNA from blood samples to identify specific genetic features that may be involved in the link between neurotransmitter levels and antisocial behavior.[41] Genetic defects in two neurotransmitters, dopamine and serotonin, have been identified in violent individuals and certain drug abusers. These defects seem to play a role in certain types of excessive and compulsive behaviors that are associated with violence.[42] Researchers speculate that the neurotransmitters affect the sensitivity of the brain to both abusable drugs and to other sources of arousal such as aggression. The use of drugs and/or aggression may then provide relief from or stimulation to brain systems that are essentially "out of balance." In other words, these individuals may attain a "neurological high" from both drug use and from antisocial behavior.[43]

Although neurotransmitter levels initially are determined by genetics, it is possible to manipulate them with drugs, such as lithium carbonate (for serotonin), reserpine (for norepinephrine) and various antipsychotic drugs (for dopamine). The research on whether these manipulations can actually reduce antisocial behavior is mixed, but includes some encouraging results.[44] Neurotransmitter levels can also be affected by changes in the environment. For example, changes in diet can significantly increase the levels of serotonin, dopamine, and norepinephrine, which could possibly reduce the tendency to engage in violent or antisocial behavior. In addition, living in very stressful conditions (such as in inner-city areas) can dramatically lower serotonin levels, which could increase the tendency to engage in these behaviors.[45]

HORMONES

In addition to neurotransmitter levels, much research has been generated relating to the effect of hormone levels on human behavior, including aggressive or criminal behavior. Interest in hormones dates back to the mid-1800s, when biochemists were first able to isolate and identify some of the physiological and psychological effects of the secretions

41. Diana Fishbein, "Selected Studies on the Biology of Antisocial Behavior," forthcoming in John Conklin, *Criminology*.

42. Ibid.

43. Ibid.

44. For a review see D. A. Brizer, "Psychopharmacology and the Management of Violent Patients," *Psychiatric Clinics of North America* 11: 551–68 (1988).

45. As mentioned earlier, some researchers have posited that property crimes have a genetic basis, whereas violent crimes may be affected by environmental conditions. Whether this holds for neurotransmitter effects is uncertain. Raine urges that future research on neurotransmitter differences clearly separate out property offenders from violent offenders, so that stronger inferences can be made. See Raine, ibid., p. 95.

of the endocrine glands (hormones).[46] Most recent attention paid to hormone levels and aggressive or criminal behavior relates to either testosterone or female premenstrual cycles.

The role of testosterone in the aggressiveness of many animal species has been well documented,[47] but a question remains as to whether testosterone plays a significant role in human aggressive and violent behavior. Raine reviews some of this literature, finding mixed results.[48] Effects of testosterone on aggression are slight when aggression is measured using personality questionnaires, but much stronger when behavioral measures of aggression are employed.[49]

A major problem with this research is that there are several possible causal paths between testosterone and aggressive behavior. In general, researchers want to know whether high testosterone levels cause increased aggression. But it is possible that the causal path is in the opposite direction: certain types of aggressive behavior might cause an increase in testosterone production.[50] Thus, aggressive individuals might have higher testosterone levels, but those higher testosterone levels do not cause the aggressive behavior. A third possibility is that some individuals might generally have normal levels of testosterone, but they may respond to certain types of situations with very large increases in testosterone. These people may have an increased tendency to engage in aggressive behavior due to their high testosterone levels, even though their testosterone levels measured as normal most of the time. A fourth possibility is that exposure of a fetus to abnormal levels of testosterone during pregnancy may result in more sensitivity to it later on. Thus, the actual level of testosterone in the person may be normal, but people who had been "sensitized" to it during pregnancy may respond more aggressively when testosterone increases, such as during puberty.[51] Fi-

46. For a review of some of the early studies of the impact of hormonal imbalances on criminal behavior, see the 3rd edition of this book.

47. For an excellent overview, see Paul Brain, "Hormonal Aspects of Aggression and Violence," in Reiss, Miczek, and Roth, eds., *Understanding and Preventing Violence*, vol. 2, op. cit., pp. 173–244.

48. Adrian Raine, *The Psychopathy of Crime*, op. cit. For another review of recent research on testosterone and aggression, see David Benton, "Hormones and Human Aggression," in Kaj Björkqvist and Pirkko Niemelä, eds., *Of Mice and Women: Aspects of Female Aggression*, Academic Press, San Diego, 1992, pp. 37–48.

49. Ibid., p. 206. In addition, effects of testosterone may be higher when saliva is used to measure testosterone, rather than blood samples. However, the study that found this had measured testosterone in females rather than in males.

50. Brain, op. cit., p. 221. See also Albert J. Reiss and Jeffrey Roth eds., *Understanding and Preventing Violence*, National Academy Press, Washington, D.C., 1993, p. 119.

51. See Diana Fishbein, "Selected Studies on the Biology of Antisocial Behavior," op. cit.

nally, social variables may intervene in the relationship between testosterone and antisocial behavior. A recent study by Booth and Osgood examines the relationships between testosterone, social integration, prior involvement in juvenile delinquency, and adult deviance.[52] They found that although there is a strong initial association between testosterone and adult deviance, the magnitude of this effect is reduced substantially when controlling for social integration. In other words, testosterone may reduce social integration, and reduced social integration is associated with higher deviance levels. In addition, testosterone is associated with juvenile delinquency, and when controlling for delinquency, the relationship between testosterone and adult deviance diminishes further. Research such as this highlights the need for more biosocial theories of criminal behavior and deviance.

Although most research on hormones and crime has focused on males, some work has examined the role hormones play in female crime, especially in connection with the menstrual cycle. Biological changes after ovulation have been linked to irritability and aggression.[53] Research is mixed on the strength of this linkage, but Fishbein's recent review of the literature suggests that at least a small percentage of women are susceptible to cyclical hormone changes, resulting in a patterned increase in hostility.[54] This patterned increase is associated with fluctuations in female hormones and a rise in testosterone, to which some women appear to be quite sensitive.

THE CENTRAL NERVOUS SYSTEM
The central nervous system contains neurons and systems that exist within the brain and spinal cord. Of particular importance in research on aggression and violence is the outer portion of the brain, the cerebral cortex. This consists of two hemispheres divided into four lobes: frontal, temporal, parietal, and occipital. Most attention paid by investigators studying antisocial behavior is to the frontal and temporal lobes, since these lobes are involved with goal-directed behavior, impulses, and emotions. Disturbances or irregularities within the frontal lobe generally influence neu-

52. Alan Booth and D. Wayne Osgood, "The Influence of Testosterone on Deviance in Adulthood: Assessing and Explaining the Relationship," *Criminology* 31(1): 93–117 (1993).

53. See R. F. Haskett, "Premenstrual Dysphoric Disorder: Evaluation, Pathophysiology and Treatment," *Progress in Neuro-Psychopharmacology and Biological Psychiatry* 11: 129–35 (1987); and E. P. Trunell and C. W. Turner, "A Comparison of the Psychological and Hormonal Factors in Women with and Without Premenstrual Syndrome," *Journal of Abnormal Psychology* 97: 429–36 (1988).

54. Diana Fishbein, "The Psychobiology of Female Aggression," *Criminal Justice and Behavior* 19: 99–126 (1992).

ropsychological performance, while the temporal lobe in general appears to involve behaviors more directly emotional in expression.

In the past, research on the relationship between the central nervous system and aggressive behavior has been done using a variety of relatively indirect measures.[55] More recently, however, more direct measures of the central nervous system have become available: brain imaging techniques. These techniques include computerized tomography (CT), magnetic resonance imaging (MRI), positron emission tomography (PET), and single photon emission tomography (SPECT). These new brain imaging procedures have been used to detect structural and functional abnormalities in both the frontal and temporal lobes.[56] After a comprehensive review of brain imaging studies, Raine concludes that[57]:

An integration of findings from these studies gives rise to the hypothesis that frontal dysfunction may characterize violent offenders while temporal lobe dysfunction may characterize sexual offending; offenders with conjoint violent and sexual behavior are hypothesized to be characterized by both frontal and temporal lobe dysfunction.

Another common way of measuring brain abnormalities is through the use of the electroencephalograph (EEG). The EEG measures electrical brain activity, and can detect abnormalities in brain wave patterns. Hundreds of studies have examined EEG activity in various types of criminals.[58] Most reviewers agree that repeat violent offenders are characterized by EEG abnormalities, but the relationship between psychopathy and EEG indicators is more uncertain.[59] Raine points out that most of this research is too broad in focus, and while it may point to some general relationship between dysfunctional behavior and EEG abnormalities, we need to know much more specific information about the processes by which brain wave activity may affect behavior.[60]

---

55. These neuropsychological measures have been used extensively in the past to study CNS abnormalities, and the findings from these studies have formed the basis for the newer, more direct research using brain imaging. For a review of neuropsychological indicators of brain dysfunction and abnormal behavior, see Raine, op. cit., pp. 103–27.

56. Raine, op. cit., p. 130.

57. Ibid., p. 155.

58. Ibid., p. 175.

59. Ibid., pp. 175–76.

60. Ibid., pp. 177–80. EEG abnormalities and EP (evoked potential) responses may be indicative of several possible problems, including CNS instability, underarousal, or subcortical epilepsy. Lumping all EEG abnormalities together is a mistake, since they may refer to different problems that may have different effects on behavior.

THE AUTONOMIC NERVOUS SYSTEM

In addition to the central nervous system, there is a relatively separate part of the nervous system, called the autonomic nervous system (ANS), which controls many of the body's involuntary functions such as blood pressure, heart and intestinal activity, and hormone levels. The autonomic nervous system is, in turn, modulated by structures within the limbic system in the brain (such as the hypothalamus) that control motivation, moods, hunger, thirst, reproductive and sexual behaviors, anger and aggression, memories, and other feeling states.

The ANS is especially active in a "fight or flight" situation, when it prepares the body for maximum efficiency by increasing the heart rate, rerouting the blood from the stomach to the muscles, dilating the pupils, increasing the respiratory rate, and stimulating the sweat glands. Lie detectors measure these functions and use them to determine whether the subject is telling the truth. The theory is that, as children, most people have been conditioned to anticipate punishment when they tell a lie. The anticipation of punishment produces the involuntary fight or flight response, which results in a number of measurable changes in heart, pulse, and breathing rate, and, because sweat itself conducts electricity, in the electric conductivity of the skin.

The anxiety reaction in anticipation of punishment has been described by some researchers as the primary socializing agent for children.[61] Children are conditioned by their parents to anticipate punishment in certain types of situations, and the anxiety they then feel (usually called conscience or guilt) often leads them to avoid those situations. Because the anxiety reaction in anticipation of punishment is essentially an autonomic nervous system function related to the fight or flight response, the level of socialization in children may depend at least in part on the functioning of that system. Specifically, if the fight or flight response is activated slowly or at low levels in situations in which punishment is anticipated, or if it fails to deactivate quickly when the situation changes, then the child will be difficult to socialize.

The first to examine this question was Eysenck, who based his discussion on Jung's concepts of introversion and extroversion as the major attitudes or orientations of the personality.[62] The introvert is oriented toward the inner, subjective world, and tends to be more quiet, pessimistic, retiring, serious, cautious, reliable, and controlled. The ex-

61. H. J. Eysenck, *Crime and Personality*, Houghton Mifflin, Boston, 1964, pp. 100–119; Gordon Trassler, "Criminal Behavior," in H. J. Eysenck, ed., *Handbook of Abnormal Psychology*, Putnam, London, 1972; Sarnoff A. Mednick, "A Biosocial Theory of the Learning of Law-Abiding Behavior," in Mednick and Christiansen, op. cit., pp. 1–8.

62. Eysenck, *Crime and Personality*, pp. 34–36.

trovert is oriented toward the external, objective world, and is more sociable, impulsive, carefree, optimistic, and aggressive. Extroverts crave excitement, like to take chances, tend to be undependable, and lose their temper easily. Eysenck notes that the diagnosis of this personality dimension is highly reliable, with self-ratings, ratings by others, and ratings by objective tests all highly consistent.

Eysenck also utilized Pavlov's concepts of excitation and inhibition.[63] Excitation means simply that the stimulus that was presented to the organism has successfully passed through the autonomic nervous system to be registered in the cortex. Obviously this concept is central to the explanation of all learning and behavior. But to explain the patterns of conditioning, Pavlov also found it necessary to postulate that something like brain fatigue occurs after a period of excitation. Conditioning was found to slow down after a period of time, but would resume at a higher level after a period of rest. Pavlov called this phenomenon inhibition.

Eysenck hypothesized that these two sets of concepts were connected, and that introverts were characterized by higher levels of excitation and/or lower levels of inhibition, whereas extroverts were characterized by the opposite. Because extroverts have lower levels of stimulation coming into the cortex, they experience "stimulus hunger," whereas introverts, whose brains receive stronger stimulation for longer periods of time, will be oriented toward "stimulus avoidance."[64] The possibility of punishment is therefore much more threatening to introverts—they experience high anxiety reactions in these situations and seek to avoid them. Extroverts, on the other hand, experience less anxiety (also termed arousal) both because they are less sensitive to pain and because they more readily seek out prohibited activities in their search for stimulation. Eysenck further argued that psychopaths are extreme extroverts and that they fail to develop adequate consciences because of the way their autonomic nervous systems function.[65]

A number of more recent studies on autonomic nervous system functioning have involved measuring the same peripheral functions that are monitored by a lie detector. For example, Mednick[66] maintains that the rate of skin conductance response (SCR) recovery—the time between when the skin conducts electrical current at its peak amplitude and when that conductance returns to normal levels—can be taken to measure the general rate of recovery in the autonomic nervous system. If so, it would

63. Ibid., pp. 68–87.
64. Ibid., p. 99.
65. Ibid., pp. 39–43.
66. Mednick, "A Biosocial Theory," op. cit., pp. 2–4.

measure the rate at which the anxiety reaction in anticipation of potential punishment is diminished following removal from the threatening situation. Mednick argues that the rate at which the anxiety dissipates is crucial, since fear reduction is the most powerful reinforcer known to psychology. When fear is dissipated quickly, the individual receives a large reinforcement for avoiding the situation of potential punishment, and conditioning is much more likely to occur.

Raine reviews studies on conditioning using skin conductance responses and concludes that "these data provide good support for Eysenck's conditioning theory of crime. . ."[67] However, he points out that in the past decade and a half, there has been little research on this topic, so that most of our data come from the late 1970s and early 1980s. He offers some ways in which skin conductance research on conditioning and criminal behavior may be improved.[68] Raine also reviewed studies (ranging from 1979 to 1990) that related skin conductance measures to general antisocial behavior, without necessarily using a conditioning framework.[69] Overall the findings are mixed, but it seems possible that the ANS does play some role in antisocial behavior.

ENVIRONMENTALLY INDUCED BIOLOGICAL COMPONENTS OF BEHAVIOR

To this point we have discussed research on hereditary factors influencing antisocial and criminal behavior (such as the family, twins, and adoption studies), and research addressing factors that may be hereditary but may also change over time due to environmental influences (such as hormones, neurotransmitter levels, and skin conductance responses to stimuli). Now we examine research on several biological factors that may influence criminal behavior but which clearly are environmental, in the sense that they have nothing to do with the person's hereditary or genetic makeup. These are drug and alcohol abuse, diet and toxins, head injury, and pregnancy or birth complications.

There are many possible types of relationships between *drug and alcohol abuse* and violent behavior: biological, psychosocial, social, cultural, and economic. For example, violence and crime may result from an addict's need to get money to buy drugs, or from "wars" between rival drug gangs over the rights to sell drugs in a certain area. Because the range of literature is so broad in these areas, we do not summarize

67. Raine, op. cit., p. 229.
68. Ibid.
69. Ibid., pp. 161–64.

it here.[70] Instead, we present a few brief comments on the strictly biological links between violence and alcohol or drug use.

Alcohol is known to temporarily increase aggressive behavior in lower doses (when people get nasty), and temporarily decrease aggressive behavior in higher doses (when people pass out).[71] Many people believe that the increased aggressiveness at lower doses is because of alcohol's "dis-inhibiting" effect—alcohol tends to release people from their inhibitions—but there is little evidence for this. An alternative explanation is that alcohol increases the production of the endocrine system, especially testosterone, but again, there is little evidence for this. Other possible neurobiological explanations involve serotonin functioning and EEG abnormalities, but experiments have yet to confirm any of these possible explanations. Some researchers believe that there may be a genetic basis for the relationship between alcohol and violence, but there is no confirmation of this to date. So while there is a strong relationship between alcohol and violence (probably the strongest of any drug), the reason for this relationship remains unclear.

Other drugs that may have a biological association with violence are opiates, amphetamines, cocaine, and hallucinogens. Opiates are known to temporarily reduce aggressive and violent behavior, although chronic use may increase the possibility of violent behavior. Withdrawal from opiates is related to aggressive behavior as well.[72] Chronic amphetamine use may provoke violent outbursts in humans, but usually only when the individuals already are prone to violent behavior.[73] There is still no direct evidence of a biological effect of cocaine use on violent behavior.[74] Marijuana use most likely decreases or does not affect violent human behavior; PCP, when used over a long term, may increase aggressive behavior; and LSD may intensify violent behavior in those already prone to aggression.[75]

Research on the relationship between *nutrition or toxins* and antisocial or aggressive behavior often is comprised of correlational studies with methodological shortcomings. Most commonly studied are sugar, cholesterol, and lead toxicity.[76]

70. For a broad review of the drug and violence literature, see Diana H. Fishbein and Susan E. Pease, *The Dynamics of Drug Abuse*, Allyn and Bacon, Boston, 1996. See also Reiss and Roth, eds., *Understanding and Preventing Violence*, op. cit., ch. 4.

71. The discussion of alcohol and violence is summarized from Reiss and Roth, ibid., pp. 189–91.

72. Ibid., p. 192.

73. Ibid.

74. Ibid., p. 194.

75. Ibid., p. 195.

Research in the 1980s showed hypoglycemia (low blood sugar), which is caused in part by excess sugar intake, to be common in habitually violent criminals. Numerous methodological problems with these studies are cited by Kanarek,[77] casting significant doubt on whether sugar intake causes antisocial behavior. Sugar has also been associated with hyperactivity in children, but again, there is reason to doubt the validity of most of this research.[78] More research that is methodologically solid, examining potential negative consequences of sugar, is needed before any conclusions should be drawn on the sugar-violence link. Research has also purported that there is a link between blood cholesterol and violent behavior, but these studies suffer from the same sorts of problems as the research on sugar and violent behavior.[79] Finally, exposure to lead in diet and environment has been shown to negatively affect brain functioning, bringing about learning disabilities and hyperactive attention deficit disorder in children, and may increase the risk for antisocial behavior.[80] Future research is certain to continue examining the linkages between lead exposure and negative behavioral consequences.

Several studies have found a correlation between *head injury* and criminal and antisocial behavior; whether the relationship is causal is another matter.[81] Such head injury can be detected by medical tests such as X-rays, CAT scans, and spinal taps. A variety of studies have found that prisoners and violent patients report a large number of head injuries involving loss of consciousness. Mednick found some support for a relationship between brain damage and violent behavior among juveniles in a study of children born at a hospital in Copenhagen between 1959 and 1961.[82] Those who later became violent delinquents had generally good medical, physical, and neurological reports during pregnancy and delivery, despite relatively poor social conditions. However, they had significantly worse physical and neurological status at 1 year of age. Similar findings were reported by Dorothy Lewis and her

76. This discussion is taken primarily from Robin B. Kanarek, "Nutrition and Violent Behavior" in Reiss, Miczek, and Roth, eds., *Understanding and Preventing Violence*, Vol. 2, op. cit., pp. 515–39.

77. Ibid., pp. 523–26.

78. Ibid., pp. 530–31.

79. Ibid., pp. 533–34.

80. Fishbein, "Selected Studies on the Biology of Antisocial Behavior," op. cit.

81. Mednick et al., "Biology and Violence," pp. 52–58.

82. Ibid., p. 55

colleagues.[83] Lewis also found a strong association between parental criminality and the presence of serious medical problems in their children. She suggested that delinquency among children with criminal parents may reflect the combined physical and psychological effects of parental neglect and battering, rather than any genetic factors.[84]

Raine discusses some possible scenarios that would account for the association between head injury and criminal behavior. For example, in abusive homes children are more likely to incur head injuries, and these homes may also be more conducive to criminal behavior among offspring raised in them.[85] Still, Raine cites evidence that the link between head injury and criminal behavior may be at least partially causal.[86] Some processes by which head injury may influence negative behaviors are: (1) increasing sensitivity to effects of alcohol; (2) decreasing cognitive and social skills; (3) causing headaches and irritability, which increase the possibility of violent outbursts; and (4) damaging the frontal and temporal lobes of the brain, increasing anxiety, anger, and hostility.[87]

Another possible source of CNS deficits (which have been linked to aggressive behavior) is *pregnancy and birth complications*. A recent study by Kandel and Mednick examined data on 216 children born between 1959 and 1961 in Copenhagen.[88] The group of 216 was selected from an original cohort of 9,125 children because their parents were schizophrenic, psychopathic, or character-disordered, and therefore they were considered to be at high risk of becoming delinquent. The research examined pregnancy complications (such as infections, chemotherapy, and jaundice) and delivery complications (such as ruptured perineum, weak secondary labor, and ruptured uterus), and measured criminal behavior with arrest records for property and violent offenses when the subjects were 20 to 22 years old. Pregnancy complications were not significantly related to offending rates, but delivery complications were related to violent offending: 80 percent of violent offenders ranked had greater than average delivery complications,

83. Dorothy Otnow Lewis et al., "Perinatal Difficulties, Head and Face Trauma, and Child Abuse in the Medical Histories of Seriously Delinquent Children," *American Journal of Psychiatry* 136 (4): 419–23 (April 1979). See also Lewis et al., "Violent Juvenile Delinquents: Psychiatric, Neurological, Psychological, and Abuse Factors," *Journal of the American Academy of Child Psychiatry* 18(2): 307–19 (1979); and Lewis, ed., *Vulnerabilities to Delinquency*, Spectrum, New York, 1981.

84. Dorothy Otnow Lewis et al., "Parental Criminality and Medical Histories of Delinquent Children," *American Journal of Psychiatry* 136(3): 288–92 (March 1979).

85. Raine, op. cit., p. 193.

86. Ibid., pp. 193–94.

87. Ibid., pp. 194–95.

88. Elizabeth Kandel and Sarnoff A. Mednick, "Perinatal Complications Predict Violent Offending," *Criminology* 29(3): 519–29: (1991).

compared to 30 percent of property offenders and 47 percent of nonof-fenders.[89] A subsequent study found that violent offending occurs most often among individuals with both a high number of delivery compli-cations and parents with psychiatric problems.[90]

IMPLICATIONS AND CONCLUSIONS

Biological theories are necessarily part of a "multiple factor" approach to criminal behavior—that is, the presence of certain biological factors may increase the likelihood but not determine absolutely that an indi-vidual will engage in criminal behaviors. These factors generate crimi-nal behaviors when they interact with psychological or social factors. Mednick, for example, has suggested a possible interaction between bi-ological and social factors[91]:

Where the social experiences of an antisocial individual are not especially an-tisocial, biological factors should be examined. The value of the biological fac-tors is more limited in predicting antisocial behavior in individuals who have experienced criminogenic social conditions in their rearing.

In the past, biologically oriented and sociologically oriented crimi-nologists have often been at odds with each other. Both sides have over-stated their own positions and refused to acknowledge partial validity in their opponents' views. This is changing, as criminologists on both sides are recognizing the need for biosocial theories that examine not only the separate contribution of sociological and biological phenomena to criminal behavior, but the interaction of these perspectives as well. This emerging synthesis of perspectives will probably benefit biological criminology, since extreme biological views often raise images of de-terminism among some audiences, who subsequently react negatively to the furthering of such research and to any policies based on it.

89. Ibid., p. 523.

90. P. Brennan, S. A. Mednick, and E. Kandel, "Congenital Determinants of Violent and Property Offending," in D. J. Pepler and K. H. Rubin, eds., *The Development and Treatment of Childhood Aggression*, Erlbaum, Hillsdale, N.J., 1993, pp. 81–92.

91. Mednick et al., "Biology and Violence," op. cit., pp. 55, 68. A similar conclusion is reached in Mednick et al., "An Example of Biosocial Interaction Research," in Mednick and Christiansen, op. cit., pp. 9–23.

CHAPTER 7

The Personality of the Offender

The term *personality* refers to the complex set of emotional and behavioral attributes that tend to remain relatively constant as the individual moves from situation to situation. This chapter examines theories that explain criminal behavior primarily in terms of the enduring personality attributes of the individual. In general, psychological and psychiatric theories include the personality of the offender within their explanations of criminal behavior. Thus, these theories are the focus of the present chapter.

Psychological and psychiatric theories also consider biological and situational factors in their explanations of criminal behavior. Much of the biological research presented in Chapter 6 has been done by psychologists and psychiatrists and can be considered as part of psychological or psychiatric theories of crime. Those theories also consider the impact of the situation on the individual, and they explain behavior by interrelating the situation with individual's biological and psychological characteristics. Situational factors, however, will be discussed in the chapters on sociological theories of criminal behavior. In addition, some psychological theories argue that criminal behavior is the result of normal learning processes. These theories are discussed below in Chapter 12.

The present chapter considers only those psychological and psychiatric theories that argue that criminal behavior originates primarily in the personalities of offenders rather than in their biology or in situation. This includes psychoanalytic theories that argue that the causes of criminal behavior are found in unconscious elements of the personality. It also includes research on the conscious personality, using a type of psychological test called the personality inventory. Finally, the present chapter discusses the antisocial personality and impulsivity as specific personality characteristics thought to be associated with criminality.

HISTORICAL BACKGROUND: PSYCHIATRY AS A SPRINGBOARD FOR PSYCHOANALYTIC THEORY

Before looking at the psychoanalytic view of the causes of criminal behavior, it is necessary to consider the differences between psychiatry in general and the psychoanalytic movement. Psychiatry grew out of the experience of medical doctors in dealing with the basic problem of mental disease. Control of the dangerous and often outrageous behavior of the mentally and emotionally disturbed has been a problem in organized societies from the earliest times. Historically it has often been indistinguishable from the control of the dangerous and often outrageous behavior of the criminal.

In early societies spiritual explanations—the influence of evil spirits or the devil—were generally accepted for both crime and insanity.[1] Yet there was an objective, naturalistic school of medical thought in ancient Greece that goes back to roughly 600 B.C. This medical thought rested on the science of Pythagoras (580–510 B.C.), Alcmaeon (550–500 B.C.), and Empedocles of Agrigentum (490–430 B.C.), and had as its most distinguished member Hippocrates (460?–?377 B.C.), the father of medicine. This last name is, of course, well known and honored for the Hippocratic oath, which is solemnly assumed by physicians today.

Pythagoras and his pupil Alcmaeon identified the brain as the organ of the mind, and conceived of mental illness as a disorder of that organ. Empedocles introduced certain explanatory principles of personality (namely, the qualities of heat, cold, moisture, and dryness; and the humors—blood, phlegm, black bile, and yellow bile) that were to be in use for hundreds of years, through the Middle Ages into almost modern times.

In this conception delirium and various other kinds of mental disorders were explained as aspects of special functions of the brain. Hysteria, mania, and melancholia were recognized, described, and prescribed for just as objectively and scientifically as were the medications suggested for a long list of wounds and other human afflictions.[2] In this

1. For good accounts of principal historical developments, see Erwin H. Ackerknecht, M.D., *A Short History of Medicine*, rev. ed., Johns Hopkins University Press, Baltimore, 1982; Brian Inglis, *A History of Medicine*, World, Cleveland, 1965; Charles Singer and E. Ashworth Underwood, *A Short History of Medicine*, Oxford University Press, New York, 1962; or George Rosen, *Madness in Society*, University of Chicago Press, Chicago, 1968.

2. "To those women suffering from hysteria, Hippocrates recommended marriage and pregnancy as general treatment, while the immediate attacks were to be met with substances causing unpleasant tastes and odors combined with purges and pessiaries." N. D. C. Lewis, *A Short History of Psychiatric Achievement*, Norton, New York, 1941, p. 35.

sense psychiatry constituted an important division of the developing field of medical knowledge from the very beginning.[3]

As knowledge of physical disease slowly grew, knowledge of mental disease did also. By the time of Sigmund Freud (1856–1939), all the basic concepts of abnormal psychology had been developed out of experience in dealing with disturbed persons. This included a distinction between *organic disorders*—for example, head injuries that leave the mind blank or that distort vision or hearing or cause a ringing in the ears, or those due to disease or degeneration, such as syphilitic paresis or the senility of old age—and *functional disorders* in which there is strange behavior but no known organic cause. Even the central concept of psychoanalysis, the *unconscious*, was developed before Freud by von Hartman (1842–1906), and was extensively utilized and further developed by Morton Prince (1854–1929).[4] Somewhat the same is true of several other ideas or concepts that have been used extensively in psychoanalysis, including repression, projection, symbolic behavior, and various notions of substitute responses. These all were part of psychiatry before Freud.[5]

SIGMUND FREUD AND PSYCHOANALYSIS

While psychiatry is as old as medicine, psychoanalysis is a relatively recent development associated with the life and work of Sigmund Freud and some of his pupils, notably Alfred Adler (1870–1937), Carl Jung (1875–1961), and Wilhelm Stekel (1868–1940). Psychoanalysis is an extremely complicated and not particularly unified set of ideas, due to the fact that Freud himself revised his most fundamental ideas at several points in his life, and his followers continued to propose revisions and extensions after his death. Nevertheless, it has had a profound impact on almost all modern thought, including philosophy, literature, and conceptions of human (and, consequently, criminal) behavior. The following is only a very brief overview of some basic ideas associated with psychoanalysis, meant to give a sense of what it is about.

3. For a good short review of the history and general development of contemporary psychiatry, see ibid., or Winfred Overholser, "An Historical Sketch of Psychiatry," *Journal of Clinical Psychopathology* 10(2): (April 1949), reprinted in Richard C. Allen, Elyce Z. Ferster, and Jesse G. Rubin, *Readings in Law and Psychiatry*, Johns Hopkins University Press, Baltimore, 1975.

4. Lewis, op. cit., p. 134; Morton Prince, *The Dissociation of a Personality: A Biographical Study in Abnormal Psychology*, Longmans, Greens, New York, 1906, reprinted by Greenwood Press, Westport, Conn., 1969; Morton Prince, *The Unconscious*, Macmillan, New York, 1914, reprinted (1921 edition) by Arno, New York.

5. See J. R. Whitwell, *Historical Notes on Psychiatry*, H. K. Lewis, London, 1936; E. A. Strecker, *Fundamentals of Psychiatry*, Lippincott, Philadelphia, 1943; Lewis, op. cit., pp. 66–159; E. C. Mann, *Manual of Psychological Medicine and Allied Nervous Disorders*, Blakiston, Philadelphia, 1883.

Sigmund Freud lived most of his life in Vienna and published most of his important ideas during the first forty years of this century.[6] Like other psychiatrists before him, he was a physician who was concerned with the medical treatment of a variety of functional disorders that seemed to be unrelated to any organic causes. Freud first adopted the idea of the unconscious, as used by earlier psychiatrists, arguing that the behaviors could be explained by traumatic experiences in early childhood that left their mark on the individual despite the fact that the individual was not consciously aware of those experiences.

As a way to treat these problems, Freud invented a technique he called "psychoanalysis." The central idea of psychoanalysis was free association: The patient relaxed completely and talked about whatever came to mind. By exploring these associations the individual was able to reconstruct the earlier events and bring them to consciousness. Once the patient was conscious of these events, Freud argued that the events would lose their unconscious power and the patient would gain conscious control and freedom in his or her life.

Freud later revised his conceptions of the conscious and unconscious, in a sense redefining the conscious as ego, and splitting the unconscious into the id and superego. *Id* was a term used to describe the great reservoir of biological and psychological drives, the urges and impulses that underlie all behavior. That includes the libido, the full force of sexual energy in the individual, as diffuse and tenacious as the "will to live" found in all animals. The id is permanently unconscious, and responds only to what Freud called "the pleasure principle"—if it feels good, do it. The *superego*, in contrast, is the force of self-criticism and conscience and reflects requirements that stem from the individual's social experience in a particular cultural milieu. The superego may contain conscious elements in the form of moral and ethical codes, but it is primarily unconscious in its operation. The superego arises out of the first great love attachment the child experiences, that with his or her parents. The child experiences them as judgmental, and ultimately internalizes their values as an *ego-ideal*—that is, as an ideal conception of what he or she should be. Finally, what Freud called the *ego* is the conscious personality. It is oriented toward the real world in which the person lives

6. A very readable account of Freud's life, interwoven with accounts of his theories and those of his companions, can be found in Peter Gay, *Freud: A Life for Our Time*, Norton, New York, 1988. A briefer but very thorough account is found in Harold I. Kaplan and Benjamin J. Sadock, *Synopsis of Psychiatry*, 6th ed., Williams and Wilkins, Baltimore, 1991, pp. 171–92. A brief account of psychoanalytic theory as applied to the explanation of crime is found in Ronald Blackburn, *The Psychology of Criminal Conduct*, John Wiley, Chichester, 1993, pp. 111–16; or Fritz Redl and Hans Toch, "The Psychoanalytic Explanation of Crime," in Hans Toch, ed., *Psychology of Crime and Criminal Justice*, Holt, Rinehart, and Winston, New York, 1979.

(termed by Freud the "reality principle"), and attempts to mediate be-tween the demands of the id and the prohibitions of the superego.[7]

Given this basic organization of the personality, Freud explored how the ego handles the conflicts between the superego and the id. The basic problem is one of guilt: The individual experiences all sorts of drives and urges coming from the id, and feels guilty about them because of the prohibitions of the superego. There are a variety of ways the individual may handle this situation. In *sublimation* the dri-ves of the id are diverted to activities approved of by the superego. For example, aggressive and destructive urges may be diverted to ath-letic activity. Sublimation is the normal and healthy way the ego han-dles the conflicts between the drives of the id and the prohibitions of the superego. In *repression*, in contrast, those drives are stuffed back into the unconscious and the individual denies that they exist. This may result in a variety of strange effects on behavior. One possible re-sult is a *reaction formation*, such as when a person with repressed sex-ual desires becomes very prudish about all sexual matters. Another re-sult might be *projection*, in which, for example, a person with repressed homosexual urges frequently sees homosexual tendencies in others.

Freud believed that these basic conflicts were played out in different ways at different points of the life cycle. Of particular interest to him were the experiences of early childhood. He argued that each infant goes through a series of phases in which the basic drives were oriented around, first, oral drives, then anal drives, and finally genital drives. Dur-ing the genital stage (around the ages of 3 and 4) the child is sexually attracted to the parent of the opposite sex and views the same-sex par-ent as competition. This is the famous Oedipus complex in boys, and the comparable Electra complex in girls. If the guilt produced by these urges is not handled adequately by the ego, it leaves a lasting imprint on the personality that affects later behavior.

The major tool Freud used to treat these problems was *transference*, the tendency for past significant relationships to be replayed during cur-rent significant relationships. As the relationship with the analyst takes on increasing significance in the patient's life, the patient will tend to replay with the analyst the earlier relationships that are presently gen-erating the problems. For example, if a patient's problems stem from an earlier traumatic relationship with a parent, the patient will tend to create a similar traumatic relationship with the analyst. Treatment then consists of straightening out the current relationship between analyst

7. Redl and Toch, op. cit.

and patient, which has the effect of also straightening out the earlier relationship the patient had with the parent.

PSYCHOANALYTIC EXPLANATIONS OF CRIMINAL BEHAVIOR

While the preceding is only a brief presentation of psychoanalytic theory, it provides the basic orientation for psychoanalytic explanations of criminal behavior. Within the psychoanalytic perspective criminal and delinquent behaviors are attributed to disturbances or malfunctions in the ego or superego. The id, in contrast, is viewed as a constant and inborn biologically based source of drives and urges; it does not vary substantially among individuals.

Freud himself did not discuss criminal behavior to any great extent. He did, however, suggest that at least some individuals performed criminal acts because they possessed an overdeveloped superego, which led to constant feelings of guilt and anxiety.[8] There is a consequent desire for punishment to remove the guilt feelings and restore a proper balance of good against evil. Unconsciously motivated errors (i.e., careless or imprudent ways of committing the crime) leave clues so that the authorities may more readily apprehend and convict the guilty party, and thus administer suitably cleansing punishment. This idea was extensively developed by later Freudians.[9] Criminality of this type is said to be appropriate for treatment through psychoanalysis, since it can uncover the unconscious sources of guilt and free the person from the compulsive need for punishment.

While excessive guilt from an *overdeveloped* superego is one source of criminal behavior within the psychoanalytic framework, August Aichhorn, a psychoanalytically oriented psychologist, suggested alternate sources for crime and delinquency based on his years of experience running an institution for delinquents.[10] He found that many children in his institution had *underdeveloped* superegos, so that the delinquency and criminality were primarily expressions of an unregulated id. Aich-

8. Sigmund Freud, "Criminals from a Sense of Guilt," in *The Standard Edition of the Complete Psychological Works of Sigmund Freud*, Hogarth Press, London, vol. 14, pp. 332–33.

9. This idea is elaborated in such works as Walter Bromberg, *Crime and the Mind: A Psychiatric Analysis of Crime and Punishment*, Macmillan, New York, 1965; Seymour L. Halleck, *Psychiatry and the Dilemmas of Crime*, Harper & Row, New York, 1967; David Abrahamsen, *The Psychology of Crime* (1960) and *Crime and the Human Mind* (1944), both published by Columbia University Press, New York; also his *Who Are the Guilty?*, Rinehart, New York, 1952; Kate Friedlander, *The Psychoanalytic Approach to Juvenile Delinquency*, Kegan Paul, Trench & Trubner, London, 1947; Erich Fromm, *Escape from Freedom*, Farrar & Rinehart, New York, 1941; Ben Karpman, *The Individual Criminal*, Nervous and Mental Disease Publishing Co., Washington, D.C., 1935; William A. White, *Crimes and Criminals*, Farrar & Rinehart, New York, 1933; and Theodor Reik, *The Compulsion to Confess*, Farrar, Straus, and Cudahy, New York, 1945.

10. August Aichhorn, *Wayward Youth*, Viking, New York, 1963.

horn attributed this to the fact that the parents of these children were either absent or unloving, so that the children failed to form the loving attachments necessary for the proper development of their superegos. Aichhorn treated these children by providing a happy and pleasurable environment, so as to promote the type of identification with adults that the child failed to experience earlier. He commented that most training schools "attempted through force, through fear of punishment, and without rewards of love to make the delinquent socially acceptable. Since most of their charges belong to the type just described, they only exaggerated what the parents had already begun and consequently they were doomed to failure."[11] Freud approved of these techniques in his foreword to Aichhorn's book, and concluded that they, rather than psychoanalysis per se, were appropriate in the case of young children and of adult criminals dominated by their instincts.[12]

Aichhorn also suggested that other types of delinquents existed, including those who, from an overabundance of love, were permitted to do anything they wanted by overprotective and overindulgent parents.[13] He did not find that there were many of these, but they required different treatment techniques than the delinquents created by the absent or excessively severe parents described above. Finally, there also were a few delinquents who had well-developed superegos but who identified with criminal parents.[14] Again, these required very different treatment techniques.

Much of later psychoanalytic theorizing with respect to criminal behavior is consistent with these three types of delinquents first suggested by Aichhorn.[15] Healy and Bronner, for example, examined 105 pairs of brothers, in which one brother was a persistent delinquent and the other was a nondelinquent.[16] They concluded that the delinquent brother had failed to develop normal affectional ties with his parents due to a variety of situational factors. Delinquency, they argued, was essentially a form of sublimation in which delinquents attempt to meet basic needs that are not being met by their families. Bowlby focused on early maternal deprivation as the origin of delinquency, arguing similarly that

11. Ibid., p. 209.

12. Sigmund Freud, Introduction, in ibid.

13. Aichhorn, op. cit., pp. 200–202.

14. Ibid., pp. 224–25.

15. Blackburn, op. cit., pp. 113–15.

16. William Healy and Augusta Bronner, *New Light on Delinquency and Its Treatment*, Yale University Press, New Haven, Conn., 1931.

the basic affectional ties had failed to form.[17] Redl and Wineman found that "children who hate" lacked factors leading to identification with adults, such as feelings of being wanted, loved, encouraged, and secure.[18] They said that these children not only lacked adequate super-egos, but their egos had been organized to defend the unregulated expression of their id desires. Redl and Wineman called this the "delinquent ego." Like Aichhorn, they recommended that these children be treated with unconditional love, to promote the identification with adults they lacked in earlier childhood.

The most common criticism of psychoanalytic theory as a whole is that it is untestable. Against this criticism, several authors have argued that Freud's ideas can be expressed in testable hypotheses, that these hypotheses have been tested in a great deal of empirical research, and that the results of the research have generally supported the theory.[19] A more specific criticism is that the psychoanalytic explanation of a particular individual's behavior often seems subjective and out of reach of objective measuring devices. These explanations are formulated after the behavior has occurred and rely heavily on interpretations of unconscious motivations. They may make a great deal of sense, but there is generally no way to determine the accuracy of the analyst's interpretation of an individual case within the framework of accepted scientific methodology. Cleckley, for example, made the following comment[20]:

When teaching young physicians in psychiatric residency training I was often also impressed by the influence of the examiners' convictions on items of experience reported by such patients. I found that some of these patients could be led on in almost any direction to report almost any sort of infantile recollection one sought to produce. . . . I have become increasingly convinced that some of the popular methods presumed to discover what is in the unconscious cannot be counted upon as reliable methods of obtaining evidence.

In addition to these criticisms of psychoanalytic theory in general, several criticisms also have been made about psychoanalytic explana-

17. John Bowlby, *Child Care and the Growth of Love*, Penguin, Baltimore, 1953. A review of research about his theory is presented in J. E. Hall-Williams, *Criminology and Criminal Justice*, Butterworths, London, 1982, pp. 59–68.

18. Fritz Redl and David Wineman, *Children Who Hate*, The Free Press, New York, 1951. See also Redl and Wineman, *Controls from Within*, The Free Press, New York, 1952.

19. Seymour Fisher and Roger P. Greenberg, *The Scientific Credibility of Freud's Theories and Therapy*, Basic Books, New York, 1977; Paul Kline, *Fact and Fantasy in Freudian Theory*, 2nd ed., Methuen, New York, 1981.

20. Hervey Cleckley, *The Mask of Sanity*, Mosby, St. Louis, 1976, pp. 406–7.

tions of crime. The central assertion of this explanation is that at least some crime is caused by "unconscious conflicts arising from disturbed family relationships at different stages of development, particularly the oedipal stage."[21] This argument may apply to some crimes that would appear "irrational," but many crimes seem quite conscious and rational and therefore not caused by unconscious conflicts. In addition, as a treatment technique, psychoanalysis requires a lengthy and usually quite expensive process that simply is not available to ordinary criminals. To date, psychoanalysis has not been particularly useful in either understanding crime or responding to it.

RESEARCH USING PERSONALITY TESTS

Commonsense notions of what constitutes personality generally have focused on qualities of the individual other than intellectual ability. Words such as *aggressive, belligerent, suspicious, timid, withdrawn, friendly, cooperative, likable, argumentative*, and *agreeable* have long been used to describe or express impressions of some of these qualities. Psychological tests to measure personality differences have been developed more or less parallel to intelligence tests. Inevitably, delinquents and criminals have been tested with these "personality inventories" to discover how their personalities differ from those of nondelinquents and noncriminals.

In 1950 Schuessler and Cressey[22] published the results of a survey of studies made in the United States during the preceding twenty-five years, in which comparisons between delinquents and nondelinquents were made in terms of scores on objective tests of personality. Somewhat less than half the studies showed that personality differences between delinquents and nondelinquents existed. But because of the doubtful validity of these studies and the lack of consistency in their results, Schuessler and Cressey stated that it was "impossible to conclude from these data that criminality and personality elements are associated."[23]

The same year that Schuessler and Cressey reached that conclusion, the Gluecks published an intensive study that compared 500 delinquent and 500 nondelinquent boys.[24] They argued that "the delinquent per-

21. Blackburn, op. cit., pp. 115–16.

22. Karl F. Schuessler and Donald R. Cressey, "Personality Characteristics of Criminals," *American Journal of Sociology* 55: 476–84 (March 1950).

23. Ibid., p. 476.

24. Sheldon Glueck and Eleanor Glueck, *Unraveling Juvenile Delinquency*, Commonwealth Fund, New York, 1950.

sonality" is not so much a matter of the presence or absence of certain characteristics, but is more a matter of the interrelatedness of these characteristics. The Gluecks summarize their impression of this interrelationship of characteristics as follows[25]:

On the whole, delinquents are more extroverted, vivacious, impulsive, and less self-controlled than the non-delinquents. They are more hostile, resentful, defiant, suspicious, and destructive. They are less fearful of failure or defeat than the non-delinquents. They are less concerned about meeting conventional expectations, and are more ambivalent toward or far less submissive to authority. They are, as a group, more socially assertive. To a greater extent than the control group, they express feelings of not being recognized or appreciated.

There are a number of desirable features in this description of the delinquent, which can be confusing from the point of view of theory. Often, theories about the "delinquent" or "criminal" personality are based on the implicit assumption that delinquents are somehow defective and therefore inferior to nondelinquents. This, of course, is the same assumption found in earlier theories related to biology and intelligence. But the Glueck's description would suggest that a delinquent may be, and often is, as attractive and socially acceptable as a nondelinquent.

Even if these findings are confusing from the standpoint of theory making, the differences between delinquents and nondelinquents nevertheless lend themselves to making statistical predictions. The Gluecks developed three prediction tables,[26] one based on factors in the social background, one based on character traits as determined by the Rorschach test, and one based on personality traits as determined in the psychiatric interview. All three are said to give impressive results. For example, only about 10 percent of juveniles in the best-score class may be expected to become delinquent, as opposed to about 90 percent in the worst-score class.[27]

---

25. Ibid., p. 275.

26. Ibid., pp. 257–71 for detailed tables.

27. Ibid., Table XX–3, p. 262. The predictive validity of a revised table was supported in studies by M. M. Craig and S. J. Glick ("Ten Years' Experience with the Glueck Social Prediction Table," *Crime and Delinquency* 9: 249–61 [1963]; and "Application of the Glueck Social Prediction Table on an Ethnic Basis," *Crime and Delinquency* 11: 175–78 [1965]) and N. B. Trevvett ("Identifying Delinquency-Prone Children," *Crime and Delinquency* 11: 186–91 [1965]). Kurt Weis ("The Glueck Social Prediction Table: An Unfulfilled Promise," *Journal of Criminal Law, Criminology and Police Science* 65: 397–404 [1974]), however, argued that its results are only slightly better than chance.

Similar results have been obtained with the Minnesota Multiphasic Personality Inventory (MMPI), which is a list of 550 statements developed to aid in psychiatric diagnosis.[28] People who take the MMPI indicate whether the statements in the test are true or false about themselves. Ten different scales are then scored and assumed to measure different aspects of the personality. These scales were originally identified by the names of the psychiatric symptoms or pathologies they were assumed to measure, such as hypochondriasis, depression, or hysteria. Since the MMPI is now often used with normal individuals, the scales are now identified by number only (Scale 1, Scale 2, etc.). The ten scores a person gets on the ten scales are then arranged into a "profile," so that no single score indicates a person's performance on the MMPI.[29]

Waldo and Dinitz examined ninety-four personality studies performed between 1950 and 1965 in an update of Schuessler and Cressey's study, and found that about 80 percent of these studies reported statistically significant differences between criminals and noncriminals.[30] The most impressive results were found with Scale 4 of the MMPI, previously called the "psychopathic deviate" scale, which consistently produced significant results. These studies generally concluded that delinquents and criminals were more "psychopathic" than nondelinquents and noncriminals.

Scale 4, however, includes statements such as "I have never been in trouble with the law," "Sometimes when I was young I stole things," "I like school," and "My relatives are nearly all in sympathy with me." On the average, nondelinquents and noncriminals responded to four of these statements differently than did criminals and delinquents. This may simply reflect differences in the situations and circumstances of their lives, rather than any increased "psychopathy" among delinquents and criminals.[31] It seems best to conclude that the differences that ap-

28. For a full discussion of the use of the MMPI, see S. R. Hathaway and P. E. Meehl, *An Atlas for the Clinical Use of the MMPI*, University of Minnesota Press, Minneapolis, 1951; for an account of its application and use in the study of delinquency, see S. R. Hathaway and E. D. Monachesi, *Analyzing and Predicting Juvenile Delinquency with the MMPI* (1953) and *Adolescent Personality and Behavior* (1963), both published by the University of Minnesota Press, Minneapolis. A more recent review of studies using the MMPI on criminals can be found in Edwin I. Megargee and Martin J. Bohn, Jr., *Classifying Criminal Offenders*, Sage, Beverly Hills, Calif., 1979.

29. For a full discussion of the profiles, see Hathaway and Meehl, *An Atlas;* a short account may be found in Hathaway and Monachesi, *Analyzing and Predicting . . . ,* pp. 19–23.

30. Gordon P. Waldo and Simon Dinitz, "Personality Attributes of the Criminal: An Analysis of Research Studies, 1950–1965," *Journal of Research in Crime and Delinquency* 4(2): 185–202 (July 1967).

31. In fact, Scale 4 had originally been constructed by listing statements that "normal" persons said were true about themselves while "psychopaths" said were not. The original "psychopathic" group consisted largely of young delinquents, so that a person who scores high on Scale 4 makes responses to the statements that are similar to the responses of a group consisting primarily of young delinquents. It should not be surprising if that person is also a delinquent.

pear between criminals and noncriminals on personality tests do not have any theoretical relevance to understanding the causes of criminal behavior or to treating it.[32]

ANTISOCIAL PERSONALITY DISORDER

In addition to appearing on personality inventories, the term psychopath is used by psychiatrists to describe individuals who exhibit a certain group of behaviors and attitudes.[33] When used in this way, the term psychopath can be considered synonymous with the more recent terms sociopath and antisocial personality disorder. The three terms are used interchangeably in this section.

The fourth edition of the official *Diagnostic and Statistical Manual* (DSM-4) of the American Psychiatric Association states that "the essential feature of Antisocial Personality Disorder is a pervasive pattern of disregard for, and violation of, the rights of others that begins in childhood or early adolescence and comes into adulthood."[34] The diagnosis may be made when there are at least three of the following six characteristics: (1) repeated violations of the law that are grounds for arrest; (2) repeated lying, use of aliases, or conning others for personal profit or pleasure; (3) impulsivity or failure to plan ahead; (4) repeated physical fights or assaults; (5) repeated failure to sustain consistent work behavior or honor financial obligations; and (6) lack of remorse.

The DSM-4 distinguishes "antisocial personality disorder" from "adult antisocial behavior," which is criminal behavior that occurs without the presence of any personality disorder. A person should be diagnosed as having "antisocial personality disorder" when these characteristics are "inflexible, maladaptive, and persistent, and cause significant functional impairment or subjective distress." The DSM-4 also states that the antisocial personality disorder "has a chronic course but may become less evident or remit as the individual grows older, particularly by the fourth decade of life."

The DSM-4 attempts to provide a fairly precise definition of the term "antisocial personality," especially so that it can be distinguished from criminality. In practice, however, Cleckley points out that "the term psychopath (or antisocial personality) as it is applied by various psychiatrists and hospital staffs sometimes becomes so broad that it can be ap-

---

32. Blackburn, op. cit., pp. 185–86; Jack Arbuthnot, Donald A. Gordon, and Gregory J. Jurkovic, "Personality," in Herbert C. Quay, ed., *Handbook of Juvenile Delinquency*, John Wiley, New York, 1987, pp. 139–83.

33. See Blackburn, op. cit., pp. 80–86; Kaplan and Sadock, op. cit., pp. 532–33.

34. *Diagnostic and Statistical Manual of Mental Disorders*, 4th ed., American Psychiatric Association, Washington, D.C., 1994, pp. 645–50.

plied to almost any criminal."[35] He argues, however, that the majority of psychopaths are not criminals, and the majority of criminals are not psychopaths. Psychopaths may be found in any profession, including business, science, medicine, and psychiatry.[36] Typical psychopaths differ from typical criminals in that their actions seem less purposeful, they cause themselves needless sorrow and shame, and they usually do not commit major crimes or crimes of violence.[37]

These terms "psychopath" and "antisocial personality" are not merely descriptions of behavior patterns, but also imply that those behaviors originate in the personality of the individual. It is possible, however, that the behaviors may be explained by factors other than personality. For example, Yablonsky argued that "core" members of violent gangs were sociopaths who led the gang in moblike violence as a way of acting out their own hostility and aggression.[38] Other gang researchers described the behavior of core gang members in a similar way, but argued that the behavior resulted from the need to create and maintain a leadership position in the gang.[39] Thus, the origin of these behaviors may not lie in personality characteristics.

Because psychiatrists tend to assume that antisocial actions originate in the personality of the offender, some psychiatrists have recommended that people with "antisocial personality disorder" be locked up until they reach middle age,[40] and even that they be executed.[41] This is because psychiatrists have no effective methods for treating this disorder, so they assume that the person will continue to commit antisocial actions if allowed to remain free. But this assumption is not supported by a study by William McCord, who has done extensive work on psychopaths and crime.[42] McCord found that delinquents who had been diagnosed as psychopathic at two juvenile institutions had only slightly worse recidi-

35. Cleckley, op. cit., p. 263.

36. Ibid., pp. 188–221.

37. Ibid., pp. 261–63.

38. Louis Yablonsky, *The Violent Gang*, Penguin, New York, 1970, pp. 236–47.

39. James F. Short, Jr., and Fred L. Stodtbeck, *Group Process and Gang Delinquency*, University of Chicago Press, Chicago, 1974, especially pp. 248–64. This material had been previously published in *Social Problems* 12: 127–40 (fall 1964).

40. E.g., Samuel B. Guze, *Criminality and Psychiatric Disorders*, Oxford University Press, New York, 1976, p. 137.

41. Charles Patrick Ewing, "Preventive Detention and Execution: The Constitutionality of Punishing Future Crimes," *Law and Human Behavior* 15(2): 139–63 (1991).

42. William McCord, *The Psychopath and Milieu Therapy*, Academic Press, New York, 1982. See also William McCord and Jose Sanchez, "The Treatment of Deviant Children: A Twenty-Five-Year Follow-Up Study," *Crime and Delinquency* 29(2): 238–53 (April 1983).

vism rates than other delinquents at the same institutions, and that several years after release the recidivism rates were identical.

PREDICTING FUTURE DANGEROUSNESS

Some psychiatrists recommend that offenders with antisocial personality disorder be locked up for extended periods of time. While this may be a reasonable policy for frequent and serious offenders, psychiatrists go further by arguing that they are able to identify these offenders through psychiatric means. If that is their claim, then their track record so far has been poor.[43]

For example, a ten-year study in Massachusetts by Kozol and associates[44] involved the use of extensive psychiatric and social casework services in the attempt to predict the future likely dangerousness of a group of high-risk offenders prior to their release from prison. As it turned out, the researchers were unable to predict nearly two thirds of the violent crime that ultimately occurred (thirty-one crimes out of forty-eight), and nearly two thirds of the persons whom they predicted would be violent (thirty-two persons out of forty-nine) were not. Because of the probable occurrence of such errors, Morris argues that it is fundamentally unjust to detain anyone on the basis of a prediction of his future behavior.[45] In addition, the idea that a person can be punished for what he *might* do rather than for what he has actually done seriously threatens the basic notions of freedom of the individual from unwarranted governmental control.[46]

Monahan extensively reviewed the clinical techniques for predicting violent behavior and concluded that it can only be done within very restricted circumstances.[47] Specifically, he concluded that it is possible to estimate the probability of a violent act in the immediate future when the person is going to remain in a situation that is essentially similar to ones in which he or she had committed violent acts in the past. Monahan presented a complex procedure for estimating this probability, which included: (1) a comparison of the circumstances the offender was likely to encounter in the near future with the circumstances in which the offender had committed violent acts in the past; (2) the recency,

---

43. For a review, see Blackburn, op. cit., pp. 328–35.

44. Harry L. Kozol, Richard J. Boucher, and Ralph F. Garofalo, "The Diagnosis and Treatment of Dangerousness," *Crime and Delinquency* 18: 371–92 (1972).

45. Norval Morris, *The Future of Imprisonment*, University of Chicago Press, Chicago, 1974, pp. 71–73.

46. Ibid., pp. 83–84.

47. John Monahan, *Predicting Violent Behavior*, Sage, Beverly Hills, Calif., 1981.

severity, and frequency of violent acts the individual had committed in the past; and (3) general statistics on the probability of violence for individuals who are similar in age, sex, race, class, history of drug abuse, residential and employment stability, and educational attainment. Monahan stated that it is not possible to predict violence over a long period of time, or to predict it when a person was moving from one situation to a very different one (e.g., on being released from prison). He also maintained that this type of prediction is entirely separate from the diagnosis of mental disease, and that if mental disease is also of interest, a separate examination must be undertaken. Finally Monahan argued that psychologists should confine themselves to estimating the probability of a violent act and should not recommend whether any official action should be taken in a given case. According to Monahan, criminal justice officials are responsible for deciding whether or not to take official actions while the role of psychologists and psychiatrists is to provide accurate information on which to base those decisions.

Psychological and psychiatric research has now turned away from the question of trying to predict whether particular people will commit acts of violence in the future. Instead, this research has turned to the more general question of identifying factors associated with an increased or decreased likelihood that a person will engage in any type of crime in the future. Most of this research has focused on delinquency rather than adult criminality, and on less serious crime rather than more serious violence, since these are considerably easier to predict.

This research shows that the strongest predictor of later delinquent behavior is earlier childhood problem behaviors such as disruptive classroom conduct, aggressiveness, lying, and dishonesty.[48] This means that the same individuals who caused the most problems when they were young children will also cause the most problems when they are adolescents and adults. The stability of behavioral problems over time suggests that these people may have certain personality characteristics, even if they do not show up on personality tests, that are associated with antisocial or troublesome behavior.

Other factors in early childhood associated with later delinquency include poor parental child management techniques, offending by parents and siblings, low intelligence and educational attainment, and separation from parents.[49] This suggests that the personality characteristic

---

48. E.g., Rolf Loeber and T. Dishion, "Early Predictors of Male Delinquency: A Review," *Psychological Bulletin* 94(1): 68–99 (1983); Rolf Loeber and Magda Stouthamer-Loeber, "Prediction," in Herbert C. Quay, ed., *Handbook of Juvenile Delinquency*, op. cit., pp. 325–82.

49. Loeber and Dishion, op. cit.; David P. Farrington, "Introduction," in Farrington, ed., *Psychological Explanations of Crime*, Dartmouth, Aldershot, England, 1994, p. xv.

may be associated with or caused by early childhood experiences. This research will be further discussed in Chapter 18 on developmental theories of criminology, but it has also led to several theories that focus on impulsivity as a key personality characteristic related to crime and delinquency.

IMPULSIVITY AND CRIME

A rather diverse group of researchers have recently suggested that impulsivity is the key personality feature associated with antisocial behavior.[50] In general, these researchers assume that impulsivity is manifested in high levels of activity (especially where the person acts without thinking), a tendency to become impatient and to seek immediate gratification, and a tendency to become distracted.[51]

One theory that focused on this characteristic was by Wilson and Herrnstein.[52] Farrington describes this as a "typical psychological explanation of crime, incorporating propositions seen in several other psychological theories."[53] In general, those propositions include the assumption that crime is inherently rewarding, so that everyone would commit it unless we were restrained by internal inhibitions. These internal inhibitions are associated with what is normally called "conscience," and are developed primarily in early childhood by parents through their childrearing practices. While criminal behavior may be directly learning through modeling by parents, peers, or the media, most crime is assumed to be the result of the failure to learn internal inhibitions against it.

Within the context of these general assumptions, Wilson and Herrnstein propose that the key individual-level factor associated with criminality is the tendency to think in terms of short-term rather than long-term consequences. The rewards from not committing crime almost

---

50. David P. Farrington, "Have Any Individual, Family, or Neighbourhood Influences on Offending Been Demonstrated Conclusively?" in Farrington, Robert J. Sampson, and P. O. Wikstrom, eds., *Integrating Individual and Ecological Aspects of Crime*, National Council for Crime Prevention, Stockholm, 1993, pp. 3–37; E. E. Gorenstein and J. P. Newman, "Disinhibitory Psychopathology," *Psychological Review* 87: 301–15 (1980); Jennifer L. White et al., "Measuring Impulsivity and Examining Its Relationship to Delinquency," *Journal of Abnormal Psychology* 103(2): 192–205 (1994); Marvin Zuckerman, "Personality in the Third Dimension," *Personality and Individual Differences* 10: 391–418 (1989); Jeffrey A. Gray, "Drug Effects on Fear and Frustration," in Leslie L. Iversen, Susan D. Iversen, and Solomon H. Snyder, eds., *Handbook of Psychopharmacology: Drugs, Neurotransmitters, and Behavior*, vol. 8, Plenum, New York, 1977.

51. White et al., op. cit.

52. James Q. Wilson and Richard J. Herrnstein, *Crime and Human Nature*, New York: Simon & Schuster, 1985. See especially ch. 7.

53. Farrington, "Introduction," op. cit., pp. xix–xx.

always are in the future, while the rewards from committing it almost always are in the present. The tendency to think in terms of short-term consequences is associated with a variety of factors, including impulsivity and low intelligence. Wilson and Herrnstein also argue that the tendency to engage in criminal actions is associated with five other types of factors: (1) certain features of family life, such as poor child-rearing techniques can produce weak internalized inhibitions; (2) membership in subcultures such as street gangs can increase the value placed on crime; (3) the mass media can directly affect aggressiveness through modeling and can indirectly affect it by convincing people they are being treated unfairly; (4) the economic system can influence that ability to achieve rewards through legitimate activity; and (5) schools can influence whether children believe they can achieve rewards through legitimate activity. Wilson and Herrnstein reviewed a massive amount of data to support their theory, but the extent to which this data support the theory has been questioned by several reviewers.[54]

Glenn Walters also proposed a theory with a strong focus on impulsivity as an enduring personality characteristic.[55] Walters defines "lifestyle criminals" as those who are characterized by "a global sense of irresponsibility, self-indulgent interests, an intrusive approach to interpersonal relationships, and chronic violation of societal rules, laws, and mores." He argues that these criminals have eight specific thinking patterns that allow them to perpetuate this pattern of actions. With *mollification*, these criminals point out the inequities and unfairnesses of life, and blame others for their own choices. The *cutoff* is some visual image or verbal cue (e.g., "f___ it") which has the effect of terminating all thought in the moment and simply allows the criminals to act without worrying about the consequences. A sense of *entitlement* means that any actions are considered justifiable to achieve what is desired. *Power orientation* means that these criminals believe it is a dog-eat-dog world, and those who are strong can do whatever they can get away with. *Sentimentality* is the tendency for these criminals to look back at all the good things they have done in their lives, and to claim that they there-

---

54. See book reviews by Lawrence E. Cohen, (*Contemporary Sociology* 16: 202–5 [March 1987]); Jack P. Gibbs (*Criminology* 23[2]: 381–88 [May 1985]); Philip Jenkins (*Contemporary Crises* 10: 329–35 [1986]); and Joseph Gusfield (*Science* 231: 413–14 [January 1986]). In addition, Michael R. Gottfredson and Travis Hirschi (*A General Theory of Crime*, Stanford University Press, Stanford, Calif., 1990) have criticized the theory as being theoretically contradictory.

55. Glenn D. Walters, *The Criminal Lifestyle: Patterns of Serious Criminal Conduct*, Sage, Newbury Park, Calif., 1990. Walters's work is based in part on the earlier description of fifty-two "thinking errors" by Samuel Yochelson and Stanton E. Samenow, *The Criminal Personality*, Jason Aronson, New York, vol. I, 1976; vol. II, 1977. For a description of Yochelson and Samenow's theory, see George B. Vold, *Theoretical Criminology*, 2nd ed. prepared by Thomas J. Bernard, Oxford University Press, New York, 1979, pp. 153–56.

fore should not be held responsible for the bad things. *Superoptimism* is the tendency to believe that nothing bad will ever happen to them, including being punished for the crimes they commit. *Cognitive indolence* means that they just don't pay attention to the details in life. *Discontinuity* means they fail to follow through on commitments, carry out intentions, and remain focused on goals over time.

A third theory with a strong focus on impulsivity is Moffitt's theory of "life-course-persistent" offenders.[56] Moffitt describes these as a small group of people who engage "in antisocial behavior of one sort or another at every stage of life." Examples of such behavior would be biting and hitting at age 4, shoplifting and truancy at age 10, drug dealing and car theft at age 16, robbery and rape at age 22, and fraud and child abuse at age 30.[57] Moffitt argues that these behaviors begin with early neuropsychological problems that are caused by factors such as drug use or poor nutrition by the mother while she is pregnant, complications at birth resulting in minor brain damage, or deprivation of affection or child abuse and neglect after birth. These neuropsychological problems then tend to generate a cycle that results in an impulsive personality style. Parents dealing with children who have these problems often have psychological deficiencies themselves, and their attempts to discipline and socialize their children tend to intensify the children's problem behaviors.[58] As the children age, these problems can directly cause problems by interfering with their ability to control their behavior and to think of the future consequences of their actions. In addition, these problems can disrupt the children's success in school, which can reduce their ability to acquire rewards in legitimate activities and increase the likelihood they will turn to illegitimate, antisocial actions for rewards. Although this theory is quite recent, a number of studies have produced supportive results.[59]

---

56. Terrie E. Moffitt, "Life-Course-Persistent and Adolescent-Limited Antisocial Behavior," *Psychological Review* 100: 674–701 (1993).

57. Ibid., p. 679.

58. Ibid., p. 682.

59. Moffitt contrasted the "life course persistent" offenders with what she called "adolescent-limited" offenders who desist from delinquency as they mature to adults. Daniel Nagan and Kenneth Land ("Age, Criminal Careers, and Population Heterogeneity," *Criminology* 31[3]: 327–62 [1993]) identified separate groups of "life course persistent" and "adolescent-limited" offenders. They also found that the "life course persistent" group can be separated into low- and high-level chronic offenders. Nagan, Land, and Moffitt ("Life-Course Trajectories of Different Types of Offenders," *Criminology* 33[1]: 111–39 [1995]) then explored the nature of these groups of offenders further. They found that adolescent-limited offenders do not completely desist from antisocial behavior after adolescence, but still engage in behaviors such as heavy drinking, drug use, fighting, and minor criminal acts. Finally, Moffit, Donald Lynam, and Phil Silva ("Neuropsychological Tests Predicting Persistent Male Delinquency," *Criminology* 32[2]: 277–300 [1994]) found that poor neuropsychological status predicts delinquency that begins in early childhood but not that which begins in adolescence.

More recently, Caspi, Moffitt and their colleagues examined personality traits in two very different groups: about 1,000 youths born in Dunedin, New Zealand, in 1972–73, and about 500 ethnically diverse 12- and 13-year-old boys from Pittsburgh.[60] They found that crime-proneness was associated with a combination of impulsivity and "negative emotionality," which they described as "a tendency to experience aversive affective states such as anger, anxiety, and irritability." Youths with "negative emotionality," they suggested, perceive more threats and dangers than other people in the normal affairs of daily life. When these youths also have "great difficulty in modulating impulses," they tend to quickly turn those negative emotions into actions. Using an analogy from the Wild West, they describe these youths as "quick on the draw."

IMPLICATIONS AND CONCLUSIONS

There is a widespread perception that some people are more likely to commit crime and that this increased likelihood remains relatively stable as these people grow older and as they move from situation to situation. This suggests that these people have some personality characteristic that is associated with crime that they carry with them through time and space.

There may be considerable truth to this widespread perception, but the research linking personality to crime has been beset with a whole host of methodological problems.[61] These problems have led many criminologists, even those who are largely favorable to this approach, to discard much of the research as meaningless. For example, Wilson and Herrnstein assert that delinquents score higher than nondelinquents on fourteen separate personality dimensions.[62] Gottfredson and Hirschi comment that this evidence is "at best, unimpressive" since most of it "is produced by attaching personality labels to differences in rates of offending between offenders and nonoffenders."[63] They conclude that "all these 'personality' traits can be explained without abandoning the conclusion that offenders differ from nonoffenders only in their tendency to offend."

---

60. Avshalom Caspi, Terrie E. Moffitt, Phil A. Silva, Magda Stouthamer-Loeber, Robert F. Krueger, and Pamela S. Schmutte, "Are Some People Crime-Prone?" *Criminology* 32(2): 163–95 (1994).

61. These are reviewed in Robert F. Kruger et al., "Personality Traits Are Linked to Crime among Men and Women: Evidence from a Birth Cohort," *Journal of Abnormal Psychology* 103(2): 328–38 (1995). See also Moffitt, op. cit., 1993. For a brief defense of trait-based personality theories, see Caspi et al., op. cit., pp. 164–65.

62. Wilson and Herrnstein, op. cit., ch. 7.

63. Gottfredson and Hirschi, op. cit., p. 209. Their own theory of crime is quite close to a personality theory, and is presented in Chapter 13.

Recent research, such as that focused on impulsivity, seems to be addressing these methodological problems, so that researchers may be closing in on personality characteristics that are actually associated with crime. On the other hand, the relation between impulsivity and crime has been the subject of a great deal of research in the past without producing the consistent results suggested by these recent studies.[64] For example, Scale 9 on the MMPI, previously described as the "hypomania" scale, is largely a measure of impulsivity, but this scale never consistently distinguished between offenders and nonoffenders. How these earlier findings can be reconciled with the more recent research on impulsivity is unclear at present.

Thus, it is not yet clear how large a role personality plays in explaining crime in general. Some individuals may be more likely to commit crime regardless of the situation they are in. But it is also true that some situations are more likely to be associated with crime, regardless of the people who are in them. To understand the behavior of most criminals and delinquents, it may be more profitable to start by analyzing the situations people find themselves in rather than the personalities they carry from situation to situation.

64. Blackburn, op. cit., pp. 191–96.

CHAPTER 8

Crime and Economic Conditions

In sharp contrast to the explanations of criminal behavior that focus on the characteristics of the individual are those theories that minimize or ignore entirely the significance of the individual's biological or psychological makeup. Perhaps the oldest and most elaborately documented of the theories with a nonindividual orientation are those that explain criminal behavior in terms of economic differences or influence. Discussions of the sad state of the poor, with arguments about the undesirable consequences of poverty such as sickness, crime, and despair, go far back into antiquity.[1] These discussions have generated a great many empirical studies concerning the relationship between poverty and crime.

Some of these studies focus on variations in economic conditions to see if they correspond to variations in crime rates. If crime is caused by poverty, so the reasoning goes, then there should be more crime in places and at times where there are more poor people. Thus these studies have compared times of economic depression with times of economic prosperity, and wealthy areas of a country with poor areas, to see if there are any systematic differences in their crime rates. Later studies looked at whether there is any systematic relationship between crime rates and unemployment rates, and whether crime is associated with economic inequality, that is, with poverty that exists next to wealth.

From the very beginning, however, there has been disagreement about the findings and debate about whether the conclusions being drawn were justified. This chapter examines some of the studies to

1. For a brief history of these arguments as they relate to crime, see Lynn McDonald, *The Sociology of Law and Order*, Faber and Faber, London, 1976.

demonstrate those disagreements and to draw conclusions about the relationship between crime and poverty.

RESEARCH ON CRIME AND ECONOMIC CONDITIONS: CONTRADICTIONS AND DISAGREEMENTS

There is an enormous amount of research on the relationship between crime and economic conditions. Many of the results of this research are inconsistent with each other and result in contradictory conclusions about the relationship between these two phenomena. The following is a brief review of a few of these studies to give a sense of the general situation.

As discussed in Chapter 3, as soon as national crime statistics were available in France in the early 1800s, attempts were made by Guerry and Quetelet to demonstrate the relationship between crime and poverty. Both compared wealthy areas of France with poor areas, expecting to find more crime in the poor areas because there were more poor people there. Neither found what he had expected. Guerry found that the wealthiest regions of France had more property crime but less violent crime. He concluded that the higher levels of property crime were caused by opportunity. There were more things to steal in the wealthy provinces. Quetelet found a similar pattern, and also suggested that opportunity might be a factor. But he also pointed to the great inequality between poverty and wealth in the wealthy provinces. This, he suggested, might generate resentment among the poor. In contrast, poor provinces tended to have less inequality because everyone was poor although people generally had enough to survive.

Since that time, hundreds of studies have been published on this subject in Europe and in the United States. These studies, extending back over a period of almost 200 years, often have given complicated and apparently contradictory results. For example, numerous studies have been done on the relationship between crime and the business cycle.[2] The thinking was that there should be more crime during times of economic downturns, when there would be more poor people, and less crime during times of economic expansions. Most of these studies, however, find that the general crime rate does not increase during economic

2. European and American studies up to 1935 are reviewed in Thorsten Sellin, *Research Memorandum on Crime in the Depression*, Social Science Research Council Bulletin No. 27, New York, 1937; reprinted by Arno Press, New York, 1972. A number of these studies are also reviewed in the first and second editions of the present book. See George B. Vold, *Theoretical Criminology*, 2nd ed., prepared by Thomas J. Bernard, Oxford University Press, New York, 1979, pp. 168–71. Abstracts of more recent studies may be found in Thomas C. Castellano and Robert J. Sampson, "Annotations and References of the Literature on the Relationship between Economic Conditions and Criminality," in Kenneth R. Danser and John H. Laub, *Juvenile Criminal Behavior and Its Relation to Economic Conditions*, Criminal Justice Research Center, Albany, N.Y., 1981.

recessions and depressions.[3] Some studies even find the opposite situation—that crime actually decreases during such periods. For example, Henry and Short found that crimes of violence in American cities from the late 1920s to the late 1940s declined during times of economic downturn, and increased during periods of economic expansion.[4]

Quetelet had pointed out that even wealthy areas may have many poor people in them. Similarly, it may be that there are more poor people even in times of economic expansion, and this would account for the increases in crime rates. A more direct measure of poverty therefore would be to count the number of poor people in a particular time or place, to see if times or places with more poor people have greater amounts of crime. Results of such studies, however, have also proved inconsistent and even contradictory.

For example, using 1970 statistics, Cho found that the percentage of people below the poverty line in the forty-nine largest cities of the United States was not associated with any of the seven index crimes reported by the FBI.[5] Jacobs reached a similar conclusion with respect to the crimes of burglary, robbery, and grand larceny.[6] In contrast, Ehrlich found that there was a positive relationship between state property crime rates for 1940, 1950, and 1960 and the percentage of households receiving less than half the median income.[7] An even stronger result was found by Loftin and Hill, who created an index of "structural poverty" including measures of infant mortality, low education, and one-parent families, as well as income.[8] They found very strong correlation between this measure and state homicide rates. Similar results using the same index of structural poverty were found in two additional studies, one of which concluded that it was strongly correlated with homicides involving families and friends but not in homicides involving strangers.[9] To make matters even more confusing, some studies have found that there

3. Sharon K. Long and Ann D. Witte, "Current Economic Trends: Implications for Crime and Criminal Justice," pp. 69–143, in Kevin Wright, ed., *Crime and Criminal Justice in a Declining Economy*, Oelgeschlager, Gunn and Hain, Cambridge, Mass., 1981.

4. Andrew F. Henry and James F. Short, Jr., *Suicide and Homicide*, The Free Press, New York, 1954.

5. Y. H. Cho, *Public Policy and Urban Crime*, Ballinger, Cambridge, Mass., 1974.

6. D. Jacobs, "Inequality and Economic Crime," *Sociology and Social Research* 66: 12–28 (Oct. 1981).

7. Isaac Ehrlich, "Participation in Illegal Activities," in Gary S. Becker and W. M. Landes, eds., *Essays in the Economics of Crime and Punishment*, Columbia University Press, New York, 1974.

8. Colin Loftin and R. H. Hill, "Regional Subculture and Homicide," *American Sociological Review* 39: 714–24 (1974).

9. Steven F. Messner, "Regional and Racial Effects on the Urban Homicide Rate: The Subculture of Violence Revisited," *American Journal of Sociology* 88: 997–1007 (1983); M. Wayne Smith and Robert Nash Parker, "Type of Homicide and Variation in Regional Rates," *Social Forces* 59(1): 136–47 (Sept. 1980). Smith and Parker argue that structural poverty is related to homicides between families and friends, but not between strangers.

are different poverty-crime relationships in different regions of the country.[10] One of these studies concluded that the results are best explained by variations in the way crimes are reported and recorded, rather than by variations in the incidence of crime.[11]

CRIME AND UNEMPLOYMENT:
A DETAILED LOOK AT RESEARCH

Many people believe that unemployment causes crime, so they believe that crime should increase when unemployment is high and decrease when unemployment is low. This popular view presumably is based on the assumption that unemployment causes poverty, and then poverty causes crime. Unemployment also is an indicator of general economic conditions, since it goes up in times of economic slowdown and goes down in times of economic expansion. The popular assumption that crime is related to the business cycle probably is based on an assumption about a relationship between crime and unemployment. A more detailed look at research on unemployment and crime is presented here both to explore this specific issue and to give a general sense of the problems that arise with research that attempts to relate crime to economic conditions.

Consider first the studies that focus on the relationship between unemployment and juvenile delinquency. A study by Glaser and Rice found that delinquency is inversely related to unemployment; that is, delinquency is high when unemployment is low and vice versa.[12] Glaser and Rice suggested that this might be because in times of unemployment parents are more available to their children. Two econometric studies, however, concluded that delinquency is directly related to unemployment, and that a 1 percent increase in unemployment results in an approximately .15 percent increase in delinquency.[13] A third econo-

10. Steven F. Messner, "Regional Differences in the Economic Correlates of the Urban Homicide Rate," *Criminology* 21(4): 477–88 (Nov. 1983); John D. McCarthy, Omer Galle, and William Zimmern, "Population Density, Social Structure, and Interpersonal Violence," *American Behavioral Scientist* 18(6): 771–89 (July–Aug. 1975); Booth, Johnson, and Choldin, op. cit.

11. Booth et al., op. cit.

12. Daniel Glaser and Kent Rice, "Crime, Age, and Employment," *American Sociological Review* 24: 679–86 (Oct. 1959). Additional support for this study can be found in Jack P. Gibbs, "Crime, Unemployment and Status Integration," *The British Journal of Criminology* 6(1): 49–58 (Jan. 1966). The study was criticized as a statistical artifact in Marcia Guttentag, "The Relationship of Unemployment to Crime and Delinquency," *Journal of Social Issues* 24(1): 105–14 (Jan. 1968).

13. Larry D. Singell, "An Examination of the Empirical Relationship Between Unemployment and Juvenile Delinquency." *The American Journal of Economics and Sociology* 26(4): 377–86 (1965); and Belton M. Fleischer, "The Effect of Unemployment on Juvenile Delinquency," *Journal of Political Economy* 71: 543–55 (Dec. 1963). Related works by Fleischer are "The Effect of Income on Delinquency," *The American Economic Review*, March 1966, pp. 118–37, and *The Economics of Delinquency*, Quadrangle Books, Chicago, 1966. This position is supported in Harold L. Votey, Jr., and Llad Phillips, "The Control of Criminal Activity: An Economic Analysis," in Daniel Glaser, ed., *Handbook of Criminology*, Rand McNally, Chicago, 1974, pp. 1065–69.

metric study found that unemployment had no effect on the criminality of urban males in the age group 14 to 24.[14] Danser and Laub used
victimization data rather than official police statistics, and concluded
that there was no relationship between juvenile delinquency and adult
unemployment, contradicting Glaser and Rice's findings.[15] They also
found that there was no relationship between delinquency and juvenile
unemployment rates, even within specific age, sex, and racial groups.
Calvin, in contrast, argues there is a close relationship between unemployment and crime for black youths, and that those who argue there
is no relationship are using incorrect data or faulty interpretations.[16]

There also have been contradictory findings on the question of the
relationship between unemployment and adult crime. Nagel found a
strong correlation between crime rates and unemployment rates when
he ranked each of the fifty states on those two measures.[17] Brenner concluded, on the basis of a study of national crime and unemployment statistics from 1940 to 1973, that a sustained 1 percent increase in unemployment results in a 5.7 percent increase in murder.[18] Berk and his
colleagues studied programs that provide unemployment benefits to released prisoners, and concluded: "For ex-offenders at least, unemployment and poverty do cause crime."[19] In contrast, a number of other authors have concluded that there is either no relationship between
unemployment and crime or that the relationship (sometimes found to
be positive and sometimes negative) is insignificant.[20]

These inconsistent and contradictory results continue to be generated by research. In 1983, Freeman reviewed eighteen of these studies
and concluded that higher unemployment rates are associated with

14. Isaac Ehrlich, "Participation in Illegitimate Activities: A Theoretical and Empirical Investigation," *Journal of Political Economy*, May–June 1973, pp. 521–64.

15. Danser and Laub, op. cit.

16. Allen D. Calvin, "Unemployment among Black Youths, Demographics, and Crime," *Crime and
Delinquency* 27(2): 234–44 (1981).

17. William G. Nagel, "A Statement on Behalf of a Moratorium on Prison Construction," *Crime
and Delinquency* 23(2): 154–72 (April 1977).

18. Harvey Brenner, *Estimating the Social Costs of National Economic Policy*, U.S. Government
Printing Office, Washington, D.C., 1976. See also a summary of his testimony before the House
Judiciary Committee's Subcommittee on Crime in *Criminal Justice Newsletter*, Oct. 10, 1977,
p. 5.

19. Richard A. Berk, Kenneth J. Lenihan, and Peter H. Rossi, "Crime and Poverty: Some Experimental Evidence from Ex-Offenders," *American Sociological Review* 45: 766–86 (Oct. 1980). See
also their *Money, Work, and Crime: Experimental Evidence*, Academic Press, New York, 1980.

20. See, for example, Long and Witte, op. cit.; D. Jacobs, "Inequality and Economic Crime," *Sociology and Social Research* 66: 12–28 (Oct. 1981); Alan Booth, David R. Johnson, and Harvey
Choldin, "Correlates of City Crime Rates: Victimization Surveys Versus Official Statistics," *Social
Problems* 25: 187–97 (1977); and Paul E. Spector, "Population Density and Unemployment," *Criminology* 12(4): 399–401 (1975).

higher crime rates, but that the relation is weak and generally insignificant.[21] His conclusion was consistent with two earlier and somewhat
smaller reviews of the research on unemployment and crime.[22] In 1987,
however, Chiricos reviewed sixty-three studies of crime and unemployment.[23] He concluded that the relationship between unemployment and
crime is positive and frequently significant, especially for property crime,
and that this effect was especially strong after 1970.[24] Chiricos also argued that the positive relation between crime and unemployment is
more likely to be found when smaller units are examined (e.g., neighborhoods) rather than larger units (e.g., nations), because these smaller
units "are more likely to be homogeneous."[25] In contrast, economic conditions in larger units often have little impact on the extent of poverty
and deprivation in particular areas.[26]

But after Chiricos's review, Land and his colleagues found consistently negative relationships between homicide and unemployment after controlling for other variables related to economic deprivation,[27] and
negative relationships more often than positive ones for robbery, and
positive but nonsignificant effects for rape and assault.[28] Commenting
on Chiricos's conclusion, Land, Cantor, and Russell suggest that all the
evidence, taken together, support the inference of a weak negative relationship between crime and unemployment from 1960 to 1980.[29] That
is, in their view, crime goes down when unemployment goes up, but
not very much. However, they agreed with Chiricos that positive relationships between crime and unemployment (crime goes up when un-

21. Richard B. Freeman, "Crime and Unemployment," ch. 6 in James Q. Wilson, ed., *Crime and Public Policy*, ICS Press, San Francisco, 198

22. Long and Witte, op. cit.; and R. W. Gillespie, "Economic Factors in Crime and Delinquency: A Critical Review of the Empirical Evidence," pp. 601–26 in House of Representatives, *Unemployment and Crime: Hearings Before the Subcommittee on Crime of the Committee on the Judiciary*, U.S. Government Printing Office, Washington, D.C., 1978. See also Thomas Orsagh, "Unemployment and Crime," *Journal of Criminal Law and Criminology* 71(2): 181–83 (summer 1980).

23. Theodore G. Chiricos, "Rates of Crime and Unemployment: An Analysis of Aggregate Research Evidence," *Social Problems* 34(2): 187–211 (April 1987).

24. Ibid., p. 203.

25. Ibid., p. 195.

26. See Kenneth C. Land, Patricia L. McCall, and Lawrence E. Cohen, "Structural Covariates of Homicide Rates: Are There Any Invariances Across Time and Space," *American Journal of Sociology* 95: 922–63 (1990).

27. Ibid.

28. Patricia L. McCall, Kenneth C. Land, and Lawrence E. Cohen, "Violent Criminal Behavior: Is There a General and Continuing Influence of the South?" *Social Science Research* 21(3): 286–310 (1992).

29. Kenneth C. Land, David Cantor, and Stephen T. Russell, "Unemployment and Crime Rate Fluctuations in the Post-World War II United States," ch. 3 in John Hagan and Ruth D. Peterson, eds., *Crime and Inequality*, Stanford University Press, Stanford, Calif., 1995, fn. 2 (p. 309).

employment goes up) are more likely to be found with smaller units of analysis and for property crimes.[30]

PROBLEMS INTERPRETING RESEARCH ON
CRIME AND ECONOMIC CONDITIONS

There are six major problems with interpreting this research, leading to all the inconsistent and contradictory conclusions reviewed above. The first problem is that *poverty is always in part a subjective condition*, relative to what others have, rather than the simple presence or absence of a certain amount of property or other measure of wealth. What one person considers poverty another may view as a level of satisfactory comfort, if not of abundance. Because of the lack of any clear definition of poverty, it has been measured in at least twenty different ways in different studies.[31] These different ways of measuring poverty can lead to the inconsistent and contradictory results reviewed above. Unemployment, too, is an unclear concept. Official unemployment rates only count people who are "able and available" for work. This often is defined in terms of having actually applied for more than one job in the previous week. People who do not actively seek work therefore are not counted as unemployed in official unemployment statistics.[32] In addition, many people are "underemployed" in low wage, dead-end jobs with terrible working conditions. Regardless of how they feel about those jobs, these people are counted as employed.[33] Thus, despite the fact that poverty and unemployment are genuine kinds of human experience, they nevertheless do not lend themselves readily to the accurate and consistent gathering of information.

The second problem is that *there are two contradictory theoretical assumptions* about the relationship between economic conditions and crime. The first assumption is that the relationship is inverse or negative; that is, when economic conditions are good, the amount of crime should be low, while when economic conditions are bad, crime should be high. That assumption is found throughout history and is still fairly commonly believed by the public.

30. Ibid., pp. 56–57.

31. Sampson and Lauritsen, op. cit., p. 5.

32. Elliott Curry, *Confronting Crime*, Pantheon, New York, 1985, ch. 4, argues that "labor market participation" is more likely to be related to crime than "unemployment." "Labor market participation" measures the number of people who are in the labor market, which includes those who are employed and those who are unemployed but "able and available" to work. This contrasts with those who have dropped out of the labor market altogether. These are the people who are not counted in unemployment statistics, and they are more likely to be involved in crime than "unemployed" people who are actively seeking work.

33. For some of the problems of counting unemployed persons, see Gwynn Nettler, *Explaining Crime*, 3rd ed., McGraw-Hill, New York, 1984, pp. 127–29.

But as described above, many studies found the opposite of that assumption. As a result, a second theoretical assumption has arisen about the relation between crime and economic conditions—that the relationship is direct or positive. This second assumption looks at criminality as an extension of normal economic activity (a criminal fringe, as it were), and therefore assumes that it increases and decreases in the same manner as other economic activity. If the second assumption is correct, the amount of crime should increase and be at its highest point when economic conditions are good, and it should decrease when economic conditions are bad.

In 1931, Morris Ploscowe used the second assumption in an attempt to explain the generally accepted belief that crime had increased throughout much of the Western world during the previous 150 years, despite an obvious increase in the economic well-being of nearly everyone.[34] Ploscowe argued that the unparalleled economic and social progress had given ordinary workers a much better economic position than they had ever enjoyed in the past, but it also brought new pressures and demands that often resulted in criminality. Ploscowe concluded: "Where increased incentives and increased occasions for illegitimate activities result from an increased amount of legitimate activity, there is apt to be an increase in crime."[35]

But Ploscowe's assumption that crime has been rising for 150 years was later contradicted in a study by Gurr and his colleagues, which found that the crime rates of London, Stockholm, and Sydney had actually decreased from the 1840s to the 1930s (Ploscowe wrote his report in 1931) and at that time were only about one-eighth of their earlier levels.[36] Gurr also found that from the 1930s to the 1970s crime had increased by approximately the same amount as the previous decrease. He speculated that some of the recent increases in crime rates may be due to more complete police reporting of crimes, but argued that, in general, these statistics reflected basic trends in the incidence of criminal behavior.

---

34. Morris Ploscowe, "Some Causative Factors in Criminality," *Report on the Causes of Crime*, vol. 1, part 1, no. 13, Report of National Commission on Law Observance and Law Enforcement, Washington, D.C., June 26, 1931, pp. 115–16.

35. Ibid., p. 114.

36. Ted Robert Gurr, *Rogues, Rebels, and Reformers*, Sage, Beverly Hills, Calif., 1976. This study also considers crime rates of Calcutta, a non-Western city that had a different pattern of crime rates. For the complete study, see Ted Robert Gurr, Peter N. Grabosky, and Richard C. Hula, *The Politics of Crime and Conflict: A Comparative History of Four Cities*, Sage, Beverly Hills, Calif., 1977. A shorter version is found in Gurr's article "Contemporary Crime in Historical Perspective: A Comparative Study of London, Stockholm, and Sydney," *Annals of the American Academy of Political and Social Science* 434: 114–36 (Nov. 1977).

Gurr considered the relationship between crime and economic conditions, and found support for both assumptions[37]:

The evidence of the city studies is that poverty *and* wealth are correlated with the incidence of common crime, not only theft but crimes against the person as well. In nineteenth century London, Stockholm, and New South Wales both theft and assault increased during periods of economic slump and declined when economic conditions improved again. Economic distress had very little effect on crime rates in either direction in the twentieth century, but as total productivity (wealth) increased, so did common crime. Evidently two separate causal processes were at work at different times.

Gurr's notion that separate causal processes may be at work at different times raises the possibility that both of these interpretations may be correct. This gives rise to the third problem, which lies in *specifying the amount of time* before economic changes are said to have an effect on criminality. Should one assume that changes in crime rates will occur at the same time as changes in economic conditions, or should one assume that there will be some period of delay, or "lag," before the crime rates are affected? Some studies find very different relationships between economic conditions and criminality when different time lags are considered.[38] The same study can then be cited as support for both contradictory theoretical assumptions simply by selecting the data at different time lags.

Cantor and Land argue that these two theoretical assumptions are correct but that they operate at different times.[39] On the one hand, they agree with the general and widely held view that unemployment increases the motivation to commit crime. Thus, higher unemployment rates should be associated with higher crime rates. But this "motivation" effect, they argue, should be "lagged" by some period of time. People only experience the full effects of unemployment after some period of time because of their own savings, support from their families and friends, and government programs such as unemployment compensation.

---

37. Gurr, *Rogues, Rebels, and Reformers*, p. 179.

38. See, for example, Dorothy Swaine Thomas, *Social Aspects of the Business Cycle*, Routledge & Kegan Paul, London, 1925, p. 143. This point is argued more extensively and with supporting data in earlier editions of the present text. See George B. Vold, *Theoretical Criminology*, Oxford University Press, New York, 1958, pp. 177–81; see also the 2nd ed., prepared by Thomas J. Bernard, 1979, pp. 176–78.

39. David Cantor and Kenneth C. Land, "Unemployment and Crime Rates in the post-World War II United States: A Theoretical and Empirical Analysis," *American Sociological Review* 50: 317–23 (1985).

On the other hand, they agree with Ploscowe's argument that economic activity is associated with increased opportunities to commit crime. When unemployment rates are higher, overall economic activity tends to be lower and there should be lower crime rates because there are fewer opportunities to commit it. But, they argue, this "opportunity" effect should occur immediately. As economic activities decline, the opportunities to commit crime decline simultaneously with them. Thus, there should be no "lag" in the effect of decreased opportunities on crime rates.

Using national data on unemployment rates and index crimes in the United States from 1946–1982,[40] these researchers found the predicted positive-negative effect for the property-related crimes of robbery, burglary, and larceny-theft. That is, in each case, they found both an immediate "opportunity" effect and a lagged "motivation" effect. Thus, when unemployment went up, robbery, burglary, and larceny-theft decreased immediately but then increased the next year. The overall impact of these two contradictory trends was negative—i.e., when unemployment increased, these crimes declined overall but not by much. Homicide and auto theft showed only the immediate negative "opportunity" effect—that is, they declined when unemployment went up but did not increase the next year. Finally, rape and assault did not seem to be associated with unemployment at all.

The fourth problem with interpreting this research relates to Chiricos's conclusion that the positive relation between crime and unemployment was more likely to be found in smaller units, such as neighborhoods and communities, rather than in larger units such as metropolitan areas and nations. The problem is *determining the size of the unit* that economic factors affect. Thus, economic conditions in a neighborhood might strongly affect crime in that neighborhood, but economic conditions in a nation might have little impact on national crime rates.

The conclusion that unemployment is associated with crime at the community level is consistent with research on the experience of people who live in areas with high unemployment. Individuals in those areas may mix crime and employment in a variety of ways, and participation in illegal work may depend considerably on the nature of the legal

---

40. Cantor and Land, op. cit. This analysis was replicated and extended, using data to 1990, in Land, Cantor, and Russell, op. cit. See also the interchange between Chris Hale and Dima Sabbagh ("Unemployment and Crime") and Cantor and Land ("Exploring Possible Temporal Relationships of Unemployment and Crime: A Comment on Hale and Sabbagh") in *Journal of Research in Crime and Delinquency* 28(4): 400–425 (1991).

work market.[41] Especially since the 1980s, the legitimate work traditionally available to "unskilled" young males in inner-city areas has declined significantly, while the illegal work available to them, particularly those associated with illegal drug markets, has expanded rapidly. The illegal work pays better and provides better working conditions than legal work, so these youths have an incentive to become involved in crime. Early involvement in crime and incarceration as an adolescent then further limits their access to legal jobs as an adult. In contrast, youths who have early successful legitimate work experiences tend to have limited access to illegal work later in life.

Fagan argued that these experiences shape the cultural and social context of inner-city adolescents[42]:

With limited access to legal work, and in segregated neighborhoods with high concentrations of joblessness, alienated views of legal work and diminished expectations for conventional success spread through social contagion and become normative. Tastes and preferences are driven by definitions of status dominated by material consumption. Violence substitutes for social control as a means to resolve disputes and attain status, increasing the likelihood either of mortality or incarceration. Legal work at low pay is defined poorly and carries a negative social stigma. With intergenerational job networks disrupted, the ability of young people to access increasingly complex labor markets with limited human capital or personal contacts foretells poor work outcomes.

The fifth problem with interpreting research on economic conditions and crime is illustrated by this description. High crime communities usually have a whole host of factors that might cause crime—poverty, unemployment, high rates of divorce and single-parent households, high population density, dilapidated housing, poor schools and other social services, frequent residential mobility and population turnover, and concentrations of racial and ethnic minorities. Any or all of these factors might cause crime, but all of them tend to be found in the same places at the same times. The problem, then, is *determining which factors actually cause crime* and which ones just happen to be there but have no

41. Jeffrey Fagan, "Legal and Illegal Work: Crime, Work and Unemployment," in Burton Weisbrod and James Worthy, eds., *Dealing with Urban Crisis: Linking Research to Action*, Northwestern University Press, Evanston, Ill., 1996. For relatively similar conclusions, see Richard B. Freeman, "The Labor Market," ch. 8 in James Q. Wilson and Joan Petersilia, eds., *Crime*, ICS Press, San Francisco, 1995.

42. Fagan, op. cit., pp. 37–38. See also John Hagan, "The Social Embeddedness of Crime and Unemployment," *Criminology* 31(4): 465–91 (1993). Hagan argues that there are different directions of causality between crime and unemployment at different levels of analysis. Macro-level theory and research tends to view unemployment as a cause of crime, but micro-level theory and research tends to view crime as a cause of unemployment. What is missing in this literature is "an understanding of the proximate causes of joblessness in the lives of individuals."

actual effect. This problem is called "multicollinearity"—i.e., a number of possible causal factors are all highly intercorrelated with each other.[43] In this situation, relatively small changes in statistical techniques can result in different conclusions about which factors have a causal impact and which do not. Thus, it can give rise to the type of inconsistent and contradictory results that are reviewed above.

To address this problem, Land and his colleagues incorporated all the variables used in twenty-one studies of homicide at city, metropolitan area, and state levels into one "baseline regression model."[44] They then "clustered" these variables to see what would "hang together" over time and place. The most important clustering of variables was around what they called "resource deprivation/affluence," which included measures of poverty and income inequality, as well as percent black and percent of children not living with both parents. While these factors are conceptually separate, the statistical techniques could not separate them from each other in the effects they had on homicide. This cluster of variables had a significant positive effect on city, metropolitan area, and state levels of homicide in 1960, 1970, and 1980, with some tendency for this effect to increase over time.

The sixth problem with interpreting research on crime and economic conditions has to do with adequately *distinguishing between concepts of poverty and economic inequality.*[45] The "resource deprivation/ affluence" cluster described above includes both poverty and economic inequality. These are quite different concepts. Poverty refers to the lack of some fixed level of material goods necessary for survival and minimum well-being. In contrast, economic inequality refers to a comparison between the material level of those who have the least in a society and the material level of other groups in that society. Countries in which everyone has an adequate material level have little or no poverty, but they may still have a great deal of economic inequality if there is a very large gap between those who have the least and those who have the most. On the other hand, countries in which everyone is poor have a great deal of poverty but little or no economic inequality.

43. Robert J. Sampson and Janet L. Lauritsen, "Violent Victimization and Offending," in Albert J. Reiss, Jr., and Jeffrey A. Roth, eds., *Understanding and Preventing Violence—Social Influences,* vol. 3, National Academy Press, Washington, D.C., 1994, p. 66; Land et al., 1990.

44. Land, McCall, and Cohen, op. cit., 1990.

45. Many studies of inequality use the Gini coefficient, which is a statistic that measures the extent to which incomes are dispersed in a society relative to the average income in that society. The coefficient ranges from "0," where everyone has equal shares of the total income, to a "1," where one person has all the income and everyone else has none. See S. Yitzhaki, "Relative Deprivation and the Gini Coefficient," *Quarterly Journal of Economics* 93: 321–24 (May 1974); and M. Bronfenbrenner, *Distribution Theory,* Aldine-Atherton, New York, 1971.

Hsieh and Pugh analyzed thirty-four studies that had been published between 1980 and 1991 that focused on the relationship between poverty, economic inequality, and violent crime.[46] The sampling units ranged from neighborhoods to nations, and most focused either on homicide or on violent crime in general, while a few focused on rape, robbery, or assault. These thirty-four studies produced seventy-six correlation coefficients relating violent crime to either poverty and economic inequality. Seventy-four of those coefficients were positive, and fifty-six of the seventy-four were at least moderately strong ($>.25$). These are very consistent results suggesting that both poverty and economic inequality are associated with higher levels of violent crime. Hsieh and Pugh concluded that these results were somewhat stronger for homicide and assault than they were for robbery and rape.

More recently, attention has turned to the specific effects of racial inequality in the United States. The issue is whether the specific inequality between blacks and whites, rather than general inequality in the entire society, has a specific effect on black crime rates. For example, Messner and Golden examined the effect of inequality between whites and blacks in the 154 largest U.S. cities.[47] First, they performed analyses similar to the one done by Land and his colleagues, as described above, and found similar results about the "resource deprivation/affluence" cluster. But then they went on to construct a measure of racial inequality, which included the gap between whites and blacks in income, education, and unemployment levels, and the extent of residential segregation. They found that increased levels of inequality between the races were associated with higher black, white, and total homicide rates, separate from the effects of the "resource deprivation/affluence" cluster. They concluded that "Racial inequality evidently affects the social order in some generalized way that increases criminogenic pressures on the entire population." Other results on this subject, however, have been very mixed.[48]

46. Ching-Chi Hsieh and M. D. Pugh, "Poverty, Income Inequality, and Violent Crime: A Meta-Analysis of Recent Aggregate Data Studies," *Criminal Justice Review* 18(2): 182–202 (1983).

47. Steven F. Messner and Reid M. Golden, "Racial Inequality and Racially Disaggregated Homicide Rates: An Assessment of Alternative Theoretical Explanations," *Criminology* 30(3): 421–45 (1992).

48. E.g., Edward S. Shihadeh and Darrell J. Steffensmeier, "Economic Inequality, Family Disruption, and Urban Black Violence," *Social Forces* 73(22): 729–51 (1994); Gary LaFree, Kriss A. Drass, and Patrick O'Day, "Race and Crime in Postwar America: Determinants of African-American and White Rates, 1957–1988," *Criminology* 30(2): 157–85 (1992); Miles D. Harer and Darrell J. Steffensmeier, "The Different Effects of Economic Inequality on Black and White Rates of Violence," *Social Forces* 70: 1035–54 (1992).

IMPLICATIONS AND CONCLUSIONS

Both poverty and inequality are clearly associated with crime, especially violent crime, but whether they *cause* crime is another matter. At present, a stronger case can be made that the level of general economic inequality in a society—i.e., the gap between its wealthiest and its poorest citizens—has a causal impact on the level of violent crime in that society.

If that is the case, then criminologists may have been looking at the wrong end of the social scale in their attempts to explain the relationship between crime and economic conditions. Poor people may have higher crime rates when there are many wealthy people around them, but they may have lower crime rates when other people around them are also poor. If this is true, then the key factor needed to explain the amount of crime in a particular location would be the number of wealthy people, not the number of poor people.[49] This would be consistent with the general trend for crime to expand along with the expansion of wealth in society.

In addition, the case for poverty as a cause of crime is much weaker than the case for economic inequality. Since the 1970s, there has been a general expansion of wealth in American society, consistent with an overall expansion of the economy. But there has also been an increasing concentration of extreme poverty in inner-city areas, leading to the development in the United States of a relatively isolated and impoverished segment of the population sometimes called "the underclass." It is within this group that the relationship between crime and economic conditions seems to have the most direct effect.[50]

Certainly, at the community level, there is a clear association between poverty and crime. For example, after reviewing numerous studies about local areas, Sampson and Lauritsen concluded that "Almost without exception, studies of violence find a positive and usually large correlation between some measure of area poverty and violence—especially homicide."[51] But in the end, they conclude that poverty itself does not directly cause crime because crime rates do not consistently increase and decrease as the number of poor people increases and decreases. Consistent with this conclusion, Sampson and Lauritsen suggest that, de-

49. E.g., Sheldon Danzinger and David Wheeler, "The Economics of Crime: Punishment or Income Redistribution," *Review of Sociology and Economics* 33: 113–31 (1975); Paul Eberts and Kent P. Schwirian, "Metropolitan Crime Rates and Relative Deprivation, *Criminologica* 5: 43–52 (Feb. 1968).

50. In general, see John Hagan and Ruth D. Peterson, "Criminal Inequality in America," and Robert J. Sampson and William Julius Wilson, "Toward a Theory of Race, Crime, and Urban Inequality," chs. 1 and 2 in Hagan and Peterson, eds., *Inequality and Crime*, Stanford University Press, Stanford, Calif., 1994. See also John Hagan, *Crime and Disrepute*, Pine Forge Press, Thousand Oaks, Calif., 1994.

51. Sampson and Lauritsen, op. cit., p. 63.

spite the overwhelming association between violence and poverty, the data suggest that the direct effect of poverty on crime is weak and probably is conditional on other community factors. They particularly point to factors involved in the processes of rapid community change. For a further discussion of these factors, we turn to one of the most important early sociological theories, that by Emile Durkheim.

CHAPTER 9

Durkheim, Anomie, and Modernization

The preceding chapter concluded that economic inequality might be associated with crime. In contrast Emile Durkheim viewed inequality as a natural and inevitable human condition that is not associated with social maladies such as crime unless there is also a breakdown of social norms or rules. Durkheim called such a breakdown *anomie* and argued that it had occurred in his own society as a result of the rapid social changes accompanying the modernization process. Like Lombroso's theories, written approximately twenty years earlier, Durkheim's theories were in part a reaction to the classical assumptions that humans were free and rational in a contractual society. But where Lombroso had focused on the determinants of human behavior within the individual, Durkheim focused on society and its organization and development.

Durkheim's theories are complex, but his influence on criminology has been great. The present chapter examines his theories and discusses them in the context of later research on the relationship between crime and modernization. But Durkheim's ideas also appear in several later chapters. In the 1920s a group of Chicago sociologists used his theories, among others, as the basis for an extensive research project linking juvenile delinquency to rapid social changes in urban areas. These studies are presented in Chapter 10. In 1938 Robert K. Merton revised Durkheim's conception of anomie and applied it directly to American society. This and other similar theories are now known as *strain* theories of crime and delinquency and are presented in Chapter 11. In 1969 Travis Hirschi returned to Durkheim's original conception of anomie and used it as the basis for his *control* theory of delinquency. Control theories are discussed in Chapter 13. Finally, Durkheim's view of "crime as normal" is the basis for social reaction views of the law-enactment process, which are discussed in Chapter 14.

EMILE DURKHEIM

Emile Durkheim (1858–1917) has been called "one of the best known and one of the least understood major social thinkers."[1] Presenting his thought is no easy task, since "the controversies which surround this thought bear upon essential points, not details."[2] For this reason it is best to approach his work by first considering the political and intellectual climate in which it evolved.

The nineteenth century in France was an age of great turmoil generated by the wake of the French Revolution of 1789 and by the rapid industrialization of French society. Speaking of these two "revolutions," Nisbet has pointed out that "In terms of immediacy and massiveness of impact on human thought and values, it is impossible to find revolutions of comparable magnitude anywhere in human history."[3] The writings of the day were filled with a "burning sense of society's sudden, convulsive turn from a path it had followed for millennia" and a "profound intuition of the disappearance of historic values—and with them, age-old securities, as well as age-old tyrannies and inequalities—and the coming of new powers, new insecurities, and new tyrannies that would be worse than anything previously known unless drastic measures were taken. . . ."[4]

Sociology had been developed by Auguste Comte in the first half of the century largely in response to the effects of these two revolutions; it was part of a more general effort to construct a rational society out of the ruins of the traditional one.[5] Sociologists saw themselves as providing a rational, scientific analysis of the monumental social changes that were occurring, in order to "mastermind the political course of 'social regeneration.' "[6] This regeneration would consist primarily of the reestablishment of social solidarity, which appeared to have substantially disintegrated in French society.

Emile Durkheim was born in a small French town on the German border, one year after the death of Comte. After completing his studies

1. Dominick LaCapra, *Emile Durkheim, Sociologist and Philosopher*, Cornell University Press, Ithaca, N.Y., 1972, p. 5.

2. Ibid., p. 5.

3. Robert A. Nisbet, *Emile Durkheim*, Prentice Hall, Englewood Cliffs, N.J., 1965, p. 20.

4. Ibid., p. 20.

5. LaCapra, op. cit., p. 41.

6. Julius Gould, "Auguste Comte," in T. Raison, ed., *The Founding Fathers of Social Science*, Penguin, Harmondsworth, U.K., 1969, p. 40.

in Paris he spent several years teaching philosophy at various secondary schools in the French provinces near Paris. He then spent a year in Germany, where he studied social science and its relation to ethics under the famed experimental psychologist Wilhelm Wundt. Durkheim's publication of two articles as a result of these studies led to the creation of a special position for him at the University of Bordeaux, where in 1887 he taught the first French university course in sociology. In 1892 Durkheim received the first doctor's degree in sociology awarded by the University of Paris, and ten years later he returned to a position at the university, where he dominated sociology until his death in 1917.

Durkheim's analysis of the processes of social change involved in industrialization is presented in his first major work, *De la division du travail social (The Division of Labor in Society)*,[7] written as his doctoral thesis and published in 1893. In it he describes these processes as part of the development from the more primitive "mechanical" form of society into the more advanced "organic" form. In the mechanical form each social group in society is relatively isolated from all other social groups, and is basically self-sufficient.[8] Within these social groups individuals live largely under identical circumstances, do identical work, and hold identical values. There is little division of labor, with only a few persons in the clan or village having specialized functions. Thus there is little need for individual talents, and the solidarity of the society is based on the uniformity of its members.

Contrasted with this is the organic society, in which the different segments of society depend on each other in a highly organized division of labor. Social solidarity is no longer based on the uniformity of the individuals, but on the diversity of the functions of the parts of the society. Durkheim saw all societies as being in some stage of progression between the mechanical and the organic structures, with no society being totally one or the other. Even the most primitive societies could be seen to have some forms of division of labor, and even the most advanced societies would require some degree of uniformity of its members.[9]

Law plays an essential role in maintaining the social solidarity of each of these two types of societies, but in very different ways. In the mechanical society law functions to enforce the uniformity of the members of the social group, and thus is oriented toward repressing any deviation from the norms of the time. In the organic society, on the other

7. Emile Durkheim, *The Division of Labor in Society*, translated by George Simpson, The Free Press, New York, 1965.

8. Raymond Aron, *Main Currents in Sociological Thought*, vol. II, translated by Richard Howard and Helen Weaver, Basic Books, New York, 1967, p. 12.

9. Ibid., pp. 12–13.

hand, law functions to regulate the interactions of the various parts of society and provides restitution in cases of wrongful transactions. Because law plays such different roles in the two types of societies, crime appears in very different forms. Durkheim argued that to the extent a society remains mechanical, crime is "normal" in the sense that a society without crime would be pathologically overcontrolled. As the society develops toward the organic form, it is possible for a pathological state, which he called anomie, to occur, and such a state would produce a variety of social maladies, including crime. Durkheim developed his concept of "crime as normal" in his second major work, *The Rules of the Sociological Method*,[10] published in 1895, only two years after *The Division of Labor;* he went on to develop anomie in his most famous work, *Suicide*,[11] published in 1897. These concepts will be explored in the following sections.

CRIME AS NORMAL IN MECHANICAL SOCIETIES

Mechanical societies are characterized by the uniformity of the lives, work, and beliefs of their members. All the uniformity that exists in a society, that is, the "totality of social likenesses," Durkheim called the *collective conscience*.[12] Since all societies demand at least some degree of uniformity from their members (in that none are totally organic), the collective conscience may be found in every culture. In every society, however, there will always be a degree of diversity in that there will be many individual differences among its members. As Durkheim said, "There cannot be a society in which the individuals do not differ more or less from the collective type."[13]

To the extent that a particular society is mechanical, its solidarity will come from the pressure for uniformity exerted against this diversity. Such pressure is exerted in varying degrees and in varying forms. In its strongest form it will consist of criminal sanctions. In weaker forms, however, the pressure may consist of designating certain behaviors or beliefs as morally reprehensible or merely in bad taste.

If I do not submit to the conventions of society, if in my dress I do not conform to the customs observed in my country and my class, the ridicule I pro-

10. Emile Durkheim, *The Rules of the Sociological Method*, translated by Sarah A. Solovay and John H. Mueller, edited by Georege E. G. Catlin, The Free Press, New York, 1965.

11. Durkheim, *Suicide*, translated by John A. Spaulding and George Simpson, edited by George Simpson, The Free Press, New York, 1951.

12. Durkheim, *Division of Labor*, p. 80, n. 10. In French, the term *conscience* has overtones of both "conscience" and "consciousness," but the term is usually translated as "collective conscience."

13. Durkheim, *Rules*, p. 70.

voke, the social isolation in which I am kept, produce, although in attenuated form, the same effects as a punishment in the strict sense of the word. The constraint is nonetheless efficacious for being indirect.[14]

Durkheim argued that "society cannot be formed without our being required to make perpetual and costly sacrifices."[15] These sacrifices, embodied in the demands of the collective conscience, are the price of membership in society, and fulfilling the demands gives the individual members a sense of collective identity, which is an important source of social solidarity. But, more important, these demands are constructed so that it is inevitable that a certain number of people will not fulfill them. The number must be large enough to constitute an identifiable group, but not so large as to include a substantial portion of the society. This enables the large mass of the people, all of whom fulfill the demands of the collective conscience, to feel a sense of moral superiority, identifying themselves as good and righteous, and opposing themselves to the morally inferior transgressors who fail to fulfill these demands. It is this sense of superiority, of goodness and righteousness, which Durkheim saw as the primary source of the social solidarity. Thus criminals play an important role in the maintenance of the social solidarity, since they are among the group of those identified by society as inferior, which allows the rest of society to feel superior.

The punishment of criminals also plays a role in the maintenance of the social solidarity. When the dictates of the collective conscience are violated, society responds with repressive sanctions not so much for retribution or deterrence, but because without them those who are making the "perpetual and costly sacrifices" would become severely demoralized.[16] For example, when a person who has committed a serious crime is released with only a slap on the wrist, the average, law-abiding citizen may become terribly upset. He feels that he is playing the game by the rules, and so everyone else should too. The punishment of the criminal is necessary to maintain the allegiance of the average citizen to the social structure. Without it the average citizen may lose his overall commitment to the society and his willingness to make the sacrifices necessary for it. But beyond this, the punishment of criminals also acts as a visible, societal expression of the inferiority and blameworthiness of the criminal group. This reinforces the sense of superiority and right-

---

14. Ibid., pp. 2–3.

15. Kurt Wolff, ed., *Emile Durkheim et al., Writings on Sociology and Philosophy*, Harper & Row, New York, 1960, p. 338.

16. Nisbet, op. cit., p. 225. See also Jackson Toby, "Is Punishment Necessary?" *Journal of Criminal Law, Criminology and Police Science* 55: 332–37 (1964).

eousness found in the mass of the people, and thus strengthens the solidarity of the society.

Crime itself is normal in society because there is no clearly marked dividing line between behaviors considered criminal and those considered morally reprehensible or merely in bad taste. If there is a decrease in behaviors designated as criminal, then there may be a tendency to move behaviors previously designated as morally reprehensible into the criminal category. For example, not every type of unfair transfer of property is considered stealing. But if there is a decrease in the traditional forms of burglary and robbery, there then may be an associated increase in the tendency to define various forms of white-collar deception as crime. These behaviors may always have been considered morally reprehensible, and in that sense they violated the collective conscience. They were not, however, considered crimes. Society moves them into the crime category because criminal sanctions are the strongest tool available to maintain social solidarity.

Since the institution of punishment serves an essential function, it will be necessary in any society.

Imagine a society of saints, a perfect cloister of exemplary individuals. Crimes, properly so called, will there be unknown; but faults which appear venial to the layman will create there the same scandal that the ordinary offense does in ordinary consciousnesses. If, then, this society has the power to judge and punish, it will define these acts as criminal and will treat them as such. For the same reason, the perfect and upright man judges his smallest failings with a severity that the majority reserve for acts more truly in the nature of an offense.[17]

Thus a society without crime is impossible. If all the behaviors that are presently defined as criminal no longer occurred, new behaviors would be placed in the crime category.[18] Crime, then, is inevitable because there is an inevitable diversity of behavior in society. The solidarity of the society is generated by exerting pressure for conformity against this diversity, and some of this pressure will inevitably take the form of criminal sanctions.[19]

Let us make no mistake. To classify crime among the phenomena of normal sociology is not merely to say that it is an inevitable, although regrettable, phenomenon, due to the incorrigible wickedness of men; it is to affirm that it is a factor in public health, an integral part of all societies.

17. Durkheim, *Rules*, pp. 68–69.
18. Ibid., p. 67.
19. Ibid., p. 67.

The abnormal or pathological state of society would be one in which there was no crime. A society that had no crime would be one in which the constraints of the collective conscience were so rigid that no one could oppose them. In this type of situation crime would be eliminated, but so would the possibility of progressive social change. Social change is usually introduced by opposing the constraints of the collective conscience, and those who do this are frequently declared to be criminals. Thus Socrates and Jesus were declared criminals, as were Mahatma Gandhi and George Washington. The leaders of the union movement in the 1920s and 1930s were criminalized, as were the leaders of the civil rights movement of the 1960s. If the demands of the collective conscience had been so rigidly enforced that no crime could exist, then these movements would have been impossible also.

Thus crime is the price society pays for the possibility of progress. As Durkheim wrote,[20]

To make progress, individual originality must be able to express itself. In order that the originality of the idealist whose dreams transcend his century may find expression, it is necessary that the originality of the criminal, who is below the level of his time, shall also be possible. One does not occur without the other.

In a similar way individual growth cannot occur in a child unless it is possible for that child to misbehave. The child is punished for misbehavior, and no one wants the child to misbehave. But a child who never did anything wrong would be pathologically overcontrolled. Eliminating the misbehavior would also eliminate the possibility of independent growth. In this sense the child's misbehavior is the price that must be paid for the possibility of personal development. Durkheim concluded[21]:

From this point of view, the fundamental facts of criminality present themselves to us in an entirely new light. Contrary to current ideas, the criminal no longer seems a totally unsociable being, a sort of parasitic element, a strange and unassimilable body, introduced into the midst of society. On the contrary, he plays a definite role in social life. Crime, for its part, must no longer be conceived as an evil that cannot be too much suppressed. There is no occasion for self-congratulation when the crime rate drops noticeably below the average level, for we may be certain that this apparent progress is associated with some social disorder.

---

20. Ibid., p. 71.
21. Ibid., p. 72.

ANOMIE AS A PATHOLOGICAL STATE IN ORGANIC SOCIETIES

To the extent that a society is mechanical, it derives its solidarity from pressure for conformity against the diversity of its members. The criminalizing of some behaviors is a normal and necessary part of this pressure. But to the extent that a society is organic, the function of law is to regulate the interactions of the various parts of the whole. If this regulation is inadequate, there can result a variety of social maladies, including crime. Durkheim called the state of inadequate regulation anomie.

Durkheim first introduced this concept in *The Division of Labor in Society*, where he argued that the industrialization of French society, with its resulting division of labor, had destroyed the traditional solidarity based on uniformity. But this industrialization had been so rapid that the society had not yet been able to evolve sufficient mechanisms to regulate its transactions. Periodic cycles of overproduction followed by economic slowdown indicated that the relations between producers and consumers were ineffectively regulated. Strikes and labor violence indicated that the relations between workers and employers were unresolved. The alienation of the individual worker and the sense that the division of labor was turning people into mere "cogs in the wheel" indicated that the relation of the individual to work was inadequately defined.[22]

Durkheim expanded and generalized his notion of anomie four years later with the publication of his most famous work, *Le Suicide*. In it he statistically analyzed data that showed that the suicide rate tends to increase sharply both in periods of economic decline and economic growth. Whereas suicide in a time of economic decline might be easily understood, the key question is why suicide would increase in a time of prosperity. Durkheim proposed that society functions to regulate not only the economic interactions of its various components, but also how the individual perceives his own needs. Durkheim's theory of anomie has been used as the basis for later explanations of crime and a variety of other deviant behaviors.[23] Because of its importance in criminology and sociology, the theory is presented here at some length, and in Durkheim's own words.[24]

a. No living being can be happy or even exist unless his needs are sufficiently proportioned to his means. In other words, if his needs require more than can

22. Durkheim, *Division of Labor*, pp. 370–73.

23. Marshall B. Clinard, ed., *Anomie and Deviant Behavior*, The Free Press, New York, 1964.

24. Reprinted with permission of The Free Press, a Division of Simon & Schuster, from *Suicide* by Emile Durkheim, translated by John A. Spaulding and George Simpson © 1951, copyright renewed by The Free Press.

be granted, or even merely something of a different sort, they will be under continual friction and can only function painfully.

b. In the animal, at least in a normal condition, this equilibrium is established with automatic spontaneity because the animal depends on purely material conditions.

c. This is not the case with man, because most of his needs are not dependent on his body. . . . A more awakened reflection suggests better conditions, seemingly desirable ends craving fulfillment. . . . Nothing appears in man's organic nor in his psychological constitution which sets a limit to such tendencies. . . . They are unlimited so far as they depend on the individual alone. . . . Thus, the more one has, the more one wants, since satisfactions received only stimulate instead of filling needs.

d. A regulative force must play the same role for moral needs which the organism plays for physical needs. . . . [S]ociety alone can play this moderating role; for it is the only moral power superior to the individual, the authority of which he accepts. . . . It alone can estimate the reward to be prospectively offered to every class of human functionary, in the name of the common interest.

e. As a matter of fact, at every moment of history there is a dim perception, in the moral consciousness of societies, of the respective value of different social services, the relative reward due each, and the consequent degree of comfort appropriate on the average to workers in each occupation. . . . Under this pressure, each in his sphere vaguely realizes the extreme limit set to his ambitions and aspires to nothing beyond. . . . Thus, an end and goal are set to the passions. . . .

f. But when society is disturbed by some painful crisis or by beneficent but abrupt transitions, it is momentarily incapable of exercising this influence; thence come the sudden rises in the curve of suicides which we have pointed out above.

g. In the case of economic disasters, indeed, something like a declassification occurs which suddenly casts certain individuals into a lower state than their previous one. Then they must reduce their requirements, restrain their needs, learn greater self-control. . . . So they are not adjusted to the condition forced on them, and its very prospect is intolerable. . . .

h. It is the same if the source of the crisis is an abrupt growth of power and wealth. Then, truly, as the conditions of life are changed, the standard according to which needs were regulated can no longer remain the same; for it varies with social resources. . . . The scale is upset; but a new scale cannot be immediately improvised. Time is required for the public conscience to reclassify men and things. So long as the social forces thus freed have not regained equilibrium, their respective values are unknown and so all regulation is lacking for a time. The limits are unknown between the possible and the impossible, what is just and what is unjust, legitimate claims and hopes and those which are immoderate. Consequently, there is no restraint upon aspirations. . . . Appetites, not being controlled by a public opinion, become disoriented, no longer recognize the limits proper to them. Besides, they are at the same time seized by a sort of natural erethism simply by the greater intensity of public life. With increased prosperity desires increase. At the very moment when traditional rules have lost their authority, the richer prize offered these appetites stimulates them and makes them more exigent and impatient of control. The state of de-regulation or anomy is thus further heightened by passions being less disciplined, precisely when they need more disciplining.

Durkheim went on to argue that French society, over the previous 100 years, had deliberately destroyed the traditional sources of regulation for human appetites.[25] Religion had almost completely lost its influence over both workers and employers. Traditional occupational groups, such as the guilds, had been destroyed. Government adhered to a policy of laissez-faire, or noninterference, in business activities. As a result human appetites were no longer curbed. This freedom of appetites was the driving force behind the French industrial revolution, but it also created a chronic state of anomie, with its attendant high rate of suicide.

ASSESSING DURKHEIM'S THEORY OF CRIME

Durkheim presented his theory of crime in the context of an overall theory of modernization—the progression of societies from the mechanical to the organic form. One of the problems with assessing his theory is that he predicted that different things would happen at different times. Specifically he argued that: (1) the punishment of crime would remain fairly stable in mechanical societies, independent of changes in the extent of criminal behavior; (2) as those societies made the transition to organic societies in the process of modernization, a greater variety of behaviors would be tolerated, punishments would become less violent as their purpose changed from repression to restitution, and there would be a vast expansion of "functional" law to regulate the interactions of the emerging organic society; and (3) in organic societies, the extent of criminal behavior would increase during periods of rapid social change. Each of these ideas has generated additional theories and research in more recent times.

Erikson reformulated Durkheim's theory about the stability of punishment in mechanical societies, based on a study of the Puritan colony in seventeenth-century Massachusetts.[26] This society had a relatively constant level of punishment throughout the century despite three "crime waves" attributed to Antinomians, Quakers, and witches. Erik-

25. Ibid., pp. 254–58.
26. Kai T. Erikson, *Wayward Puritans*, John Wiley, New York, 1966.

son concluded[27]: "When a community calibrates its control machinery to handle a certain volume of deviant behavior it tends to adjust its . . . legal . . . definitions of the problem in such a way that this volume is realized."

Blumstein and his colleagues attempted to demonstrate a similar process in modern societies.[28] They examined imprisonment rates in the United States from 1924 to 1974, in Canada from 1880 to 1959, and in Norway from 1880 to 1964, arguing that these rates remained stable over the time periods and that the stability was maintained by adjusting the types of behaviors that resulted in imprisonment. Later studies either failed to find a similar effect or have criticized the research methods of studies that do find an effect.[29] More recently, the explosion of incarceration in the United States associated with the "get tough" era has clearly demonstrated that punishment in the United States is no longer "stable," if it ever was. For example, before 1970, the imprisonment rate in the United States had generally remained somewhere around 100 prisoners for every 100,000 people in the population, whether crime rates were high or low. Since then, however, the imprisonment rate has been steadily rising and at midyear 1996 it was 615 prisoners for every 100,000 people in the population.

Durkheim's theory, however, does not predict that punishment levels in modern industrialized societies will remain constant, since those cannot be considered mechanical societies. The Puritan colony in Massachusetts can reasonably be considered such a society, so that Erikson's study supports Durkheim's theory while the others neither support nor challenge it. On the other hand, Erikson's interpretation has been challenged by Chambliss, who suggests that "his conclusion is hardly sup-

---

27. Ibid., p. 26.

28. Alfred Blumstein and Jacqueline Cohen, "A Theory of the Stability of Punishment," *Journal of Criminal Law and Criminology* 64: 198–207 (June 1973); Alfred Blumstein, Jacqueline Cohen, and Daniel Nagin, "The Dynamics of a Homeostatic Punishment Process," *Journal of Criminal Law and Criminology* 67: 317–34 (Sept. 1977); and Alfred Blumstein and Soumyo Moitra, "An Analysis of the Time Series of the Imprisonment Rate in the States of the United States: A Further Test of the Stability of Punishment Hypothesis," *Journal of Criminal Law and Criminology* 70: 376–90 (Sept. 1979). See also Nils Christie, "Changes in Penal Values," in Christie, ed., *Scandinavian Studies in Criminology*, vol. 2, Scandinavian University Books, Oslo, 1968, pp. 161–72. For a review of these studies, see Allen E. Liska, "Introduction," in Liska, ed., *Social Threat and Social Control*, State University of New York Press, Albany, N.Y., 1992, pp. 13–16.

29. M. Calahan, "Trends in Incarceration in the United States," *Crime and Delinquency* 25: 9–41 (1979); David F. Greenberg, "Penal Sanctions in Poland," *Social Problems* 28: 194–204 (1980); David Rauma, "Crime and Punishment Reconsidered: Some Comments on Blumstein's Stability of Punishment Hypothesis," *Journal of Criminal Law and Criminology* 72: 1772–98 (1981); Richard A. Berk, David Rauma, Sheldon L. Messinger, and T. F. Cooley, "A Test of the Stability of Punishment Hypothesis," *American Sociological Review* 46: 805–29 (1981); and Richard A. Berk, David Rauma, and Sheldon L. Messinger, "A Further Test of the Stability of Punishment Hypothesis," in John Hagan, ed., *Quantitative Criminology*, Sage, Beverly Hills, Calif., 1982, pp. 39–64.

ported by the data he presents."[30] Erikson, following Durkheim, had described the three crime waves as being generated by the need to establish the moral boundaries of the community. Chambliss pointed out that each of these crime waves occurred when the power and authority of the ruling groups were threatened. He concluded:

> Deviance was indeed created for the consequences it had. But the consequences were not "to establish moral boundaries"; rather, they aided those in power to maintain their position. . . . Erikson gives no evidence that any of these crime waves actually increased social solidarity except through the elimination of alternative centers of authority or power.

Durkheim made three arguments about crime during the process of transition from mechanical to organic societies: a greater variety of behaviors would be tolerated, punishments would become less violent as their purpose changed from repression to restitution, and there would be a vast expansion of "functional" law to regulate the interactions of the emerging organic society. Wolfgang has stated that contemporary American society illustrates Durkheim's first argument about the increasing tolerance for diversity in more advanced societies: "My major point is that we are currently experiencing in American culture, and perhaps in Western society in general, an expansion of acceptability of deviance and a corresponding contraction of what we define as crime."[31] A similar argument has been made more recently by conservative commentators who argue that Western societies are losing all their morals.

With respect to Durkheim's second argument, Spitzer found that more developed societies were characterized by severe punishments, while simple societies were characterized by lenient punishments, which is the opposite of what Durkheim predicted.[32] Spitzer's findings are consistent with several studies that have found that rural areas in Western societies before modernization were characterized by fairly high levels of violence, and also by a considerable degree of tolerance for it.[33] It was only after modernization, with the concentration of populations in anonymous cities, that societies began to punish violence consistently and severely. Durkheim may have derived his idea from the fact that

---

30. William J. Chambliss, "Functional and Conflict Theories of Crime," in Chambliss and Milton Mankoff, eds., *Whose Law? What Order?*, John Wiley, New York, 1976, pp. 11–16.

31. Marvin E. Wolfgang, "Real and Perceived Changes in Crime," in Simha F. Landau and Leslie Sebba, *Criminology in Perspective*, D. C. Heath, Lexington, Mass., 1977, pp. 27–38.

32. Steven Spitzer, "Punishment and Social Organization," *Law and Society Review* 9: 613–37 (1975).

33. See, for example, Howard Zehr, *Crime and Development of Modern Society*, Rowman & Litlefield, Totowa, N.J., 1976.

punishments in European societies were becoming much less severe at the time, due to the reforms introduced by Beccaria and other classical theorists. But the extremely harsh punishments that had been imposed prior to those reforms were not associated with simple, undeveloped societies, but rather with absolute monarchies. Those types of punishments were not found in earlier, simpler societies.[34]

Third, Durkheim predicted a great expansion in functional law as modern societies attempt to regulate all their new functions. In his case study of four cities from 1800 to the present, Gurr found "the veritable explosion of laws and administrative codes designed to regulate day-to-day interactions, in domains as dissimilar as trade, public demeanor, and traffic."[35] While some of this was generated by "the functional necessity of regulating the increased traffic and commercial activities of growing cities," as Durkheim had argued, Gurr also found that a great deal of other legislation was passed defining and proscribing new kinds of offenses against morality and against "collective behavior" such as riots and protests.[36] Gurr argued that the new offenses against morality arose primarily from the effort to apply middle-class values to all social groups, while the offenses against collective behavior arose from efforts of the elite groups to maintain their power.[37]

Finally, Durkheim argued that the source of high crime rates in organic societies lay in normlessness or anomie generated by the rapid social changes associated with modernization. Durkheim's theory of anomie led to the later ecological, strain, and control theories of crime, so that the assessment of this argument must, to a certain extent, await the presentation of those theories in Chapters 10, 11, and 13. But those theories do not directly link the breakdown of social norms to the processes of modernization, as did Durkheim's theory. Durkheim's theory of anomie is therefore assessed here in the context of his theory of modernization.

Durkheim attributed the high rates of crime and other forms of deviance in his own society to the normlessness generated by the French and Industrial revolutions. One very basic criticism of this argument is that crime in France was not rising at the time. Lodhi and Tilly conclude that between 1831 and 1931 the incidence of theft and robbery declined in France, citing a massive decline in the statistics for serious

---

34. Michel Foucault, *Discipline and Punish*, Pantheon, New York, 1977, pp. 3–69. See also Philippe Ariès, *Centuries of Childhood*, Knopf, New York, 1962, ch. 1, for a discussion of the tendency to idealize the past as harmonious and peaceful.

35. Ted Robert Gurr, *Rogues, Rebels, and Reformers*, Sage, Beverly Hills, Calif., 1976, p. 180.

36. Ibid., p. 177.

37. Ibid., pp. 93–115.

property crime during that period.[38] The statistics for violent crime remained approximately stable over the same period, with some tendency toward a decline. Durkheim had formulated his theory of anomie in the context of a study of suicide rates, not crime rates. Having done so, he simply presumed that crime was also increasing, although he nowhere presented data to support his conclusion. McDonald argues that the statistics showing decreases in crime rates were available to Durkheim, as well as to other prominent criminologists of the time who also presumed that crime rates were increasing, but that none of them took any notice[39]: "Marxists of that time were no more willing to admit that social and economic conditions were improving than Durkheimians that industrialization and urbanization did not inevitably lead to higher crime."

Recent research has led to a generally accepted conclusion that economic development is associated with increases in property crime but with decreases in violent crime.[40] For example, Neuman and Berger reviewed seventeen cross-national crime studies and concluded that urbanism and industrialization are both associated with increased property crime, but neither was associated with increases in violent crime.[41] In addition, they found no support for the argument that the increases in property crime were caused by the change from traditional to modern values. All of this is inconsistent with Durkheim's basic argument.

Neuman and Berger therefore question the continued dominance of Durkheim's theory in explaining the link between modernization and crime. They suggest that much more attention be paid to the role of economic inequality in this process, as opposed to Durkheim's emphasis on the breakdown of traditional values. They point out that the relationship between economic inequality and homicide is "the most consistent finding in the literature,"[42] and suggest that criminologists examine the large literature on the relation between inequality and eco-

38. A. Q. Lodhi and Charles Tilly, "Urbanization, Crime and Collective Violence in Nineteenth Century France," *American Journal of Sociology* 79: 297–318 (1973). See also A. V. Gatrell and T. B. Hadden, "Criminal Statistics and Their Interpretations," in E. A. Wrigley, ed., *Nineteenth-Century Society*, Cambridge University Press, Cambridge, U.K., 1972, pp. 336–96.

39. Lynn McDonald, "Theory and Evidence of Rising Crime in the Nineteenth Century," *British Journal of Sociology* 33: 404–20 (Sept. 1982), p. 417.

40. For a review, see Gary D. LaFree and Edward L. Kick, "Cross-National Effects of Development, Distributional and Demographic Variables on Crime: A Review and Analysis," *International Annals of Criminology* 24: 213–36 (1986). A single recent study found that, with proper controls for the age structure of populations and for region, both homicide and theft rates rise with modernization. See Suzanne T. Ortega et al., "Modernization, Age Structure, and Regional Context: A Cross-National Study of Crime," *Sociological Spectrum* 12: 257–77 (1992).

41. W. Lawrence Neuman and Ronald J. Berger, "Competing perspectives on Cross-National Crime: An Evaluation of Theory and Evidence," *Sociological Quarterly* 29(2): 281–313 (1988).

42. Ibid., p. 296.

nomic development.[43] The basic finding of this literature is that in developing nations, foreign investment by multinational corporations and dependency on exports of raw material slow long-term economic growth and increase economic inequality. The economic inequality, then, increases both criminal behavior and the criminalization of that behavior by criminal justice agencies. This is particularly true in moderately repressive, as opposed to highly repressive or democratic regimes. They conclude that "future studies should examine the relationship that exists between multinational penetration, inequality, and type of regime."

A study by Bennett also challenged Durkheim's theory as the explanation of the linkage between crime and modernization.[44] Durkheim had argued that crime is caused by rapid social change. If that is true, Bennett reasoned, then: (1) the rate of increase in crime would be directly proportional to the rate of growth in the society; (2) both theft and homicide should increase during periods of rapid growth; and (3) the level of development itself (i.e., whether the country is underdeveloped or advanced) should not affect crime rates as long as the country is not rapidly changing. Using data from fifty-two nations from 1960 to 1984, Bennett then showed that the rate of growth does not significantly affect either homicide or theft, and that the level of development itself, independent of the rate of growth, significantly affects theft offenses but not homicides. Bennett concludes: "These findings refute the Durkheimian hypotheses."[45]

CONCLUSION

Durkheim's influence has been extremely broad in criminology and sociology. His primary impact was that he focused attention on the role that social forces play in determining human conduct at a time when the dominant thinking held either that people were free in choosing courses of action or that behavior was determined by inner forces of biology and psychology. Although the focus on social forces is now the dominant view used to explain crime, it was considered quite radical at the time.[46]

---

43. Ibid., pp. 298–99. A still different causal path was suggested by Sethard Fisher ("Economic Development and Crime," *American Journal of Economics and Sociology* 46[1]: 17–34 [1987]) who argued that crime is associated with the unplanned drift of rural populations into urban areas and with changes in elite groups as the society attempts to modernize and achieve economic growth.

44. Richard R. Bennett, "Development and Crime," *Sociological Quarterly* 32(3): 343–63 (1991).

45. Ibid., p. 356.

46. See the chapter on Durkheim in Ian Taylor, Paul Walton, and Jock Young, *The New Criminology*, Harper, New York, 1973, pp. 67–90.

There is now considerable evidence that the basic patterns of crime found in the modern world can only be explained by a theory that focuses on modernization as a fundamental factor. Shelley reviewed studies of crime and modernization and found that the same changes in crime patterns that occurred first in Western Europe have reoccurred in Eastern European socialist nations and in the emerging nations of Asia, Africa, and Latin America as they have undergone modernization.[47] She concluded: "The evidence . . . suggests that only the changes accompanying the developmental process are great enough to explain the enormous changes that have occurred in international crime patterns in the last two centuries."

Many of the changes that have accompanied the modernization process, however, are not those predicted by Durkheim's theory. Premodern societies were characterized by high levels of violent crime, in contrast to Durkheim's arguments about their stability. There appears to have been a long-term decline in crime over the last several hundred years as the process of modernization has occurred, something that Durkheim's theory does not predict.[48] Short-term increases in that long-term decline occurred in the early stages of urbanization and industrialization, but those short-term increases seem to have been associated with the retention, not the breakdown, of rural culture. Gurr argues that other sources of short-term increases in crime rates include wars and growths in the size of the youth population.[49] Thus Durkheim may have been right in pointing to modernization as a fundamental factor in the explanation of crime, but he did not accurately describe the effect that it has.

On the other hand, Durkheim's basic argument was that modernization is linked to crime through the breakdown of social norms and rules—that is, he associated crime with the absence of social controls. It may be that Durkheim's argument itself is correct but that Durkheim was wrong in assuming that premodern societies had strong social controls and little crime. In contrast, it now seems more likely that they had little social control and a great deal of crime, especially violent crime. The long-term decline in violent crime may then be explained by the

47. Louise I. Shelley, *Crime and Modernization*, Southern Illinois University Press, Carbondale, Ill., 1981, pp. 141–42.

48. See Steven F. Messner, "Societal Development, Social Equality, and Homicide," *Social Forces* 61: 225–40 (1982).

49. Ted Robert Gurr, "Historical Forces in Violent Crime," in Michael Tonry and Norval Morris, eds., *Crime and Justice*, vol. 3, University of Chicago Press, Chicago, 1981, pp. 340–46. See also Gurr, "On the History of Violent Crime in Europe and America," in Hugh David Graham and Ted Robert Gurr, eds., *Violence in America*, 2nd ed., Sage, Beverly Hills, Calif., 1979.

continuously increasing level of social controls associated with increasing modernization.[50] The relationship between crime and social controls will be further explored in Chapter 13. At the same time, the long-term increase in property crime may be associated with increasing opportunities that industrialization and urbanization provides. This relationship will be further explored in Chapter 10.

50. This is basically Gurr's interpretation. See the sources in n. 49.

The Ecology of Crime

One of Durkheim's arguments was that rapid social change was associated with increases in crime due to the breakdown of social controls. This idea was one of several used by members of the Department of Sociology at the University of Chicago in the 1920s in their attempt to pinpoint the environmental factors associated with crime and to determine the relationship among those factors. However, instead of focusing on rapid change in entire societies, they focused on rapid change in neighborhoods.

Their procedure involved correlating the characteristics of each neighborhood with the crime rates of that neighborhood. This first large-scale study of crime in America produced a mass of data and a large number of observations about crime that led directly to much of the later work in American criminology. Since this research was based on an image of human communities taken from plant ecology, it became known as the Chicago School of Human Ecology.

THE THEORY OF HUMAN ECOLOGY

The term *ecology*, as it is used today, is often linked to the idea of protecting the natural environment. In its original meaning, however, it is a branch of biology in which plants and animals are studied in their relationships to each other and to their natural habitat. Plant life and animal life are seen as an intricately complicated whole, a web of life in which each part depends on almost every other part for some aspect of its existence. Organisms in their natural habitat exist in an ongoing balance of nature, a dynamic equilibrium in which each individual must struggle to survive. Ecologists study this web of interrelationships and interdependencies in an attempt to discover the forces that define the activities of each part.

Human communities, particularly those organized around a free-market economy and a laissez-faire government, could be seen to resemble this biotic state in nature. Each individual struggles for his or her survival in an interrelated, mutually dependent community. The Darwinian law of survival of the fittest applies here as well.

Robert Park proposed a parallel between the distribution of plant life in nature and the organization of human life in societies.[1] He had been a Chicago newspaper reporter for twenty-five years and had spent much of that time investigating social conditions in the city. Chicago at that time had a population of over 2 million; between 1860 and 1910 its population had doubled every ten years, with wave after wave of immigrants. Park was appointed to the Sociology Department at the University of Chicago in 1914. From the study of plant and animal ecology he derived two key concepts that formed the basis of what he called the "theory of human ecology."

The first concept came from the observations of the Danish ecologist Warming, who noted that a group of plants in a given area might have many characteristics that, in combination, were similar to those of an individual organism.[2] Warming called such groups "plant communities." Other ecologists argued that the plant and animal life in a given habitat tended to develop a "natural economy" in which different species are each able to live more prosperously together than separately. This is called "symbiosis," or the living together of different species to the mutual benefit of each. Since each plant and animal community was said to resemble an organism, the balance of nature in the habitat was said to resemble a super-organism.

Park's work as a newspaperman had led him to view the city in a similar way—not merely as a geographic phenomenon, but as a kind of "super-organism" that had "organic unity" derived from the symbiotic interrelations of the people who lived within it.[3] Within this super-organism Park found many "natural areas" where different types of people lived. These natural areas, like the natural areas of plants, had an organic unity of their own. Some of them were racial or ethnic communities, such as "Chinatown," "Little Italy," or the "Black Belt." Other natural areas included individuals in certain income or occupational

---

1. Park's background and a review of the theory of human ecology are presented in Terence Morris, *The Criminal Area*, Humanities Press, New York, 1966, pp. 1–18. See also Winifred Raushenbush, *Robert E. Park: Biography of a Sociologist*, Duke University Press, Durham, 1979; and Amos H. Hawley, "Human Ecology," *International Encyclopedia of the Social Sciences*, vol. 4, Macmillan and The Free Press, New York, 1968, pp. 328–37.

2. Eugenius Warming, "Plant Communities," in Robert E. Park and Ernest W. Burgess, *Introduction to the Science of Sociology*, University of Chicago Press, Chicago, 1969, pp. 175–82.

3. Robert E. Park, *Human Communities*, The Free Press, Glencoe, Ill., 1952, p. 118.

groups, or they were industrial or business areas. Still other areas were physically cut off from the rest of the city by railroad tracks, rivers, major highways, or unused space. Symbiotic relationships existed not only among the people within a natural area (where the butcher needed the baker for bread and the baker needed the butcher for meat), but also among the natural areas within the city. Each natural area was seen as playing a part in the life of the city as a whole.

The second basic concept Park took from plant ecology involved the process by which the balance of nature in a given area might change. A new species may invade the area, come to dominate it, and drive out other life forms. For example, a cleared field in one of the southern states will first be covered with tall weeds. Later this field will be invaded and dominated by broomsedge and, even later, by pine trees. Finally the field will stabilize as an oak-hickory forest. Ecologists call this process "invasion, dominance, and succession."

This process can also be seen in human societies. The history of America is a process of invasion, dominance, and succession by Europeans into the territory of Native Americans. And in cities one cultural or ethnic group may take over an entire neighborhood from another group, beginning with the shift of only one or two residents. Similarly, business or industry may move into and ultimately take over a previously residential neighborhood.

The processes of invasion, dominance, and succession were further explored by Park's associate, Ernest Burgess, who pointed out that cities do not merely grow at their edges. Rather, they have a tendency to expand radially from their center in patterns of concentric circles, each moving gradually outward. Burgess described these concentric circles as "zones."

Zone I is the central business district, while Zone II is the area immediately around it. Zone II generally is the oldest section of the city, and it is continually involved in a process of invasion, dominance, and succession by the businesses and industry that are expanding from Zone I. Houses in this zone are already deteriorating, and will be allowed to deteriorate further because they will be torn down in the foreseeable future to make way for incoming business and industry. Since this is the least desirable residential section of the city, it is usually occupied by the poorest people, including the most recent immigrants to the city. Zone III is the zone of relatively modest homes and apartments, occupied by workers and their families who have escaped the deteriorating conditions in Zone II. The final zone within the city itself is Zone IV, the residential districts of single-family houses and more expensive apartments. Beyond the city limits are the suburban areas and the satellite cities, which constitute Zone V, the commuter zone. Each of these five zones is growing and thus is gradually moving outward into the territory occupied by the next zone, in a process of invasion, dominance, and succession.

Natural areas occur within each zone, and often are linked to natural areas in other zones. For example, Burgess noted the location in Chicago's Zone II where Jewish immigrants initially settled. Zone III was an area of Jewish workers' homes that was constantly receiving new residents from Zone II and at the same time was constantly losing residents to more desirable Jewish neighborhoods in Zones IV and V.[4]

Within the framework of these ideas Park and his colleagues studied the city of Chicago and its problems. They attempted to discover "the processes by which the biotic balance and the social equilibrium are maintained once they are achieved, and the processes by which, when the biotic balance and the social equilibrium are disturbed, the transition is made from one relatively stable order to another."[5]

RESEARCH IN THE "DELINQUENCY AREAS" OF CHICAGO

Park's theories were used as the basis for a broadly ranging study of the problem of juvenile delinquency in Chicago by Clifford R. Shaw. The problem of crime and delinquency had become of increasing concern to social scientists in the 1920s because the country was gripped in a crime wave generated by resistance to Prohibition, a problem that was particularly severe in Chicago.

Shaw worked as a probation and parole officer during this period and became convinced that the problem of juvenile delinquency had its origin in the juvenile's "detachment from conventional groups" rather than in any biological or psychological abnormalities.[6] Following his appointment to the Institute for Juvenile Research in Chicago, Shaw devised a strategy, based on the theory of human ecology, to study the process by which this "detachment from conventional groups" occurred.

---

4. Ernest W. Burgess, "The Growth of the City," in Park, Burgess, and Roderick D. McKenzie, Jr., *The City*, University of Chicago Press, Chicago, 1928, p. 62.

5. Robert E. Park, "Human Ecology," *American Journal of Sociology* 42: 158 (1936).

6. James F. Short, Jr., "Introduction to the Revised Edition," in Clifford R. Shaw and Henry D. McKay, *Juvenile Delinquency and Urban Areas*, University of Chicago Press, Chicago, 1969, p. xlvii. Additional background material on Shaw and his colleague Henry McKay can be found in Jon Snodgrass, "Clifford R. Shaw and Henry D. McKay: Chicago Criminologists," *British Journal of Criminology* 16: 1–19 (Jan. 1976). A detailed assessment of their impact on criminology can be found in Harold Finestone, "The Delinquent and Society: The Shaw and McKay Tradition," in James F. Short, ed., *Delinquency, Crime and Society*, University of Chicago Press, Chicago, 1976, pp. 23–49; and Finestone, *Victims of Change: Juvenile Delinquency in American Society*, Greenwood, Westport, Conn., 1977, pp. 77–150.

Because he saw delinquents as essentially normal human beings, he believed that their illegal activities were somehow bound up with their environment. Therefore the first stage of his strategy involved analyzing the characteristics of the neighborhoods that, according to police and court records, had the most delinquents. But even in the worst of these neighborhoods only about 20 percent of the youth were actually involved with the court. Shaw therefore compiled extensive "life histories" from individual delinquents to find out exactly how they had related to their environment.

Shaw first published his neighborhood studies in 1929 in a volume entitled *Delinquency Areas*, and he subsequently published more of his research in two studies coauthored with Henry D. McKay, *Social Factors in Juvenile Delinquency* (1931) and *Juvenile Delinquency and Urban Areas* (1942). Shaw and McKay reached the following conclusions as a result of studying neighborhoods:

1. *Physical Status:* The neighborhoods with the highest delinquency rates were found to be located within or immediately adjacent to areas of heavy industry or commerce. These neighborhoods also had the greatest number of condemned buildings, and their population was decreasing. The population change was assumed to be related to an industrial invasion of the area, which resulted in fewer buildings being available for residential occupation.[7]

2. *Economic Status:* The highest rates of delinquency were found in the areas of lowest economic status as determined by a number of specific factors, including the percentage of families on welfare, the median rental, and the percentage of families owning homes.[8] These areas also had the highest rates of infant deaths, active cases of tuberculosis, and insanity. But Shaw and McKay concluded that economic conditions did not in themselves *cause* these problems. This conclusion was based on the fact that the rates of delinquency, of adult criminality, of infant deaths, and of tuberculosis for the city as a whole remained relatively stable between 1929 and 1934, when the Great Depression hit, and there was a tenfold increase in the number of families on public or private assistance. Median rentals, welfare rates, and other economic measures continued to show that the areas with the highest concentrations of these problems were in the lowest economic status relative to other areas of the city. These problems appeared to be associated with the least privileged groups in society, regardless of the actual economic conditions of that society as a whole.

3. *Population Composition:* Areas of highest delinquency were consistently associated with higher concentrations of foreign-born and African-American

7. Clifford R. Shaw and Henry D. McKay, *Juvenile Delinquency and Urban Areas*, University of Chicago Press, Chicago, 1969, p. 145.
8. Ibid., pp. 147–52.

heads of families.[9] To determine the precise role of racial and ethnic factors in the causation of delinquency, Shaw and McKay further analyzed these data. They found that certain inner-city areas in Zone II remained among those with the highest delinquency rates in the city despite shifts of almost all the population of these areas. In 1884 approximately 90 percent of the population in these areas was German, Irish, English, Scottish, or Scandinavian. By 1930 approximately 85 percent of the population was Czech, Italian, Polish, Slavic, or other. In spite of this dramatic shift in ethnic populations, these eight areas continued to have some of the highest delinquency rates in the city. At the same time there was no increase in delinquency rates in the areas into which the older immigrant communities moved.

They also found that, within similar areas, each group, whether foreign-born or native, recent immigrant or older immigrant, black or white, had a delinquency rate that was proportional to the rate of the overall area. No racial, national, or nativity group exhibited a uniform characteristic rate of delinquency in all parts of the city. Each group produced delinquency rates that ranged from the lowest to the highest in the city, depending on the type of area surveyed. Although some variation associated with the group could be seen, it was apparent that the overall delinquency rate of a particular group depended primarily on how many individuals of that group resided in "delinquency areas." Shaw and McKay concluded[10]:

In the face of these facts it is difficult to sustain the contention that, by themselves, the factors of race, nativity, and nationality are vitally related to the problem of juvenile delinquency. It seems necessary to conclude, rather, that the significantly higher rates of delinquents found among the children of Negroes, the foreign born, and more recent immigrants are closely related to existing differences in their respective patterns of geographical distribution within the city. If these groups were found in the same proportion in all local areas, existing differences in the relative number of boys brought into court from the various groups might be expected to be greatly reduced or to disappear entirely.

In addition to this research, Shaw compiled and published a series of "life histories" of individual delinquents, including *The Jackroller* (1930), *The Natural History of a Delinquent Career* (1931), and *Brothers in Crime* (1938). The basic findings of these histories are summed up in the following points.

9. Ibid., p. 155.
10. Ibid., pp. 162–63.

1. Delinquents, by and large, "are not different from large numbers of persons in conventional society with respect to intelligence, physical condition, and personality traits."[11]

2. In delinquency areas "the conventional traditions, neighborhood institutions, public opinion, through which neighborhoods usually effect a control over the behavior of the child, were largely disintegrated."[12] In addition, parents and neighbors frequently approved of delinquent behavior, so that the child grew up "in a social world in which [delinquency] was an accepted and appropriate form of conduct."[13]

3. The neighborhoods included many opportunities for delinquent activities, including "junk dealers, professional fences, and residents who purchased their stolen goods" and "dilapidated buildings which served as an incentive for junking." There was also a "lack of preparation, training, opportunity, and proper encouragement for successful employment in private industry."[14]

4. Delinquent activities in these areas began at an early age as a part of play activities of the street.[15]

5. In these play activities, there is a continuity of tradition in a given neighborhood from older boys to younger boys.[16] This tradition includes the transmission of such different criminal techniques as jackrolling, shoplifting, stealing from junkmen, or stealing automobiles, so that different neighborhoods were characterized by the same types of offenses over long periods of time.[17]

6. The normal methods of official social control could not stop this process.[18]

7. It was only later in a delinquent career that the individual began "to identify himself with the criminal world, and to embody in his own philosophy of life the moral values which prevailed in the criminal groups with which he had contact."[19] This was due both to the continuous contact the delinquent had with juvenile and adult criminals on the street and in correctional institutions, and to rejection and stigmatization by the community.

11. Clifford R. Shaw, *Brothers in Crime*, University of Chicago Press, Chicago, 1938, p. 350. See also Shaw's *The Jackroller*, University of Chicago Press, Chicago, 1930, p. 164; and *The Natural History of a Delinquent Career*, University of Chicago Press, Chicago, 1931, p. 226.

12. Shaw, *Natural History*, p. 229. See also *The Jackroller*, p. 165, and *Brothers in Crime*, p. 358.

13. Shaw, *Brothers in Crime*, p. 356. See also Shaw and McKay, op. cit., p. 172; *The Jackroller*, p. 165; and *Natural History*, p. 229.

14. Ibid., p. 356.

15. Shaw, *Brothers in Crime*, pp. 354, 355; *Natural History*, p. 227; *The Jackroller*, p. 164. See also Short, op. cit., p. xli.

16. Shaw and McKay, op. cit., pp. 174–75.

17. Ibid., p. 174.

18. Shaw, *Natural History*, p. 233; *Brothers in Crime*, p. 260; Shaw and McKay, op. cit., p. 4.

19. Shaw, *Natural History*, p. 228. See also *The Jackroller*, pp. 119, 165; *Brothers in Crime*, p. 350.

Shaw concluded that delinquency and other social problems are closely related to the process of invasion, dominance, and succession that determines the concentric growth patterns of the city.[20] When a particular location in the city is "invaded" by new residents, the established symbiotic relationships that bind that location to a natural area are destroyed. Ultimately this location will be incorporated as an organic part of a new natural area, and the social equilibrium will be restored. Meanwhile the natural organization of the location will be severely impaired.

These "interstitial areas" (so called because they are *in between* the organized natural areas) become afflicted with a variety of social problems that are directly traceable to the rapid shift in populations. The formal social organizations that existed in the neighborhood tend to disintegrate as the original population retreats. Because the neighborhood is in transition, the residents no longer identify with it, and thus they do not care as much about its appearance or reputation. There is a marked decrease in "neighborliness" and in the ability of the people of the neighborhood to control their youth. For example, in an established neighborhood, a resident who is aware that a child is getting into trouble may call that child's parents or may report that child to the local authorities. But because new people are continuously moving into the interstitial area, residents no longer know their own neighbors or their neighbors' children. Thus children who are out of their parents' sight may be under almost no control, even in their own neighborhood. The high mobility of the residents also means that there is a high turnover of children in the local schools. This is disruptive both to learning and to discipline. Finally, the area tends to become a battleground between the invading and retreating cultures. This can generate a great deal of conflict in the community, which tends to be manifested in individual and gang conflicts between the youth of the two cultures.

Although other areas only periodically undergo this process, areas in Zone II are continually being invaded both by the central business district and by successive waves of new immigrants coming into the city from foreign countries and from rural areas. These new immigrants already have many problems associated with their adjustment to the new culture. In addition, the neighborhood into which the immigrant moves is in a chronic state of "social disorganization." This presents the immigrant with many additional problems, and there is almost no help available to solve any of them. Thus recent immigrants tend to have a wide

---

20. Morris, op. cit., pp. 77, 78; Ian Taylor, Paul Walton, and Jock Young, *The New Criminology*, Harper & Row, New York, 1973, pp. 110–14.

range of social problems, including delinquency among their youth. These problems are resolved as recent immigrants acquire some of the resources necessary both to solve their own problems and to move into the better-established neighborhoods of Zone III, with its natural processes of social control.

POLICY IMPLICATIONS

Because Shaw believed that juvenile delinquency was generated by social disorganization in interstitial areas, he did not believe that treatment of individual delinquents would have much effect in reducing overall delinquency rates. Rather, he thought that the answer had to be found in "the development of programs which seek to effect changes in the conditions of life in specific local communities and in whole sections of the city."[21] In Shaw's view these programs could only come from organizations of neighborhood residents, so that the natural forces of social control could take effect. Thus, in 1932, he launched the Chicago Area Project, which established twenty-two neighborhood centers in six areas of Chicago.[22] Control of these centers rested with committees of local residents rather than with the central staff of the project, and local residents were employed as staff.

These centers had two primary functions. First, they were to coordinate such community resources as churches, schools, labor unions, industries, clubs, and other groups in addressing and resolving community problems. Second, they were to sponsor a variety of activity programs including recreation, summer camping and scouting activities, handicraft workshops, discussion groups, and community projects.[23] Through these activities the project sought "to develop a positive interest by the inhabitants in their own welfare, to establish democratic bodies of local citizens who would enable the whole community to become aware of its problems and attempt their solution by common action."[24]

The Chicago Area Project operated continuously for twenty-five years, until Shaw's death in 1957, but its effect on delinquency in these areas was never precisely evaluated.[25] A similar project in Boston was

---

21. Shaw and McKay, op. cit., p. 4.

22. See Solomon Kobrin, "The Chicago Area Project—A 25–Year Assessment," *Annals of the American Society of Political and Social Science*, March 1959, pp. 19–29; or Anthony Sorrentino, "The Chicago Area Project After 25 Years," *Federal Probation*, June 1959, pp. 40–45. A review of this and other similar programs is found in Richard Lundman, *Prevention and Control of Juvenile Delinquency*, 2nd ed., Oxford, New York, 1993, ch. 3.

23. Shaw and McKay, op. cit., p. 324.

24. Morris, *The Criminal Area*, p. 83.

25. Short, op. cit., p. xlvi.

carefully evaluated by Walter B. Miller over a three-year period.[26] Here it was found that the project was effective in achieving many admirable goals. It established close relationships with local gangs and organized their members into clubs, it increased their involvement in recreational activities, it provided them with access to occupational and educational opportunities, it formed citizens' organizations, and it increased interagency cooperation in addressing community problems.

The goal of all these activities, however, was to reduce the incidence of delinquent behavior. To assess the impact of the project on the behavior of the youth, Miller analyzed the daily field reports of the outreach workers, which included a description of the activities of each youth. The behaviors were then classified as "moral" or "immoral" (where "immoral" meant disapproval by the community, but not necessarily a violation of the law) and as "legal" or "illegal." It was found that the ratio of moral to immoral behaviors remained relatively constant throughout the project, and that, although the total number of illegal acts decreased slightly during the project, the number of major offenses by boys increased. In addition, data were compiled on the number of court appearances made by each youth before, during, and after contact with the project, and these data were compared with the number of court appearances by a control group. There was almost no difference in these statistics. Miller concluded that the project had had a "negligible impact" on delinquency.[27] The failure of this and other similar projects led Lundman to conclude that it was likely that "the Chicago Area Project also failed to prevent juvenile delinquency."[28]

RECENT THEORY AND RESEARCH ON NEIGHBORHOODS AS CAUSES OF CRIME

Despite the failure of the Chicago Area Project to prevent delinquency, criminologists have continued to argue that neighborhoods themselves are important as causes of crime and delinquency and that they are appropriate targets for crime prevention programs. To a considerable extent, this continuing focus is the result of Shaw and McKay's discovery of *residential succession*, the fact that neighborhoods often retain their high crime and delinquency rates despite total turnovers in population.

---

26. Walter B. Miller, "The Impact of a 'Total-Community' Delinquency Control Project," *Social Problems* 10: 168–91 (fall 1962).

27. Ibid., p. 187.

28. Lundman, op. cit., p. 81.

Bursik and Webb tested this concept using data on Chicago neighborhoods directly comparable to that of Shaw and McKay.[29] They found that the residential succession argument was supported by data from 1940 to 1950. However, after 1950 all neighborhoods undergoing racial change were characterized by high delinquency rates, regardless of their delinquency rates before the change. Bursik and Webb interpret their finding in terms of community stability. At the time Shaw and McKay wrote, the zones of transition were found exclusively in the inner-city areas, and the process of dispersion to outlying residential areas was gradual. This "natural" process was disrupted in more recent times as African Americans attempted to follow in the footsteps of other ethnic groups. Strong white resistance to any blacks moving into the neighborhood would be followed by total white flight and total racial turnover in a very short time. In such situations social institutions disappeared entirely or persevered but were resistant to including the new residents, resulting in the high delinquency rates associated with social disorganization. Bursik and Webb found that, after the neighborhoods had stabilized, they "had delinquency rates not much different than would have been expected from their previous patterns."[30] This finding was consistent with several other studies that found that delinquency rates were increasing in African-American neighborhoods that had recently undergone residential changes but were decreasing in African-American neighborhoods that had been stable for some time.[31]

Beginning with an assumption about residential succession, Stark asked what it is about neighborhoods themselves that is associated with high crime rates, independent of the people who live there. As an answer to this question, he presented a formal theory in thirty integrated propositions.[32] These thirty propositions focused on five structural aspects of urban neighborhoods: density (many people in a small area), poverty (people have little money), mixed use (residences, industries, and stores are all in the same place), transience (people frequently move into, out of, and around the neighborhood) and dilapidation (the buildings themselves are falling apart). Stark argues that, in a variety of ways, these five structural characteristics increase moral cynicism among com-

29. Robert J. Bursik, Jr., and Jim Webb, "Community Change and Patterns of Delinquency," *American Journal of Sociology* 88(1): 24–42 (1982).

30. Ibid., p. 39.

31. Robert E. Kapsis, "Residential Succession and Delinquency," *Criminology* 15(4): 459–86 (Feb. 1978). See also more recent findings by McKay reported in the 1969 edition of Shaw and McKay, op. cit., p. 345, and interesting comments by Snodgrass, op. cit., pp. 5–6.

32. Rodney Stark, "Deviant Places: A Theory of the Ecology of Crime," *Criminology* 25(4): 893–909 (Nov. 1987).

munity residents, provide more opportunities to commit crime, increase motivations to commit crime, and decrease informal surveillance by which crime in a community is held in check. As a consequence, crime-prone people are attracted to the neighborhood, while law-abiding people get out if they can. This results in high crime rates that tend to persist even when there are complete turnovers in the people who live there.

Similarly, Sampson reviewed recent research on the relation between neighborhoods and crime in an attempt to determine how community structures and cultures create different crime rates.[33] Poor neighborhoods have higher crime rates, but Sampson found that poverty itself is not related to crime. Rather, poverty combined with residential mobility (i.e., frequent moves by residents) seems to be associated with higher levels of violent crime. Neighborhood rates of family disruption (divorce rates and rates of female-headed households) are strongly and consistently related to rates of violence. Neighborhoods with high percentages of African Americans have higher crime rates, but race itself tends to drop out when family disruption and poverty are taken into account. Finally, neighborhoods with high population density, many apartments, and high concentrations of individuals who do not live within a family situation tend to have higher rates of crime and violence.

Sampson explained this pattern of research findings with Shaw's concept of social disorganization. Sampson defined social disorganization as the inability of the community to realize its common values. An example would be when community residents oppose drug use but cannot get rid of the drug dealers who have taken over a nearby corner or house for a drug market. There may be a variety of reasons that some communities cannot realize their common values, but one reason is the lack of what Coleman calls "social capital"—i.e., networks of relationships among people that facilitate common actions and make possible the achievement of common goals.[34] In general, when there are many social relationships among community residents (i.e., a lot of "social capital"), there is less crime. This is because no one wants crime in their own neighborhood, and the social relationships allow people to achieve their common goal of driving the crime out.

33. Robert J. Sampson, "The Community," pp. 193–216 in James Q. Wilson and Joan Petersilia, eds., *Crime*, ICS Press, San Francisco, 1995. See also Sampson and Janet Lauritsen, "Violent Victimization and Offending: Individual, Situational, and Community-Level Risk Factors," pp. 1–114 in Albert J. Reiss and Jeffrey A. Roth, eds., *Understanding and Preventing Violence*, vol. 3, National Academy Press, Washington, D.C., 1994.

34. James Coleman, "Social Capital in the Creation of Human Capital," *American Journal of Sociology* 94 (Supplement): 95–120, 1988.

Sampson then proposed a causal sequence that ties all this research together in a way that resembles Shaw's earlier work.[35] Poverty, family disruption, and residential instability are community characteristics that result in anonymity and the lack of relationships among neighborhood residents and low participation in community organizations and in local activities. Because of this "low social capital," neighbors are not able to exert effective control over public or common areas, such as streets and parks, and so they are free to be taken over by criminals. In addition, local teenagers have considerable freedom because the anonymity of the neighborhood means that they and their friends are unknown to adults even though they may be only a short distance from their homes. All of this results in increased crime and violence in the neighborhood, independent of the people who live there. The high crime and violence then promotes further disintegration of the community, as law-abiding residents withdraw from community life and try to move out of the neighborhood.

At least some of the concentration of crime among African Americans, according to Sampson, is caused by differences in the neighborhoods in which they live. About 38 percent of poor blacks live in extremely poor neighborhoods, where the above processes are likely to occur, and only 16 percent of poor blacks live in neighborhoods that are not poor. In contrast, poor whites are much more widely dispersed in society. Only about 7 percent of poor whites live in extremely poor neighborhoods, while around 70 percent of them live in neighborhoods that are not poor at all. The "worst" urban contexts in which whites reside, in terms of poverty and family disruption, are considerably better than the average urban contexts in which blacks reside.[36] To the extent that neighborhoods themselves have a causal impact on crime, this would produce marked differences in the crime rates of these two groups.

Sampson proposed a variety of policy recommendations that are focused on "changing places, not people." These include targeting "hot spots" in the community where there is frequent criminal activity; stopping the "spiral of decay" by cleaning up trash, graffiti, and so on; increasing the social relationships between adults and teenagers through organized youth activities; reducing residential mobility by enabling residents to buy their homes or take over management of their apartments; scatter public housing in a broad range of neighborhoods rather than

35. Ibid., pp. 200–201.

36. Ibid., pp. 201–2; Robert Sampson and William Julius Wilson, "Toward a Theory of Race, Crime, and Urban Inequality," in John Hagan and Ruth Peterson, eds., *Crime and Inequality*, Stanford University Press, Stanford, Calif., 1995.

concentrating it in poor neighborhoods; maintain and increase urban services, such as police, fire, and public health services, especially those aimed at reducing child abuse and teen pregnancy; and generally increase community power by promoting community organizations. He conceded that such programs have had limited success in the past, but argued that small successes can produce cumulative changes that result in a more stable community in the long run.

SITUATIONAL CONTEXTS OF CRIME

The term "situation" refers to the immediate setting in which behavior occurs, and "situational analysis" refers to the search for regularities in relationships between behaviors and situations.[37] Neighborhoods are one situational context that can influence the occurrence of crime. Recent research has looked at a variety of other situational contexts to explain both the likelihood that crimes will occur and the likelihood that particular people will be victimized by them.

Essentially, these theories assume that there are always people around who will commit a crime if given a chance, so they do not explain the motivation to commit crime. Rather, they explain the situations and circumstances in which motivated offenders find that they have the opportunity to commit a crime. Therefore, these theories sometimes are called "opportunity theories" of crime.

For example, looting often accompanies large-scale disasters such as floods, earthquakes, violent storms, wars, and riots. Home owners and store owners flee the disaster, leaving their property unprotected. The police often are busy with more pressing matters, such as saving human lives. Many people who normally would not commit crime take advantage of the opportunities in the situation and steal whatever they think they can get away with.

The preceding example would be a theory of "situational selection," in that it describes the types of situations that motivated offenders select to commit their crimes.[38] In general, motivated offenders consider ease of access to the target, the likelihood of being observed or caught, and the expected reward. This perspective assumes that offenders are largely rational in their decision-making processes, so it is associated with "rational choice" explanations of crime.[39]

---

37. For a review, see Christopher Birkbeck and Gary LaFree, "The Situational Analysis of Crime and Deviance," *Annual Review of Sociology* 19:113–37 (1993).

38. Ibid., pp. 124–26.

39. Ibid. See also Darrell B. Cornish and Ronald V. G. Clarke, eds., *The Reasoning Criminal: Rational Choice Perspectives on Offending*. Springer-Verlag, New York, 1986.

A similar approach has been used to explain differences in the rates at which groups are victimized.[40] Hindelang and his colleagues argued that the differences in risks of victimization are associated with differences in "lifestyles," which they describe in terms of "routine daily activities, both vocational activities (work, school, keeping house, etc.) and leisure activities."[41] In general, they argue that people who are younger, male, unmarried, poor, and black have higher risks of victimization than people who are older, female, married, wealthy, and white because each of these groups has an increased tendency to be away from home, especially at night, to engage in public activities while away from home, and to associated with people who are likely to be offenders.[42] All this leads to increased risk of property and personal victimization.

Hindelang and his colleagues argued that the routine activities of some groups expose them to much greater risks of victimization than others. Similarly, Cohen and Felson argue that certain changes in the modern world have provided motivated offenders with a greatly increased range of opportunities to commit crime.[43] They point out that most violent and property crimes involve direct contact between the offender and the "target"—i.e., the person or property of the victim.[44] These crimes therefore require the convergence in time and space of a motivated offender, a suitable target, and the absence of a capable guardian (e.g., police) to prevent the crime. Most criminology theories assume that changes in crime rates reflect changes in the number

40. Michael J. Hindelang, Michael R. Gottfredson, and James Garofalo, *Victims of Personal Crime*, Ballinger, Cambridge, Mass., 1978. James Garofalo, "Reassessing the Lifestyle Model of Criminal Victimization," in Michael Gottfredson and Travis Hirschi, eds., *Positive Criminology: Essays in Honor of Michael J. Hindelang*, Sage, Beverly Hills, Calif., 1987, updates the theory and argues that there is no substantive difference between the "lifestyle" and the "routine activities" approaches. See also Michael G. Maxfield, "Lifestyle and Routine Activity Theories of Crime," *Journal of Quantitative Criminology* 3(4): 275–82 (1987).

41. Ibid., p. 241.

42. For a good summary, see Robert F. Meier and Terance D. Miethe, "Understanding Theories of Criminal Victimization," in Michael Tonry, ed., *Crime and Justice: An Annual Review of Research* 17: 459–99 (1993). See also Birkbeck and LaFree, op. cit.

43. Lawrence E. Cohen and Marcus Felson "Social Change and Crime Rate Trends: A Routine Activity Approach," *American Sociological Review* 44: 588–608 (1979). Where Cohen and Felson focused on crime rate trends of predatory crimes, Felson has extended this approach to a broader range of crimes and examined the implications of routine activities for individual offending. See Marcus Felson, "Linking Criminal Choices, Routine Activities, Informal Control, and Criminal Outcomes," pp. 119–28 in Cornish and Clarke, op. cit.; Marcus Felson, *Crime and Everyday Life*, Pine Forge Press, Thousand Oaks, Calif., 1994; and Felson and Michael R. Gottfredson, "Social Indicators of Adolescent Activities Near Peers and Parents," *Journal of Marriage and the Family* 46:709–14 (1984).

44. Some crimes do not involve direct contact—e.g., many white-collar crimes. Cohen and Felson do not explain these types of crime, but the organization of the modern world obviously has made crimes without direct contact much more available to motivated offenders.

of motivated offenders or changes in the strength of their motivation. But Cohen and Felson argue that changes in the crime rates instead may be explained in terms of changes in the availability of targets and in the absence of capable guardians. This is exactly what happens when looting follows a disaster—there is no increase in criminal motivation, but suddenly there are many available targets and no capable guardians.

Cohen and Felson argue that there have been a great increase in the availability of targets and in the absence of capable guardians in the modern world as a result of changes in "routine activities"—i.e., how normal people live their lives, including activities related to work, home life, child rearing, education, and leisure. When people are home, they function as "guardians" for their own property. But the routine activities of modern life have led to the "dispersion of activities away from family and household." This means that many households no longer have "capable guardians" for extended and fairly predictable periods of time. In addition, there has been a large increase in goods that are portable and therefore suitable as a target for thieves. For example, Cohen and Felson calculate that, in 1975, $26.44 in motor vehicles and parts were stolen for each $100 of these goods that were consumed. In comparison, $6.82 worth of electronic appliances were stolen for every $100 consumed, and 12¢ worth of furniture and nonelectronic household durables. The vast differences in these amounts is due to the suitability of these items as targets for theft. Cohen and Felson then demonstrated that changes in crime rates in the United States from 1947 to 1974 could be explained largely by these trends. That is, in 1947, people were home more of the time and more of what they owned was like furniture, while by 1974 people were away from home more of the time and more of what they owned was like cars and electronic appliances. So despite large increases in crime over that time period, there may be no changes in offender motivations at all.

The routine activities approach offers an alternative to Durkheim's theory of modernization as an explanation for changes in crime rates as nations undergo economic development. As discussed in the preceding chapter, Durkheim explained these changes primarily in terms of the breakdown of traditional values and beliefs. Neuman and Berger reviewed seventeen studies that compared Durkheim's and the routine activities approaches, and found only weak support for either one.[45] Bennett also compared the two, using data from fifty-two nations from

---

45. W. Lawrence Neuman and Ronald J. Berger, "Competing Perspectives on Cross-National Crime," *The Sociological Quarterly* 29(2): 281–313 (1988).

1960 to 1984.[46] In general, he found that neither approach could account for changes in homicide rates, since homicide was not affected either by developmental level or the rate of growth. But the changes in theft rates were consistent with the routine activities approach—i.e., more development was associated with more theft, independent of the rate of growth at which the development was occurring. He also found a "threshold" point at a very high level of development, at which further economic development did not seem to be associated with more theft. Bennett suggested that this was probably due to a variety of "adaptive social mechanisms" that began to become effective at that point, such as "theft target hardening (e.g., better locks, higher fences, burglar alarms), development of community watches increasing surveillance over goods, and more effective police strategies and tactics (e.g., community-oriented policing)."[47]

CONCLUSIONS

The Chicago School of Human Ecology can be described as a gold mine that continues to enrich criminology today. The individual case studies remain classic portrayals of delinquents and their social worlds, the urban research methods have led to a wide variety of empirical studies, and the social disorganization theory forms the basis for several other theories in contemporary criminology.

Despite the richness of this historic legacy, the ecological approach to crime was somewhat stagnant for many years. Recently, however, there has been a veritable explosion of new theory and research that has ecological theory as its foundation. The basic point of this new theory and research is that crime cannot be understood without also understanding the context in which it occurs. The immediate contexts are the neighborhoods in which people live and the situations that their lifestyles frequently place them in, while the broadest context is formed by the routine activities found in the entire society.

Ultimately, all these studies implicitly rely on a view of society as having an organic unity that includes symbiotic relationships among all its various parts. Crime is part of that symbiotic unity and so it can only be understood in the context of its relation to the activities in the rest of the organism. As Meier and Miethe state, this whole line of research suggests that there is a "symbiotic relationship between conventional and illegal activities" in such a way that "victims and offenders are in-

46. Richard R. Bennett, "Development and Crime," *The Sociological Quarterly* 32(3): 343–63 (1991).

47. Ibid., p. 356.

extricably linked in an ecology of crime."[48] Thus, criminologists must look to the social contexts to understand the parallel processes by which victims come to experience the risk of crime and offenders come to be motivated to commit crime.

48. Meier and Miethe, op. cit., p. 495.

CHAPTER 11

Strain Theories

In adapting Durkheim's theory to American society, Shaw and McKay retained Durkheim's argument about rapid social change but shifted the focus from societies to neighborhoods. Robert K. Merton also adapted Durkheim's theory to American society, but he shifted the focus away from rapid social change. Instead, he argued that there were certain relatively stable social conditions that were associated with the higher overall crime rates in American society, as well as with the higher rates of crime in the lower social classes. Merton used the term "social structural strain" to describe those social conditions, so that the theories that followed Merton's lead have come to be known as "strain theories."

ROBERT K. MERTON AND ANOMIE IN AMERICAN SOCIETY

Durkheim had analyzed anomie as a breakdown in the ability of society to regulate the natural appetites of individuals. Merton, in an article first published in 1938,[1] argued out that many of the appetites of individuals are not "natural," but rather originate in the "culture" of American society. At the same time, the "social structure" of American society limits the ability of certain groups to satisfy those appetites. The result is "a definite pressure on certain persons in the society to engage in nonconformist rather than conformist conduct."[2]

---

1. Robert K. Merton, *Social Theory and Social Structure*, The Free Press, Glencoe, Ill., 1968, p. 186. The most recent presentation and discussion of this theory is found in Merton, "Opportunity Structure: The Emergence, Diffusion, and Differentiation as Sociological Concept, 1930s–1950s," in Freda Adler and William Laufer, eds., *Advances in Criminological Theory: The Legacy of Anomie Theory*, vol. 6, Transaction Press, New Brunswick, N.J., 1995, pp. 3–78. For a discussion of the relationship between Durkheim's and Merton's theories, see Thomas J. Bernard, "Merton vs. Hirschi: Who Is Faithful to Durkheim's Heritage?" in Adler and Laufer, op. cit., pp. 81–90.

2. For definitions of structure and culture in Merton's theory, see Merton, "Opportunity Structure," op. cit., pp. 6–7.

Merton began by pointing out that the culture of any society defines certain goals it deems "worth striving for."[3] There are many such goals in every society, and they vary from culture to culture. Perhaps the most prominent culture goal in American society, however, is to acquire wealth. This might be regarded merely as a "natural aspiration," as Durkheim maintained. But American culture encourages this goal far beyond any intrinsic rewards the goals itself might have. Accumulated wealth is generally equated with personal value and worth and is associated with a high degree of prestige and social status. Those without money may be degraded even if they have personal characteristics that other cultures may value, such as age or spiritual discipline.

In addition, whereas Durkheim said that culture functioned to limit these aspirations in individuals (although at certain times it did not do this well), Merton argued that American culture specifically encourages all individuals to seek the greatest amount of wealth. American culture is based on an egalitarian ideology that asserts that all people have an equal chance to achieve wealth. Although all individuals are not expected to achieve this goal, all are expected to try. Those who do not may be unfavorably characterized as "lazy" or "unambitious."[4]

Cultures also specify the approved norms, or institutionalized means, all individuals are expected to follow in pursuing the culture goals. These means are based on values in the culture, and generally will rule out many of the technically most efficient methods of achieving the goal. For example, in American culture the institutionalized means that should be used to achieve wealth can generally be identified as "middle-class values" or "the Protestant work ethic." They include hard work, honesty, education, and deferred gratification. The use of force and fraud, which may be more efficient methods of gaining wealth, is forbidden.[5]

Merton argued that because all persons cannot be expected to achieve the goals of the culture, it is very important that the culture place a strong emphasis on the institutionalized means and the necessity of following them for their own value.[6] These means must provide some intrinsic satisfactions for all persons who participate in the culture. This is similar to the situation in athletics, in which the sport itself must provide enjoyment, even if the person does not win. The phrase "It's not whether you win, it's how you play the game" expresses the notion that

3. Merton, *Social Theory and Social Structure*, op. cit., p. 187.

4. Ibid., p. 193.

5. Ibid., p. 187.

6. Ibid., p. 188.

the primary satisfaction comes from following the institutionalized means (rules) rather than achieving the goal (winning).

In athletics, however, the goal of winning may be unduly emphasized, so that there is a corresponding deemphasis on the rewards provided by the sport itself. In this situation ("It's not how you play the game, it's whether you win") the institutionalized means are placed under a severe strain. Merton argues that this is the situation in American culture regarding the goal of achieving wealth.[7] The goal has been emphasized to the point that the institutionalized means are little reward in themselves. The person who adheres to these methods—that is, hard work, education, honesty, deferred gratification—receives little social reward for it unless he or she also achieves at least a moderate degree of wealth as a result. But the person who achieves wealth, even if it is not by the approved means, still receives the social rewards of prestige and social status. This situation places a severe strain on the institutionalized means, particularly for those persons who cannot achieve wealth through their use.

This strain falls on a wide variety of people in the society, but it tends to be more concentrated among persons in the lower class. In that group the ability to achieve wealth is limited not only by the talents and efforts of the individual, but by the social structure itself. Only the most talented and the most hard-working individuals from this class can ever expect to achieve wealth through the use of the institutionalized means. For the majority of persons this possibility is simply not realistic, and therefore the strain can be most severe. By the same token, the strain is least apparent among those in the upper classes, in which, using the same institutionalized means, a person of moderate talents can achieve a degree of wealth with only moderate efforts.

For certain groups, then, a severe strain on the cultural values arises because (1) the culture places a disproportionate emphasis on the achievement of the goal of accumulated wealth and maintains that this goal is applicable to all persons, and (2) the social structure effectively limits the possibilities of individuals within these groups to achieve this goal through the use of institutionalized means. This contradiction between the culture and the social structure of society is what Merton defines as anomie.[8]

Merton therefore used a *cultural argument* to explain the high rate of crime in American society as a whole, and a *structural argument* to

7. Ibid., p. 190.
8. Ibid., p. 216.

TABLE 11–1   Merton's Typology of Modes of Individual Adaptation*

Modes of Adaptation	Culture Goals	Institutional Means
I. Conformity	+	+
II. Innovation	+	−
III. Ritualism	−	+
IV. Retreatism	−	−
V. Rebellion	±	±

*Key: + signifies "acceptance," − signifies "rejection," and ± signifies "rejection of prevailing values and substitution of new values."

explained the concentration of crime in the lower classes.[9] The high level of crime in American society was explained in terms of "cultural imbalance"—the imbalance between the strong cultural forces that valued the goal of monetary success and the much weaker cultural forces that valued the institutional means of hard work, honesty, and education. However, Merton described American culture as relatively uniform throughout the class structure, so that everyone is similarly pressured to achieve wealth and everyone has a relatively weak allegiance to the institutionalized means. Thus "cultural imbalance" does not explain why the lower classes in America have higher crime rates than the upper classes. Merton therefore used social structure, not culture, to explain why lower-class people in America have higher crime rates than upper-class people. That explanation focused on the distribution of legitimate opportunities in the social structure—that is the ability to achieve wealth through institutionalized means. Merton argued that those opportunities were relatively concentrated in the higher classes and relatively absent in the lower classes. The distribution of criminal behavior is said to be a sort of mirror image of the distribution of legitimate opportunities, being relatively concentrated in the lower classes and relatively absent in the upper classes.

There are various ways in which an individual can respond to this problem of anomie, depending on his attitude toward the culture goals and the institutionalized means. Merton describes these options as conformity, innovation, ritualism, retreatism, and rebellion (Table 11–1).[10]

9. These cultural and structural arguments are presented in propositional form in Thomas J. Bernard, "Testing Structural Strain Theories," *Journal of Research in Crime and Delinquency* 24(4): 264–70 (1987).

10. Reprinted with permission of The Free Press, a Division of Simon & Schuster, from *Social Theory and Social Structure*, Revised and Enlarged Edition by Robert K. Merton. Copyright © 1967, 1968, by Robert K. Merton.

To the extent that a society is stable, most persons in it will choose conformity, which entails acceptance of both the culture goals and the institutionalized means. These persons strive to achieve wealth through the approved methods of middle-class values and will continue to do so whether or not they succeed.

Most crime that exists in society, however, will probably take the form of innovation. Persons who innovate retain their allegiance to the culture goal of acquiring wealth (since this is so heavily emphasized), but they find that they cannot succeed at this through the institutionalized means. Therefore they figure out new methods by which wealth can be acquired. Businessmen may devise different forms of white-collar crime entailing fraud and misrepresentation, or they may cheat on their income tax. Workers may systematically steal from their place of employment. Poor people may develop illegal operations, such as gambling, prostitution, or drug dealing, or they may burglarize and rob. In each of these cases the individual has retained his commitment to the culture goal, but is pursuing it through unapproved means.

This situation is very similar to that described by the classical thinkers, who maintained that since humans were hedonistic, they would always choose the most technically efficient methods of achieving their goals, unless limited by punishments, imposed by society.[11] Although the classical thinkers thought this was the normal condition of people, Merton argued that it was the condition only when the cultural goals were overemphasized to the point that the norms broke down.

A third possible adaptation involves rejecting the possibility of ever achieving wealth, but retaining allegiance to the norms of hard work, honesty, etc. This is the adaptation of those persons who wish to "play it safe." They will not be disappointed by failure to achieve their goals, since they have abandoned them. At the same time they will never find themselves in any trouble since they abide by all the cultural norms. This is the perspective of "the frightened employee, the zealously conformist bureaucrat in the teller's cage"[12] and tends to be found most frequently among persons in the lower middle class. These persons have achieved a minimum level of success through the institutionalized means, but have no real hope of achieving anything more. The fear of losing even this minimum level locks them into their adaptation.

The fourth adaptation—retreatism—involves simply dropping out of the whole game. Dropouts neither pursue the cultural goals nor act according to the institutionalized means. Those who choose this adapta-

11. Merton, op. cit., p. 211.
12. Ibid., p. 204.

tion include "psychotics, autists, pariahs, outcasts, vagrants, vagabonds, tramps, chronic drunkards and drug addicts."[13] Merton points out that this adaptation does not necessarily arise from a lack of commitment to the culture. It can also occur when there is a strong commitment to both the goals and the means, but no real possibility of achieving success.

> There results a twofold conflict: the interiorized moral obligation for adopting institutional means conflicts with pressures to resort to illicit means (which may attain the goal) and the individual is shut off from means which are both legitimate and effective. The competitive order is maintained, but the frustrated and handicapped individual who cannot cope with this order drops out.

Rebellion is the last of the possible adaptations to the problem of anomie. Here the person responds to his frustrations by replacing the values of the society with new ones. These new values may be political, in which the goals are, for example, the achievement of a socialist society, and the approved means might involve violent revolution. On the other hand these values might be spiritual, in which the goals entail the achievement of certain states of consciousness, and the means involve fasting and meditation. Or the values might be in one of any number of other areas. The basic point is that this person ceases to function as a member of the existing society and begins to live within an alternate culture.

These adaptations do not describe personality types. Rather they describe an individual's choice of behaviors in response to the strain of anomie. Some individuals may consistently choose one adaptation, such as low-level bureaucrats who respond to their situation through ritualism. But the same bureaucrats may occasionally innovate by stealing small amounts from their employers, or they may occasionally retreat through the use of alcohol. Other persons develop patterns of behavior involving the use of several adaptations simultaneously. For example, a professional criminal (innovation) may also consistently use narcotics (retreatism) while at the same time promoting a militant, revolutionary philosophy (rebellion). These behaviors might not be seen as consistent with each other unless it is understood they are all responses to the anomic situation the individual faces.

These same adaptations may be seen in other situations in which there is a discrepancy between the emphasis placed on the goals and the means to achieve them. In athletics, if the goal of winning is overem-

---

13. Ibid., p. 207.

phasized, those who cannot win within the institutionalized means (rules) may be strongly motivated to cheat (innovate), they may merely continue playing without hope of winning (ritualism), they may quit playing altogether (retreatism), or they may attempt to get a different game going (rebellion). Students are often faced with a strong overemphasis of the goal of achieving high grades, and may resort to similar adaptations. Deviant behavior among scientists has been analyzed in terms of an overemphasis on the goal of originality in scientific research.[14] Those who cannot achieve this goal may resort to various adaptive behaviors such as "reporting only the data which support an hypothesis, making false charges of plagiarism, making self-assertive claims, being secretive lest one be forestalled, occasionally stealing ideas, and in rare cases, even fabricating data."[15]

Finally, Merton makes the point that "the foregoing theory of anomie is designed to account for some, not all, forms of deviant behavior customarily described as criminal or delinquent."[16] The intention of the theory is to focus attention on one specific problem, "the acute pressure created by the discrepancy between culturally induced goals and socially structured opportunities," and does not attempt to explain all the diverse behaviors that at one time or another are prohibited by the criminal law.

A number of theorists have attempted to extend and refine Merton's theories. The most significant of these attempts was by Richard Cloward, writing in 1959.[17] Whereas Merton focuses on the fact that lower-class people had limited access to legal means of achieving success goals, Cloward pointed out that these same people often had very broad access to illegal means that existed in their neighborhoods. The local pawn shop, which would fence stolen goods; the junkyard, which would take that hot car off your hands; the numbers racket; and the drug and prostitution rings all provided illegal opportunities to achieve the success goals of society. Cloward also pointed out that the mere presence of an opportunity is not enough unless you have been introduced to the ways of taking advantage of it.[18] This "learning structure" had been described

14. Robert K. Merton, "Priorities in Scientific Discovery: A Chapter in the Sociology of Science," *American Sociological Review* 22: 635–59 (Dec. 1957). See also Harriet Zuckerman, "Deviant Behavior and Social Control in Science," in Edward Sagarin, ed., *Deviance and Social Change*, Sage, Beverly Hills, Calif., 1977, pp. 87–138.

15. Clinard, op. cit., p. 23.

16. Merton, *Social Theory and Social Structure*, p. 195.

17. Richard A. Cloward, "Illegitimate Means, Anomie, and Deviant Behavior," *American Sociological Review* 24: 164–76 (April 1959).

18. Ibid., p. 168.

by Shaw and McKay in their studies of delinquency areas and by Sutherland in his theory that crime is normal, learned behavior; and Cloward regarded his formulation as a consolidation of these three approaches. Merton agreed with Cloward's theory, regarding it as a substantial extension of his own theory.[19]

STRAIN AS THE EXPLANATION OF GANG DELINQUENCY

Merton's reformulation of anomie theory focused on the special strains under which certain segments of the population are placed, and used those strains to explain criminality. This type of argument has also been used in two major theories to explain urban, lower-class, male gang delinquency, one by Albert Cohen and the other by Richard Cloward and Lloyd Ohlin.

In his work with juveniles, Cohen found that most delinquent behavior occurred in gangs rather than individually, and that most of it was "non-utilitarian, malicious, and negativistic."[20] This type of delinquency, in contrast to most adult crime, seemed to serve no useful purpose. Juvenile gangs stole things they did not want or need, vandalized and maliciously destroyed property, and participated in gang wars and unprovoked assaults. Purposeless crimes could not be explained by Merton's theory, which argued that crimes had the purpose of acquiring money, although by illegitimate means. Cohen believed that these actions were methods of gaining status among the delinquent's peers, but then he had to ask why these behaviors were "a claim to status in one group and a degrading blot in another."[21] He concluded that gangs have a separate culture from the dominant culture, with a different set of values for measuring status. The question that Cohen then addressed was why and how this separate culture had evolved.

Merton described people as seeking the cultural goal of success. In a similar way Cohen saw youths as seeking the goal of status among their peers. He utilized the classic distinction between achieved status, which is earned in competition with one's own age and sex group, and ascribed status, which is acquired by virtue of one's family, such as when one's father is an important person. Competition for achieved status normally takes place within the school. Cohen saw the school as a solidly middle-

---

19. Robert K. Merton, "Social Conformity, Deviation and Opportunity Structures: A Comment on the Contributions of Dubin and Cloward," *American Sociological Review* 24: 188 (April 1959).

20. Albert K. Cohen, *Delinquent Boys: The Culture of the Gang*, The Free Press, New York, 1955. For an analysis of the theory and a statement of its major arguments in propositional form, see Bernard, "Testing Structural Strain Theories," op. cit. Merton discusses and analyzes the theory in "Opportunity Structure," op. cit., pp. 33–44.

21. Ibid., p. 27.

class institution, permeated by the values of its middle-class teachers and administrators. Status in school was judged on the basis of such values as ambition, responsibility, achievement (especially in the areas of academic work and athletics), deferred gratification, rationality, courtesy, ability to control physical aggression, constructive use of time, and respect for property.[22]

A youth who has no ascribed status by virtue of his family, and who typically loses in the competition for achieved status, is placed under a severe strain. He can continue to conform to middle-class values, but he must then be content with a low-status position among his peers. Or he can rebel against middle-class values and set up a new value structure according to which he can increase his status and self-worth. Youths who rebel in such a way tend to come together to form a group in order to validate their choices and reinforce their new values. The delinquent gang is such a group. It is a spontaneous development in which a number of youths, each of whom faces a similar problem (low status), together create a common solution to that problem.

Lack of status may affect youths in different social classes, but, like Merton's anomie, it disproportionately affects youths from the lower class. These youths generally have no ascribed status from their families, since their parents normally have low-status occupations. At the same time they are at a disadvantage in competing for achieved status in schools. Lower-class children often have internalized values different from those of middle-class children prior to entering the school. When measured against these values, they perform poorly and must either adjust to these new values or reject them. Thus members of delinquent gangs will generally be lower-class children. And because the gang is primarily rebelling against middle-class values, it takes on the "negativistic" character noticed by Cohen.

Merton's and Cohen's theories differ in several respects. Merton emphasized the utilitarian nature of crime, focusing on innovation as a response to the social structural pressures, whereas Cohen sought to explain the nonutilitarian character of much delinquency. Cohen's theory is similar to the "rebellion" adaptation proposed by Merton, but it differs in that the particular form the rebellion takes is determined by a reaction against middle-class values. In Merton's theory rebellion may take any one of a number of different forms. Finally, Cohen saw the choice of rebellion as linked to the choices of other members of the group, whereas Merton portrayed the choice of an adaptation as an individual response.

22. Ibid., pp. 88–91.

TABLE 11–2   Cloward and Ohlin's Classification of Lower-Class Youth

Categories of Lower-Class Youth	Orientation of Lower-Class Youth	
	Toward Membership in Middle Class	Toward Improvement in Economic Position
Type I	+	+
Type II	+	−
Type III	−	+
Type IV	−	−

Cloward and Ohlin sought to resolve the conflicts between the theories of Merton and Cohen, and also to integrate with these two theories the ideas of the Chicago Ecologists and of Edwin Sutherland.[23] Whereas Merton had argued that lower-class youths strive for monetary success and Cohen that they strive for status, Cloward and Ohlin argued that these were separate strivings which could operate independently of each other. They proposed four categories of lower-class youths, as shown in Table 11–2.[24] Youths who seek an increase in status are seen as striving for membership in the middle class, while other youths seek an improvement in their economic position without seeking to change their class association.

Cohen claimed that most delinquency is committed by boys of Type I and Type II, who are striving to increase their status. Cloward and Ohlin agreed that when pressures toward delinquency arose among these boys, they were likely to be of the type described by Cohen, that is, reactions against the middle-class values in which the boy believes, but with which he is unable to conform due to social structural pressures. But they argue that these boys do not constitute the major group of delinquents, since their values generally are consistent with those of middle-class authorities. Instead, the most serious delinquents are of Type III. These youths are oriented toward conspicuous consumption, "fast cars, fancy clothes, and swell dames," goals that are phrased solely in economic terms and not in terms of middle-class lifestyles. These youths experience the greatest conflict with middle-class values, since they "are looked down upon both for what they do *not* want (i.e., the

23. Richard A. Cloward and Lloyd E. Ohlin, *Delinquency and Opportunity: A Theory of Delinquent Gangs*, The Free Press, New York, 1960. For an analysis of the theory and a statement of its major arguments in propositional form, see Bernard, "Testing Structural Strain Theories," op. cit. Merton discusses and analyzes the theory in "Opportunity Structure," op. cit., pp. 44–71.

24. Reprinted with permission of The Free Press, a Division of Simon & Schuster, from *Delinquency and Opportunity* by Richard A. Cloward and Lloyd Ohlin. © 1960 by The Free Press; copyright renewed 1988 by Richard A. Cloward and Lloyd E. Ohlin.

middle-class style of life) and for what they *do* want (i.e., 'crass materialism').ʺ[25] These are the youths, Cloward and Ohlin claim, who have been repeatedly described in the literature of juvenile delinquency. Finally, Cloward and Ohlin argue that Type IV youths, although they may incur criticism from middle-class authorities for their "lack of ambition," generally stay out of trouble because they tend to avoid middle-class institutions and people as much as possible.

Cloward and Ohlin then refer to the earlier extension of Merton's theory by Cloward to explain the particular form of delinquency that these Type III youths will commit. It is assumed that there are no legitimate opportunities for these youths to improve their economic position. If illegitimate opportunities are presented, as described by Cloward, then these youths will tend to form "criminal" gangs, in which the emphasis is on production of income. If, however, neither legitimate nor illegitimate opportunities are available, then the youths' frustration and discontent will be heightened. In addition, lack of opportunities is often a symptom of a lack of social organization (whether legitimate or illegitimate) in the community, which means there will be fewer controls on the youths' behavior. In this circumstance the youths will tend to form a violent, or "conflict," gang to express their anger. This is the source of the "non-utilitarian, malicious, and negativistic" activity described by Cohen. Finally, Cloward and Ohlin describe a "retreatist subculture" similar to Merton's "retreatist" adaptation and similarly populated with "double failures." Youths in this subculture were unable to achieve the economic improvement they sought, whether because of lack of opportunity or because of internal prohibitions against the use of illegitimate means. They also fail in the resort to conflict and violence. This group turns to alcohol or to drugs, and drops out.

POLICY IMPLICATIONS

During the 1960s, strain theories came to dominate criminology, and eventually had a great impact on federal policy toward crime and delinquency.[26] After Robert Kennedy, who was then attorney general of the

25. Cloward and Ohlin, op. cit, p. 97.

26. For a brief review of the attempt to implement Cloward and Ohlin's ideas in federal policy, see LaMar T. Empey, *American Delinquency*, rev. ed., Dorsey, Homewood, Ill., 1982, pp. 240–45. For more extended accounts, see Peter Maris and Martin Rein, *Dilemmas of Social Reform*, 2nd ed., Aldine, Chicago, 1973; James F. Short, Jr., "The Natural History of an Applied Theory: Differential Opportunity and Mobilization for Youth," in N. J. Demerath, ed., *Social Policy and Sociology*, Academic Press, New York, 1975, pp. 193–210; Joseph J. Helfgot, *Professional Reforming: Mobilization for Youth and the Failure of Social Science*, Heath, Lexington, Mass., 1981; and Stephen M. Rose, *The Betrayal of the Poor: The Transformation of Community Action*, Schenkmann, Cambridge, Mass., 1972.

United States, read Cloward and Ohlin's book, he asked Lloyd Ohlin to help develop a new federal policy on juvenile delinquency. The result was the passage of the Juvenile Delinquency Prevention and Control Act of 1961, which was based on a comprehensive action program developed by Cloward and Ohlin in connection with their book. The program included improving education, creating work opportunities, organizing lower-class communities, and providing services to individuals, gangs, and families. The program was later expanded to include all lower-class people and became the basis of Lyndon Johnson's War on Poverty. Although billions of dollars were spent on these programs, the only clear result seems to have been the massive political resistance that was generated against this attempt to extend opportunities to people without them. The programs, having failed to achieve their goals, were eventually dismantled by Richard Nixon.

Since no genuine extension of opportunities ever took place, this failure might be attributed to the opposition the programs encountered. Rose has offered an alternative interpretation of the failure of these programs.[27] The War on Poverty was based on strain theories, which argue that crime and poverty have their origins in social structural arrangements. Therefore, these theories imply that the solution to the problems of crime and poverty require social structural change. As originally conceived, the War on Poverty was designed to change social structural arrangements, not to change individual people. However, most of these programs were taken over by the bureaucracies of poverty-serving agencies, who immediately acted to protect and enhance their own bureaucratic interests. As a consequence, when the poverty programs were actually implemented, virtually all of them were designed to change poor people, and very few were designed to change social structural arrangements. Rose maintains that the War on Poverty failed because its original purpose was subverted as it was transformed to serve the interests of the established poverty-serving bureaucracies. Thus, he entitles his book *The Betrayal of the Poor*.

THE DECLINE AND RESURGENCE OF STRAIN THEORIES

After the failure of strain-based federal policies of the 1960s, strain theories were subjected to a great deal of scrutiny and to a very large number of criticisms. Some of the criticisms were theoretical, focusing on the adequacy of their terms and concepts, while other criticisms were empirical, focusing on whether the theories are supported by research.

27. Rose, op. cit.

The most extensive criticisms were made by Kornhauser in an influential book published in 1978.[28] She described the central element of "strain" theories as the assertion that stress or frustration causes crime and delinquency. The source of this stress or frustration was said to be the "gap" between what criminals and delinquents want (aspirations) and what they expect to get (expectations). She then argued that strain in this sense is evenly spread throughout society and is not greater among the poor. This is because, no matter how rich people are, they always want more than they can get[29]:

Compare a millionaire with a strong need to make his second million fast to a struggling clerk with a strong need to find a few thousand dollars for a down payment on a house. Whose need is greater? Who is more strained?

She also attacked the cultural arguments in strain theories. For example, she rejected Merton's argument that American culture values the goal of economic success more than the institutionalized means of honesty and hard work.[30] On the one hand, she interpreted the desire for economic succes·, ; a natural desire not requiring cultural supports. On the other hand, she argued that culture itself should be defined in terms of a design for a moral order that is passed as a valued heritage from generation to generation. Defined this way, economic success cannot be a component of any culture. Thus, in her view, American culture does not *value* monetary success. Rather, it values hard work and honesty, but those values are extremely weak and are overwhelmed by the natural desires for economic success. Fi· ally, she reviewed a large number of studies that generally were interpreted as supporting strain theories and concluded instead that they largely contradicted them. For example, she reviewed empirical research on the aspirations and expectations of delinquents and argued that it showed that delinquency is associated with both low expectations and low aspirations.[31] She maintained that such youths would not be "strained" since there is no gap between what they want and what they expect to get. These criticisms were widely accepted in criminology, resulting is a general decline of interest in strain theories.

28. Ruth Rosner Kornhauser, *Social Sources of Delinquency*, University of Chicago Press, Chicago, 1978, pp. 139–80. Some of the basic conceptions were found in an earlier work by Travis Hirschi, *Causes of Delinquency*, University of California Press, Berkeley, 1969, pp. 4–8. However, Hirschi cites a 1963 paper by Kornhauser as the source of those ideas.

29. Kornhauser, op. cit., p. 47.

30. Ibid., pp. 162–65.

31. Kornhauser, op. cit., pp. 167–80.

In 1984, Bernard attacked the validity of Kornhauser's criticisms of strain theories.[32] He argued that strain is not evenly spread throughout society but rather is concentrated in the lower class. He also argued that strain theories should be interpreted primarily as structural rather than cultural theories.[33] To illustrate his argument, Bernard cited Liebow's study of a group of African-American men who regularly met on a particular corner in a blighted area of inner-city Washington, D.C.[34] Liebow argued that the values these men held were not cultural in that they were not passed from generation to generation as a valued heritage. Rather, each man experienced the same failures in jobs, marriages, and life in general; each man generated "public fictions" to defend himself against those failures (e.g., "I got divorced because I was too much of a man for any one woman"); and each man supported the others in maintaining those fictions. It is those public fictions that have been interpreted by sociologists as "lower-class culture." Liebow concluded: "What appears as a dynamic, self-sustaining cultural process is, in part at least, a relatively simple piece of social machinery which turns out, in a rather mechanical fashion, independently produced look-alikes."[35] Bernard argued the strain theories of Merton, Cohen, and Cloward and Ohlin should also be viewed as describing "a relatively simple piece of social mechinery" in which individuals confront socially structured situations that they do not necessarily understand and cannot control. These individuals end up thinking and acting in similar ways, even though each is "independently produced."

Finally, Bernard argued that the studies Kornhauser cited as falsifying strain theories either said nothing about them or actually supported them.[36] For example, Kornhauser cited research showing that delinquents did not have a greater gap between their aspirations and their expectations than nondelinquents. Bernard pointed out that these studies asked youths about aspirations and expectations related to obtaining more education and high status jobs. But Cloward and Ohlin had specifically argued that delinquents do not have such aspirations and instead wanted "fast cars, fancy clothes, and swell dames." Later research by Farnsworth and Leiber found that, when measured in strictly monetary

---

32. Thomas J. Bernard, "Control Criticisms of Strain Theories: An Assessment of Theoretical and Empirical Adequacy," *Journal of Research in Crime and Delinquency* 21(4): 353–72 (Nov. 1984). See also the discussion of Kornhauser on pp. 199–201 of the third edition of this text.

33. Bernard, "Control Criticisms," op. cit., pp. 357–59.

Kornhauser (op. cit.) had favorably cited this study in her critique of strain theories.

34. Elliot Liebow, *Tally's Corner*, Little, Brown, Boston, 1967.

35. Ibid., p. 223.

36. Bernard, "Control Criticisms," op. cit., pp. 359–66.

terms, the gap between aspirations and expectations was associated with delinquency.[37]

Also in 1984, Cullen published a theoretical book that reinterpreted the major strain theories of Merton, Cohen, and Cloward and Ohlin.[38] Cullen argued that Merton actually proposed two different theories— one at the individual level and the other at the societal level. At the individual level, Cullen agreed with Kornhauser that, according to Merton's theory, people in situations of social structural strain would feel frustrated and those feelings would motivate them to act in deviant ways.[39] But Cullen argued that "a variety of social circumstances structure when participation in a form of deviance will be possible." These include societal-level conditions, such as technological advances and historical transformations, that determine the illegitimate opportunities that are available generally at a given time and place; specific illegitimate opportunities that become available to specific people at specific times and places (e.g., the Columbian drug cartel); social psychological factors such as values, norms, and cultural stereotypes in the person's cultural environment; and whether particular kinds of "deviant" actions are defined as criminal at a given time and place (e.g., drug use).[40] Cullen described these as "structuring" variables since they channel the motivated person (i.e., one who is pressured or stressed or strained or frustrated) either toward or away from crime in response to that motivation. These social circumstances, which have nothing to do with stress or frustration, are the central explanatory variables in so-called "strain" theories.[40] Thus, Cullen rejected the word "strain" as characteristic of these theories and substituted the word "structuring."[41]

At the aggregate level, Cullen argued that Merton proposed a separate theory in which criminals are not described as stressed or frustrated at all[42]:

Merton did not maintain that an unregulated individual has to experience any special stress or pressure to become deviant. . . In the place of (the "strained" deviant), Merton substituted a thoroughly classical view of the deviant, argu-

---

37. Margaret Farnsworth and Michael J. Lieber, "Strain Theory Revisited: Economic Goals, Educational Means, and Delinquency," *American Sociological Review* 54: 263–74 (April 1989).

38. Francis T. Cullen, *Rethinking Crime and Deviance Theory: The Emergence of a Structuring Tradition*, Rowman and Allanheld, Totowa, N.J., 1983.

39. Ibid., pp. 36–37.

40. Ibid., pp. 162–66.

41. Francis T. Cullen, "Were Cloward and Ohlin Strain Theorists?" *Journal of Research in Crime and Delinquency* 25(3): 214–41 (1988).

42. Cullen, 1984, pp. 80–82.

ing that the deregulated or anomic actor is free to choose any course of conduct. The only guide to the person's activity is the rational calculation of the costs and benefits of the various means available. Deviant behavior now occurs when illegitimate means are the 'technically most effective procedure' that can be employed to secure a desired end. As Merton has noted, this attenuation of institutional controls creates a "situation erroneously held by the utilitarian philosophers to be typical of society, a situation in which the calculations of personal advantage and fear of punishment are the only regulating agencies."

This "anomie theory" operates at the societal level, linking social structural characteristics to rates and distributions of deviant behavior.

STRAIN IN INDIVIDUALS AND IN SOCIETIES: NEGATIVE EMOTIONS AND INSTITUTIONAL ANOMIE

Cullen's interpretation makes it clear that the term "strain" can be used in two completely different ways. First, it can refer to characteristics of a society: a situation in which the social structure fails to provide legitimate means to achieve what the culture values. Second, it can refer to feelings and emotions that an individual experiences: feelings of stress or frustration or anxiety or depression or anger. The line of argument connecting these two meanings is that people in situations of "social structural strain" (i.e., people who cannot achieve culturally valued goals through legitimate means provided by the social structure) may feel "strained" (i.e., may feel stressed, frustrated, anxious, depressed, and angry), and feelings then are the actual cause of the higher crime rates associated with those people. There is disagreement about whether the original strain theories of Merton, Cohen, and Cloward and Ohlin included this line of argument or not.[43] But regardless of whether they did, new "strain" theories using both types have appeared recently.

At the individual level, Agnew has proposed a "general strain theory" that focuses on negative relationships with others.[44] He argued that these negative relationships generate negative emotions in the person, and the negative emotions then cause crime. This is a general theory of

43. See the interchange between Bernard and Agnew in *Journal of Research in Crime and Delinquency* 24(4): 262–90 (Nov. 1987). Agnew argued that each of the traditional strain theories necessarily contained this individual-level argument. In contrast, Bernard argued that these theories did not make any individual-level argument in which frustration in individuals causes those individuals to commit crime. Related to this disagreement, Merton's most recent statement ("Opportunity Structures, op. cit., p. 9) includes a statement that "the basic point" of theories in the anomie tradition "centers on *rates* of structurally generated and constrained behavior, not on the behavior of this or that individual." See also ibid., p. 27.

44. Robert Agnew, "Foundation for a General Strain Theory of Crime and Delinquency," *Criminology* 30: 47–87 (1992).

crime, but Agnew used it specifically to explain why adolescents engage in delinquency and drug use.

Negative relationships include relationships in which other people prevent a person from achieving a valued goal, take away something valued that the person already has, or impose on the person something that is "noxious" and unwanted. According to Agnew, previous strain theories have focused on relationships in which people were prevented from reaching their valued goals, such as monetary success and status. Agnew, however, focuses on relationships in which the person is presented with a "noxious" situation and is unable to escape from it—i.e., "relationships in which others do not treat the individual as he or she would like to be treated. . ." These can include a wide variety of relationships, but for adolescents they often are associated with living at home and being in school. Unlike adults, adolescents cannot legally leave these relationships if they experience them as "noxious"—if they do, they can be arrested for truancy or running away. These relationships then generate a variety of negative emotions, such as disappointment, depression, fear, and anger. It is these negative emotions that Agnew defines as "strain."

Delinquency and drug use are both ways of coping with and managing the "strain" of these negative emotions. Delinquency may be a way that the adolescents have of achieving their valued goals, of retrieving what is being taken away from them, or of removing themselves from the negative relationship. Alternately, delinquency may be a means for retaliating against those who are the source of the negative relationships. Finally, drug use may be a means of managing the negative emotions directly, rather than addressing the negative relationships themselves. Thus, Agnew explains delinquency and drug use as coping responses to interpersonal problems.

Several tests of Agnew's basic argument have produced largely supportive results, finding that negative relationships and stressful life events were associated with a wide variety of delinquent behaviors.[45] In addition, one study found that delinquent behavior is more successful than nondelinquent behavior as a technique for managing the negative emotions associated with negative relationships.[46] That is, given the

45. Robert Agnew and Helene Raskin White, "An Empirical Test of General Strain Theory," *Criminology* 30: 475–99 (1992); and Raymond Paternoster and Paul Mazerolle, "General Strain Theory and Delinquency: A Replication and Extension," *Journal of Research in Crime and Delinquency* 31: 235–63 (1994). See also two earlier articles by Agnew, "A Revised Strain Theory of Delinquency," *Social Forces* 64: 151–67 (1985); and "A Longitudinal Test of the Revised Strain Theory," *Journal of Quantitative Criminology* 5: 373–87 (1989).

46. Timothy Brezina, "Adapting to Strain: An Examination of Delinquent Coping Responses," *Criminology* 34(1): 39–60 (Feb. 1996).

same level of negative relationships, youths who engage in delinquency experience "modest relief" from the negative emotions compared to youths who obey the law.

At the societal level, Messner and Rosenfeld have presented an "institutional anomie" theory that is similar to Merton's.[47] They explain the high levels of crime in American society by pointing to "the American dream," which they describe as "a broad cultural ethos that entails a commitment to the goal of material success, to be pursued by everyone in society, under conditions of open, individual competition."[48] Like Merton, they argue that this cultural ethos generates intense cultural pressures for monetary success. At the same time, the American Dream does not strongly prohibit people from using more efficient illegal means to achieve monetary success.[49]

Messner and Rosenfeld diverge from and extend Merton's theory in two ways. First, they argue that redistributing legitimate opportunities may actually increase, rather than decrease, the pressures toward criminal behavior unless the culture, with its emphasis on the goal of monetary success at the expense of following the institutional means, also changes.[50] Expanding opportunities may change who wins and who loses in the competition for monetary success, but there will still be losers. People who lose this competition have no one to blame but themselves and their own inadequacies. This may put even more pressure on them to commit crime (i.e., achieve monetary success through illegitimate means) than if they could blame an unfair "system."

A second divergence from Merton's theory involves Messner and Rosenfeld's explanation of the overemphasis on monetary success in American culture. They point to the overwhelming influence of economic institutions in American society, and argue that other institutions, such as families, schools, and even politics, tend to be subservient to the economy[51]:

---

47. Steven F. Messner and Richard Rosenfeld, *Crime and the American Dream*, Wadsworth, Belmont, Calif., 1994. The term "institutional anomie" is taken from Mitchell B. Chamlin and John K. Cochran, "Assessing Messner and Rosenfeld's Institutional Anomie Theory," *Criminology* 33(3): 411–29 (Aug. 1995), which found partial support for the theory. See also the comment by Gary Jensen and reply by Chamlin and Cochran in *Criminology* 34(1): 129–34 (Feb. 1996).

48. Ibid., p. 6. Merton ("Opportunity Structures," op. cit., p. 7) states that the 1938 version of his theory "centers on the interaction between aspirations for upward mobility being normatively defined as legitimate for all—'the American Dream'—*and* on structural differentials in the probability of actually realizing those aspirations. . . ."

49. Messner and Rosenfeld, op. cit., p. 85.

50. Ibid., pp. 99–101.

51. Ibid., pp. 85–86.

The reason that prosocial cultural messages tend to be overwhelmed by the anomic tendencies of the American Dream is because of the dominance of the economy in the institutional balance of power. A primary task for noneconomic institutions such as the family and schools is to inculcate beliefs, values, and commitments other than those of the marketplace. But as these noneconomic institutions are relatively devalued and forced to accommodate to economic considerations, as they are penetrated by economic standards, they are less able to fulfill their distinctive socialization functions successfully.

They therefore propose a number of policies to strengthen these institutions in their relations to the economy, and to weaken the impact of the economy on them.[52] First, Messner and Rosenfeld argue that families in American society are heavily driven by economic concerns, to the extent that the family as a social institution is relatively unable to influence the behavior of its members. Families can be strengthened in their relation to the economy by implementing policies such as family leave, job sharing for husbands and wives, flexible work schedules, and employer-provided child care.[52] These policies provide parents with some freedom from the demands of the economy, and parents then are able to spend more time and energy on family concerns. Schools have become subservient to the economy. Good jobs usually require high school or college degrees, so many students stay in school because they want a good job in the future, and not because they want an education. As teachers respond to this demand from students, the entire educational enterprise tends to become driven by the job market. If job success were less tied to number of years in school, then students who were not really interested in acquiring an education could drop out of school and go to work, and schools then could actually focus on education as a goal. Political institutions also have tended to be subservient to the economy, and Messner and Rosenfeld recommend that other elements of political life be emphasized. For example, the creation of a national service corps would engage young people in the life of the community in ways that emphasize collective goals other than material success. The economy itself could also be modified so as to reduce somewhat its control of individuals. Messner and Rosenfeld point to the mixed economies of Western Europe and Japan, which ensure that a level of material well-being is not totally dependent on economic performance. Finally, at the cultural level, goals other than material success must be given greater prominence in our society, especially activities such as parenting, teaching, and serving the community. In general, Messner and Rosenfeld suggest an increased emphasis on mutual support and col-

52. Ibid., pp. 102–11.

lective obligations in American society, and a decreased emphasis on individual rights, interests, and privileges.

CONCLUSION

Strain theories argue that certain social structural arrangements are associated with higher crime rates. That is, they focus on changing the "relatively simple piece of social machinery" that is producing criminals and delinquents in American society, rather than changing the criminals and delinquents after they have been produced.

The failure of the War on Poverty illustrates that the policy implications of strain theories may be difficult to achieve in the real world. The problem is that patterns of self-interest always develop around existing social structural arrangements.[53] People who benefit from those arrangements protect their self-interests by resisting social change. Messner and Rosenfeld's policy recommendations may be more politically appealing than the policies associated with the War on Poverty because they emphasize strengthening families and schools. To some extent, these policies may appeal to both liberals and conservatives.[54] On the other hand, the thrust of their recommendations is to reduce the overwhelming influence of the economy in American society. The rhetoric in recent elections suggests that economic concerns almost totally dominate the political process, and that government policies are overwhelmingly directed toward promoting economic growth. It does not seem likely that, in the near future, the American people would be willing to compromise economic growth in order to promote "the general welfare."

There is no question that the problems described by strain theories are complex. It is not merely a matter of talented individuals confronted with inferior schools and discriminatory hiring practices. Rather, a good deal of research indicates that many delinquents and criminals are untalented individuals who cannot compete effectively in complex industrial societies.[55] When viewed in the light of that research, strain theories can be interpreted as suggesting that untalented people want many of the same things as talented people but find they cannot obtain these

---

53. Talcott Parsons, *Politics and Social Structure*, The Free Press, New York, 1969, p. 95.

54. Messner and Rosenfeld, op. cit., pp. 101–2.

55. See, for example, Richard J. Herrnstein and Charles Murray, *The Bell Curve*, The Free Press, New York, 1994, for a general argument that America is spinning toward a society radically divided between the talented and the untalented, with the talented totally in control of the economy and the untalented having very high rates of crime. Like Messner and Rosenfeld, Herrnstein and Murray recommend that the dominance of the economy in American society be reduced to prevent a catastrophe.

things through legitimate means. Some of them therefore attempt to obtain those things through criminal activity. From this perspective, strain theories would seem to pose some disturbing questions for public policy. Do untalented people have the same rights as talented people to want material goods, the respect of their peers, and power and control over their own lives? Would society be well-advised to provide untalented as well as talented people with legitimate opportunities to obtain these things? Or is the economy so dominant in American society that we cannot even consider such questions?

CHAPTER 12

Learning Theories

This chapter focuses on the role of normal learning in the generation of criminal behavior. It includes theories about ideas and behaviors that can be learned and that support and encourage law violation. It also includes theories about the processes by which the learning of these ideas and behaviors takes place. Finally, it includes theories about cultures and subcultures that contain ideas supportive of criminal behavior within particular groups.[1]

Learning and cultures played important roles in the strain theories described in the last chapter. Merton, and later Messner and Rosenfeld, linked crime to ideas in the dominant American culture. Cohen described how a separate negativistic subculture arose among gang boys who deliberately inverted the values of the dominant American culture. Cloward pointed out that the mere presence of an opportunity, whether legitimate or illegitimate, was meaningless unless the person also had learned how to take advantage of it. These strain theories, however, focus on the social structural conditions that give rise to the learning of these ideas and behaviors in the first place.[2]

---

1. In the past, these theories were described as "cultural deviance" theories. This term was based on the argument that the cultures themselves could be deviant, and that individuals who conform to such deviant cultures will therefore commit crimes. This term and the interpretation associated with it originated in Ruth Rosner Kornhauser ("Theoretical Issues in the Sociological Study of Juvenile Delinquency," unpublished manuscript, Center for the Study of Law and Society, Berkeley, Calif., 1963; *Social Sources of Delinquency*, University of Chicago Press, Chicago, 1978). The use of this term and the interpretation of the theories associated with it have been extensively criticized. See Ross L. Matsueda, "The Current State of Differential Association Theory," *Crime & Delinquency* 34(3): 277–306 (July 1988); and Thomas J. Bernard and Jeffrey B. Snipes, "Theoretical Integration in Criminology," in Michael Tonry, ed., *Crime and Justice: An Annual Review of Research*, University of Chicago Press, Chicago, 1996, pp. 327–30. For a recent discussion of this issue, see Ronald L. Akers, "Is Differential Association/Social Learning Cultural Deviance Theory," and the response by Travis Hirschi, "Theory Without Ideas: Reply to Akers," in *Criminology* 34(2): 229–56 (May 1996).

2. In particular, see the discussion of Liebow's theory in Chapter 11, p. 171.

In contrast, the learning theories described in this chapter focus on the content of what is learned and the processes by which that learning takes place. Some of these learning theories briefly point to the structural conditions that give rise to the learning in the first place, while others describe those structural conditions more extensively. But in each case, the theories focus on the learning itself rather than on the underlying structural conditions. In that sense, "strain" and "learning" theories are complementary with each other, but they have different emphases.[3]

BASIC PSYCHOLOGICAL APPROACHES TO LEARNING

Learning refers to habits and knowledge that develop as a result of the experiences of the individual in entering and adjusting to the environment.[4] These are to be distinguished from unlearned or instinctual behavior, which in some sense is present in the individual at birth and determined by biology.

One of the oldest formulations about the nature of learning is that we learn by association.[5] Aristotle (384–322 B.C.) argued that all knowledge is acquired through experience and that none is inborn or instinctive. Basic sensory experiences become associated with each other in the mind because they occur in certain relationships to each other as we interact with the object. Aristotle formulated four laws of association that described those relationships: the law of similarity; the law of

3. See the description of structure and process in Ronald Akers, *Deviant Behavior: A Social Learning Approach*, Wadsworth, Belmont, Calif., 1985, p. 66. Bernard and Snipes (op. cit., pp. 332–35) extend Akers's argument.

4. Basic information about learning theories may be found in Gordon H. Bower and Ernest R. Hilgard, *Theories of Learning*, Prentice Hall, Englewood Cliffs, N.J., 1981; Stewart H. Hulse, Howard Egeth, and James Deese, *The Psychology of Learning*, 5th ed., McGraw-Hill, New York, 1980; Robert C. Bolles, *Learning Theory*, 2nd ed., Holt, Rinehart, and Winston, New York, 1979; Winifred F. Hill, *Learning: A Survey of Psychological Interpretations*, 3rd ed., Crowell, New York, 1977. These theories are briefly reviewed in Gwynn Nettler, *Explaining Crime*, 3rd ed., McGraw-Hill, New York, 1984, pp. 296–300.

5. For a detailed account of the development of associationism, see J. R. Anderson and Gordon H. Bower, *Human Associative Memory*, Winston and Sons, Washington, D.C., 1973. Concise accounts can be found in Hulse, Egeth, and Deese, op. cit., pp. 2–4, and Bower and Hilgard, op. cit., pp. 2–4. The major alternative to associationism began with Plato (427?–347 B.C.), who emphasized the rational aspects of human learning. See Bower and Hilgard, op. cit., pp. 4–8; and Hulse, Egeth, and Deese, op. cit., pp. 4–8. Where Aristotle broke complex learning down to its simplest components, Plato argued that the whole was greater than the sum of its parts. He emphasized the inborn capacity of the human mind to organize raw sense data, and his ideas appear in modern times in the form of Gestalt psychology. This school has gained support recently from research on "species-specific" behaviors. See Keller Breland and Marian Breland, "The Misbehavior of Organisms," *American Psychologist* 16: 681–84 (1961); M. E. P. Seligman, "On the Generality of the Laws of Learning," *Psychological Review* 77: 406–18 (1970); J. Garcia and R. Koelling, "Relation of Cue to Consequence in Avoidance Learning," *Psychonomic Science* 4: 123–24 (1966). However, this view has not been applied to crime, so it is not presented here.

contrast; the law of succession in time; and the law of coexistence in space. The most complex ideas, according to Aristotle, are all built out of these simple associations between sensory experiences.

Associationism has been the dominant learning theory through the centuries to the present time. It was elaborated by such philosophers as Hobbes, Locke, and Hume, and was the basis for the first experiments on human memory, carried out by Ebbinhaus,[6] as well as for the first experiments on animal learning, carried out by Thorndike.[7] The *behaviorist* revolution substituted observable stimuli and responses for the mental images and ideas of earlier times, but retained the basic idea that learning is accomplished through association. At the present time a major controversy among learning theorists is between such behavioral theorists and the *cognitive* theorists, who retain the original Aristotelian notion that learning takes place because of the association of ideas and factual knowledge.[8] Where behaviorists argue that we acquire habits through the association of stimuli with responses, cognitive theorists argue that we acquire factual knowledge through the association of memories, ideas, or expectations. Behaviorists argue that learning occurs primarily through trial and error, while cognitive theorists describe learning as taking place through insight into problem solving. Despite these and other controversies between behavioral and cognitive learning theories, both can be traced back to Aristotle's original ideas about association as the basis of learning.

There are three basic ways that individuals learn through association. The simplest way is *classical* conditioning, as originally described by Pavlov. Some stimuli will reliably produce a given response without any prior training of the organism. For example, a dog will consistently salivate when presented with meat. Pavlov consistently presented meat to dogs along with some other stimulus that did not by itself produce the salivation—for example, the sound of a bell. He found that after a few pairings the sound of the bell itself was sufficient to produce salivation in the dog. What Pavlov demonstrated was that behaviors could be learned by association: If the sound of a bell is associated consistently with the presentation of the meat, then the dog learns to salivate at the sound of the bell alone.

In classical conditioning the organism is passive and learns what to expect from the environment. In *operant* conditioning the organism is

6. H. Ebinghaus, *Memory*, Teachers College, New York, 1913; reprinted by Dover, New York, 1964.

7. E. L. Thorndike, "Animal Intelligence," *Psychological Review Monograph Supplement* 2(8): (1898).

8. Bower and Hilgard, op. cit., pp. 15–17.

active and learns how to get what it wants from the environment. Operant conditioning is associated with B. F. Skinner and is now probably the dominant learning theory in psychology. Operant conditioning uses rewards and punishments to reinforce certain behaviors. For example, rats may be taught to press a lever by rewarding that behavior with a food pellet or by punishing with an electric shock its failure to push the lever. The rat learns to operate on its environment by associating rewards and punishments with its own behaviors. Thus operant conditioning is another way of learning by association.

While both classical and operant conditioning are associated with the behaviorist school of learning theory, a third theory describing how people learn by association attempts to combine both operant conditioning and elements from cognitive psychology. Called *social learning* theory, it emphasizes the point that behavior may be reinforced not only through actual rewards and punishments, but also through expectations that are learned by watching what happens to other people. Bandura, for example, argues that "virtually all learning phenomena resulting from direct experiences can occur on a vicarious basis through observation of other persons' behavior and its consequences for them."[9] While classical and operant conditioning are both tested extensively with animal experiments, social learning theory is more focused on human learning, since it directs attention to higher mental processes.

TARDE'S LAWS OF IMITATION

An early criminologist who presented a theory of crime as normal learned behavior was Gabriel Tarde (1843–1904).[10] Tarde rejected Lombroso's theory that crime was caused by biological abnormality, arguing that criminals were primarily normal people who, by accident of birth, were brought up in an atmosphere in which they learned crime as a way of life. He phrased his theory in terms of "laws of imitation," which were similar to Aristotle's laws of learning except that they focused on associations among individuals rather than associations among sensations within one individual. Like Aristotle's original theory, Tarde's theory was essentially a cognitive theory in which the individual was said to learn ideas through the association with other ideas, and behavior was said to follow from those ideas.

9. Albert Bandura, *Principles of Behavior Modification*, Holt, Rinehart, and Winston, New York, 1969, p. 118.

10. The following account is taken from Margaret S. Wilson Vine, "Gabriel Tarde," in Hermann Mannheim, ed., *Pioneers in Criminology*, 2nd ed., Patterson Smith, Montclair, N.J., 1972, pp. 292–304. See also Don Martindale, *The Nature and Types of Sociological Theory*, Houghton Mifflin, Boston, 1960, pp. 305–9; and Jack H. Curtis, "Gabriel Tarde," in Clement S. Mihanovich, ed., *Social Theorists*, Bruce, Milwaukee, 1953, pp. 142–57.

Tarde's first law was that people imitate one another in proportion to how much close contact they have with one another. Thus imitation is most frequent, and changes most rapidly, in cities. Tarde described this as "fashion." In rural areas, in contrast, imitation is less frequent and changes only slowly. Tarde defined that as "custom." Tarde argued that crime begins as a fashion and later becomes a custom, much like any other social phenomenon.

The second law of imitation was that the inferior usually imitates the superior. Trade traced the history of crimes such as vagabondage, drunkenness, and murder, and found that they began as crimes committed by royalty, and later were imitated by all social classes. Similarly, he argued that many crimes originated in large cities, and were then imitated by those in rural areas.

The third law of imitation was that the newer fashions displace the older ones. Tarde argued, for example, that murder by knifings had decreased while murder by shooting increased.

Tarde's theory was important at the time for its role in opposing Lombroso's theories. It retains some importance for us at the present time, since it was the first attempt to describe criminal behavior in terms of normal learning rather than in terms of biological or psychological defects. From this point of view, the major problem with the theory is that it was based on such a simplistic model of learning. This was the state of learning theory at the time that Tarde wrote. A later theory with some elements of the same basic idea—criminal behavior is the result of normal learning—was presented by Sutherland. Although the model of learning on which the theory was based is also relatively simple, Sutherland's theory continues to have a profound impact on criminology.

SUTHERLAND'S DIFFERENTIAL ASSOCIATION THEORY

Edwin H. Sutherland (1883–1950) was born in a small town in Nebraska and received his bachelors degree from Grand Island College there.[11] He taught for several years at a small Baptist college in South Dakota before leaving to obtain his PhD from the University of Chicago. Sutherland's interests were primarily focused on problems of unemployment, and that was the subject of his dissertation. Following his graduation he taught for six years at a small college in Missouri, and then went to the University of Illinois, where his department chair suggested that he write a book on criminology. The result was the first edition of *Criminology*, published in 1924.

11. See George B. Vold, "Edwin Hardin Sutherland: Sociological Criminologist," *American Sociological Review* 16(1): 3–9 (Feb. 1951).

Sutherland's theory of criminal behavior emerged gradually in several editions of this book, as he formulated his thinking on the subject and systematized his presentation of that thinking.[12] He was influenced in this endeavor by a report on criminology written by Jerome Michael and Mortimer J. Adler, which appeared in 1933 and severely criticized the state of criminological theory and research.[13] Sutherland was extremely annoyed by the report, and responded to it by attempting to create a general theory that could organize the many diverse facts known about criminal behavior into some logical arrangement. The first brief statement of that general theory appeared in the second edition of *Criminology*, published in 1934. In the third edition of the book, published in 1939, Sutherland made a more systematic and formal presentation of his theory, and further expanded and clarified it in the fourth edition, appearing in 1947. The theory has remained unchanged since that edition, and consists of the following nine points[14]:

1. Criminal behavior is learned. . . .

2. Criminal behavior is learned in interaction with other persons in a process of communication. . . .

3. The principal part of the learning of criminal behavior occurs within intimate personal groups. . . .

4. When criminal behavior is learned, the learning includes: (a) techniques of committing the crime, which are sometimes very complicated, sometimes very simple; (b) the specific direction of the motives, drives, rationalizations, and attitudes. . . .

5. The specific directions of the motives and drives is learned from definitions of the legal codes as favorable or unfavorable. In some societies an individual is surrounded by persons who invariably define the legal codes as rules to be observed, while in others he is surrounded by persons whose definitions are favorable to the violation of the legal codes. . . .

6. A person becomes delinquent because of an excess of definitions favorable to violation of law over definitions unfavorable to violation of law. This is the principle of differential association. . . .

7. Differential associations may vary in frequency, duration, priority, and in-

---

12. For an account of the development of the theory, see Ross Matsueda, op. cit., pp. 278–84.

13. Jerome Michael and Mortimer J. Adler, *Crime, Law, and Social Science*, Harcourt, Brace, New York, 1933. Sutherland's reaction to this report is discussed in the "Introduction" (by Gilbert Geis) to a reprint edition published by Patterson Smith, Montclair, N.J., 1971. See also Donald R. Cressey, "Fifty Years of Criminology," *Pacific Sociological Review* 22: 457–80 (1979).

14. Edwin H. Sutherland *Criminology*, 4th ed., Lippincott, Philadelphia, 1947, pp. 6–7. The most recent edition is Edwin H. Sutherland, Donald R. Cressey, and David F. Luckenbill, *Principles of Criminology*, 11th ed., General Hall, Dix Hills, N.Y., 1992, where the theory appears on pp. 88–90.

tensity. This means that associations with criminal behavior and also associations with anticriminal behavior vary in those respects. . . .

8. The process of learning criminal behavior by association with criminal and anticriminal patterns involves all of the mechanisms that are involved in any other learning. . . .

9. While criminal behavior is an expression of general needs and values, it is not explained by those general needs and values, since noncriminal behavior is an expression of the same needs and values. Thieves generally steal in order to secure money, but likewise honest laborers work in order to secure money. The attempts by many scholars to explain criminal behavior by general drives and values, such as the happiness principle, striving for social status, the money motive, or frustration, have been, and must continue to be, futile, since they explain lawful behavior as completely as they explain criminal behavior. They are similar to respiration, which is necessary for any behavior, but which does not differentiate criminal from noncriminal behavior.

Sutherland's theory has two basic elements. The *content* of what is learned includes specific techniques for committing crimes; appropriate motives, drives, rationalizations, and attitudes; and more general "definitions favorable to law violation." All these are cognitive elements; that is, they are all ideas rather than behaviors. In addition, the *process* by which the learning takes place involves associations with other people in intimate personal groups. Both elements of Sutherland's theory are derived from "symbolic interactionism," a theory developed by George Herbert Mead (1863–1931), who was on the faculty at the University of Chicago while Sutherland was getting his doctorate there.[15]

Sutherland's description of the content of what is learned was derived from Mead's argument that "human beings act toward things on the basis of the meanings that the things have for them."[16] In Mead's theory a cognitive factor—"meanings"—determines behavior. Mead then argued that people construct relatively permanent "definitions" of their situation out of the meanings they derive from particular experiences.[17] That is, they generalize the meanings they have derived from particular situations, and form a relatively set way of looking at things. It is because of these different "definitions" that different people in similar sit-

---

15. For a review of Mead's thought, see Herbert Blumer, *Symbolic Interactionism*, Prentice Hall, Englewood Cliffs, N.J., 1969. The theory is briefly reviewed in George B. Vold, *Theoretical Criminology*, 2nd ed., prepared by Thomas J. Bernard, Oxford University Press, New York, 1979, pp. 255–58.

16. Blumer, op. cit., pp. 2–3.

17. Cf. W. I. Thomas, *The Unadjusted Girl*, Little, Brown, Boston, 1923, pp. 41–53. For a more recent discussion, see Peter McHugh, *Defining the Situation*, Bobbs-Merrill, Indianapolis, 1968.

uations may act in very different ways. To cite an old example, two brothers may grow up in identical terrible situations but one may become a drug lord while the other becomes a priest. Drawing on this theory, Sutherland argued that the key factor determining whether people violate the law is the meaning they give to the social conditions they experience, rather than the conditions themselves. Ultimately, whether a person obeys or violates the law depends on how they *define* their situation.

Sutherland's description of the process by which definitions are learned was also derived from Mead's theory. Mead had argued that "the meaning of such things is derived from, or arises out of, the social interaction one has with one's fellows."[18] Following Mead's theory, Sutherland argued that the meaning of criminal acts, whether murder or shoplifting, marijuana smoking or income tax evasion, prostitution or embezzlement, arises primarily from the meanings given those acts by other people with whom the individual associates in intimate personal groups. In an attempt to explain why some associations were more important than others for the learning of these definitions, Sutherland also argued that those associations vary in "frequency, duration, priority, and intensity."

Sutherland also discussed the general social conditions underlying the differential association process. In the 1939 version of his theory Sutherland described those general social conditions in terms of *culture conflict*, where that term meant that different groups in a society have different ideas about appropriate ways to behave.[19] *Social disorganization* was then introduced to describe the presence of culture conflict in a society, the term taken from general sociological theories, including the Chicago School of Human Ecology.[20]

In the 1949 and final version of his theory Sutherland rejected the term *social disorganization* and replaced it with the term *differential social organization*. Social disorganization implies that there is an absence of organization. In contrast with that implication, Sutherland argued that there are numerous divergent associations organized around different interests and for different purposes. Under this condition of divergent, differential social organizations, it is inevitable that some of these groups will subscribe to and support criminal patterns of behavior, others will be essentially neutral, and still others will be definitely anticriminal and self-consciously law-abiding.[21]

18. Blumer, op. cit.

19. Sutherland, *Criminology*, 1939 ed., p. 7.

20. Ibid., p. 8.

21. Ibid.

Because of some confusion about the term *culture conflict*, Sutherland's coauthor, Donald R. Cressey, substituted the term *normative conflict* after Sutherland's death. Norms are socially accepted rules about how people are supposed to act in specific situations and circumstances.[22] Normative conflict, then, refers to the situation in which different social groups (i.e., differential social organization) hold different views about appropriate ways to behave in specific situations and circumstances. In making this substitution, Cressey stated that he was clarifying, not changing, the meaning of Sutherland's argument.

Sutherland's theory, then, states that in a situation of differential social organization and normative conflict, differences in behavior, including criminal behaviors, arise because of differential associations. That is really only another way of saying that a person who associates with Methodists is likely to become a Methodist, a person who associates with Republicans is likely to become a Republican, and a person who associates with criminals is likely to become a criminal.

RESEARCH TESTING SUTHERLAND'S THEORY

In Sutherland's theory, crime and delinquency are caused by associating with other people who transmit "definitions" that favor violations of the law. Research testing this theory has tended to focus on the explanation of juvenile delinquency rather than on the explanation of adult criminality. In general, this is because delinquency is largely a group phenomenon in that juveniles are likely to commit crime and delinquency in the company of other juveniles.[23]

While this fact is consistent with Sutherland's theory, it does not in itself demonstrate that delinquency is *caused by* the transmission of "definitions" through associating with other delinquents. It may be, as Sheldon and Eleanor Glueck said, that "birds of a feather flock together"[24]— that is, delinquents may select as friends other youths whose values and behaviors are similar to their own. If that is the case, then delinquency "causes" delinquent friends, but delinquent friends do not cause delinquency. Related to this is the obvious fact that not everyone who associates with criminals and delinquents adopts or follows the criminal pattern. What, then, is the difference in the quality of the associations that

22. Donald R. Cressey, "Culture Conflict, Differential Association, and Normative Conflict," in Marvin E. Wolfgang, ed., *Crime and Culture*, John Wiley, New York, 1968, pp. 43–54.

23. In general, see Albert J. Reiss, Jr., "Co-offender Influences on Criminal Careers," in Alfred Blumstein, Jacqueline Cohen, Jeffrey Roth, and Christy Visher, eds., *Criminal Careers and "Career Criminals,"* vol. 2, National Academy Press, Washington, D.C., 1986, pp. 145–52.

24. Sheldon Glueck and Eleanor T. Glueck, *Unraveling Juvenile Delinquency*, Commonwealth Fund, New York, 1950, p. 164.

in one instance lead to acceptance of "definitions favorable to law violation" but in another leads only to an acquaintance with but not acceptance of them. Sutherland suggested that the "frequency, duration,
priority, and intensity" of associations determined how much impact
they had on a person, and he supported this argument with case histories and with self-appraisal statements by various individuals who had
followed a criminal pattern.[25] Finally, Sheldon Glueck also questioned
whether Sutherland's theory was inherently untestable, asking, "Has
anyone actually counted the number of definitions favourable to violation of law and definitions unfavourable to violation of law, and demonstrated that in the predelinquency experience of the vast majority of
delinquents and criminals, the former exceed the latter?"[26] In 1960,
Sutherland's coauthor Donald Cressey agreed that, at the broadest level,
differential association theory is untestable.[27]

In 1988, however, Matsueda asserted that differential association theory can be tested and that a considerable amount of research supports
it.[28] First, he argued that a variety of studies have found that juveniles
who report having more delinquent friends also report committing more
delinquent acts, and that these studies provide general support for the
theory. Second, Matsueda stated that a number of studies have focused
on the content of definitions favorable to law violation and showed that
these definitions are associated with increased tendencies to engage in
criminal and delinquent behavior. Matsueda says that these definitions
are not "oppositional values that repudiate the legitimacy of the law and
make crimes morally correct."[29] Rather, they are disagreements with
the larger culture about the specific situations in which the laws should
apply. For example, Matsueda describes the legal defenses to crime,
such as self-defense and insanity, as "prototypical definitions favorable
to crime," but states that these are included in the law rather than excluded from it.[30] Third, Matsueda argues that recent advances in statistical techniques have found support for the complex causal structure

25. See, for example, Edwin H. Sutherland, *White Collar Crime*, Dryden, New York, 1949,
pp. 222–56.

26. Sheldon Glueck, "Theory and Fact in Criminology: A Criticism of Differential Association,"
British Journal of Delinquency 7: 92–109 (Oct. 1956).

27. Donald Cressey, "Epidemiology and Individual Conduct," *Pacific Sociological Review* 3: 47–58,
(1960).

28. Matsueda, "The Current State of Differential Association Theory," op. cit., pp. 284–87. See
also James D. Orcutt, "Differential Association and Marijuana Use," *Criminology* 25(2): 341–58
(May 1987).

29. Matsueda, op. cit., p. 296.

30. Ibid., p. 301, fn. 11; see also fn. 6.

in Sutherland's theory, especially involving the ratio of definitions favorable and unfavorable to violating the law.[31]

A great deal of modern theory and research in criminology can be traced to Sutherland's original formulation. Cultural and subcultural theories are based on Sutherland's arguments about normative conflict and focus on the *content* of what is learned. These theories retain the cognitive orientation of Sutherland's original theory and examine the role of ideas in causing criminal behaviors. Other theories, however, focus on the learning *process* that Sutherland described rather than on the content of the ideas that were said to be learned. These theories tend to be associated with the more modern theories of learning, although at least some of them retain Sutherland's emphasis on differential association. These two branches of modern theory and research are presented in the next two sections.

THE CONTENT OF LEARNING: CULTURAL AND SUBCULTURAL THEORIES

In Sutherland's theory the actual causes of criminal behavior are *ideas*— the definitions favorable to law violation. Cultural and subcultural theories also focus on the role of ideas in causing criminal behaviors. These theories, like Sutherland's, may explore the sources of those ideas in general social conditions, but they are characterized by the argument that it is the ideas themselves, rather than the social conditions, that directly cause criminal behavior.[32]

Walter B. Miller presented one such cultural theory, focusing on the explanation of gang delinquency.[33] He argued that the lower class has a separate, identifiable culture distinct from the culture of the middle

---

31. The studies he cites here are Orcutt, op. cit.; Matsueda, "Testing Control Theory and Differential Association," *American Sociological Review* 47: 489–504 (1982); Matsueda and Karen Heimer, "Race, Family Structure, and Delinquency," *American Sociological Review* 52: 826–40 (1988); Elton F. Jackson, Charles R. Tittle, and Mary Jean Burke, "Offense-Specific Models of the Differential Association Process," *Social Problems* 33: 335–56 (1986); and Charles R. Tittle, Mary Jean Burke, and Elton F. Jackson, "Modeling Sutherland's Theory of Differential Association," *Social Forces* 65: 405–32 (1986). More recently, Mark Warr ("Age, Peers, and Delinquency," *Criminology* 31[1]: 17–40 [Feb. 1993]) argued that differential associations can explain the relation between age and crime. In particular, he found support for Sutherland's concept of duration, but argued that it was the recency rather than the priority of delinquent friends that had an impact on delinquent behavior.

32. In contrast, the strain theories of Cohen and of Cloward and Ohlin both use the term *subculture*, but both locate the primary causes of criminal behavior directly in social conditions. There are common thinking patterns that arise among delinquents, but the thinking patterns are not the cause of the criminal behavior. In strain theories, both the thinking patterns and the criminal behaviors are caused by the same social structural forces. See Chapter 11.

33. Walter B. Miller, "Lower Class Culture as a Generating Milieu of Gang Delinquency," *Journal of Social Issues* 14(3): 5–19 (1958).

class, and that this culture has a tradition at least as old as that of the middle class. Where the middle class has "values" such as achievement, the lower class has "focal concerns" that include *trouble* (getting into and staying out of trouble are dominant concerns of lower-class people); *toughness* (masculinity, endurance, strength, etc., are all highly valued); *smartness* (skill at outsmarting the other guy; "street sense" rather than high IQ); *excitement* (the constant search for thrills, as opposed to just "hanging around"); *fate* (the view that most things that happen to people are beyond their control, and nothing can be done about them); and *autonomy* (resentment of authority and rules). Miller described this lower-class culture as a "generating milieu" for gang delinquency because it interacts with several social conditions typically found in poor areas. Lower-class families are frequently headed by females, so that male children do not have a masculine role model in the family. These boys may then acquire an exaggerated sense of masculinity. In addition, crowded conditions in lower-class homes means that the boys tend to hang out on the street, where they form gangs. The delinquent nature of much gang activity is then a rather obvious consequence of the way the boys think, that is, of the lower-class culture and its focal concerns.

A general theory of criminal violence was presented by Wolfgang and Ferracuti, called the "subculture of violence."[34] This theory relied to some extent on Wolfgang's earlier study of homicide in Philadelphia.[35] Wolfgang had found that a significant number of the homicides that occurred among lower-class people seemed to result from very trivial events that took on great importance because of mutually held expectations about how people would behave. Wolfgang interpreted these events in theoretical terms taken from Sutherland's theory[36]:

The significance of a jostle, a slightly derogatory remark, or the appearance of a weapon in the hands of an adversary are stimuli differentially perceived and interpreted by Negroes and whites, males and females. Social expectations of response in particular types of social interaction result in differential "definitions of the situation." A male is usually expected to defend the name or honor of his mother, the virtue of womanhood . . . and to accept no derogation about his race (even from a member of his own race), his age, or his masculinity. Quick resort to physical combat as a measure of daring, courage, or defense of status appears to be a cultural expression, especially for lower socio-economic class males of both races. When such a culture norm response is elicited from

34. Marvin E. Wolfgang and Franco Ferracuti, *The Subculture of Violence*, Sage, Beverly Hills, Calif., 1981.

35. Marvin E. Wolfgang, *Patterns in Criminal Homicide*, University of Pennsylvania Press, Philadelphia, 1958.

36. Ibid., pp. 188–89.

an individual engaged in social interplay with others who harbor the same response mechanism, physical assaults, altercations, and violent domestic quarrels that result in homicide are likely to be common.

Wolfgang and Ferracuti generalized the findings of this and a number of other studies on criminal violence into an overall theory that was designed to explain one type of homicide, the passion crimes that were neither planned intentional killings nor manifestations of extreme mental illness.[37] They described underlying conflicts of values between the dominant culture and this subculture of violence. For example, people in the subculture of violence tend to value honor more highly than people in the dominant culture. On the other hand they tend to value human life less highly. There are also normative conflicts between the subculture of violence and the dominant culture. Those refer to "rules" about what behaviors are expected in response to the trivial jostles or remarks that were the cause of so many homicides. Those norms are backed up with social rewards and punishments: People who do not follow the norms are criticized or ridiculed by other people in the subculture, and those who follow them are admired and respected. These norms take on a certain life of their own, independent of whether they are approved by the individuals who follow them, since the failure to follow the norms may result in the person becoming a victim of the violence. Thus each individual may respond to a situation violently because he or she expects the other individual to respond violently, even if neither person approves of the violence. In this sense the subculture of violence is similar to a wartime situation in which "it is either him or me."[38]

Wolfgang and Ferracuti, like Sutherland, argued that the immediate causes of these passion homicides are ideas—values, norms, and expectations of behavior. Like Sutherland, they agreed that these ideas had originated in general social conditions, and suggested that theories such as those by Cohen, Cloward and Ohlin, or Miller might explain the origin of the subculture. They themselves, however, refused to speculate on how the subculture of violence had arisen.[39] That question was not vital to their theory, since the cause of the violent behaviors was

---

37. Wolfgang and Ferracuti, op. cit., p. 141. The theory itself is presented in seven points on pp. 158–61, and is summarized on pp. 314–16. A similar theoretical approach, focusing on cultural differences in disputatiousness (the tendency to define negative interactions as grievances and to demand reparations for them) and aggressiveness (the tendency to pursue a grievance and to use force to settle the dispute), is presented in David F. Luckenbill and Daniel P. Doyle, "Structural Position and Violence: Developing a Cultural Explanation," *Criminology* 27(3): 419–36 (Aug. 1989).

38. Ibid., p. 156.

39. Ibid., p. 163.

said to be the ideas themselves rather than the social conditions that had generated those ideas in the past. Essentially they argued that the subculture had arisen in the past for specific historical reasons, but that it was transmitted from generation to generation as a set of ideas after those original social conditions had disappeared. Thus their policy recommendations did not require dealing with general social conditions, but only required doing something to break up the patterns of ideas that constituted the subculture of violence. For example, one of their major policy recommendations was to disperse the subculture by scattering low-income housing projects throughout the city rather than concentrating them in inner-city areas.[40] Once the subculture was dispersed, individuals would gradually be assimilated into the dominant culture and the violent behaviors would cease to occur.

The subculture of violence thesis has generated a large amount of additional theory and research, especially with respect to explaining higher levels of violent crime in the American South and among blacks. A number of theorists have argued that there is a Southern subculture of violence that has its historical roots in the exaggerated sense of "honor" among Southern gentlemen, the institutionalized violence associated with maintaining a part of the population in slavery, the defeat at the hands of Northerners in the Civil War, the subsequent economic exploitation of Southern states by the North, and so on.[41] As with Wolfgang and Ferracuti's theory, these studies argue that the subculture of violence arose in the South for a variety of historical reasons, but that it continues now because the ideas are passed from generation to generation, although the conditions that originally gave rise to the ideas no longer exist.[42]

40. Ibid., p. 299.

41. See, for example, S. Hackney, "Southern Violence," in Hugh D. Graham and Ted Robert Gurr, eds., *The History of Violence in America*, Bantam, New York, 1969, pp. 505–27; and R. D. Gastil, "Homicide and a Regional Subculture of Violence," *American Sociological Review* 36: 412–27 (June 1971).

42. Recent research on race, region, and homicide rates has focused this argument considerably. Overall homicide rates are higher in the South than in other regions of the country, but the West has the highest homicide rates for both whites and blacks. See Patrick W. O'Carroll and James A. Mercy, "Regional Variation in Homicide Rates: Why Is the West So Violent," *Violence and Victims* 4: 17–25 (1989); and Gregory S. Kowalski and Thomas A. Petee, "Sunbelt Effects on Homicide Rates," *Sociology and Social Research* 75: 73–79 (1991). This is because blacks have higher homicide rates than whites, and the South has a higher proportion of blacks in the population. But Southern blacks themselves are not more violent than blacks elsewhere in the country. In fact, black homicide rates are lower in the South than in any other region of the country. Thus, there is no "southern subculture of violence" among the black population there. On the other hand, there may be such a subculture among the whites there. Whites in Western states have higher homicide rates than whites in the South, but this is largely due to the high homicide rates for Hispanic whites. Homicide rates for non-Hispanic whites are highest in the South. Thus, if there is a southern subculture of violence, it affects non-Hispanic whites only. See Candice Nelsen, Jay Corzine, and Lin Huff-Corzine, "The Violent West Re-Examined," *Criminology* 32(1): 149–61 (Feb. 1994).

Lynn A. Curtis presented a subcultural theory of violence among American blacks that is essentially an adaptation of Wolfgang and Ferracuti's theory.[43] According to Curtis, "the central impulse mechanism" underlying the subculture of violence is an exaggerated view of "manliness."[44] This is combined with a "brittle defensiveness" that leads to heated standoffs in situations that others would find trivial. Some individuals have good verbal skills and may handle these confrontations without resort to physical force. Others, however, lack verbal skills, and physical violence becomes their only option. This results in a high number of murders and assaults among friends and in families.[45] The same exaggerated view of manliness leads to frequent and almost routine sexual demands on women. Men who have good verbal skills will use words to manipulate women to obtain sex. Others may simply resort to physical force, resulting in a high incidence of rapes.[46]

Curtis's adaptation of Wolfgang and Ferracuti's theory made an important change in the basic theoretical orientation in that he tied the subculture of violence more closely to the general social conditions that generate it. The historical conditions that had a role in forming the black subculture of violence include all the factors involved in forming the Southern subculture of violence, since most blacks in northern cities originally migrated from the South. But Curtis also argued that current social conditions are involved. He included the use of repressive violence by police in black ghettoes and the general absence of legitimate opportunities. Curtis described culture as a key intervening variable between these current social conditions and the behaviors of each individual.[47] Each individual independently experiences these social conditions, and to a certain extent his or her behavior is a direct response to the social conditions. But each individual also learns ideas and interpretations of these conditions from others who face similar conditions, and to a certain extent his or her behavior is a response to those ideas and interpretations.

Thus, Curtis's theory is partly a cultural theory like Wolfgang and Ferracuti's, describing the direct causal impact of ideas on behaviors, and is partly a structural theory like the strain theories presented in the last chapter, describing the direct causal impact of general social conditions on behaviors. Curtis's policy recommendations reflected this double causation. Unlike Wolfgang and Ferracuti, Curtis argued that

43. Lynn A. Curtis, *Violence, Race, and Culture*, Heath, Lexington, Mass., 1975.

44. Ibid., p. 37.

45. Ibid., pp. 49–67.

46. Ibid., pp. 69–86.

47. Ibid., pp. 17–19.

the general social conditions that are responsible for producing the sub-culture of violence must be addressed, in addition to attempts to mod-ify the subculture of violence itself.[48]

Bernard focused even more directly on the structural conditions gen-erating cultural beliefs in his theory of angry aggression.[49] Like Wolf-gang and Ferracuti's theory, his theory attempted to explain extremely violent responses, especially homicides, to trivial conflicts and insults. Bernard's theory was based on biological and psychological research about physiological arousal, which is the body's "fight or flight" response to being threatened.[50] He argued that a large and well-established body of research indicates that people who are chronically aroused will tend to interpret a wider variety of events as threatening and to respond to those events more aggressively than other people. In other words, chron-ically aroused people tend to see threats everywhere and respond to threats more aggressively than other people.

Bernard then argued that poverty, urban environments, and dis-crimination are structural conditions that all result in chronic arousal in the people who experience them. Poor African Americans who live in inner-city areas experience all three of these conditions, so these peo-ple would interpret a wide variety of events as threatening, and would respond to those events with considerable aggression. In addition, these inner-city areas are socially isolated from the rest of society. In that sit-uation, people would tend to see threats from and respond aggressively to other people in the immediate environment, even if those other peo-ple have done nothing threatening. This creates a highly dangerous en-vironment, which further increases everyone's arousal and thus increases everyone's tendency to see threats everywhere and to respond with ag-gression. Social isolation also means that these chronically aroused and highly aggressive people interact mainly with each other. In such a sit-uation, these patterns of thinking (seeing threats everywhere, respond-ing with extreme violence) tend to become subcultural, in the sense that they separate from the structural conditions that originally gave rise to them and are passed from person to person in interpersonal communi-cations. The result is what Bernard calls "the subculture of angry ag-gression."

48. Ibid., pp. 119–23.

49. Thomas J. Bernard, "Angry Aggression among the Truly Disadvantaged," *Criminology* 28(1): 73–96 (Feb. 1990). See also Bernard, "The Intent to Harm," pp. 23–41 in Anna Victoria Wilson, ed., *Homicide: The Victim/Offender Connection*, Anderson, Cincinnati, 1993.

50. See the discussion of the "flight or fight" response in the section on the autonomic nervous system in Chapter 6, p. 81.

Matsueda and his colleagues argued that all subcultural theories should include an account of the structural conditions that give rise to them[51]:

The salience of values, whether subcultural or cultural, is an important link between social structure and individual behavior. . . . Any theory of subcultures that ignores social structure is incomplete and will fail to predict when individuals who have been exposed to the values of the subculture will act on those values. . . Subcultures, then, are intimately tied to structural opportunities. Because structural opportunities affect crime partly through affecting subcultures, any structural explanation of crime that ignores subcultures is incomplete.

THE LEARNING PROCESS: SOCIAL LEARNING THEORY

While cultural and subcultural theories are derived from Sutherland's arguments about the content of what is learned, other theory and research has focused on his description of the learning process. Several authors have maintained Sutherland's view that criminal behavior is normally learned behavior, but have updated the conception of what is involved in "normal learning" to include arguments found in more modern learning theories.[52] In particular, these more recent theories drop Sutherland's argument that the principal part of normal learning takes place in intimate personal groups, although they may retain that as one important source of learning. These theories argue that learning can also take place through direct interactions with the environment, independent of associations with other people, through the principles of operant conditioning. In addition to changing the description of the learning process, the more recent theories also change the description of the content of what is learned. Specifically, these theories switch from Sutherland's original cognitive orientation that only ideas are learned, and adopt the more recent theoretical orientation that behaviors themselves can be directly learned through both operant conditioning and social learning.

The most important such reformulation is by Ronald Akers, in what he describes as "differential reinforcement" or "social learning" theory. In an original article with Burgess, Akers rewrote the principles of dif-

---

51. Ross L. Matsueda, Rosemary Gartner, Irving Piliavin, and Michael Polakowski, "The Prestige of Criminal and Conventional Occupations," *American Sociological Review* 57: 752–70 (Dec. 1992). This is not inconsistent with Sutherland's theory, since he gave a brief account of such structural conditions himself. See Sutherland, *Criminology*, 4th ed., op. cit., pp. 69–75.

52. See Daniel Glaser, "Criminality Theories and Behavioral Images," *American Journal of Sociology* 61: 433–44 (March 1956); and C. R. Jeffery, "Criminal Behavior and Learning Theory," *Journal of Criminal Law, Criminology and Police Science* 56: 294–300 (Sept. 1965).

ferential association into the language of operant conditioning.[53] This reformulation held that "criminal behavior is learned both in nonsocial situations that are reinforcing or discriminative and through that social interaction in which the behavior of other persons is reinforcing or discriminative for criminal behavior."[54] The addition of "nonsocial situations" constitutes a recognition that the environment itself can reinforce criminality, aside from the person's "social interactions" with other individuals. But Burgess and Akers maintain, with Sutherland, that "the principal part of the learning of criminal behavior occurs in those groups which comprise the individual's major source of reinforcement."[55]

Akers later revised and updated this theory, and expanded the principles of operant conditioning to include modeling, or social learning, theory,[56] which argues that a great deal of learning among humans takes place by observing the consequences that behaviors have for other people. Akers's formulation of social learning theory focused on four major concepts.[57] The most important source of social learning, according to Akers, is *differential association*. This refers to the patterns of interactions with others who are the source of definitions that are either favorable or unfavorable to violating the law. Akers retained Sutherland's argument that differential associations vary according to priority, duration, frequency, and intensity, but argued that it includes both the direct transmission of the definitions through interpersonal communication, and the indirect transmission through identification with more distant reference groups. The *definitions* themselves, according to Akers, reflect the meanings one attaches to one's own behavior. "General" definitions reflect overall religious, moral, or ethical beliefs, while "specific" definitions reflect the meanings that one applies to a particular behavior (e.g., smoking marijuana, burglarizing a house, killing the witnesses to an armed robbery). *Differential reinforcement* refers to the actual or anticipated consequences of a given behavior. People do things that they think will result in rewards or will avoid punishments in the future and they don't do things that they think will result in punishments. These rewards and punishments can be social (approval or disapproval by other people) or nonsocial (e.g., getting high or getting sick

53. Robert L. Burgess and Ronald L. Akers, "A Differential Association—Reinforcement Theory of Criminal Behavior," *Social Problems* 14: 128–47 (fall 1968).

54. Ibid., p. 146.

55. Ibid., p. 140.

56. Ronald L. Akers, *Deviant Behavior: A Social Learning Approach*, 3rd ed., Wadsworth, Belmont, Calif., 1985, pp. 39–70.

57. Ronald L. Akers, *Criminological Theories*, Roxbury, Los Angeles, 1994, pp. 94–107. This includes a brief and excellent summary of the theory.

on drugs). Finally, *imitation* involves observing what others do. Whether or not a behavior will be imitated depends on the characteristics of the person being observed, the behavior the person engages in, and the observed consequences of that behavior.

Akers also proposed a specific sequence of events by which the learning of criminal behavior is said to take place.[58] The sequence originates with the differential association of the individual with other individuals who have favorable definitions of criminal behavior, who model criminal behaviors for the person to imitate, and who provide social reinforcements for those behaviors. Thus, the initial participation of the individual in criminal behavior is explained primarily by differential association, definitions, imitation, and social reinforcements. After the person has begun to commit criminal behaviors, differential reinforcements determine whether the behaviors are continued or not. These includes both social and nonsocial reinforcements in the form of the rewards and punishments directly experienced by the individual as a consequence of participating in the criminal behavior, and also the rewards and punishments the person experiences vicariously, by observing the consequences that criminal behavior has for others.

Akers maintains that the social learning process explains the link between social structural conditions and individual behaviors.[59] For example, economic inequality, the modernization process, social disorganization, and social structural strain have all been linked to criminal behavior in Chapters 8, 9, 10, and 11 above. Akers argues that structural conditions such as these affect crime by affecting a person's differential associations, definitions, models, and reinforcements.

Finally, Akers reviews a large volume of research to argue that "almost all research on social learning theory has found strong relationships in the theoretically expected direction. . . . When social learning theory is tested against other theories using the same data collected from the same samples, it is usually found to account for more variance in the dependent variables than the theories with which it is being compared."[60] In particular, he argues that research supports the "typical" sequence in which social learning operates, in which criminal behaviors are acquired through differential associations, definitions, imitation, and social reinforcements, and then are maintained through social and nonsocial reinforcements.

---

58. Ronald L. Akers, Marvin D. Krohn, Lonn Lanza-Kaduce, and Marcia Radosevich, "Social Learning and Deviant Behavior," *American Sociological Review* 44: 636–55 (1979).

59. Ronald L. Akers, "Linking Sociology and Its Specialties," *Social Forces* 71: 1–16 (1992); Akers, *Criminological Theories*, op. cit., pp. 101–2.

60. Akers, *Criminological Theories*, ibid., pp. 102–7.

IMPLICATIONS

Sutherland's theory has had a massive impact on criminology. At the time it was written criminology was dominated by physicians and psychiatrists who searched for the causes of criminal behavior in biological and psychological abnormalities. Sutherland's theory, more than any other, was responsible for the decline of that view and the rise of the view that crime is the result of environmental influences acting on biologically and psychologically normal individuals.

To assess this school of thought it is necessary to distinguish between Sutherland's theory itself and the more modern learning theories that have followed it. To a considerable extent Sutherland's theory was based on an outdated theory of learning. His argument that learning consists entirely in ideas ("definitions") and that the principal part of learning occurs in differential associations in intimate personal groups must be assessed in terms of general research on the nature of human learning. The field of learning theory has its own controversies and to some extent Sutherland's theory, as a cognitive theory, must do its own battle with other cognitive theories and with the more popular behavioral theories. There is no reason to think that Sutherland's theory will emerge triumphant from that battle. Quite to the contrary, there are many reasons to believe that, as a learning theory, Sutherland's theory has virtually no importance whatsoever. Sutherland, after all, was not a learning theorist and was not particularly familiar with the major theory and research on human learning that was going on at the time.[61]

Sutherland's legacy to criminology is not his specific learning theory but his argument that criminal behavior is normal learned behavior. The task Sutherland focused on, and the task still facing criminologists today, is to explore the implications of that argument for criminology. In the first edition of this book Vold argued that the logical implication of Sutherland's theory is that crime must be viewed in the context of political and social conflict[62]:

If criminal behavior, by and large, is the normal behavior of normally responding individuals in situations defined as undesirable, illegal, and therefore criminal, then the basic problem is one of social and political organization and the established values or definitions of what may, and what may not, be per-

---

61. For conflicting reactions to this assertion in an earlier edition of the present book, see Orcutt, op. cit., and Warr, op. cit. It is interesting that at the time Sutherland wrote the final version of differential association theory, he was located at Indiana University, where in a nearby building B. F. Skinner was conducting the experiments that would revolutionize learning theory.

62. George B. Vold, *Theoretical Criminology*, Oxford University Press, New York, 1958, p. 202; see also the 2nd ed. prepared by Thomas J. Bernard, 1979, pp. 247–48. For a similar argument, see Matsueda, op. cit., pp. 298–99.

mitted. Crime, in this sense, is political behavior and the criminal becomes a member of a "minority group" without sufficient public support to dominate and control the police power of the state.

Sutherland seemed to draw a similar implication from his theory. After making the first systematic presentation of the theory in 1939, he turned his attention to white-collar crime and retained that focus until his death.[63] Sutherland argued that white-collar crimes are normal learned behaviors and that there are no essential differences between those behaviors and the behaviors of lower-class criminals when viewed from the perspective of causation. The differences in official crime rates between the upper and lower classes arise because upper-class people have sufficient political power to control the enactment and enforcement of criminal laws. When their normal learned behaviors are socially harmful, these behaviors either are not defined as wrongs at all or are defined as civil wrongs. But when the normal learned behaviors of lower-class people are socially harmful, these behaviors are defined and processed as crimes. Thus, lower-class people end up with high official crime rates, while upper-class people end up with low official crime rates. Further discussion of this implication will be presented in Chapter 15 on conflict criminology.

CONCLUSIONS

Sutherland described criminal behavior as normal learned behavior and went on to make specific assertions about the nature of normal learning. He asserted that normal learning primarily involves the learning of ideas and beliefs in the process of associating with other people. Behaviors, including criminal behaviors, follow from and are a product of those ideas and beliefs.

The adequacy of Sutherland's assertions can only be assessed in the context of general theories and research about human learning. In general, it seems reasonable to conclude that ideas and beliefs learned in association with other people do have a direct causal impact on criminal behaviors. However, criminal behaviors may also be associated with other types of normal learning. More recent learning theories of criminal behavior, such as Akers's social learning theory, retain Sutherland's view that criminal behavior is normal learned behavior but more adequately incorporate modern learning principles in the description of the normal learning process.

63. Edwin H. Sutherland, "White Collar Criminality," *American Sociological Review* 5: 1–12 (Feb. 1940); "Is 'White Collar Crime' Crime?" *American Sociological Review* 10: 132–39 (April 1945); and *White Collar Crime*.

To assert that criminal behavior is directly caused by beliefs does not deny that there are structural sources for beliefs—that is one of the most fundamental propositions in sociology. The question is whether those beliefs attain some life of their own as causes of behavior in general and as causes of criminal behavior in particular. The most reasonable position at the present time seems to be that adopted by Curtis and by Matsueda and his colleagues: that culture functions as a crucial intervening variable between social structure and individual behavior.[64] That is, ideas and beliefs—including "definitions" of behavior, expectations about how to behave in particular situations, social approval or valuation of certain behaviors, and social responses that back up those expected and approved behaviors with rewards and punishments—have a direct causal impact on behavior, independent of their social structural sources.

64. Curtis, op. cit., pp. 17–19; Matsueda, Gartner, Piliavin, and Polakowski, op. cit., pp. 767–68. For the argument that beliefs have no direct causal impact on criminal behavior, see Kornhauser, *Social Sources of Delinquency*, op. cit., pp. 207–10.

CHAPTER 13

Control Theories

Many theories of criminal behavior assume that people naturally obey the law if left to their own devices, and argue that there are special forces—either biological, psychological, or social—that drive people to commit crime. Control theories take the opposite approach. They assume that all people naturally would commit crimes if left to their own devices. The key question, then, is why most people do *not* commit crimes. Control theories answer that question by focusing on special "controlling" forces that restrain the person from committing crimes. These forces break down in certain situations, resulting in crime and other "uncontrolled" behaviors. Thus individuals are said to commit crime because of the weakness of forces restraining them from doing so, not because of the strength of forces driving them to do so.

The control perspective is a broad point of view found in many different theories in biology, psychology, and sociology.[1] This chapter examines a number of recent sociological theories that take the control perspective and are described as control theories. These theories are especially important as explanations of delinquency, since most of the research supporting them has been done with juvenile populations. Control theories, however, may also be used to explain adult criminality.

---

1. For example, Eysenck's biological theory of autonomic nervous system functioning (described in Chapter 6) takes the control perspective, since it describes the conditions under which punishment either inhibits or fails to inhibit the natural drives toward criminal behavior. Aichhorn's psychological theory (described in Chapter 7) argued that most delinquency resulted from unrepressed id forces that were freed because of an inadequate superego. This theory explains the differences in behavior in terms of differences in the controlling forces found in the superego, not differences in the driving forces found in the id. Finally, Durkheim's sociological theory of anomie (see Chapter 9) described the breakdown of social restraints on behaviors that are motivated by unlimited human needs. This theory falls into the control perspective because it describes the driving forces behind criminal behaviors (unlimited human needs) as the same at all times and places, and explains differences in the amount of crime on the basis of differences in the restraining forces (societal restraints).

EARLY CONTROL THEORIES: REISS TO NYE

In 1951 Albert J. Reiss published an article in which he examined a number of factors related to the control perspective to see if they might be used to predict probation revocation among juvenile offenders.[2] Reiss reviewed the official court records of 1,110 white male juvenile probationers between the ages of 11 and 17. He found that probation revocation was more likely when the juvenile was psychiatrically diagnosed as having weak ego or superego controls and when the psychiatrist recommended either intensive psychotherapy in the community or treatment in a closed institution. Reiss argued that such diagnoses and recommendations were based on an assessment of the juvenile's "personal controls"—that is, the ability to refrain from meeting needs in ways that conflicted with the norms and rules of the community. In addition, he found that probation revocation was more likely when juveniles did not regularly attend school, and when they were described as behavior problems by school authorities. Reiss argued that these were a measure of the acceptance or submission of the juvenile to "social controls"—i.e., the control of socially approved institutions.[3]

Reiss's theory influenced later control theories, but his findings in support of that theory were quite weak. A variety of factors related to family and community controls over the juvenile did not predict probation revocation. The strongest associations were found between probation revocation and the diagnoses and recommendations of the psychiatrists. Reiss argued that the failure of personal controls explained both phenomena, thus accepting at face value the theoretical framework of the psychiatrists. But such an explanation is tautological unless it is supported by some additional evidence about the strength or weakness of personal controls.[4] The association of probation revocation with truancy and school problems was much weaker and can be explained from other perspectives besides control theory.

In 1957 Jackson Toby introduced the concept of "stakes in conformity"—i.e., how much a person has to lose when he or she breaks the law.[5] He argued that all youths are tempted to break the law, but

2. Albert J. Reiss, "Delinquency as the Failure of Personal and Social Controls," *American Sociological Review* 16: 196–207 (April 1951).

3. Ibid., p. 206.

4. Cf. Travis Hirschi, *Causes of Delinquency*, University of California Press, Berkeley, 1969, pp. 11 and 198, n. 4.

5. Jackson Toby, "Social Disorganization and Stake in Conformity: Complementary Factors in the Predatory Behavior of Hoodlums," *Journal of Criminal Law, Criminology and Police Science* 48: 12–17 (May–June 1957). A similar concept was presented in a later article by Scott Briar and Irving Piliavin, "Delinquency, Situational Inducements, and Commitment to Conformity," *Social Problems*, summer 1965, pp. 35–45.

some youth risk much more than others when they give in to those temptations. Youths who do well in school not only risk being punished for breaking the law, but they also jeopardize their future careers. Thus they have high "stakes in conformity." In contrast, youths who do poorly in school risk only being punished for their offense, since their future prospects are already dim. Thus they have less to lose when they break the law—i.e., lower "stakes in conformity." Toby also argued that peer support for deviance can develop in communities that have a large number of youths with low stakes in conformity, so that the community develops even higher crime rates than would be expected by considering the stakes in conformity of the individual youths. Conversely, youths in suburbs who have low stakes in conformity normally obtain no support from their peers for delinquency. Thus these youths may be unhappy, but usually do not become delinquent.

Toby focused on how well the youth did in school, but he stated: "In all fairness, it should be remembered that the basis for school adjustment is laid in the home and the community."[6] The following year, F. Ivan Nye published a study that focused on the family as the single most important source of social control for adolescents.[7] He argued that most delinquent behavior was the result of insufficient social control, and that delinquent behavior "caused" by positive factors was relatively rare.[8] *Social control* was used as a broad term that included direct controls imposed by means of restrictions and punishments, internal control exercised through conscience, indirect control related to affectional identification with parents and other noncriminal persons, and the availability of legitimate means to satisfy needs.[9] With respect to the final type of social control, Nye argued that "if all the needs of the individual could be met adequately and without delay, without violating laws, there would be no point in such violation, and a minimum of internal, indirect, and direct control would suffice to secure conformity."

Nye surveyed 780 boys and girls in grades 9 through 12 in three towns in the state of Washington to test the theory. Included in the survey were a wide variety of questions on family life, as well as seven items intended to measure delinquency. Those seven items were: skipped school without a legitimate excuse; defied parents' authority to their face; took things worth less than $2; bought or drank beer, wine, or liquor (including at home); purposely damaged or destroyed public or

6. Ibid., p. 14.
7. F. Ivan Nye, *Family Relationships and Delinquent Behavior*, John Wiley, New York, 1958.
8. Ibid., p. 4.
9. Ibid., p. 5–8.

private property; and had sexual relations with a person of the opposite sex.[10] On the basis of how often they said they had committed these acts since the beginning of grade school, about one fourth of the youths were placed in a "most delinquent" group, and the remainder in a "least delinquent" group.[11]

Nye found that youths in the "most delinquent" group were more likely to be given either complete freedom or no freedom at all, to have larger sums of money available, to be rejecting of their parents and to disapprove of their parents' appearance, to describe their parents as being seldom cheerful and often moody, nervous, irritable, difficult to please, dishonest, and who "took things out" on the youth when things went wrong. Youths whose mothers worked outside the home and who were rejected by their parents were slightly more likely to fall in the "most delinquent" group. In contrast, youths in the "least delinquent" group were significantly more likely to come from families that attended church regularly, did not move often, and were from rural areas. They were likely to be the oldest or only child, from a small family, to have a favorable attitude toward their parents' disciplinary techniques and toward recreation with their parents, to agree with their parents on the importance of a variety of values, to be satisfied with the allocation of money by their parents, and to get information and advice concerning dating and religion from their parents. In all, Nye tested 313 relationships between youths and their parents. He found that 139 of those were consistent with his control theory, 167 were not significant, and only seven were inconsistent with it.[12]

Nye's contribution to the development of control theory was quite significant because of the theory he proposed and because he undertook a broad empirical test of the theory. His findings in support of the theory are impressive, but one can question the extent to which they apply to groups that are normally referred to as delinquents. Nye's sample did not include any youths from large cities, and included only negligible numbers of nonwhite youths or youth with foreign-born parents. Toby pointed out that "the group which Professor Nye calls 'most delinquent' would be considered nondelinquents by many criminologists."[13] Also, because the questionnaire was administered in high schools, the sample would not include any youths age 15 or younger who were more

10. Ibid., pp. 13–14.

11. See ibid., pp. 15–19, and Nye and James F. Short, Jr., "Scaling Delinquent Behavior," *American Sociological Review* 22: 26–31 (June 1957).

12. Nye, *Family Relationships*, p. 155.

13. Jackson Toby, "Review of *Family Relationships and Delinquent Behavior* by F. Ivan Nye," *American Sociological Review* 24: 282–83 (Feb. 1959).

than one year behind in school (they would still be in grade school), or any youths age 16 or over who had legally dropped out of school. Only two behaviors on the questionnaire constituted criminal offenses: taking things worth less than $2 and purposely damaging or destroying public or private property. Thus the results of Nye's study might be interpreted as describing the effect of family relationships on minor delinquent activities among basically nondelinquent youths.

Toby also pointed out that Nye's research apparently assumes that the same causal processes would be involved with more serious delinquents, but that other researchers might very well disagree with the assumption. Finally, Toby noted that a response bias among the youths answering the questionnaire could account for many of Nye's findings. Youths who were more willing to report their delinquent activities may also have been more willing to describe the less desirable aspects of their family life. Other youths may have both underreported their delinquent activities and described their family life in more positive terms. Thus the study would show that better family relationships are associated with fewer delinquent activities. Toby concluded that Nye's results should be interpreted with great caution.

MATZA'S DELINQUENCY AND DRIFT

While the early control theories presented above have been soundly criticized, they provided the basic concepts and framework for the modern control theories of David Matza and Travis Hirschi. Those control theories present a strong challenge to the more common view that juvenile delinquency is caused by special biological, psychological, or social factors.

In *Delinquency and Drift* Matza stated that traditional theories of delinquency emphasize constraint and differentiation: Delinquents are said to be different from nondelinquents in some fundamental way, and that difference constrains them to commit their delinquencies.[14] In some theories the differences are said to be biological or psychological, and the constraint takes the form of compulsion. In other theories the differences are said to be social and the constraint takes the form of commitment to delinquent values. Matza maintained that these theories predicted and explained too much delinquency. Most of the time delinquents are engaged in routine, law-abiding behaviors just like everyone else, but if you believe the picture painted in these theories, delinquents should be committing delinquencies all the time. In addition, these theories cannot account for the fact that most delinquents

14. David Matza, *Delinquency and Drift*, John Wiley, New York, 1964, pp. 1–27.

"age out" of delinquency and settle down to law-abiding lives when they reach late adolescence or early adulthood. The factors that supposedly explained the delinquency are still present (for example, lack of legitimate opportunities), but the delinquency itself disappears.[15]

Matza proposed an alternate image for delinquents that emphasizes freedom and similarity rather than constraint and differentiation. That image was *drift*.[16] Drift is said to occur in areas of the social structure in which control has been loosened, freeing the delinquent to respond to whatever conventional or criminal forces happen to come along. The positive causes of delinquency, then, "may be accidental or unpredictable from the point of view of any theoretical frame of reference, and deflection from the delinquent path may be similarly accidental or unpredictable."[17] Within the context of such an image a theory of delinquency would not attempt to describe its positive causes, but rather would describe "the conditions that make delinquent drift possible and probable," that is, the conditions under which social control is loosened. Matza did not deny that there were "committed" and "compulsive" delinquents, as described by the traditional theories. However, he argued that the vast majority of delinquents were "drifters" who were neither.

Matza's criticism of traditional theories of delinquency focused on the sociological argument that their behaviors are generated by commitment to delinquent values. Matza argued that delinquents portray themselves this way because they are unwilling to appear "chicken."[18] But private interviews reveal that delinquents do not value delinquent behavior itself. Rather, they describe the behavior as morally wrong but argue that there are extenuating circumstances, so that their own delinquent actions are "guiltless."[19] The delinquent's portrayal of these circumstances is similar to, but much broader than, the extenuating circumstances defined in the law relating to intent, accident, self-defense, and insanity. Thus the delinquent does not reject conventional moral values, but "neutralizes" them in a wide variety of circumstances so that he is able to commit delinquent actions and still consider himself guiltless. This *sense of irresponsibility* is reinforced by the ideology of the juvenile court, which declares that juveniles are not responsible for their actions.

15. For a discussion of age and crime, see Chapter 17, pp. 286, 288–89.
16. Matza, op. cit., pp. 27–30.
17. Ibid., p. 29.
18. Ibid., pp. 33–59.
19. Ibid., pp. 59–98.

The sense of irresponsibility is the immediate condition that makes delinquent drift possible, but the delinquent is prepared to accept the sense of irresponsibility by a pervasive *sense of injustice*.[20] Just as the sense of irresponsibility is derived from a broad interpretation of conventional legal standards for extenuating circumstances, so the sense of injustice is derived from a broad interpretation of conventional legal standards for justice. For example, by conventional legal standards of justice it is necessary to prove beyond a reasonable doubt that a given individual has committed a given criminal act. The delinquent uses excessively legalistic standards to argue that "they didn't prove it." Thus he may passionately argue that he was unjustly treated even though he admits that he committed the act.

Once the moral bind of the law has been loosened by the sense of irresponsibility and the sense of injustice, the juvenile is in a state of drift and is then free to choose among a variety of actions, some delinquent, some lawful. At this point Matza suggests that there are some "positive" causes of delinquency in the sense that there are reasons why the juvenile chooses delinquent, as opposed to lawful, behaviors.[21] The juvenile feels that he exercises no control over the circumstances of his life and the destiny awaiting him. In such a mood he moves to make something happen, to experience himself as a cause of events. This mood of desperation provides the motivation to commit new acts of delinquency. Once those actions have been committed, he is motivated to continue committing them because he has learned the moral rationalizations necessary to consider himself guiltless, and because he has learned the technical means to carry out the offenses.

HIRSCHI'S SOCIAL CONTROL THEORY

The theorist who is most closely identified with control theory is Travis Hirschi. In his 1969 book entitled *Causes of Delinquency*, Hirschi argued that it is not necessary to explain the motivation for delinquency, since "we are all animals and thus all naturally capable of committing criminal acts."[22] He then proposed a comprehensive control theory that individuals who were tightly bonded to social groups such as the family, the school, and peers would be less likely to commit delinquent acts.[23] The most important element of the social bond is *attachment—*

---

20. Ibid., pp. 101–77. See also Marvin Krohn and John Stratton, "A Sense of Injustice?" *Criminology* 17(4): 495–504 (Feb. 1980).

21. Matza, op. cit., pp. 181–91. Compare with Hirschi, *Causes of Delinquency*, pp. 33–34.

22. Hirschi, op. cit., p. 31.

23. Ibid., pp. 16–34.

i.e., affection for and sensitivity to others. Attachment is said to be the basic element necessary for the internalization of values and norms, and thus is related to Reiss's conception of personal controls and Nye's conceptions of internal and indirect controls. A second element is *commitment*, the rational investment one has in conventional society and the risk one takes when engaging in deviant behavior. Commitment is similar to what Toby described as a "stake in conformity." The third element is *involvement* in conventional activities. This variable is based on the common sense observation that "idle hands are the devil's workshop," and that being busy restricts opportunities for delinquent activities. The final element of the social bond is *belief*. Matza had argued that delinquents had conventional moral beliefs, but neutralized them with excuses so that they could commit delinquent acts without feeling guilty. Hirschi, in contrast, argued that "there is variation in the extent to which people believe they should obey the rules of society, and, furthermore, that the less a person believes he should obey the rules, the more likely he is to violate them."[24] Thus Matza's theory had emphasized that delinquents are tied to the conventional moral order and must free themselves from it to commit delinquent acts, while Hirschi's theory assumes that they are free from the conventional order to begin with.

Like Nye, Hirschi tested his theory with a self-report survey. The sample consisted of about 4,000 junior and senior high school youths from a county in the San Francisco Bay area. The questionnaire contained a variety of items related to family, school, and peer relations, as well as six items that served as an index of delinquency.[25] Three of those six items referred to stealing (things worth less than $2, things worth between $2 and $50, and things worth more than $50), while the other three asked whether the youth had ever "taken a car for a ride without the owner's permission," "banged up something that did not belong to you on purpose," and "beaten up on anyone or hurt anyone on purpose" (not counting fights with a brother or sister). Youths were given one point for each of the six offenses they reported committing in the last year, regardless of how often they reported committing it.[26] Hirschi also used school records and official police records as data for the study.

Hirschi was particularly concerned to test the adequacy of his theory against theories that argued the motivation for delinquency was to be found in social strain (such as Merton's, Cohen's, or Cloward and

24. Ibid., p. 26.
25. Ibid., p. 54.
26. Ibid., p. 62. This was defined as the "recency" index, and was used throughout the study.

Ohlin's) and theories that explained delinquency in terms of cultural or group influence (such as Sutherland's or Miller's).[27] Each of these three types of theories explains many well-known facts about delinquency such as that delinquents do poorly in school, but each proposes a different chain of causation. Much of Hirschi's book is devoted to testing the different chains of causation found in the three types of theories.

Hirschi reported that, in general, there was no relationship between reported delinquent acts and social class, except that children from the poorest families were slightly more likely to be delinquent.[28] In addition, he found only minimal racial differences in self-reported delinquency, although their official arrest rates were substantially different.[29] Hirschi concluded that these findings were most difficult to reconcile with strain theories, since those were explicitly class-based theories.[30]

Hirschi then analyzed the effects of attachment to parents, schools, and peers on reported delinquent acts. He found that, regardless of race or class, and regardless of the delinquency of their friends, boys who were more closely attached to their parents were less likely to report committing delinquent acts than those who were less closely attached.[31] That finding is consistent with control theory but inconsistent with cultural theories, where attachment to deviant friends or deviant parents would theoretically be associated with increased reporting of delinquency. Hirschi also found that youths who reported more delinquent acts were more likely to have poor verbal scores on the Differential Aptitude Test, to get poor grades in school, to care little about teachers' opinions, to dislike school, and to reject school authority. He argued that these findings are consistent with control theory, since such boys would be free from the controlling forces of schools. However, he argued that they were inconsistent with strain theories such as Cohen's, since the most "strained" youths would be those who did poorly but who continued to care about success in the school. Youths who did poorly and did not care about school success would not be "strained."[32] He

27. Strain theories are reviewed in Chapter 11 of this book, while what Hirschi called "cultural deviance" theories are reviewed in Chapter 12. One of the arguments made in Chapter 12 is that the description of these theories as cultural deviance theories is inaccurate. This argument implies that Hirschi's test is invalid.

28. Hirschi, op. cit., pp. 66–75.

29. Ibid., pp. 75–81.

30. Ibid., pp. 226–27.

31. Ibid., pp. 97, 99.

32. Hirschi admits that his formulation may not adequately test strain because of Cohen's idea of reaction formation: Boys may care about school success, but if they are unable to succeed, they may then deny that they care at all. However, Hirschi argues that such an argument is virtually impossible to falsify; ibid., pp. 124–26.

also found that boys who reported more delinquent acts were less attached to their peers than were boys who reported fewer delinquent acts. Again Hirschi argued that this finding is consistent with control theory, since attachment to peers would be conducive to delinquency only if those peers valued delinquent behavior. However, it is inconsistent with cultural theories, where the assumption is made that the motivation for delinquency is passed through intimate, personal relationships. Hirschi found that association with delinquent companions could increase delinquent behavior, but only when social controls had been weakened. Youths with large stakes in conformity are unlikely to have delinquent friends, and when they do have such friends, they are unlikely to commit delinquent acts themselves. For youths with low stakes in conformity, however, the greater the exposure to "criminal influences," the more delinquent activities the youth reported.[33]

Having examined the effect of attachment on reported delinquent acts, Hirschi examined the effects of the other three elements of his theory. He found that the educational and occupational aspirations of delinquents are lower than nondelinquents, as are the educational and occupational expectations. This finding is consistent with control theory, since youths with low aspirations and low expectations have little commitment to conformity—that is, they risk little by committing delinquent acts. In contrast, the findings are inconsistent with strain theories since, according to those theories, youths with high aspirations but low expectations should be the most strained and therefore the most delinquent. Hirschi found that "the higher the aspiration, the lower the rate of delinquency, regardless of the student's expectations."[34] Hirschi also found that youths who worked, dated, spent time watching TV, reading books, or playing games were more likely to report delinquencies.[35] That finding was the opposite of what was expected from his theory, since these behaviors represent involvement in conventional activities. Hirschi did find, however, that boys who spent less time on homework, reported being bored, spent more time talking to friends, and riding around in cars were more likely to report delinquent acts. These can be considered measures of the lack of involvement in conventional activities. Finally, Hirschi found a strong correlation between reported delinquent activities and agreement with the statement "It is alright to get around the law if you can get away with it."[36] He took this

33. Ibid., pp. 159–61.
34. Ibid., p. 183.
35. Ibid., p. 190.
36. Ibid., pp. 202–3.

to be a measure of the extent to which boys believe they should obey the law. He also found support for the neutralizing beliefs that Matza had described as freeing the delinquent from the moral bind of the law, although he argued that "the assumption that delinquent acts come before the justifying beliefs is the more plausible causal ordering with respect to many of the techniques of neutralization."[37] Finally, Hirschi found no support for a separate lower-class culture as described by Miller. Hirschi found instead that these beliefs are held by academically incompetent youths, whether lower or middle class, and that academically competent youths, whether lower or middle class, held what are often called "middle-class values." Thus he concluded that lower-class values are not cultural in that they are not transmitted as a valued heritage. Rather, they "are available to all members of American society more or less equally; they are accepted or rejected to the extent they are consistent or inconsistent with one's realistic position in that society."[38] Thus Hirschi believes that "the class of the father may be unimportant, but the class of the child most decidedly is not.[39]

ASSESSING SOCIAL CONTROL THEORIES

Social control theories, especially Hirschi's, have generated a large number of empirical studies, many of which have supported the theory.[40] But many of these tests have focused on relatively trivial offenses committed by essentially nondelinquent youths. Both Hirschi's study and Nye's study, as reported above, are of this type. Hirschi admits that some theorists may hold that "delinquents are so obviously underrepresented among those completing the questionnaires that the results need not be taken seriously."[41] However, he argues that including serious delinquents would have made the final relationships even stronger. Such an argument is valid only if the same causal processes are at work for se-

---

37. Ibid., p. 208.

38. Ibid., p. 230.

39. Ibid., p. 82.

40. For a general review of studies, see Kimberly L. Kempf, "The Empirical Status of Hirschi's Control Theory," pp. 143–85 in Freda Adler and William S. Laufer, eds., *New Directions in Criminological Theory: Advances in Criminological Theory*, vol. 4, Transaction Press, New Brunswick, N.J., 1993. However, two more recent longitudinal studies by Robert Agnew have suggested that the effects of control variables may have been overestimated in cross-sectional studies. See "Delinquency: A Longitudinal Test," *Criminology* 23(1): 47–59 (1985); and "A Longitudinal Test of Social Control Theory and Delinquency," *Journal of Research in Crime and Delinquency* 28(2): 126–56 (1991).

41. Hirschi, op. cit., p. 41. See Thomas J. Bernard, "Control Criticisms of Strain Theories," *Journal of Research in Crime and Delinquency* 21(4): 353–72 (Nov. 1984), for an argument that there were few serious delinquents in Hirschi's sample to begin with, and that he lost most of his data on them due to nonresponse.

riously delinquent youths as for basically nondelinquent but "wild" youths. If different processes are at work, then the inclusion of serious delinquents would weaken Hirschi's results. This is the same criticism that Toby raised about Nye's earlier study, and it is consistent with Matza's argument that serious delinquents may not be "drifters," but instead may be committed or compulsive.

A remark in Hirschi's book illustrates the problem. Hirschi found that increased involvement in conventional activities was related to more delinquency, which is the opposite of what his theory predicted[42]:

Something is wrong with our theory. The difficulty, it seems, is that the definition of delinquency used here is not the definition that makes the involvement hypothesis virtually tautological. When Cohen, for example, says the delinquent gang "makes enormous demands upon the boy's time," he is of course not saying that delinquency as here defined takes an enormous amount of the boy's time. In fact, as defined, delinquency requires very little time: *the most delinquent boys in the sample may not have devoted more than a few hours in the course of a year to the acts that define them as delinquent.*

Control theory may adequately explain delinquency in boys who spend only a few hours per year engaged in it, but whether it explains delinquency among the boys that Cohen was talking about is another question entirely.

This problem is related to the control theory assumption that criminal and delinquent behaviors are "naturally motivated," and that there are no outside pressures generating them. It is relatively easy and appealing to think of the trivial offenses in Hirschi's and Nye's studies as being naturally motivated, requiring no other explanation than that they are "fun." But that image is less appealing when one considers the aggressive and violent nature of much serious gang delinquency and adult criminality.

Social control theories ultimately attribute such serious criminality to our innately aggressive and violent animal heritage. But the question of whether humans are inherently peaceful or inherently aggressive has been the subject of debate for over 2,000 years by philosophers, theologians, psychologists, sociologists, anthropologists, and now criminologists.[43] The debate is by no means resolved at the present time, and

42. Hirschi, op. cit., p. 190 (emphasis added). Hirschi (ibid., p. 46) defines delinquency as follows: "Delinquency is defined by acts, the detection of which is thought to result in punishment of the person committing them by agents of the larger society." Under that definition, virtually all youths may be classified as delinquents. Toby ("Review," op. cit.) raised a similar problem with Nye's definition of delinquency.

43. See Thomas J. Bernard, *The Consensus-Conflict Debate: Form and Content in Social Theories*, Columbia University Press, New York, 1983.

to that extent it is not possible to evaluate fully the control theory explanation of crime.

Despite this ongoing debate, there appears to be a growing agreement on a narrower issue that concerns the type of violence and aggression that is defined as serious crime. Even those who hold the view that aggression is an innate human characteristic now also argue that serious criminal behavior represents a degeneration of the aggressive instincts caused by biological or social pathologies.[44] If this view ultimately prevails, then social control theory could only be applied to less serious forms of delinquency and crime.

FROM SOCIAL CONTROL TO SELF-CONTROL: GOTTFREDSON AND HIRSCHI'S GENERAL THEORY OF CRIME

In 1990, Michael Gottfredson and Travis Hirschi published *A General Theory of Crime*,[45] claiming that all types of crime can be explained by "low self-control" coupled with availability of opportunities. "Self-control" is conceived as internal to the individual, whereas "social control," on which Hirschi focused in his 1969 theory, is largely external to the individual. In the new theory, "social controls" are relevant to explaining criminal behavior only to the extent that they influence self-control, which is instilled in individuals by around age 8 and remains relatively constant after that.

Gottfredson and Hirschi first make some assertions about "the characteristics of ordinary crimes": They are said to be acts that involve simple and immediate gratification of desires but few long-term benefits, are exciting and risky but require little skill or planning, and generally produce few benefits for the offender while causing pain and suffering for the victim.[46] Second, they describe the characteristics of people who would commit these kinds of actions: they "will tend to be impulsive, insensitive, physical (as opposed to mental), risk-taking, short-sighted, and nonverbal."[47] These characteristics not only lead them to engage in a variety of "ordinary crimes," but also result in other similarities in behavior—e.g., these people will tend to smoke and drink heavily and to be involved in many accidents.[48] Third, Gottfredson and Hirschi ar-

---

44. Luigi Valzelli, *Psychobiology of Aggression and Violence*, Raven Press, New York, 1981, ch. 4. This view would be consistent with the finding, as discussed in Chapter 11, that research on serious delinquency provides considerable support for the basic contentions of strain theories.

45. Michael Gottfredson and Travis Hirschi, *A General Theory of Crime*, Stanford University Press, Stanford, Calif., 1990.

46. Ibid., pp. 15–44; 89–91.

47. Ibid., pp. 90–91.

48. Ibid., p. 94.

gue[49]: "Since these traits can be identified prior to the age of responsibility for crime, since there is considerable tendency for these traits to come together in the same people, and since the traits tend to persist through life, it seems reasonable to consider them as comprising a stable construct useful in the explanation of crime." They call this stable construct "low self-control." Fourth, Gottfredson and Hirschi argue that ineffective child rearing is the most important contributor to low self-control.[50] Adequate child rearing, which results in high self-control in the child, occurs when the child's behavior is monitored and any deviant behavior is immediately recognized and punished. Essentially, external controls on the child's behavior eventually are internalized by the child in a process described as "socialization." An additional source of socialization, especially important for those who do not receive adequate socialization through their families, is the school.

Gottfredson and Hirschi go on to argue that low self-control explains many of the known relationships between delinquency and other factors. For example, they argue that the relationship between delinquent peers and delinquency is explained by the fact that low self-control juveniles are likely to seek out others with low-self control as a peer group.[51] On the relationship between delinquency and poor school performance, they argue that individuals who lack self-control do not perform well in school and therefore tend to leave or avoid it.[52] Finally, those with low self-control will have difficulties keeping jobs, which explain any relationship between unemployment and criminal behavior.[53]

Gottfredson and Hirschi argue that self-control is relatively constant in the individual after the age of about 8, but they recognize that there may be a great deal of change in the rates at which individuals commit crime.[54] These variations cannot, within their theory, be explained by changes in the person's self-control, since self-control stays constant throughout the person's life. So Gottfredson and Hirschi argue that variations in crime are explained by variation in opportunities for different types of criminal and noncriminal behaviors. For example, in a community with few opportunities for property crime, low self-control people will engage in little property crime but will engage in other sorts of low self-control behavior.

49. Ibid.

50. Ibid., p. 97.

51. Ibid., pp. 157–58.

52. Ibid., pp. 162–63.

53. Ibid., p. 165.

54. The major variation found in individuals is the age-crime curve. For a discussion of Gottfredson and Hirschi's position on this issue, see Chapter 17, pp. 286, 288–89.

One problem area for this theory is found in organized criminal behavior, since it could be argued that organized criminals do not lack self-control. Gottfredson and Hirschi therefore devote a chapter to debunking this argument. In their view, "organized crime" is not really organized, and any apparent organization is short-lived and consists of unstable temporary alliances.[55] Furthermore, they claim that the reason for the failure of many cooperative attempts at criminality is that the individuals involved lack self-control. They discount the importance of organized drug dealing by arguing that for every successful organized effort, there are hundreds of failed efforts.

A General Theory of Crime has generated some heated discussion among criminologists, and has been subjected to several empirical tests. Probably the most sweeping criticism is by Akers, who argues that the theory is tautological.[56] According to Akers, the only way to determine whether people have "low self-control" is to see whether they engage in "low self-control" behaviors, including criminal behavior. If they engage in those behaviors, then the behaviors themselves are said to be explained by the person's "low self-control." Akers argued that, until low self-control is operationalized in terms other than these actions, the theory will remain tautological.[57]

Hirschi and Gottfredson respond[58]:

In our view, the charge of tautology is in fact a compliment; an assertion that we followed the path of logic in producing an internally consistent result. . . . We started with a conception of crime, and from it attempted to *derive* a conception of the offender. . . . What makes our theory *peculiarly* vulnerable to complaints about tautology is that we explicitly show the logical connections between our conception of the actor and the act, whereas many theorists leave this task to those interpreting or testing their theory. . . . In a comparative framework, the charge of tautology suggests that a theory that is nontautological is preferable. But what would such a theory look like? It would advance definitions of crime and of criminals that are independent of one another. . . .

55. Gottfredson and Hirochi, op. cit., p. 213.

56. Ronald Akers, "Self-Control as a General Theory of Crime," *Journal of Quantitative Criminology* 7(2): (1991).

57. This is tautological because other concepts could replace "low self-control" without changing the argument itself. For example, one could argue that these behaviors are "subcultural" instead of "low self-control." Evidence for the existence of the subculture would be found in the behavior of the people who were supposedly in it, but then the behaviors themselves would be explained by the subculture. Control theorists have made this exact criticism against so-called "cultural" theories in criminology, including Akers's theory. See Chapter 12.

58. Hirschi and Gottfredson, "Commentary: Testing the General Theory of Crime," *Journal of Research in Crime and Delinquency* 30(1): 52–53 (1993).

Hirschi and Gottfredson go on to say that Akers misunderstands the concept of low self-control: "We see self-control as the barrier that stands between the actor and the obvious momentary benefits crime provides."[59]

The scope of Hirschi and Gottfredson's theory has also been challenged, particularly their statement that the theory is meant to explain all crimes. Several scholars have questioned whether low self-control can explain white collar crime, for example, although Gottfredson and Hirschi argue it can.[60] Because many wonder whether low self-control by itself can explain such wide variations in different types of crimes, criminologists naturally are interested in how differential opportunity structures may interact with low self-control to produce variations in crime rates. But as Barlow notes, the opportunity part of Gottfredson and Hirschi's theory is insufficiently developed, and does not answer such questions.[61]

There have been several tests of Gottfredson and Hirschi's general theory to date.[62] All have examined linkages between low self-control and criminal acts or analogous behaviors. The studies have used somewhat different ways of measuring low self-control, but typically attempt to operationalize characteristics such as impulsivity, risk seeking, physical activities, self-centeredness, and temper. The behaviors explained by low self-control have included cutting classes, drinking, smoking, gambling, various forms of delinquency and adult criminal behavior, and drunk driving. All these studies have found at least some support for Gottfredson and Hirschi's theory, and some have found fairly strong

---

59. Ibid., p. 53.

60. See Darrell Steffensmeier, "On the Causes of White-Collar Crime: An Assessment of Hirschi and Gottfredson's Claims," *Criminology* 27(2): 345–57 (1989). Although this article was published before Hirschi and Gottfredson's book, it was based on earlier articles that laid the foundation for the book.

61. Hugh Barlow, "Explaining Crimes and Analogous Acts, or the Unrestrained Will Grab at Pleasure Whenever They Can," *Journal of Criminal Law and Criminology"* 82(1): 229–42 (1991).

62. B. J Arneklev, H. G. Grasmick, C. R. Tittle, and R. J. Bursik, Jr., "Low Self-Control and Imprudent Behavior," *Journal of Quantitative Criminology* 9(3): 225–47 (1993); D. Brownfield and A. M. Sorenson, "Self-Control and Juvenile Delinquency: Theoretical Issues and an Empirical Assessment of Selected Elements of a General Theory of Crime," *Deviant Behavior: An Interdisciplinary Journal* 14: 243–64 (1993); Grasmick, Tittle, Bursik, Jr., and Arneklev, "Testing the Core Empirical Implications of Gottfredson and Hirschi's General Theory of Crime," *Journal of Research in Crime and Delinquency* 30(1): 5–29 (1993); C. Keane, P. S. Maxim, and J. J. Teevan, "Drinking and Driving, Self-Control, and Gender: Testing a General Theory of Crime," *Journal of Research in Crime and Delinquency* 30(1): 30–46 (1993); M. Polakowski, "Linking Self- and Social Control with Deviance: Illuminating the Structure Underlying a General Theory of Crime and Its Relation to Deviant Activity," *Journal of Quantitative Criminology* 10(1): 41–78 (1994); P. B. Wood, B. Pfefferbaum, and Arneklev, "Risk-Taking and Self-Control: Social Psychological Correlates of Delinquency," *Journal of Crime and Justice* 16(1): 111–30 (1993); J. Gibbs and D. Giever, "Self-Control and Its Manifestations among University Students: An Empirical Test of Gottfredson and Hirschi's General Theory," *Justice Quarterly* 12(2): 232–55 (1995).

support. However, there have been few attempts to control for alternate explanations from other theories.

None of these tests has examined the link between child-rearing and low self-control as a stable construct in the individual. Perhaps the theory's most controversial component is its argument that self-control is essentially stable by the age of 8 or so, having been determined by child-rearing practices. Until this argument is tested, a general assessment of the theory cannot be made.[63]

The primary advantage of Gottfredson and Hirschi's theory is also its chief point of vulnerability: its simplicity. The idea that a single simple concept can explain the entire range of criminal behavior is quite appealing, and many criminologists are enthused about this possibility. But other criminologists argue that criminal behavior is far too complex to be explained by a single theory, particularly a simple one.

CONCLUSIONS

Social control theories appeal to criminologists for several reasons. First, they provide criminologists with very testable theories. Many other criminological theories, in contrast, are much more difficult to test in that their concepts and variables (like "an excess of definitions favorable to law violation") are very difficult to operationalize. Second, social control theories have been linked from the outset with a new research technique, the self-report survey. That research technique has consistently produced results that support the basic contentions of the theories. The combination of a testable theory with a research technique that produces supportive results is very attractive, to say the least.

A number of criminologists have concluded that social control theories in general, and Hirschi's social control theory in particular, is supported by empirical research.[64] That conclusion, however, does not seem warranted either by general research on human behavior or by specifically criminological research focusing on the explanation of criminal and delinquent behavior. A more restricted but better-supported assessment is that social control theories are generally supported by one type of data—self-report surveys—and that they provide a good explanation of one type of crime, the less serious forms of juvenile delinquency. However, they are not as yet supported by

63. For the view that change does matter, see John H. Laub and Robert J. Sampson, "Turning Points in the Life Course: Why Change Matters to the Study of Crime," *Criminology* 31(3): 301–25 (Aug. 1993). See the discussion of their theory in Chapter 17, pp. 296–98.

64. E. g., William R. Arnold and Terrance M. Brungardt, *Juvenile Misconduct and Delinquency*, Houghton Mifflin, Boston, 1983; Ruth Rosner Kornhauser, *Social Sources of Delinquency*, University of Chicago Press, Chicago, 1978.

studies that focus directly on more serious delinquency or on adult criminality.

Hirschi's new theory, coauthored with Gottfredson, is much broader in its scope, claiming to explain all types of crime, but it has not been as extensively tested because it is so recent. As this testing takes place, we should learn more about the capacity of the control perspective to explain a broader range of criminal and deviant behavior.

CHAPTER 14

The Meaning of Crime

Symbolic interactionism was briefly discussed in Chapter 12 of this book, since it forms the basis of Sutherland's differential association theory.[1] Its key argument is that human actions are best understood in terms of the *meaning* that those actions have for the actors, rather than in terms of preexisting biological, psychological, or social conditions. These meanings are to some extent created by the individual, but primarily they are derived from intimate personal interactions with other people. That is, people first construct meanings in relation to situations they find themselves in, and then they act toward those situations in ways that make sense within the context of their meanings.

Using a general focus on meaning as the key to understanding actions, criminologists in the symbolic interactionist tradition make theoretical arguments in four general areas related to criminology: (1) the effect that defining an individual as a criminal has on that individual's behavior; (2) the meaning of crime to criminals; (3) the processes by which general categories of behavior are defined as crimes in the criminal law and specific people and events are defined as criminal by criminal justice agencies; and (4) the meaning of crime in the context of state power. In each case, the focus is on the meaning that people attribute to crime and criminals, and actions are understood as a product of those meanings.

THE MEANING OF CRIME TO THE SELF: LABELING THEORY

One of the most important "meanings" within symbolic interaction theory is the meaning that people give to themselves—i.e., their self-

---

1. This theory was more extensively summarized in the second edition of this book. See George B. Vold, *Theoretical Criminology*, 2nd ed., prepared by Thomas J. Bernard, Oxford University Press, New York, 1979, pp. 255–58.

image. People may define themselves as handsome, cowardly, kindly, faithful, smart, worthless, or all of the above. They then act toward themselves according to the meanings they have for themselves. Each person's self-image is constructed primarily through interactions with other people. That is what Mead called "the self as a social construct"[2] and what Cooley called "the looking glass self."[3] Cohen describes this point of view well[4]:

We may lay claims to being a certain sort of person, but this claim must make sense in terms of the culture of those we are dealing with, and we must make these claims stick. To lay a claim is to say, in effect: "I am such-and-such a sort of person; I invite you to deal with me on this basis; you may expect certain things of me." To make the claim stick, we must validate it by meeting the cultural criteria of the role. We know we have done this when others, by their responses, indicate acceptance of us as valid specimens of the role. In so doing, we also confirm our conception of ourselves.

One might expect that people who commit criminal behaviors would think of themselves as criminals—that is, have a criminal self-image. In fact, many of them do not. Yochelson and Samenow found that even the most hardened, consistent offenders were unwilling to admit that they were criminals, although they could easily recognize criminality in others.[5] Cameron pointed out that nonprofessional shoplifters often deny that their actions constitute theft, and tend to rationalize their behavior as "merely naughty or bad" or as "reprehensible but not really criminal."[6] Cressey's analysis of embezzlement is quite similar.[7] Embezzlers are people who hold positions of trust and normally conceive of themselves as upstanding citizens. Therefore they must define their actions as "only borrowing the money" before they can proceed. Matza

2. For discussion of Mead's view, see Bernard N. Meltzer, "Mead Social Psychology," in Jerome G. Manis and Bernard N. Meltzer, eds., *Symbolic Interaction*, Allyn and Bacon, Boston, 1967, pp. 9–13. For an application of Mead's theory to the explanation of juvenile delinquency, see Ross L. Matsueda, "Reflected Appraisals, Parental Labeling, and Delinquency: Specifying a Symbolic Interactionist Theory," *American Journal of Sociology* 97: 1577–611, 1992; and Karen Heimer and Ross L. Matsueda, "Role-Taking, Role Commitment, and Delinquency: A Theory of Differential Social Control," *American Sociological Review* 59: 365–90 (June 1994).

3. Charles H. Cooley, *Human Nature and the Social Order*, Charles Scribner's Sons, New York, 1902, pp. 183–85, 196–99, reprinted in Manis and Meltzer, op. cit., pp. 217–19.

4. Albert K. Cohen, *Deviance and Control*, Prentice-Hall, Englewood Cliffs, N.J., 1966, p. 98.

5. Samuel Yochelson and Stanton E. Samenow, *The Criminal Personality*, vol. I, Jason Aronson, New York, 1976, p. 19.

6. Mary Cameron Owen, *The Booster and the Snitch*, The Free Press, New York, 1964, pp. 159, 161, 168.

7. Donald R. Cressey, *Other People's Money: A Study of the Social Psychology of Embezzlement*, The Free Press, Glencoe, Ill., 1953.

and Sykes argue that most juvenile delinquents do not have an overt commitment to delinquent values and do not conceive of themselves as criminals.[8] Their own delinquent behavior contradicts their self-image, and therefore they often justify the behavior by arguing that it is "not really criminal." Five "techniques of neutralization" may be used in this way: denial of responsibility ("It wasn't my fault"); denial of injury ("They can afford it"); denial of victims ("They had it coming"); condemn the condemners ("Everyone is crooked anyway"); and appeal to higher loyalties ("I did it for the gang"). Police who use illegal violence justify it in terms of the need to accomplish their jobs.[9] Illegal activities by government agencies may be justified in terms of "national security." Antiwar activists who committed illegal acts stated that the "real criminals" were the ones who were running the war. And, in general, Chambliss and Seidman state: "It is a truism that every person arrested for crime perceives himself as innocent, for there are always circumstances which to him seem to place his action outside the appropriate definition of the crime."[10]

These examples illustrate the fact that criminal behaviors are frequently committed by persons who do not conceive of themselves as criminals. To maintain a noncriminal self-image, these persons "define the situation" so that they can maintain that their actions are not really crimes. They are then free to continue committing criminal behaviors without changing their self-image.

The maintenance of a noncriminal self-image is very important to most people. Pressure to accept a criminal self-image depends in part on the number of others who define the person as a criminal, and the process of informing others is frequently used as a technique of social control. For example, consider the case of a person who has a noncriminal self-image, but who is caught shoplifting and is brought to the store office. Store officials communicate to the person that "you *are* a shoplifter." This is threatening to the person precisely because the self is constructed in the process of interacting with others, including the store officials. The officials can increase the power of the threat by increasing the number of persons who know about the new identity. The ultimate threat to the identity, however, involves the process of arrest and conviction in which the person is officially declared to be a crimi-

8. Gresham M. Sykes and David Matza, "Techniques of Neutralization: A Theory of Delinquency," *American Sociological Review* 22: 667–70 (Dec. 1957).

9. William A. Westley, "Violence and the Police," *American Journal of Sociology* 59: 34–41 (July 1953).

10. William J. Chambliss and Robert B. Seidman, *Law, Order and Power*, Addison-Wesley, Reading, Mass., 1971, p. 71.

nal in the view of the society at large. From this point of view a criminal trial can be interpreted as a "status degradation ceremony" in which the public identity of the person is lowered on the social scale. Garfinkel maintains that literally every society has such ceremonies as a method of social control, and that the structure of these ceremonies is essentially similar although the societies differ dramatically.[11]

Criminal behavior that occurs in the context of a noncriminal self-image may originate in any number of biological, psychological, or social factors in the person's life. Lemert calls such a person a "primary deviant."[12] But criminal behavior generates a negative social reaction in other people, which attacks the person's noncriminal self-image. If the person is unwilling or unable to stop the criminal behavior, then at some point it may be necessary to reorganize the self-image to incorporate the criminal behavior—that is, to take on a criminal self-image. This may be done as a defense against the attacks of the social reaction, since those who already think of themselves as criminals or as juvenile delinquents are less threatened when other people define them that way. Lemert calls such a person a "secondary deviant."[13] The redefinition of self opens the door to full participation in the criminal life and allows the person to make a commitment to a criminal career. At this point, Lemert argues, criminal behavior is no longer generated by the various biological, psychological, and social factors in the person's life, but is generated directly by the person's criminal self-image.

Criminal justice agencies, as the institutionalized means of social reaction, may play a role in the process by which a person comes to accept a criminal self-image. These agencies "label" people as criminals in formal status degradation ceremonies, as well as in informal interactions. Once applied, Becker has argued, the criminal label overrides other labels, so that other people think of the person primarily as a criminal.[14] Such a person may then be forced into criminal roles because of

11. Harold Garfinkel, "Conditions of Successful Degradation Ceremonies," *American Journal of Sociology* 61(5): 420–24 (March 1965).

12. Edwin M. Lemert, *Human Deviance, Social Problems, and Social Control*, Prentice Hall, Englewood Cliffs, N.J., 1967, pp. 17, 40.

13. Lemert, op. cit., pp. 40–64; also Lemert, *Social Pathology*, McGraw-Hill, New York, 1951, pp. 75–76.

14. Howard S. Becker, *Outsiders—Studies in the Sociology of Deviance*, Free Press of Glencoe, New York, 1963, pp. 32–33. See also Kai T. Erikson, "Notes on the Sociology of Deviance," *Social Problems* 9: 311 (spring 1962). An example would be Ray's argument that a cured heroin addict relapses in part because other people continue to treat him as an addict. See Marsh B. Ray, "The Cycle of Abstinence and Relapse among Heroin Addicts," *Social Problems* 9: 132–40 (fall 1961).

public stereotypes about criminals.[15] For example, on release from prison a person may be unable to obtain legitimate employment due to the criminal conviction and may then return to crime to survive. Finally, those who have been labeled criminal may associate primarily with other people who have been similarly labeled, either because they are all institutionalized together or because other people refuse to associate with them.[16] Membership in an exclusively criminal group can increase the likelihood that individuals will resort to a criminal self-image rather than attempt to retain a noncriminal self-image.

This discussion represents one of the basic arguments of the so-called labeling approach to crime: that the formal and informal processes of social control can have the effect of increasing criminal behavior because the labeling process increases the likelihood that the person will develop a criminal self-image. Several criticisms of the labeling approach should be mentioned. First, labeling theorists sometimes have overemphasized the importance the official labeling process can have. As Akers has remarked[17]:

One sometimes gets the impression from reading this literature that people go about minding their own business, and then—"wham"—bad society comes along and slaps them with a stigmatized label. Forced into the role of deviant the individual has little choice but to be deviant.

Second, labeling theory generally portrays the deviant as resisting the deviant label, and accepting it only when it can no longer be avoided. Although this may be true in some cases, in others it would appear that the deviant identity is actively sought and that the person may form a deviant identity without ever having been officially or unofficially labeled. For example, youths who join a delinquent gang may form a deviant identity centered on their gang activities. Although official labeling may make it harder to change that identity in the future, it would not have pushed the youth into the identity in the first place, and there is no particular reason to believe that failure to label the youth would lead him to seek a law-abiding identity instead.

Third, it is generally recognized that for the typical, law-abiding member of society who has a noncriminal self-image, the labeling or stig-

---

15. Becker, op. cit., pp. 34–35.

16. Ibid., pp. 37–39.

17. Ronald L. Akers, "Problems in the Sociology of Deviance: Social Definitions and Behavior," *Social Forces* 46: 455–65 (1967).

matizing function of the criminal court is the primary technique of social control and is much more important than the actual imposition of punishments.[18] The average citizen is deterred from committing most crimes because he or she fears the conviction itself rather than the punishment associated with it. This is why courts are frequently able to suspend sentence or impose such minor punishments as small fines or unsupervised probation with no loss of effectiveness. Only in cases in which conviction does not hold a stigma—for example, traffic offense cases—do the courts rely heavily on the actual imposition of punishments in the social control of the average citizen. Reducing the stigmatizing or labeling effects of the criminal court could possibly lead to an increase in the incidence of criminal behaviors and to an increase in the imposition of other, harsher punishments for those behaviors. Thus the basic question is not whether the labeling function creates crime, but whether it creates more crime than it eliminates. Although this is a very complicated question to analyze, it seems probable that labeling does not create more crime than it eliminates.[19]

More recently, Matsueda offered a labeling theory of delinquency that focused on the labels applied to juveniles by their parents, rather than by criminal justice agents.[20] He found that delinquency is significantly affected by juveniles' perception that other people think of them as "rule-violators," and that this perception itself is significantly affected by the actual label that parents place on the youth. In a later study, Heimer and Matsueda found that delinquency results largely from the juvenile assuming the role of delinquent, rather than from being labeled a rule-violator by parents.[21] One of the most important factors in taking on this role is the youth's perception that others see him or her as a rule violator, and other factors associated with delinquency tend to operate through the role-taking[22]:

Youths who are from older, nonblack, urban residents, and from nonintact homes commit more initial delinquent acts than others, which increases the chances that their parents will see them as rule-violators. In turn, labeling by parents increases the likelihood that these youths will affiliate with delinquent

18. Franklin E. Zimring and Gordon J. Hawkins, *Deterrence*, University of Chicago Press, Chicago, 1973, pp. 190–94.

19. Charles R. Tittle, "Labelling and Crime: An Empirical Evaluation," in Walter R. Gove, ed., *The Labelling of Deviance—Evaluating a Perspective*, John Wiley, New York, 1975, pp. 181–203.

20. Matsueda, op. cit.

21. Heimer and Matsueda, op. cit.

22. Ibid., pp. 381–82.

peers and see themselves as rule-violators from the standpoint of others, which ultimately increases the likelihood of future delinquent behavior.

Heimer and Matsueda also found that black youths commit fewer initial delinquent acts than nonblack youth but that, controlling for prior delinquency, black youths are more likely to be labeled as "rule violators" by their parents. This then leads to increased views of the self as a rule-violator and increased associations with delinquent peers, both of which increase the likelihood of delinquency in the future. Thus, with black youths, Heimer and Matsueda found some support for the traditional labeling argument that criminal labels are applied to youths who are not especially delinquent, and then those labels generate higher levels of delinquency in the future.

THE MEANING OF CRIME TO THE CRIMINAL: KATZ'S *SEDUCTIONS OF CRIME*

A very different theory based on symbolic interactionism is by Jack Katz in his book *Seductions of Crime*.[23] Katz argues that criminologists have traditionally explained crime in terms of "background" variables such as race, class, gender, urban location, and so on. But he argues that it is far more important to understand the "foreground" variable of what it feels like to commit a crime when you are committing it. Over and over, Katz asks: What are people trying to do when they commit a crime?[24] That is, Katz focuses on the meaning that crime has for the criminal.

Katz looks at a wide variety of sources, including biographies and autobiographies of criminals, journalistic accounts, and participant observation studies, and tries to read into these accounts the real explanation that the criminal has for the criminal behavior. He then applies this technique to five types of crimes: passion murders, adolescent property crime, gang violence, persistent robbery, and cold-blooded murder. In each case, he finds that the criminal is engaged in a "project"—i.e., is trying to accomplish something by committing the crime. That project is primarily moral—i.e., involves right and wrong, justice and injustice. It therefore involves emotions that have strong moral components: humiliation, righteousness, arrogance, ridicule, cynicism, defilement, and vengeance. In each case, the criminal action itself is fundamentally an attempt to transcend a moral challenge faced by the criminal in the immediate situation.

23. Jack Katz, *Seductions of Crime: Moral and Sensual Attractions in Doing Evil*, Basic, New York, 1988.
24. Ibid., p. 9.

The moral challenge faced by the passion killer, Katz finds, is "to escape a situation that is otherwise inexorably humiliating."[25] Rather than accept this humiliation, the killer engages in "righteous slaughter," which the killer interprets as participating in some higher form of good. Adolescents who engage in shoplifting and petty vandalism engage in a melodrama in which "getting away with it" demonstrates personal competence in the face of persistent feelings of incompetence. Adolescents who engage in urban gang violence generally come from poor families who have recently arrived from rural areas, and who therefore are humbled by the rational environment of the city and are deferential to the people who inhabit it. In response to this moral challenge, these adolescents are deliberately irrational in their own actions and arrogantly dominating in relation to other people. They thereby create a "territory" for themselves in the city, both in geographic and in moral terms. Those who persistently engage in robbery must become "hardmen" who take total control of the immediate situation by being willing to back their intentions violently and remorsely.[26] Robbery therefore transcends the total lack of control these robbers experience in the rest of their lives— i.e., they experience their lives as completely out of control or as controlled by the "system." Finally, cold-blooded killers have a pervasive sense of having been defiled by conventional members of society, who for years have treated them as pariahs and outcasts. In their minds, these killers finally exact vengeance for this defilement by "senselessly" killing some of those conventional members of society.

In each case, then, engaging in crime involves transcending a moral challenge and achieving a moral dominance. This moral transcendence produces a "thrill" that is experienced during the actual commission of the crime as sensual, seductive, magic, creative, even compelling. Beyond these "moral and sensual attractions in doing evil," Katz argues that there really are no general explanations for crime and deviance. But Tittle suggests that there may be some further similarities among the different types of crime described by Katz: "All appear to involve efforts to escape control exercised by others or dictated by circumstances, and they all seem to express efforts to impose control back over proximate people and circumstances."[27] According to Tittle, then, Katz's descriptions also suggest that a fundamental meaning of crime for the criminal is to escape the control of others and to impose control on others.

25. Ibid.

26. Ibid., p. 218.

27. Charles R. Tittle, *Control Balance: Toward a General Theory of Deviance*, Westview, Boulder, Col., 1995, p. 279. See also John Braithwaite, "Control Balance and the Sociology of Deviance," forthcoming in *Theoretical Criminology*.

THE MEANING OF CRIME TO THE LARGER SOCIETY: DEVIANCE AND SOCIAL REACTION

Legally speaking, societies "create" crime by passing laws.[28] For example, if criminal laws are passed concerning political contributions or truth in advertising or pollution control, then whole classes of crimes exist where none existed before. If laws against marijuana smoking or homosexuality or public drunkenness are repealed, then whole classes of crimes simply disappear. In every society there are people who kill their spouses if they find them having an affair. Some societies define this as murder, others find it regrettable but understandable, and still others consider it honorable behavior. Thus, whether a particular act is defined and processed as criminal depends on the meaning that act is given by agents of the larger society.

Social reaction theorists view the process of defining actions as crimes as part of the more general process in society of defining and suppressing deviance. Societies define deviance by declaring (either formally or informally) certain human behaviors to be "bad," and then by attempting to minimize or eliminate these behaviors. Because the specific behaviors chosen for this process vary widely from time to time and from place to place, social reaction theorists maintain that the process of defining and suppressing deviance is itself important to social solidarity, independent of the particular behaviors involved.[29] The process works by simplifying the problems of good and evil for the average member of society.[30] Defining the deviants as evil and inferior implies that the remaining members of society are good and superior, thus strengthening their commitment to each other. Combating the evil of deviance consolidates individuals into a tightly knit group and makes it possible for them to use the most ignoble methods to control deviance without questioning these methods. Thus the average member of society is not faced with difficult moral choices, which might undermine a commitment to the path society has taken.

28. See Clayton A. Hartjen, *Crime and Criminalization*, Praeger, New York, 1974, pp. 1–39, for a discussion of this view.

29. This point was originally made by Durkheim in his discussion of "crime as normal." See ch. 9, pp. 126–29. See also Erikson, op. cit.; Erikson, "On the Sociology of Deviance," in *Wayward Puritans*, John Wiley, New York, 1966, pp. 3–19; Nachman Ben-Yehuda, *Deviance and Moral Boundaries: Witchcraft, the Occult, Science Fiction, Deviant Sciences and Scientists*, University of Chicago Press, Chicago, 1985; and Erich Goode and Nachman Ben-Yehuda, *Moral Panics: The Social Construction of Deviance*, Blackwell, Oxford, U.K., 1994. For similar approaches applied to specific types of crimes, see Gary LaFree, *Rape and Criminal Justice: The Social Construction of Sexual Assault*, Wadsworth, Belmont, Calif., 1989; and J. Philip Jenkins, *The Social Construction of Serial Murder*.

30. This description is taken from the description of the benefits of anti-Semitism in J.-P. Sartre, *Anti-Semite and Jew*, Schocken, New York, 1965, as described by Thomas S. Szasz, *The Manufacture of Madness*, Harper & Row, New York, 1970, pp. 270–72.

The behavior of the individual is the normal criterion used to select those who will be defined as deviants in a society, but the process works in exactly the same way when other criteria are used. "Heretical" beliefs have been used as a criterion for selecting deviants in a number of societies, including the early Puritan colonies on Massachusetts Bay.[31] Hitler defined deviance on the basis of race and attempted a "final solution" by exterminating the Jews. Sometimes deviant behaviors are imagined and attributed to particular individuals. For example, in Renaissance Europe approximately one-half million persons were executed as witches,[32] and in the great purge under Stalin, millions of loyal Soviet citizens were declared traitors or saboteurs and were executed or shipped to Siberia.[33] Szasz argues that these all represent various manifestations of a deep-seated need for people to ritually expel evil from their communities, and that in primitive communities this took the form of the ritual destruction of a scapegoat.[34]

Campaigns to define and suppress deviance are always launched in the name of benefiting the whole society, but they are often promoted and supported primarily by those who benefit directly. For example, Chambliss's analysis of the law of vagrancy indicates that it was originally created in England shortly after the Black Death had wiped out approximately 50 percent of the population.[35] The result was a serious labor shortage and a great increase in wages. The vagrancy statute made it a crime to give alms to any person who was unemployed while being of sound mind and body, and required that any such person serve any landowner who needed him at the wage level paid before the Black Death. Up to this time beggars had been common and tolerated in England, and there is little doubt that they were defined as criminals to provide a source of cheap labor for landowners.

Sometimes the benefits of a campaign against deviance are primarily the acquisition of political or bureaucratic power. An example can be found in the campaign to define narcotics users as criminals.[36] In the nineteenth century narcotics were widely available in the form of patent

---

31. Erikson, *Wayward Puritans*, op. cit.

32. Elliott P. Currie, "Crimes Without Criminals: Witchcraft and Its Control in Renaissance Europe," *Law and Society Review* 3(1): 7–32 (Aug. 1968).

33. Walter D. Connor, "The Manufacture of Deviance: The Case of the Soviet Purge, 1936–1938," *American Sociological Review* 37: 403–13 (Aug. 1972).

34. Szasz, *The Manufacture of Madness*, op. cit., pp. 260–75.

35. William J. Chambliss, "A Sociological Analysis of the Law of Vagrancy," *Social Problems* 12(1): 66–77 (fall 1964).

36. Donald T. Dickson, "Bureaucracy and Mortality: An Organizational Perspective on a Moral Crusade," *Social Problems* 16(2): 143–56 (fall 1968). For other examples, see Isadore Silver, ed., *The Crime Control Establishment*, Prentice Hall, Englewood Cliffs, N.J., 1974.

medicines, and addiction was viewed more or less as alcoholism is today—addicts were tolerated and pitied, but not considered criminals. In an attempt to control narcotics distribution, Congress passed the Harrison Narcotics Act in 1914, which required that official records be kept on all sales and distribution of narcotics, and that a nominal tax of one cent per ounce be paid. There is no indication in the law of any legislative intent to restrict or deny addicts access to legal drugs, and the law was passed with little publicity. A narcotics bureau was set up in the Internal Revenue Division of the Treasury Department to enforce the registration procedures and collect the tax. From this tiny beginning the narcotics control bureaucracy promoted its own growth and expansion by launching an extensive public relations campaign against narcotics use and by sponsoring a series of court cases that resulted in the reinterpretation of the Harrison Act so that all narcotics use was declared illegal. As a result of these efforts "The Narcotics Division succeeded in creating a very large criminal class for itself to police . . . instead of the very small one Congress has intended."[37]

Sometimes the benefits of a campaign against deviance are not so much economic as symbolic. Gusfield has analyzed the temperance movement and the resulting enactment of Prohibition as a "symbolic crusade" to reassert the traditional values of rural, middle-class Protestants over the increasing influence of urban, lower-class Catholics in national life.[38] This law created a huge class of criminals by forbidding the manufacture, sale, or transportation of alcoholic beverages, and resulted in the establishment of organized crime syndicates to meet the demand for illegal alcohol. The volume of crime created by this act was so great that it ultimately had to be repealed. Campaigns for and against homosexual rights also can be viewed as symbolic crusades.[39] Opponents of gay rights are asserting traditional moral and religious values regarding sexual behavior. They want homosexuals to be officially recognized as deviants, and want the right to discriminate against them in specific situations, such as when hiring teachers for high schools. Proponents of gay rights are asserting such values as tolerance, liberality, and respect for the rights of minority groups, and are fighting to have discrimination against homosexuals declared illegal. Thus they want official recognition that those who practice such discrimination are deviants, and that homosexuals are not. For homosexuals, the success of their campaign

---

37. Rufus King, "The Narcotics Bureau and the Harrison Act: Jailing the Healers and the Sick," *Yale Law Journal* 62: 736–49 (1953), p. 738, quoted in Dickson, op. cit., p. 151.

38. Joseph Gusfield, *Symbolic Crusade*, University of Illinois Press, Urbana, 1963.

39. See "Battle Over Gay Rights," *Newsweek*, June 6, 1977.

would also lead to practical economic benefits in such areas as housing and employment.

Since campaigns against deviance usually result in the redistribution of benefits from some groups (the deviants) to others (the promoters and supporters of the campaigns), it seems likely that the social solidarity produced depends at least partially on the solidification of power relationships between groups in the society. This is most apparent when two competing groups are attempting to define each other as deviants, as is the case with the "battle for gay rights." One group will succeed in defining the other as deviant only if it is able to generate sufficient power to overcome the support the other group has. This group then obtains the support of the official social control agencies, which normally has the effect of solidifying their power base and institutionalizing their dominance over the other group. In most campaigns against deviance, the role of power is not as apparent because deviants are normally isolated, disorganized, and almost powerless. For example, merchants have traditionally been a powerful group in society, and laws have reflected the maxim "Let the buyer beware." If consumers had been a powerful group instead (and they are now becoming one), the saying might have been "Let the seller beware." Neither approach is inherently more just than the other. The effect of laws has traditionally been to define those who steal from the merchant as dishonest, and to define those from whom the merchant steals as stupid. There is a negative social reaction to both behaviors, but whether this reaction becomes translated into law depends on the relative power of the opposing groups.

Liazos points out that deviance theorists frequently state that those who define others as deviants must be more powerful than the deviants themselves.[40]

But this insight is not developed. In none of the 16 [textbooks in the field of deviance] is there an extensive discussion of how power operates in the designation of deviance. Instead of a study of power, of its concrete uses in modern, corporate America, we are offered rather fascinating explorations into the

---

40. Alexander Liazos, "The Poverty of the Sociology of Deviance: Nuts, Sluts and 'Preverts,' " *Social Problems* 20(1): 103–20 (summer 1972), especially p. 115. Since Liazos made this comment, several books have been published in the area of deviance that focus on power relations. See Pat Lauderdale, ed., *A Political Analysis of Deviance*, University of Minnesota Press, Minneapolis, 1980; and Edwin M. Schur, *The Politics of Deviance: Stigma Contests and the Uses of Power*, Prentice Hall, Englewood Cliffs, N.J., 1980. See also Ruth-Ellen Grimes and Austin Turk, "Labeling in Context: Conflict, Power and Self-Definition," in Marvin D. Krohn and Ronald L. Akers, eds., *Crime, Law, and Sanctions*, Sage, Beverly Hills, Calif., 1978, pp. 39–58; and the readings in H. Laurence Ross, ed., *Law and Deviance*, Sage, Beverly Hills, Calif., 1981.

identities and subcultures of "deviants," and misplaced emphasis on the middle-level agents of social control.

STATE POWER AND THE MEANING OF CRIME: CONTROL-OLOGY

The theories of deviance and social reaction described in the last section began with explaining deviance itself, but increasingly focused on explaining the social reaction to the deviance and the power of the reacting groups to make the deviant definitions stick. One group of theorists took this trend all the way to its logical end point, so that they no longer attempted to explain deviance at all and focused all their attention on the groups who defined other people as deviant. They evolved the view that criminal justice agencies are part of a much broader range of social control mechanisms, including welfare, mental health, education, and the mass media, all of which are used by the state for the purposes of controlling "problem" populations. In 1979, Ditton introduced the term "control-ology" to refer to this group of theories.[41]

The foundation of this group of theories was built by Michel Foucault, a French philosopher.[42] In his work *Madness and Civilization*,[43] Foucault argued that seemingly more humane mental institutions had replaced the apparently more coercive prisons in modern societies as the central instrument of state control. This movement was packaged and sold by the state as a more humane, enlightened, reasonable responses to deviance, but Foucault argued it was actually a way to expand the scope of state control and the subtlety with which that control could be operated.

In his later book *Discipline and Punish*,[44] Foucault expanded his argument by focusing on the earlier development of prisons in the 1700s. Foucault argued that prisons arose at that time to replace a vast system of torture and execution, in which state power was manifested primarily through public spectacles in which havoc was wreaked on the body of the condemned person. That system of torture and execution did not include extensive safeguards, such as we have today, to ensure that these punishments were not carried out on innocent people. The fundamental idea, according to Foucault, was not specifically to punish or deter

---

41. Jason Ditton, *Controlology: Beyond the New Criminology*, Macmillan, London, 1979.

42. These comments are based on Erich Goode, *Deviant Behavior* 4th ed., Prentice Hall, Englewood Cliffs, N.J., 1994, pp. 132–38.

43. Michel Foucault, *Madness and Civilization: A History of Insanity in the Age of Reason*, Mentor, New York, 1967.

44. Michel Foucault, *Discipline and Punish*, Vintage, New York, 1979.

criminals, but to manifest state power. If it turned out that the person was innocent, it only demonstrated that state power was absolute and that no one was safe from it.

But for a variety of reasons, in the 1700s, this type of exhibition of state power began to cause problems. In particular, instead of making the crowds docile and afraid, these public spectacles became the occasion for riots against the arbitrary injustice of the state. Therefore, the state transformed the way it exerted its control over the people. Instead of public spectacles, the infliction of punishments was moved behind high walls, hidden from public view. Instead of being directed at the body of the offender through physical torture and execution, state control was redefined as "rehabilitation" and directed at the souls and minds of offenders.

This constituted a shift in the direction of the looking. Under the old system of torture and execution, the state put on a spectacle with the body of the accused, at which the crowd looked. The crowd then went away with a knowledge of the massive, overwhelming power of the state. Under the new system of imprisonment, the state prevented the crowd from seeing anything with its high walls. At the same time, the state looked into the soul of the prisoner, discovered the evil and sickness that was lurking there, and rooted it out.

Garland later criticized Foucault's analysis for having a great many historical inaccuracies,[45] but the themes that Foucault identified persisted nevertheless in a broad range of works, including Garland's. Goode identified these themes as follows.[46] First, social control itself, and state control in particular, is an important topic for scientific theory and research. It is not sufficient to say, as many people do, that the state's efforts to control deviants are appropriate and functional and natural and should be viewed as a given in every society. Second, the state attempts to maintain its legitimacy by packaging its control efforts so that they appear to be reasonable, humane, and necessary. But always hidden within this "velvet glove" is an iron fist whose ultimate goal is to control troublesome populations. In particular, there are always specific groups who pursue their own economic and political agendas in the context of these social control functions, usually at the expense of other, less powerful groups. Third, the broad range of social control activities all ultimately are directed and manipulated by the state, even when some aspects of them, such as the mass media, are technically

45. David Garland, *Punishment and Welfare: A History of Penal Strategies*, Gower, Aldershott, England, 1985.

46. Goode, op. cit., pp. 134–36.

outside state jurisdiction. Fourth, these various state control mechanisms therefore have a general unity, despite their appearance of diversity. That is, ultimately all the various state control mechanisms mentioned above work in a coherent way to achieve a widespread control over the entire society.

In some ways, contrologists have more in common with the Marxist criminologists who will be discussed below in Chapter 16. On the other hand, beginning with Foucault, these theorists have focused very strongly on the meaning that criminals and deviants have for the dominant groups who exert state control over them, and the meaning of the diverse actions that these dominant groups take to control these troublesome people. This leads them to focus heavily on the thinking and words of the dominant groups—what control-ologists call the "universe of discourse."[47] And in many ways, their thinking originated in the social reaction argument that those who define others as deviant must have more power than the deviants themselves, and that they may not be doing this for the benefit of society generally but rather for the benefit of themselves personally. In that sense, these theorists more appropriately are placed in this chapter rather than in the chapter on critical criminology.

IMPLICATIONS AND CONCLUSIONS

Theories that focus on the meaning of crime seem inevitably to end up discussing the issue of power. Even Tittle's comment on Katz's work suggests that issues of power are embedded in this type of explanation, even if they are not explicitly brought out. The "control-ologists" described in the previous section most directly focus on the relative power of deviants and the groups who define them as such. On the other hand, they do so in the context of a fairly Marxist orientation that focuses strongly on the state and its subservience to economically powerful groups.

A more general approach to the role of power in the definition of crime would simply argue that the general concept of social reaction combines and confuses two separate phenomena: the official reaction of the social control agencies and the personal reaction of particular individuals and groups in society. Individuals and groups construct behavioral norms based on their own moral values and personal self-interests, and react to specific behaviors as deviant when those behaviors violate their norms. These individuals and groups then compete among themselves in an attempt to have their norms enforced by the official

47. Ibid., p. 134.

social control agencies. Their success in this competition depends directly on the degree of power they possess and are willing to use. Official policies are the result of the conflict and compromise process among these groups. To the extent that the group is successful in having its norms enforced by the social control agencies, it arrogates to itself the right to speak in the name of the entire society. But the mere fact that one group has sufficient power to define another group as deviant does not imply that there is any broad consensus on the matter (there may or may not be) and does not preclude the possibility that the other group may be able to reverse the power distribution in the future. This is the approach taken in conflict criminology, which is the subject of the next chapter.

CHAPTER 15

Conflict Criminology

Throughout the long history of thinking about human societies, social theorists have repeatedly presented two contrasting views that have very different implications for criminology.[1] In the *consensus* view, society is said to be based on a consensus of values among its members, and the state is said to be organized to protect the general public interest. To the extent that societies are composed of groups with conflicting values and interests, the organized state is said to mediate between these conflicting groups and to represent the values and interests of society at large. The contrasting *conflict* view has a history as long as that of the consensus view and is also based on the argument that societies are composed of groups with conflicting values and interests. However, the organized state is not said to represent the values and interests of the society at large. Rather, it is said to represent the values and interests of groups that have sufficient power to control the operation of the state. Thus, the basic argument of conflict criminology is that there is an inverse relation between power and official crime rates: people with less power are more likely (and people with more power are less likely) to be officially defined and processed as criminals.

SELLIN'S CULTURE CONFLICT THEORY

In 1938, Thorsten Sellin presented a criminology theory focused on the conflict of "conduct norms." Conduct norms are cultural rules that require certain types of people to act in certain ways in certain circumstances—e.g., what a man is supposed to do if he finds his wife

---

1. A history of the consensus-conflict debate, going back to Plato and Aristotle, can be found in Thomas J. Bernard, *The Consensus-Conflict Debate: Form and Content in Social Theories*, Columbia University Press, New York, 1983.

in bed with another man.[2] In simple, homogeneous societies, many of these conduct norms are enacted into law and actually represent a consensus in the society. But in more complex societies, there will be overlap and contradiction between the conduct norms of different cultural groups. Sellin defined "primary cultural conflicts" as those occurring between two different cultures.[3] These conflicts could occur at border areas between two divergent cultures; or, in the case of colonization, when the laws of one culture are extended into the territory of another; or, in the case of migration, when members of one cultural group move into the territory of another."Secondary cultural conflicts" occur when a single culture evolves into several different subcultures, each having its own conduct norms.[4] In each of these cases law would not represent a consensus of the various members of the society, but would reflect the conduct norms of the dominant culture.

VOLD'S GROUP CONFLICT THEORY

Twenty years later, in the original edition of *Theoretical Criminology*, George B. Vold presented a group conflict theory focused on the conflict of interests. Vold's theory is based on a view of human nature that holds that people are fundamentally group-involved beings whose lives are both a part of and a product of their group associations. Groups are formed out of situations in which members have common interests and common needs that can best be furthered through collective action. New groups are continuously being formed as new interests arise, and existing groups weaken and disappear when they no longer have a purpose to serve. Groups become effective action units through the direction and coordination of the activities of their members. Groups come into conflict with one another as the interests and purposes they serve tend to overlap, encroach on one another, and become competitive. Conflict between groups tends to develop and intensify the loyalty of group members to their respective groups.

Implicit in this social-psychological view of human nature is a *social process* view of society as a collection of groups held together in a dynamic equilibrium of opposing group interests and efforts. There is a more or less continuous struggle to maintain, or to improve, the place of one's own group in the interaction of groups. Conflict is therefore one of the principal and essential social processes in the continuous and

2. Thorsten Sellin, *Culture Conflict and Crime*, Social Science Research Council, New York, 1938, pp. 32–33.

3. Ibid., pp. 63, 104.

4. Ibid., p. 105.

ongoing functioning of society. These social interaction processes grind their way through varying kinds of uneasy adjustment to a more or less stable equilibrium of balanced forces, called social order or social organization. The adjustment, one to another, of the many groups of varying strengths and of different interests is the essence of society as a functioning reality.

The conflict between groups seeking their own interests is especially visible in legislative politics, which is largely a matter of finding practical compromises between antagonistic groups in the community. Conflicts between opposing group interests exist in the community before there is any legislative action. As one group lines up against another, both may seek the assistance of the organized state to help them defend their rights and protect their interests. This general situation of group conflict gives rise to the familiar cry "There ought to be a law!" which is essentially the demand by one of the conflicting groups that the power of the organized state be used to support them in their conflict with the other group. Naturally, the other group, against whom the proposed law is directed, opposes its passage. Whichever group interest can marshal the greatest number of votes will determine whether or not there will be a new law to hamper and curb the interests of the opposing group.

Once the new law has been passed, those who opposed the law in the legislature understandably do not take kindly to efforts at law enforcement. They are more likely to violate the law, since it defends interests and purposes that are in conflict with their own. Those who promoted the law, in contrast, are more likely to obey it and more likely to demand that the police enforce it against violators, since the law defends interests and purposes they hold dear. In other words, those who produce legislative majorities win control of the police power of the state and decide the policies that determine who is likely to be involved in the violation of laws.

Thus the whole process of lawmaking, lawbreaking, and law enforcement directly reflects deep-seated and fundamental conflicts between group interests and the more general struggles among groups for control of the police power of the state. To that extent, criminal behavior is the behavior of *minority power groups*, in that these groups do not have sufficient power to promote and defend their interests and purposes in the legislative process.

Group conflict theory points to one of the fundamental conditions of life in organized political society, and suggests that a considerable amount of crime is intimately related to group conflict situations. For these situations the criminal behavior of the individual is best viewed

in the context of the course of action required for the group to maintain its position in the struggle with other groups. A sociology of conflict therefore is the basis for understanding and explaining this kind of
criminal behavior. On the other hand, Vold argued that group conflict
theory is strictly limited to those kinds of situations in which the individual criminal acts flow from the collision of groups whose members
are loyally upholding the in-group position. Such a theory does not explain many kinds of impulsive and irrational criminal acts that are quite
unrelated to any battle between different interest groups in organized
society.

QUINNEY'S THEORY OF THE SOCIAL REALITY OF CRIME

Vold's group conflict theory influenced most of the more recent conflict theories that followed. Among those is Richard Quinney's theory
of "the social reality of crime," which is expressed in six propositions[5]:

Proposition 1 (Definition of Crime): Crime is a definition of human conduct
that is created by authorized agents in a politically organized society.
Proposition 2 (Formulation of Criminal Definitions): Criminal definitions describe behaviors that conflict with the interests of the segments of society that
have the power to shape public policy.
Proposition 3 (Application of Criminal Definitions): Criminal definitions are
applied by the segments of society that have the power to shape the enforcement and administration of criminal law.
Proposition 4 (Development of Behavior Patterns in Relation to Criminal Definitions): Behavior patterns are structured in segmentally organized society in
relation to criminal definitions, and within this context persons engage in actions that have relative probabilities of being defined as criminal.
Proposition 5 (Construction of Criminal Conceptions): Conceptions of crime
are constructed and diffused in the segments of society by various means of
communication.
Proposition 6 (The Social Reality of Crime): The social reality of crime is constructed by the formulation and application of criminal definitions, the development of behavior patterns related to criminal definitions, and the construction of criminal conceptions.

Each of Quinney's propositions is derived from earlier work in criminology or sociology. The first proposition is based on the labeling theory view that deviance is defined by the social reaction to it. The second and third propositions are drawn from Vold's group conflict theory.
There is, however, a major difference between the two theories. Vold

---

5. Richard Quinney, *The Social Reality of Crime*, Little, Brown, Boston, 1970, pp. 15–23.

discussed conflict between organized interest groups, whereas Quinney discussed conflict between "segments" of society. Segments are said to share the same values, norms, and ideological orientations, but they may or may not be organized in defense of those commonalities.[6] Some segments, such as business and labor, have been organized into interest groups for many years, but other segments, such as women, older people, poor people, and homosexuals, have organized themselves only recently. There are also segments of society that have only minimal organization, such as young people, and segments that have no organization at all, such as prisoners and the mentally ill. Because of this difference, Quinney used conflict theory to explain all crime instead of merely some of it.[7]

Quinney's fourth proposition relies on Sutherland's differential association theory. Different segments of society are said to have different behavior patterns and normative systems, each of which is learned in its own social and cultural setting. The probability that any individual will violate the criminal law depends, to a large extent, on how much power and influence his segment has in enacting and enforcing laws.

Quinney's two final propositions rely on contemporary sociology of knowledge, which holds that the world in which humans live is primarily subjective and socially constructed.[8] He argued that the term *crime* can be taken to refer to concrete happenings that individuals personally experience, or it can refer to conceptions of reality that are created and communicated to individuals through various forms of social interaction, including the media. Different conceptions of crime can be created and communicated as part of the political process of promoting a particular set of values and interests. For example, consumer and ecology groups may argue that the "real criminals" are corporate executives. Community organizers in inner-city neighborhoods argue that the "real criminals" are the absentee landlords and greedy store owners. But these conceptions of crime are generally disregarded because the people who hold them do not have very much power. Conceptions of crime held by people with a great deal of power, however, are widely accepted by other people in the society as their own view. This legitimizes the au-

---

6. Ibid., p. 38.

7. Vold had specifically excluded "impulsive, irrational acts of a criminal nature that are quite unrelated to any battle between different interest groups in organized society" (Vold, op. cit., p. 219). Quinney, on the other hand, would hold that even irrational and impulsive people represent a segment of society who have common values, norms, and ideological orientations, even if this segment is not organized into any interest group.

8. See particularly Peter L. Berger and Thomas Luckmann, *The Social Construction of Reality*, Doubleday, Garden City, N.Y., 1966.

thority of power segments and allows them to carry out policies in the name of the common good that really promote their own interests.

TURK'S THEORY OF CRIMINALIZATION

Where Quinney focused on explaining how the social reality of crime is constructed, Austin Turk proposed a conflict analysis of how power groups achieve authority and legitimacy in society.[9] Although consensus theorists maintained that social order arose from the internalization of the norms embodied in the law, Turk argued that social order is based in a consensus-coercion balance maintained by the authorities. Authorities must prevent this balance from shifting to either "an excessively coercive, power relationship or an excessively consensual, egalitarian relationship."[10] To the extent that they are able to prevent this, people in the society will become conditioned to live with the social roles of authorities and subjects in such a way that no one will question these roles. It is this conditioning that underlies the social order in all societies, or the stability of an authority relationship.

Turk's "theory of criminalization" specified "the conditions under which cultural and social differences between authorities and subjects will probably result in conflict, the conditions under which criminalization will probably occur in the course of conflict, and the conditions under which the degree of deprivation associated with becoming a criminal will probably be greater or lesser."[11] Turk first distinguished between cultural norms and social norms. Cultural norms are associated with verbal formulations of values (e.g., the law as written), and social norms with actual behavior patterns (e.g., the law as enforced).[12] Conflict will be most likely when there is "close agreement between the cultural norm announced by authorities and their actual behavior patterns, and similarly high congruence between the way in which subjects who possess the attribute or commit the act evaluate it and their social norms."[13] As long as there is a cultural or social difference between authorities and subjects to begin with, the probability of conflict will be greatest when the subjects have a full-blown language and philosophy with which to defend their behaviors.[14]

The likelihood of conflict is also affected by the degree of organiza-

9. Austin T. Turk, *Criminality and Legal Order*, Rand McNally, Chicago, 1969.

10. Ibid., p. 42.

11. Ibid., p. 53.

12. Ibid., pp. 36–38.

13. Ibid., p. 55.

14. Ibid., p. 57.

tion and the level of sophistication of both authorities and subjects.[15] Authorities are presumed to be organized, since organization is a prerequisite for achieving and retaining power. Conflict will be more likely when subjects are organized, since group support makes an individual less willing to back down. The term *sophistication* is used by Turk to mean "knowledge of patterns in the behavior of others which is used in attempts to manipulate them." Conflict is more likely when either subjects or authorities are less sophisticated, since the more sophisticated subjects will be able to achieve their goals without precipitating a conflict with the superior powers of the state, and the less sophisticated authorities will have to rely more strongly on overt coercion to achieve their goals rather than more subtle, alternative tactics.

Given these conditions that affect the likelihood of conflict between authorities and subjects, Turk goes on to discuss the conditions under which it will be more likely that this conflict will result in the criminalization of the subjects. The primary factor, Turk argues, will be the meaning the prohibited act or attribute has for the first-line enforcers (i.e., the police), and the extent to which the higher-level enforcers (i.e., the prosecutors and judges) agree with the evaluation of the police.[16] If all levels of enforcers find the prohibited act or attribute very offensive, then it is likely that there will be high arrest rates, high conviction rates, and severe sentences. If, due to class and status differences between police and the higher-level enforcers, police find the behavior offensive but the higher-level enforcers do not, there will likely be more severe deprivation associated with arrests, but low conviction rates and less severe sentences. If police find the behavior inoffensive but higher-level enforcers find it offensive, then there will be low arrest rates but high conviction rates and severe sentences.

The second factor affecting criminalization will be the relative power of the enforcers and resisters.[17] In general, criminalization will be greatest when the enforcers have great power and the resisters are virtually powerless.

The third factor affecting criminalization rates is what Turk calls the "realism of the conflict moves," which relates to how likely an action taken by the subjects or authorities may improve the potential for their ultimate success. Turk states that unrealistic conflict moves by either party will tend to increase criminalization, which is a measure of the overt conflict between the two groups.

15. Ibid., pp. 58–61.
16. Ibid., pp. 65–67.
17. Ibid., pp. 67–70.

CHAMBLISS AND SEIDMAN'S ANALYSIS OF
THE CRIMINAL JUSTICE SYSTEM

In recent years a number of criminologists have analyzed the functioning of the criminal justice system from the perspective of conflict theory.[18] One such analysis is Chambliss and Seidman's *Law, Order, and Power*.[19] These authors note that the consensus perspective and the conflict perspective provide radically different versions of how the criminal justice system actually functions. Therefore they examined the day-to-day functioning of that system to determine which (if either) of the two models could be considered correct. Specifically, they sought to discover whether the power of the state (as embodied in the criminal justice system) is "a value-neutral framework within which conflict can be peacefully resolved," as described by consensus theory, or whether, as conflict theory would have it, "the power of the State is itself the principal prize in the perpetual conflict that is society."[20]

The criminal justice process begins with the legislative activity of law-making. Consensus theory would describe this process as "a deliberative assembly of one nation, with one interest, that of the whole, where, not local purposes, nor local prejudices, ought to guide, but the general good, resulting from the general reason of the whole."[21] The authors argue, however, that "every detailed study of the emergence of legal norms has consistently shown the immense importance of interest-group activity, *not 'the public interest,'* as the critical variable in determining the content of legislation."[22] In addition, when the law expresses moral values rather than economic interests, they will be the values of some groups rather than others. Chambliss and Seidman maintain that "the higher a group's political and economic position, the greater is the probability that its views will be reflected in the laws."[23]

Rule making in the criminal justice system also occurs in the appellate courts, where decisions establishing precedents have the effect of

18. See, for example, Stuart A. Scheingold, *The Politics of Law and Order: Street Crime and Public Policy*, Longman, New York, 1984; Stuart L. Hills, *Crime, Power, and Morality: The Criminal Law Process in the United States*, Chandler, New York, 1971; Richard Quinney, *Critique of Legal Order*, Little, Brown, Boston, 1973; Erik Olin Wright, *The Politics of Punishment*, Harper & Row, New York, 1973; Clayton A. Hartjen, *Crime and Criminalization*, Praeger, New York, 1974; Barry Krisberg, *Crime and Privilege*, Prentice Hall, Englewood Cliffs, N.J., 1975; and Harold E. Pepinsky, *Crime and Conflict*, Academic Press, New York, 1976.

19. William J. Chambliss and Robert B. Seidman, *Law, Order, and Power*, Addison-Wesley, Reading, Mass., 1971.

20. Ibid., p. 4.

21. Edmund Burke, *Works*, H. J. Bohn, London, 1893, p. 447; quoted in Chambliss and Seidman, op. cit., p. 63.

22. Chambliss and Seidman, op. cit., p. 73.

23. Ibid., pp. 473–74.

creating law. These decisions concern "trouble cases" where no law clearly applies to the case or where more than one law can be seen to apply. Appellate courts are examined closely because it is said that they "are the institution *par excellence* for which society most carefully cherishes the idea of value-neutrality."[24]

These rule-making decisions have always been justified in written opinions by referring to factors beyond the personal values of the judge. Originally judges referred to "natural law" to support their decisions, but it later became apparent that the natural law described by the judges really embodied their personal values.[25] Later justifications have usually been phrased in terms of preexisting laws and the principles embodied in those laws.[26] Dissenting opinions, however, can just as well be justified on legalistic grounds as can majority opinions, indicating that the decision is actually being based on other factors. There is now a move to justify these decisions on the basis of what is best for society,[27] but judgments about what is "best" depend on a set of values. Roscoe Pound, the originator of this school of thought, attempted to state the common values that would underlie these judicial decisions, but his formulation did not meet with widespread acceptance and has been criticized as reflecting primarily his own personal values.[28] Therefore the authors conclude that, in the last analysis, judges must rely on their personal values when they create rules in deciding "trouble cases."[29]

Chambliss and Seidman give a number of reasons why the values of appellate judges will be primarily oriented to the wealthy rather than to the poor.[30] Appellate judges are largely from the more privileged segments of society. They are usually lawyers who have been trained in law schools by the "casebook" method. This method confines the issues studied to those raised in earlier litigation, which are predominantly issues related to the wealthy. As lawyers, future judges tend to focus on cases involving the wealthy, since these are the clients who are able to pay high legal fees. Successful lawyers who become trial judges will have achieved a socially prominent position. They can be expected to socialize with the more privileged classes and become more attuned to their

24. Ibid., p. 75.
25. Ibid., pp. 125–28.
26. Ibid., pp. 128–31.
27. Ibid., pp. 131–45.
28. Ibid., pp. 141–42.
29. Ibid., p. 151.
30. Ibid., pp. 95–115.

needs. Promotion of a trial judge to the appellate level is inevitably tied in one way or another to the political process, so that those trial judges who do not deal appropriately with the politically powerful will often not be promoted.

Thus there are many subtle pressures encouraging judges to consider, carefully and thoroughly, issues related to persons of power and wealth. But there are also organizational pressures to restrict the total amount of litigation before the court to prevent overloading the docket. These pressures, together with the fact that appeals to higher court depend in part on the ability of the defendant to pay for the cost of the litigation, have the result that the majority of case law concerns issues relating only to the wealthy and powerful.

The examination of the functioning of law enforcement agencies focuses on the bureaucratic nature of those organizations and their connections to the political structure. The authors summarize their theory in the following points[31]:

1. The agencies of law-enforcement are bureaucratic organizations.

2. An organization and its members tend to substitute for the official goals and norms of the organization's ongoing policies and activities, which will maximize rewards and minimize the strains on the organization.

3. This goal-substitution is made possible by:

   a) the absence of motivation on the part of the role-occupants to resist pressures toward goal-substitution

   b) the pervasiveness of discretionary choice permitted by the substantive criminal law, and the norms defining the roles of the members of the enforcement agencies

   c) the absence of effective sanctions for the norms defining the roles in those agencies.

4. Law enforcement agencies depend for resource allocation on political organizations.

5. It will maximize rewards and minimize strains for the organization to process those who are politically weak and powerless, and to refrain from processing those who are politically powerful.

6. Therefore it may be expected that the law-enforcement agencies will process a disproportionately high number of the politically weak and powerless, while ignoring the violations of those with power.

Chambliss and Seidman conclude that both in structure and in function the law operates in the interests of existing power groups. The public

31. Ibid., p. 269.

interest is represented only to the extent that it coincides with the interests of those power groups.[32]

MCGARRELL AND CASTELLANO'S
INTEGRATIVE CONFLICT MODEL

In 1991, McGarrell and Castellano proposed a three-level analysis of the criminal law formulation process.[33] Their theory is based in part on Chambliss and Seidman's theory as described above.[34]

The first level of the theory describes the "structural foundations" of crime and conflict in societies.[35] McGarrell and Castellano describe societies as "differentiated" if they are characterized by such factors as heterogeneity (i.e., having people who differ in race, ethnicity, religion, and urbanization) and inequality (both economic and political). They then argue that greater differentiation is associated with more interpersonal and intergroup conflict. This higher level of conflict in turn leads to a greater use of criminalization as a method of dealing with the conflicts. Certain cultural beliefs, such as beliefs in punitiveness, individual responsibility, and the vigilante tradition, can interact with high social differentiation to produce even greater criminalization.[36]

The second level of the theory focuses on the enforcement of criminal laws. Crime, which is produced by factors described by the first level of the theory, results in both victimization of individuals and increased media attention to crime as a social problem.[37] The increased media attention results in feelings of "vicarious victimization"—people who are not actually victims of crime may still feel victimized because they hear about the victimization other people. Both actual and vicarious victimization increases fear of crime, which in turn results in a more punitive response by the criminal justice system. The increased enforcement of laws then increases official crime rates, which can then further increase fear and vicarious victimization.

The third level of the theory addresses the enactment of criminal laws. Media attention and fear of crime make the public policy arena so unstable that "A slight dislocation, a random event, a vocal political

---

32. Ibid., p. 503.

33. Edmund McGarrell and Thomas Castellano, "An Integrative Conflict Model of the Criminal Law Formulation Process," *Journal of Research in Crime and Delinquency* 28(2): 174–96 (1991).

34. Besides Chambliss and Seidman's *Law, Order, and Power* (op. cit.), the theory is based on Scheingold's *The Politics of Law and Order* (op. cit.), and John F. Galliher and John Cross's *Morals Legislation Without Morality: The Case of Nevada*, Rutgers University Press, New Brunswick, N.J., 1983.

35. McGarrell and Castellano, pp. 184–85.

36. Ibid.

37. Ibid., pp. 185–87.

opportunist, or a disgruntled governmental bureaucrat, can trigger events which mobilize the political arena to consider and enact crime legislation and policy."[38] The new legislation defines even more behaviors as criminal or increases the punitive response of the system. As a result, official crime statistics, media attention, and fear of crime again increase and the cycle continues.

HAGAN'S STRUCTURAL CRIMINOLOGY

Several types of theories in criminology, including conflict theory, suggest that power is important in explanations of crime. But tests of these theories often focus only on the people who are defined as criminals, and ignore the people who have the power to define others as criminal. In 1989, John Hagan published a book which argues that crime must be explained in terms of "power relations" rather than powerlessness itself.[39] That is, Hagan focuses on the relationship between the power of those who are defined as criminals and the power of whose who define others as criminals. Hagan describes his work as "structural criminology" rather than "conflict theory," but it is consistent with conflict theory's major argument: those with less power are more likely to be defined as criminal and those with more power are less likely.

Hagan begins by linking social structure to power relations in a society:

Social structure is formed out of relations between actors. . . Structural relations organized along vertical, hierarchical lines of power are of greatest interest to criminologists. Perhaps this is because crime itself implies a power relationship. To perpetrate a crime is often to impose one's power on others, while to be punished for a crime is to be subjected to the power of others. . . Structural criminology is distinguished by its attention to power relations, and by the priority it assigns them in undertaking research on crime.[40]

Hagan then presents a number of stand-alone articles, each with different coauthors,[41] which explore power relations in three different areas: class and criminality, criminal sentencing, and the family and delinquency.

---

38. Ibid., p. 188.

39. John Hagan, *Structural Criminology*, Rutgers University Press, New Brunswick, N.J., 1989. The seminal piece is by Hagan and Alberto Palloni, "Toward a Structural Criminology: Method and Theory in Criminological Research," *Annual Review of Sociology* 20: 431–49 (1986).

40. Hagan, pp. 1–2.

41. Each article is coauthored by Hagan and one or more of the following: Celesta Albonetti, Duane Alwin, A. R. Gillis, John Hewitt, Alberto Palloni, Patricia Parker, Ruth Peterson, and John Simpson.

Hagan argues that research rarely treats social class as a relational concept. He then constructs a measure of class that attempts to distinguish it in terms of its relation to the economic system and other people within it.[42] Hagan and Albonetti ask whether different class types are more or less likely to perceive injustice in the criminal justice system.[43] They also consider race as a potentially influencing factor, and control for a number of other variables. They find that independent of race, unemployed workers are more likely than members of the other classes to perceive injustice. They also find that race and class interact, in that African Americans in the professional-managerial category are most likely to perceive injustice. They offer the possible explanation that African Americans in this category may experience the most income discrimination, which may in turn make them more likely to sense injustice in other political arenas.[44]

Another research area explored structurally by Hagan and his colleagues is the sentencing of convicted offenders. One chapter addresses the interplay between racial status and socio-political conceptions of who the true villains are in narcotics offending.[45] Hagan and Peterson attempt to make sense of the finding that over time African Americans have received less discrimination in sentencing. One explanation is that the system has approached equality. An alternative explanation focuses on the area of drug offending. Over time, drug users have come to be defined as victims while high-level drug dealers have come to be defined as villains. Since African Americans are more likely to be users than high-level dealers, they are less likely to receive punitive sanctions.

Analysis of subsets of drug offenders (big dealers versus ordinary users), however, shows that when African Americans are sentenced as dealers, they receive stiffer penalties than whites, whereas when they are sentenced as users, they actually receive smaller sentences than their white counterparts.[46] A possible interpretation of this finding is that blacks are only systemically discriminated against when they commit threatening or villainous behavior. Analysis that fails to take into account changes in societal interpretations of drug offenses over time and power notions such as threat may well fail to uncover race effects in sentencing.

42. Hagan, pp. 125–27.

43. Perceived injustice is measured by ten attitudinal questions, such as whether police treat poor suspects differently than affluent suspects, or whether courts are influenced by political considerations.

44. Hagan, pp. 139–41.

45. Ibid., ch. 3.

46. Ibid., p. 95.

A third area of research Hagan discusses pertains to the relationship between family variables and delinquency. One structural theory proposed to explain why females have been consistently found to be less criminal than males is power-control theory.[47] This theory argues that parents control daughters more than sons, which makes it likely that boys will engage in more risky behavior than girls. Additionally, this disproportional controlling behavior will be greatest in patriarchal families, in which the father has more power than the mother. Individual delinquency rates are thus viewed as a product of two levels of distribution of power—power relations in society (the workplace) and power relations in the family. The first tests of power-control theory, focusing on forms of delinquent behavior involving calculation, have generally found support for it.[48]

Hagan's notion of a structural criminology is not (and perhaps is not intended to be) very coherently developed at this point. The series of research pieces in the work are loosely tied together, and even the notion of power relations is liberally interpreted. At times it seems that "structural criminology" means merely that research and theory should consider interactions between variables rather than simply examining direct influences of frequently examined constructs on some outcome. By and large, though, Hagan is advocating research that goes beyond a superficial analysis of criminological and criminal justice issues, by beginning with an informed view of relations between social actors and institutions (particularly relations in terms of relative power), by taking historical and social context into account, and by incorporating methodology that appropriately fits theory. Structural criminology is relevant to much more than conflict criminology, but is likely to revive interest in conflict theory and perhaps improve the course of research based on conflict perspectives.

BLACK'S BEHAVIOR OF LAW

Whereas Hagan studies power relations between social actors, Donald Black's *Behavior of Law*[49] explores several different types of relationships among social entities. Black describes law (i.e., governmental social control) as a quantitative variable, so that there can be more law at some times and places and less law at other times and places. Thus, re-

---

47. The original work on power-control theory is by Hagan, A. R. Gillis, and J. Simpson, "The Class Structure of Gender and Delinquency: Toward a Power-Control Theory of Common Delinquent Behavior," *American Journal of Sociology* 90: 1151–78 (1985).

48. Hagan, chps. 7–9.

49. Donald Black, *The Behavior of Law*, Academic Press, New York, 1976.

porting a crime, making an arrest, deciding to prosecute, deciding to convict, and sentencing someone to prison all represent increases in the quantity of law.

In addition, Black argues that law can vary according to its style. Although Black mostly discusses penal law, he notes that law can also be compensatory, therapeutic, or conciliatory. Penal law is enforced by a group against an offender; with compensatory law the victim demands payment; with therapeutic law the deviant entity takes action on his or her own behalf; and in conciliatory law various parties work together to resolve imbalances.[50] Black's goal is to explain variation in the quantity and style of law.[51]

Black explores five social dimensions of social life—stratification, morphology, culture, organization, and social control. Stratification is the "vertical distance between the people of a social setting" and is best measured by the difference in average wealth between each person or groups and every other person or group, or by the difference between the lowest and highest levels of wealth.[52] Morphology is the "horizontal aspect of social life, the distribution of people in relation to one another, including their division of labor, networks of interaction, intimacy, and integration."[53] Culture is the "symbolic aspect of life, including expressions of what is true, good, and beautiful. . . . Examples are science, technology, religion, magic, and folklore. . . . Culture includes aesthetic life of all sorts, the fine arts and the popular, such as poetry and painting, clothing . . . architecture, and even the culinary arts."[54] Organization is the "corporate aspect of social life, the capacity for collective action."[55] Finally, social control "is the normative aspect of social life. It defines and responds to deviant behavior, specifying what ought to be. . . . Law is social control . . . but so are etiquette, custom, ethics, bureaucracy, and the treatment of mental illness."[56]

Within each dimension Black forms hypotheses about law. In the case of stratification, Black argues that the higher a person is in on the ladder of stratification, the more the person is able to invoke law on his or her behalf. In addition, the further apart two people are in terms of stratification, the more law the higher ranked person can exercise over

---

50. See ibid., pp. 4–5.

51. Ibid., pp. 3–4.

52. Ibid., p. 13.

53. Ibid., p. 37.

54. Ibid., p. 61.

55. Ibid., p. 85.

56. Ibid., p. 105.

the other. For example, if a corporate executive claims to be victimized by a street bum, more law would be exercised against the bum than if the executive claims to be victimized by another corporate executive or if the bum claims to be victimized by the corporate executive.

Morphology concerns the relational distance between people, or the degree to which they participate in each other's lives. Black argues that the relationship between law and relational distance is curvilinear: "Law is inactive among intimates, increasing as the distance between people increases but decreasing as this reaches the point at which people live in entirely separate worlds."[57] Hermits rarely need or use law since they live in an entirely separate world, and married couples do not invoke law against each other unless their intimacy with each other breaks down. Law is greater, says Black, when the relational distance is somewhere between intimacy and isolation.

One of Black's hypotheses concerning culture is that law is greater in a direction toward less culture than toward more culture, and furthermore, that the amount of cultural distance linearly affects the amount of law. Using education as a measure of culture, for example, if an offender is less educated than the victim, more law will be invoked to address the victimization, and the most law of all will be used when the difference in education between the offender and the victim is greatest.[58] On the other hand, if the offender is more educated than the victim, less law will be used to address the victimization, and the least law of all will be used when the difference in education between the offender and victim is greatest.

Similarly, Black argues that law varies directly with organization. If offenders are more organized than their victims (e.g., if the offender is a corporation and the victim is an individual), less law would be used to address the victimization. In addition, the most law would be used when the organizational distance between the offenders and victims is the greatest. But if the offenders are less organized than the victims (e.g., the offender is an individual and the victim is a corporation), the reverse is true: more law would be used to address the victimization, and the most law would be used when the organizational distance between the victims and offenders is greatest. Black uses these propositions to explain relatively light sanctions directed toward white-collar offenders.

Finally, Black argues that law will be greater where other forms of social control are weaker. All in all, across the five social dimensions,

57. Ibid., p. 41.
58. Ibid., pp. 65–66.

Black forms over twenty hypotheses about how law varies in quantity and style. His evidence for each is primarily anecdotal, including anthropological examples from a variety of sources, but he does not perform any systematic test of the hypotheses.

In his preface to *The Behavior of Law*, Black states: "This book does not judge the variation of law, nor does it recommend policy of any kind. Rather, it is merely an effort to understand law as a natural phenomenon. . . ."[59] But in a later book on the subject, *Sociological Justice*,[60] Black does judge variations in the quantity and style of law as being "wrong" in some sense. He therefore recommends three types of policy reforms to reduce social variation in law: legal cooperatives, desocialization of law, and starvation of law. In the first reform, people would join subsidized legal cooperatives, reducing corporate advantages in the legal system. Each co-op would consist of a variety of people so that relations among the co-ops themselves would be relatively equal. Informal social control may come about within the co-ops, as those who cause the group expensive legal costs may be expelled. Of course, this could also work to perpetuate social variations in law, if groups are quick to expel undesirable individuals. Black's second reform would make social information about offenders unavailable to criminal justice system actors handling cases. For example, jurors would not be allowed to actually see offenders, witnesses, or victims. All testimony would be done electronically, so that evidence would be stripped of social characteristics such as dialect or education. Black's third proposal is to "starve" the law. Basically, he argues that if the law has only the barest minimum in resources, then people will be forced to rely on other mechanisms for dealing with conflicts, such as conflict resolution. While there are serious flaws with each of these proposals, the book's purpose is noble: to eliminate social factors from the behavior of law.[61]

An initial attempt to test Black's theory raised conceptual questions about the "seriousness" of an offense. Gottfredson and Hindelang found that variation in Black's social dimensions did not significantly predict variation in the quantity of law, which instead was predicted primarily by the seriousness of the offense.[62] Black responded that describing a crime as "serious" is itself influenced by the five social dimensions and that, in practice, the term "serious" means that the action receives a

59. Ibid., p. x.

60. Donald Black, *Sociological Justice*, Oxford University Press, New York, 1989.

61. See Thomas J. Bernard, "Review Essay: Donald Black's *Sociological Justice*," *The Critical Criminologist* 3(2): 7–8, 13–14 (Summer 1991).

62. Michael Gottfredson and Michael Hindelang, "A Study of the Behavior of Law and Theory and Research in the Sociology of Law," *American Sociological Review* 44: 3–18 (1979).

large quantity of law.[63] Gottfredson and Hindelang responded that if this is true, Black's theory cannot be tested unambiguously.[64] The confusion around how to deal with seriousness has hampered subsequent attempts to test Black's theory, and to date, there remains no comprehensive, accepted test.[65]

On the other hand, some recent research looks at relationships between actors, rather than looking at absolute social status without regard to relative position. For example, one study of court disposition patterns uses Hagan's structural criminology as a theoretical point of departure, and employs some of Black's propositions, in attempting to show how the relationship between victim and offender may influence criminal justice reaction to behavior. Jamieson and Blowers found a greater probability of dismissal of cases with less organized victims, especially when the suspected offenders were more organized.[66] This finding is consistent with Hagan's idea that power differentials—one being organization—may influence reaction to behavior, and with Black's proposition that law varies with organization.

Black does not mention conflict theory in any of his works on the behavior of law; nor has his work been identified as conflict theory elsewhere. Yet, some of the core propositions of his theory are consistent with conflict notions, in that they imply that more powerful social actors have more ability to use law against less powerful actors. Black's theory probably has not been conceived as a conflict theory for at least two reasons. First, Black simply states his propositions as purely sociological laws, without imputing either individual or structural motivation. Conflict theory assumes disproportionate treatment has a purpose attached to it—namely, to protect the interests of the more powerful. Second, Black's theory is much broader than conflict theory. Conflict theory generally pertains to power relations, whereas Black's theory pertains to differences across several types of social relationships, some involving power and some not.

---

63. Black, "Common Sense in the Sociology of Law," *American Sociological Review* 44: 18–27 (1979).

64. Gottfredson and Hindelang, *American Sociological Review* 44: 27–37 (1979).

65. But see Larry Hembroff, "Testing Black's Theory of Law," *American Journal of Sociology* 93: 322–47 (1987); and Gloria Lessan and Joseph Sheley, "Does Law Behave?," *Social Forces* 70: 655–78 (1992). For a discussion of this issue, see Thomas J. Bernard, "The Black Hole—Sources of Confusion for Criminologists in Black's Theory," *Social Pathology* 1(3): 218–27 (Fall 1995).

66. Katherine Jamieson and Anita Neuberger Blowers, "A Structural Examination of Misdemeanor Court Disposition Patterns," *Criminology* 31(2): 243–62 (1993).

A UNIFIED CONFLICT THEORY OF CRIME

In this section we attempt to bring together some of the most important concepts from the various conflict theories, creating an integrated or unified theory. The following conflict theory is derived principally from the theories of Vold, Quinney, and Chambliss and Seidman presented in this chapter.[67] Furthermore, it incorporates some of Hagan's and Black's ideas about power relations, and it is generally consistent with McGarrell and Castellano's ideas about the effects of differentiation on crime and criminal justice.

VALUES AND INTERESTS IN COMPLEX SOCIETIES

1. A person's *values* (i.e., beliefs about what is good, right, and just, or at least excusable) and *interests* (i.e., what rewards or benefits the person) are generally shaped by the conditions in which the person lives.

2. Complex, highly differentiated societies are composed of people who live under very different conditions.

3. Therefore, the more complex and differentiated the society, the more that people within the society have different and conflicting values and interests.

PATTERNS OF INDIVIDUAL ACTION

4. People tend to act in ways that are consistent with their values and interests. That is, they tend to act in ways that they think are good, right, and just, or at least excusable. They also tend to act in ways that benefit themselves personally.

5. When values and interests conflict, people tend to adjust their values to come into line with their interests. Over time, people tend to believe that the actions that benefit themselves personally are really good, right, and just, or at least excusable.

6. Because the conditions of one's life (and therefore one's values and interests) tend to be relatively stable over time, people tend to develop relatively stable patterns of action that benefit them personally and that they believe are good, right, and just, or at least excusable.

THE ENACTMENT OF CRIMINAL LAWS

7. The enactment of criminal laws is part of a conflict and compromise process in which organized groups (and, to a much less extent, private individuals) attempt to promote and defend their values and interests.

---

67. Earlier versions can be found in Thomas J. Bernard, "The Distinction Between Conflict and Radical Criminology," *Journal of Criminal Law and Criminology* 72(1): 362–79 (spring 1981), and pp. 286–87 of the third edition of the present book.

8. Specific criminal laws usually represent a combination of the values and interests of many different groups rather than the values and interests of one particular group. Nevertheless, the greater a group's political and economic power, the more the criminal law in general tends to represent the values and interests of that group.

9. Therefore, in general, the greater a group's political and economic power, the less likely it is that the actions consistent with the values and interests of group members will violate the criminal law, and vice versa.

THE ENFORCEMENT OF CRIMINAL LAWS

10. In general, the more political and economic power a person has, the more the person is able to obtain official intervention from law enforcement agencies when he or she is victimized by someone else.

11. In addition, the more political and economic power a person has, the more difficult it is for official law enforcement agencies to process the person when he or she victimizes someone else.

12. Therefore, in general, law enforcement agencies tend to process individuals with less, rather than more, political and economic power. Specifically, the greater the power differential between the victim and the offender, the more likely an offender will be processed if the offender is less powerful than the victim, and the less likely the offender will be processed if the offender is more powerful than the victim.

THE DISTRIBUTION OF OFFICIAL CRIME RATES

13. Because of the processes of criminal law enactment and enforcement described above, the official crime rates of individuals and groups will tend to be inversely proportional to their political and economic power, independent of any other factors that might also influence the distribution of official crime rates (e.g., social, psychological, or biological factors affecting the behavior of offenders or the behavior of criminal justice agents).

This theory presents a theoretical chain that begins with general social structural characteristics, moves through the processes by which individuals in similar social structural locations learn similar patterns of behavior, and concludes by relating those patterns of behavior to the processes of enacting and enforcing criminal laws to explain the distribution of official crime rates.[68] Because it combines and interrelates a

---

68. Akers (ibid., pp. 61–68) makes a similar argument about structural sources of behavior and social processes of learning those behaviors. His argument is described in Chapter 12, p. 197. We extend the theoretical chain to the distribution of official crime rates.

theory of criminal behavior with a theory of the behavior of criminal law, the above theory is described as a "unified theory of crime."

TESTING CONFLICT THEORY

Tests of conflict theory have suffered from three major problems. First, they have been far too methodologically simplistic. Second, they have not been well guided theoretically, and have been unable to distinguish between alternative explanations. Finally, they have treated all conflict theories alike, attempting to test some "lump sum" conflict theory, without paying attention to the specific propositions of different types of conflict theories. The first problem has been largely overcome, but the latter two have not.

Probably the most common way of testing conflict theory has been to attempt to link race and equity of criminal justice decisions.[69] Researchers either explicitly or implicitly assume that if conflict theory is valid, then minorities (such as African Americans) will be treated harsher by the criminal justice system, since they have relatively less power, and the majority race will attempt to maintain its power by oppressing the threatening minority races.

One frequently researched criminal justice outcome is sentencing, both in terms of the decision to incarcerate and the length of the sentence, if incarcerated. In the 1960s and early 1970s, many researchers concluded that blacks were sentenced more severely than whites. The notion that racial discrimination in sentencing was widespread was dampened in the 1970s, as a result of better social science. Hagan's review of many of the findings supporting racial discrimination noted that: (1) the studies did not control for legal factors; and (2) they did not incorporate measures of association.[70] In the first case, studies were not allowing for the possibility that black defendants may be charged with more serious crimes than whites, and may have more serious criminal records (although see our discussion of "seriousness" above). Disparities in sentencing, then, may be solely attributed to differences in legal characteristics of the case and offender. Hagan discovered that once studies began to control for such factors, the effect of race disappeared. Second, early studies reported statistically significant differences between black and white sentences, but did not report the extent of the differences. With several hundred cases in a data set, the difference be-

---

69. This is not to say that testing race effects is the only way conflict theory has been tested. Class and unemployment are other variables commonly examined in tests of conflict theory. Race is, however, probably the most visibly researched.

70. John Hagan, "Extra-legal Attributes and Criminal Sentencing: An Assessment of a Sociological Viewpoint," *Law and Society Review* 8: 357–83 (1974).

tween thirty days in prison (for whites) and thirty-two days (for blacks) would be statistically significant, but would not be as serious a problem of discrimination as might appear. Hagan calculated measures of the strength of racial differences, and found that in previous studies, very little disparity had been observed.

Beginning in the late 1970s, more sophisticated multivariate methodologies, controlling for many possible influences on sentencing, have reduced the prevalence of findings of racial differences. Also, some explanations alternative to blatant discrimination have been supported. For example, blacks have been shown to receive harsher sentences because they are less likely to make bail, since they are less affluent, and this reduces their ability to provide an effective defense.[71] Other researchers have found that blacks are sentenced to prison more often than whites, because they could not afford private attorneys.[72]

The advancement of research methodologies, allowing for more sophisticated examinations of multivariate relationships, still has not helped overcome a more fundamental problem with tests of conflict theory: The same finding may be interpreted in more than one way. If a direct effect of race on the decision to arrest or the length of a sentence is found, controlling for hosts of other factors, what does this mean? It could be evidence of widespread racial prejudice in society, manifested in unequal treatment of minorities by criminal justice system actors. On the other hand, it could represent systematic and institutionalized protection of those in power (whites) from the threatening group (blacks). Most research testing conflict theory haphazardly draws on the actual theoretical premises, assuming support for conflict theory when a finding such as unequal treatment of different races is discovered.

Another avenue of research testing conflict theory also suffers from an inability to distinguish between alternative explanations. Macro level threat theory attempts to show that in areas where minorities pose an increasing threat to the status quo, law enforcement is focused more exclusively on minorities, and police strength or activity is greater.[73] Research in this vein commonly tests such hypotheses as: an increase in

---

71. Alan Lizotte, "Extra-legal Factors in Chicago's Criminal Courts: Testing the Conflict Model of Criminal Justice," *Social Problems* 25: 564–80 (1978). Some would interpret this finding as support for conflict theory, viewing the use of pricey bail as an economically based mechanism for treating "undesirables," or threatening individuals more harshly.

72. Cassia Spohn, J. Gruhl, and Susan Welch, "The Effect of Race on Sentencing: A Reexamination of an Unsettled Question," *Law and Society Review* 16: 72–88 (1981–82).

73. For a broad review of many different types of social threat theory, see Allen Liska, *Social Threat and Social Control*, SUNY Press, Albany, N.Y., 1992.

the relative proportion of blacks in a city will result in an increase in the number of police officers or number of arrests made. A positive association between percentage of minorities and police activity or strength is typically viewed as support for this branch of conflict theory. However, other explanations are also compatible with such a finding. For example, nonwhites may *want* more police than whites, or they may *need* more police than whites.[74] If crime occurs disproportionately in poor and minority-dominated areas, potential victims—minorities—may voice desire for greater police strength, as the minority population in their neighborhood increases. Also, minorities may face different sorts of social problems, and may need more social services. If this is true, and they are politically viable, an increase in their relative size may result in greater police attention, for reasons not relevant to conflict theory. Research to date has had a very difficult time distinguishing conflict-based interpretations from nonconflict interpretations of the same finding.[75]

Finally, few attempts are made to test well-constructed conflict theories. As shown in this chapter, not all conflict theories look the same. Most empirical research on conflict theory, however, is not careful to specify which conflict propositions from which conflict theories it is testing. Lanza-Kaduce and Greenleaf have recently attempted to show exactly how Turk's theory of norm resistance can be operationalized and tested with encounters between police and citizens.[76] They specifically demonstrate how such concepts as cultural and behavioral norm congruence, sophistication, organization, and "realism of moves" can be operationalized, such that one can predict whether conflict and criminalization will occur in police-citizen encounters. Although they save the actual empirical work for others, their effort is encouraging, in that it shows that a particular conflict theory can be tested empirically, if the researcher is careful to be true to the original theory.

POLICY IMPLICATIONS

Conflict criminology implies that greater equality in the distribution of power among groups in society should result in greater equality in the

---

74. David Greenberg, R. C. Kessler, and Colin Loftin, "Social Inequality and Crime Control," *Journal of Criminal Law and Criminology* 76: 684–704 (1985).

75. Urban research of this nature is further complicated by the possible co-occurrence of social disorganization and conflict processes. A recent development in criminological research paying special attention to community dynamics has attempted to integrate social disorganization and conflict notions, but is still in a formative stage. See the *Law and Society Review*, special issue on "Crime, Class, and Community—An Emerging Paradigm," 27(2): (1993).

76. Lonn Lanza-Kaduce and Richard Greenleaf, "Police-Citizen Encounters: Turk on Norm Resistance," *Justice Quarterly* 11(4): 605–624 (1994).

distribution of official crime rates. Crime rates should be redistributed for two reasons. First, there should be a general reduction in the crime rates of groups that presently have high crime rates, as those groups use their newly acquired power to legally pursue and defend their values and interests. Second, there should also be a general increase in the crime rates of groups that presently have low crime rates, as those groups find their ability to pursue and defend their values and interests increasingly hindered by other groups.

Within the context of conflict theory, the specific process by which a redistribution of power can be effected is through the establishment of organized groups by which the presently unorganized aggregates of individuals would be able to pursue and defend their values and interests.[77] This implication bears a resemblance to the policy implication of control theory, since it entails bonding the previously isolated individual to a group that will interact with other groups according to mutually agreed on rules. The difference is that control theory generally implies that the individual be bonded to "conventional" groups, whereas conflict criminology implies that the individual should be bonded to other individuals who have similar values and interests and who occupy similar social structural locations. To the extent that a particular individual is considered deviant rather than conventional, the group that best represents his or her values and interests will also be considered deviant rather than conventional. The view that the best solution to social conflict lies in the representation of diverse aggregates of individuals by an equally diverse number of organized groups under conditions of relative equality is the reason why conflict theory in general is most comfortable with pluralist democracy as a form of government.[78]

The organization of interest groups out of previously unorganized aggregates of individuals is a difficult process that is frequently subject to severe abuses. Especially at their beginnings, these groups are often taken over by the most aggressive members, who make unrealistic and ultimately unproductive demands on behalf of their members, while reaping many personal benefits for themselves. This pattern can be found, for example, in the history of a number of American labor unions, and it is for reasons such as these that many wardens oppose the for-

77. Dahrendorf, op. cit., pp. 225–27.

78. Bernard, "The Distinction Between Conflict and Radical Criminology"; Bernard, *The Consensus-Conflict Debate.*

mation of prisoner unions.[79] These types of problems are especially severe when the groups of people being organized have been defined as deviant by their society. Sagarin argues that such groups generally either promote overconformity to conventional norms as a means of soliciting approval from society, or seek to change societal attitudes and instill pride in the deviant by "thumbing their noses" at society.[80] Nevertheless, Irwin argues that such groups should be allowed to form in prisons in order to reduce the level of violence associated with conflicts there,[81] and Murton argues that where such groups have been successfully organized the violence associated with prison conflicts has decreased markedly.[82] More equality has also been shown to reduce violence in youth institutions,[83] and "mediating structures" have been shown to reduce violence associated with youth crime in the community.[84]

CONCLUSION

Conflict criminology asserts that there is a general tendency for power and official crime rates to be inversely related. The more power an individual or group has, the lower its official crime rates tend to be, while the less power an individual or group has the higher its official crime rates tend to be.

In the context of that assertion, it is interesting to consider Lord Acton's famous observation that power corrupts, and absolute power corrupts absolutely. Power may corrupt, but official criminalization requires that there be some greater power that is able to define that corruption as criminal. Otherwise, no matter how corrupt the action is, it either will not be defined as a crime in the criminal law, or the person will not be processed as a criminal through the criminal justice system. Absolute power may corrupt absolutely, but people with absolute power are never officially defined as criminals.[85]

79. J. E. Baker, "Inmate Self-Government," *Journal of Criminal Law, Criminology and Police Science* 55: 39–47 (1964). Sometimes wardens oppose inmate self-government because it genuinely represents the interests of the inmates and therefore challenges the interests of the prison administration. See G. T. Tyrner-Stastny and C. Stastny, "The Changing Political Culture of a Total Institution," *Prison Journal* 57: 43–55 (1977).

80. Edward Sagarin, *Odd Man In*, Quadrangle, Chicago, 1969.

81. John Irwin, *Prisons in Turmoil*, Little, Brown, Boston, 1980.

82. Thomas O. Murton, *The Dilemma of Prison Reform*, Holt, Rinehart and Winston, New York, 1976.

83. Craig A. McEwan, *Designing Correctional Organizations for Youths*, Ballinger, Cambridge, Mass., 1978.

84. Robert L. Woodson, *A Summons to Life: Mediating Structures and the Prevention of Youth Crime*, Ballinger, Cambridge, Mass., 1981.

85. See Thomas Hobbes, *Leviathan*, E. P. Dutton, New York, 1950, ch. 18, p. 148.

CHAPTER 16

Critical Criminology

The term "critical criminology" has been described as "an umbrella designation for a series of evolving, emerging perspectives" that are "characterized particularly by an argument that it is impossible to separate values from the research agenda, and by a need to advance a progressive agenda favoring disprivileged peoples."[1] This chapter examines three of these emerging perspectives—Marxist, postmodernist, and feminist criminologies.

These perspectives share the view, along with the conflict theories presented in the last chapter, that inequality of power is causally connected to the problem of crime. But these three approaches go further than conflict theories by making specific arguments about the sources of power in societies. Marxism generally locates power in ownership of the means of production, postmodernism locates it in the control over language systems, and feminism locates it in patriarchy.[2] Each of these approaches therefore implies that the crime problem can only be solved if these power structures are changed. Thus, these approaches are all "radical" in the sense that they are associated with political agendas that involve deep and fundamental social change.

These theories are difficult to summarize for two reasons. First, these areas of theorizing are extremely complex, which leads to profound disagreements among different theorists within the same area. Second, theorists in these areas may frequently change their own positions as their thinking develops. Thus, one theorist may take one position at one time and a different position only a short time later. Consequently one can

---

1. Martin D. Schwartz and David O. Friedrichs, "Postmodern Thought and Criminological Discontent: New Metaphors for Understanding Violence," *Criminology* 32:221–46 (May 1994).

2. See Werner Einstadter and Stuart Henry, *Criminological Theory*, Harcourt Brace, Fort Worth, 1995, ch. 10–12.

only summarize some of the major themes, but a great many arguments must be left out.

MARXISM AND MARXIST CRIMINOLOGY

Karl Marx (1818–1883) wrote in the immediate aftermath of the massive social changes brought about by the Industrial Revolution. In one lifespan (approximately 1760–1840), the world as it had been for a thousand years suddenly changed.[3] Marx attempted to explain why those profound changes had occurred when they did, and to give some sense of what was coming next.[4] His theory linked economic development to social, political, and historical change, but did not deal with the problem of crime in any significant way.

The principal conflict that Marx presented in his theory, and on which the theory is based, was the conflict between the material forces of production and the social relations of production.[5] The term *material forces of production* generally refers to a society's capacity to produce material goods. This includes technological equipment and the knowledge, skill, and organization to use that equipment. The term *social relations of production* refers to relationships between people. These include property relationships, which determine how the goods produced by the material forces of production are distributed—that is, who gets what.

The development of the material forces of production is relatively continuous throughout history, since it consists in the development of technology, skills, etc. The social relations of production, however, tend to freeze into particular patterns for long periods of time. When first established, the social relations enhance the development of the material forces of production, but as time goes by they become increasingly inconsistent with them and begin to impede their further development. At some point the social relations change abruptly and violently, and new social relations are established that once again enhance the development of the material forces of production.

Marx used this general model to explain the profound changes that had just occurred in European societies. When the social relations of feudalism were first established, they were "progressive" in the sense

3. Michel Foucault, *Discipline and Punish*, Pantheon, New York, 1977.

4. This account of Marx's theory is taken from Thomas J. Bernard, *The Consensus-Conflict Debate: Form and Content in Social Theories*, Columbia, New York, 1983, pp. 95–98. Other summaries of Marx's work can be found in David Greenberg, *Crime and Capitalism*, Mayfield, Palo Alto, Calif., 1980, pp. 13–17; and Richard Quinney, *Class, State and Crime*, 2nd ed., Longman, New York, 1980, pp. 41–51.

5. A summary of this argument is found in Karl Marx, *Critique of Political Economy* (1859), English translation, International Library, New York, 1904, pp. 11–13.

that they were necessary for the further development of the material forces of production. After a thousand years, however, the material forces of production had developed extensively, but the social relations had hardly changed at all. At that point the social relations of feudalism were hindering the further development of the material forces of production. The massive changes of the Industrial Revolution reflected a sudden and violent restructuring of the social relations of production. The new social relations—bourgeois capitalism—were "progressive" in the sense that they were necessary for the further development of the material forces of production.

Having analyzed the causes of the violent and abrupt social changes that had just been completed, Marx went on to use his theory to predict what would happen next. The material forces of production would continue to develop under capitalism, but the social relations would remain fixed, just as they had under feudalism. As the development of the material forces proceeded, the social relations of capitalism would increasingly become a hindrance rather than a help to the further development of the material forces. Ultimately, Marx predicted, there would be a sudden and violent restructuring of those social relations in which capitalism would be replaced by socialism.

Marx was fairly specific on why he thought that would happen. The logic of capitalism is "survival of the fittest," so that the "fittest" gobble up the "less fit." As part of this process, property is increasingly concentrated into fewer and fewer hands, and more and more people become wage laborers instead of working for themselves. At the same time, increasing mechanization in business and industry means that fewer workers are needed, so that there is an increasing pool of underemployed and unemployed workers. Because so many workers are available who want jobs, those who have jobs can be paid low wages because they can be replaced by others who will work for less.

In the long run, this means that capitalist societies will tend to polarize into two conflicting groups. One of these groups consists of the people who, as they gobble up their competitors, own an increasing portion of the property in the society. As Marx said: "One capitalist always kills many."[6] Thus the number of people in this group will grow smaller over time as some of them get gobbled up by others. As this group becomes smaller, it grows richer and richer. The other group, consisting of employed and unemployed wage laborers, keeps getting larger over time. But as unemployment increases with increasing mechanization, real wages tend to decrease because the supply of labor exceeds the de-

6. Karl Marx, *Capital*, vol. 1, International, New York, 1967, p. 763.

mand for it. Thus, while this group becomes larger and larger over time, it also grows poorer and poorer.

Thus, Marx argued, capitalist societies would inevitably tend to polarize into two groups, one growing smaller and smaller while getting richer and richer, and the other growing larger and larger while getting poorer and poorer. This tendency toward polarization is what Marx called the "contradiction" in capitalism, and as it became more extreme, it would act as a greater hindrance to the further development of the material forces of production. A revolutionary restructuring of the social relations of production would be inevitable at some point. That restructuring, according to Marx, would consist of establishing collective ownership of the means of production and instituting centralized planning to end the cycles of overproduction and depression that plague capitalism.[7]

Marx did not discuss the problem of crime or its relation to the economic system at length, although he did address the subject in several passages.[8] Hirst argues that Marx's idea of crime centered on the concept of demoralization.[9] Marx believed that it was essential to human nature that people be productive in life and in work. But in industrialized capitalist societies there are large numbers of unemployed and underemployed people. Because these people are unproductive, they become demoralized and are subject to all forms of crime and vice. Marx called these people the *lumpenproletariat*.

In another passage, Marx argued against the classical philosophy that was dominant in his day,[10] which held that all people freely and equally joined in a social contract for the common good, and that the law represented a consensus of the general will. Marx maintained that this view ignored the fact that unequal distribution of wealth in a society produced an unequal distribution of power. Those with no wealth have no power in the formation of the social contract, whereas those with great wealth can control it to represent their own interests. Thus Marx did not see crime as the willful violation of the common good, but as "the

7. See, in general, Karl Marx, *Critique of the Gotha Programme*, International, New York, 1970. See also D. Ross Gandy, *Marx and History: From Primitive Society to the Communist Future*, University of Texas Press, Austin, 1979, pp. 72–95.

8. For discussions of Marx's views of crime, see Ian Taylor, Paul Walton, and Jock Young, *The New Criminology*, Harper and Row, New York, 1973, pp. 209–36. Original passages from Marx and Engels can be found in Maureen Cain and Alan Hunt, eds., *Marx and Engels on Law*, Academic Press, New York, 1979; or Paul Phillips, *Marx and Engels on Law and Laws*, Barnes and Noble, Totowa, N.J., 1980.

9. Paul Q. Hirst, "Marx and Engles on Law, Crime, and Morality," in Ian Taylor, Paul Walton, and Jock Young, eds., *Critical Criminology*, Routledge and Kegan Paul, London, 1975.

10. Karl Marx and Friedrich Engles, *The German Ideology*, Lawrence and Wishart, London, 1965, pp. 365–67.

struggle of the isolated individual against the prevailing conditions."[11] This is sometimes called the *primitive rebellion* thesis, since it implies that crime is a "primitive" form of rebellion against the dominant social order that eventually might develop into conscious revolutionary activity.

An early Marxist criminologist, Willem Bonger, provided an extensive theory of crime in his book *Criminality and Economic Conditions*, published in 1916.[12] Bonger argued that the capitalist economic system encouraged all people to be greedy and selfish and to pursue their own benefits without regard for the welfare of their fellows. Crime is concentrated in the lower classes because the justice system criminalizes the greed of the poor while it allows legal opportunities for the rich to pursue their selfish desires. He argued that a socialist society would ultimately eliminate crime because it would promote a concern for the welfare of the whole society and would remove the legal bias that favors the rich.

After the mid-1920s Marxist criminology virtually disappeared from the English-speaking world,[13] and reappeared in the late 1960s in connection with the radical social climate of the times.[14] These versions of Marxist criminology tended to portray criminals in terms of Marx's "primitive rebellion" thesis—that is, criminals engaged in crime as an unconscious form of rebellion against the capitalist economic system. They also tended to have an "instrumentalist" view of the criminal justice system—i.e., the enactment and enforcement of criminal laws are solely the "instruments" of a unified and monolithic ruling class that conspires to seek its own advantage at the expense of other groups.

These simplistic views of criminals and criminal justice were criticized by other Marxists as misinterpreting Marx's thought.[15] Block and Chambliss, for example, criticized the early theories for their simplistic portrayal of the "ruling class" as a unified and monolithic elite; for the argument that the enactment and enforcement of laws reflects only the interests of this ruling class; and for the argument that criminal acts are

---

11. Ibid., p. 367.

12. Willem Bonger, *Criminality and Economic Conditions*, Little, Brown, Boston, 1916; reprinted by Agathon, New York, 1967. See also the excellent Introduction by Austin Turk in the abridged edition, Indiana University Press, Bloomington, 1969. See also the brief discussion of Bonger and other early Marxist criminologists in Greenberg, op. cit., pp. 11–12.

13. Greenberg, op. cit., p. 1.

14. See, for example, Richard Quinney, *Critique of Legal Order*, Little, Brown, Boston, 1973; Quinney with John Wildeman, *The Problem of Crime*, 2nd ed., Harper & Row, New York, 1977; Taylor, Walton, and Young, *The New Criminology*, and *Critical Criminology*.

15. Hirst, op. cit.; also R. Serge Denisoff and Donald McQuarie, "Crime Control in Capitalist Society: A Reply to Quinney," *Issues in Criminology* 10(1): 109–19 (spring 1975).

a political response to conditions of oppression and exploitation.[16] Greenberg raised some of the same criticisms and also pointed out that these theories ignored studies that showed a widespread consensus on legal definitions of crime; that underprivileged people are most frequently victims of crime by other underprivileged people, so that they have an interest in the enforcement of criminal laws; and that it is unrealistic to expect that crime will be eliminated in socialist societies.[17] Greenberg later described these theories as primarily political statements associated with New Left politics of the 1960s and the early 1970s rather than as genuine academic arguments about the nature of crime.[18] With the collapse of the New Left in the early 1970s, "leftists who retained their political commitments dug in for the long haul." Some turned to community organizing while others turned to Marxist theory to deepen their understanding of the broader social processes. Greenberg concludes: "By the mid 1970s, a specifically Marxian criminology began to take shape."[19] This new and more rigorous Marxist criminology attempts to relate criminal behavior and crime policies to the political economy of the particular societies in which they occur, and relies primarily on historical and cross-cultural studies for support, since only in such studies can societies with different political economies be compared.

In this more rigorous Marxist criminology, the "instrumentalist" view of criminal justice has given way to a more complex "structuralist" view that is more consistent with Marx's theory, as developed by Althusser and others.[20] In this view the primary function of the state is not to directly serve the short-term interests of capitalists, but rather to ensure that the social relations of capitalism will persist in the long run. This requires that many different interests be served at different times, to prevent the rise of conditions that will lead to the collapse of capitalism. Thus, on any particular issue, including the enactment and enforcement of criminal laws, the actions of the state may serve other in-

16. Alan A. Block and William J. Chambliss, *Organizing Crime*, Elsevier, New York, 1981, pp. 4–7. For a much harsher but less substantive criticism of these early theories, see Tony Platt, "Crime and Punishment in the United States: Immediate and Long-Term Reforms from a Marxist Perspective," *Crime and Social Justice*, winter 1982, pp. 38–45.

17. David F. Greenberg, "On One-Dimensional Criminology," *Theory and Society* 3: 610–21 (1976).

18. Greenberg, *Crime and Capitalism*, pp. 6–10.

19. Ibid., p. 10.

20. A useful summary of the instrumentalist vs. structuralist views of the state and the legal order is found in William Chambliss and Robert Seidman, *Law, Order, and Power*, 2nd ed., Addison-Wesley, Reading, Mass., 1982, pp. 306–9. Chambliss and Seidman then propose their own "dialectical, institutionalist" model on pp. 309–16.

terests besides those of the owners of the means of production. Nevertheless, the owners of the means of production can still be described as a ruling class in that the organized state serves their economic interests in the long run, and they have an excessive amount of political power in comparison to other groups, with a disproportionate ability to get the state to serve their interests in the short run.

In addition, the "primitive rebellion" explanation of criminal behavior has given way to a number of explanations within the context of the Marxist theory that are quite similar to explanations found in more traditional criminological theories, except that they link their basic concepts to a broader view of political-economic systems and the historical processes in which those systems change.[21] For example, Greenberg presented a class-based theory of delinquency that has some similarities to so-called strain theories of delinquency.[22] Strain theories describe *class* in terms of the economic or occupational status of the parents, but Greenberg used the traditional Marxist view that class should be defined in terms of the relationship to the means of production. Juveniles occupy a unique position with respect to the means of production in that they are excluded from economically productive activity but are required to engage in extensive training for their future productive role. Thus they can be described as comprising a class of their own. Membership in this class is associated with a number of special strains. Exclusion from the labor market means that they cannot finance the leisure activities that are valued in the peer culture, which leads to stealing to generate desired funds. At the same time, many youths have negative and degrading experiences in schools, which provoke hostile and aggressive responses. Finally, some youths have deep-seated anxieties about achieving the status expected of adult males in our culture, which leads to the establishment of alternate status structures in which status is achieved through criminal acts. Greenberg concluded that programs to reduce delinquency would have little effect unless they were accompanied by broader changes in the capitalist economic system. Later, however, he commented that his conclusion may have been too pessimistic, and pointed to the system of apprenticeships in

21. See Michael J. Lynch and W. Byron Groves, *A Primer in Radical Criminology*, Harrow and Heston, Albany, N.Y., 1989.

22. David F. Greenberg, "Delinquency and the Age Structure of Society," in Greenberg, *Crime and Capitalism*, pp. 118–39. See also M. Colvin and J. Pauly, "A Critique of Criminology: Toward an Integrated Structural-Marxist Theory of Delinquency Production," *American Journal of Sociology* 89(3): 513–51 (1983).

Switzerland, where delinquency is low, and suggested that such a system may have some beneficial effects.[23]

While Greenberg's theory described special strains generating crime and delinquency, other theories have described crime in capitalist societies in terms of the breakdown of social controls. Friedrichs,[24] for example, argued that the effectiveness of a legal order depends largely on the extent to which it is perceived to be "legitimate." He then pointed out that American society is widely described as being in a crisis of legitimacy, indicated by a significant erosion of faith in leaders and in governmental institutions, disillusionment with the basic values on which those institutions are based, and the perception that those institutions are ineffective. In such a situation there is a general rise in various types of illegal behavior, including crime, riots, and revolutionary activity. The state has no choice but to respond to these activities with increasingly coercive and repressive measures, but the long-term effect of these responses is to worsen the crisis. Thus the crisis of legitimacy is a "contradiction" in the sense that it cannot be resolved without changing the basic structural arrangements of capitalism.

While these Marxist views use causal descriptions similar to those found in strain and control theories, the most common Marxist view is similar to those found in the traditional criminology theories that describe criminal behavior as socially learned. These Marxist theories describe criminal behaviors as the rational responses of rational individuals confronted with a situation structured by the social relations of capitalism. This view is consistent with the general view found in Marxist theory that, in general and in the long run, individuals act and think in ways that are consistent with their economic interests.

One such description of criminal behavior was by Gordon, who fo-

---

23. Greenberg, *Crime and Capitalism*, p. 66. Other Marxist criminologists have suggested that high-crime groups are under special strains in the context of a capitalist economic system. For example, Richard Quinney (*Class, State and Crime*, op. cit., pp. 59–62) described street crimes as crimes of "accommodation" to capitalist social relations in the sense that they are the actions of people who have been brutalized by the conditions of capitalism. These criminals reproduce the exploitative relations of capitalism in their own criminal activities—that is, they treat their victims the way they themselves have been treated. Quinney's description relies on Marx's arguments about the lumpenproletariat, as described above.

24. David O. Friedrichs, "The Law and the Legitimacy Crisis," in R. G. Iacovetta and Dae H. Chang, eds., *Critical Issues in Criminal Justice*, Carolina Press, Durham, N.C., 1979, pp. 290–311. See also Friedrichs, "The Legitimacy Crisis: A Conceptual Analysis," *Social Problems* 27(5): 540–55 (1980). Other radical articles that have a control orientation include John R. Hepburn, "Social Control and the Legal Order," *Contemporary Crises* 1: 77–90 (1977); and Raymond J. Michalowski and Edward W. Bohlander, "Repression and Criminal Justice in Capitalist America," *Sociological Inquiry* 46(2): 99–104 (1976).

cused on the economic precariousness of capitalist societies.[25] Gordon argued that crime is simply a way to make money for poor people, who are faced with situations of chronic unemployment and underemployment in low-paying and demeaning jobs. The violent nature of these crimes is a result of the fact that, unlike more powerful groups, poor people do not have the option to steal in more sophisticated ways, that is, with a pen rather than with a gun.

Gordon argued that organized crime was similarly a rational response to economic conditions in which there was a demand for illegal goods and services. This type of business is available to poorer people as a method of making money, whereas other legitimate forms of business are largely unavailable. Chambliss used a similar view in his extensive analysis of organized crime in Seattle.[26] Chambliss argued that at one time most of these goods and services were legal and that they were declared illegal for various historical reasons, but the demand for them did not disappear. He also pointed out that in our political system politicians have a strong need to generate funds to run for political office, and that, at the same time, they control the conditions under which laws against these illegal goods and services are enforced. This creates a very strong pressure for a coalition between politicians and organized crime figures, and Chambliss claimed that he found such a coalition at the heart of organized crime in Seattle. Chambliss was fairly pessimistic about the possibilities for reform to eliminate such crime, except to argue that decriminalization would be helpful. However, he said that most reforms replaced the people in key positions but did nothing about the basic political-economic forces (demand for illegal goods and services, need for money by politicians) that gave rise to organized crime in the first place. As the new "reform" people responded to those same forces, they tended to do the same kinds of things done by the corrupt politicians they had replaced.

In a later book with Block, Chambliss generalized some of his arguments, relating various types of crime to the political-economic systems of societies in which they occur.[27] They argued that every political-economic system contains contradictions that cannot be resolved without changing the fundamental structure of the society. Crime in a society is essentially a rational response to those contradictions. The problem with crime control policies in general is that they attempt to deal with

25. David M. Gordon, "Class and the Economics of Crime," *Review of Radical Political Economics* 3: 51–75 (summer 1971). See also Gordon, "Capitalism, Class, and Crime in America," *Crime and Delinquency* 19: 163–86 (April 1973).

26. William J. Chambliss, *On the Take: From Petty Crooks to Presidents*, Indiana University Press, Bloomington, 1978.

27. Block and Chambliss, op. cit.

the symptoms without changing the basic political-economic forces that generate those symptoms to begin with.[28]

As Marxist criminologists have rejected the "primitive rebellion" theory of criminal behavior and "instrumentalist" view of criminal justice, they have attempted to take a more realistic approach to the problems of crime and the possible responses of criminal justice. Called "left realism," these criminologists recognize that crime causes serious problems for working class citizens and that criminal justice agencies can respond to those problems even if the capitalist economic system is not overthrown.[29] These criminologists have therefore made a variety of policy recommendations that are not that different from the recommendations of mainstream (if liberal) criminologists, such as better policing[30] the prosecution of white-collar offenders,[31] reforming prisons,[32] regulating (as opposed to criminalizing) street prostitution,[33] and addressing the major health, housing, and educational needs of inner cities as a long-term strategy for dealing with the drug problem.[34]

POSTMODERNISM AND POSTMODERNIST CRIMINOLOGY

Modernism is associated with what is described above in the early chapters of this book as the "naturalistic" approach to the world. One part of the "naturalistic" approach is a view of science as an objective process directed toward predicting and controlling the world.[35] As stated above, most criminology is "modernist" or "naturalistic" in this sense.

28. Greenberg, *Crime and Capitalism*, pp. 23–25.

29. Platt (op. cit., p. 40), for example, states: "In general, the New Left either glossed over 'street' crime as an invention of the FBI to divert attention away from corporate crimes or romanticized it as a form of primitive political rebellion. But as we well know from both experience and knowledge, 'street' crime is not a fiction, but rather a very real and serious problem, especially in the superexploited sectors of the working class and its reserve army of labor. . . . This [earlier view] was irresponsible and dangerous, a reflection of the profound alienation of the New Left from the daily conditions of life in working class communities."

30. R. Kinsey, J. Lea, and Jock Young, *Losing the Fight Against Crime*, Blackwell, Oxford, 1986. T. Mattiesen (*The Politics of Abolition*, Martin Robertson, London, 1990) even suggested that realist criminology placed all its faith in better policing as the major means to reduce crime.

31. David O. Friedrichs, *White Collar Crime in Contemporary Society*, Wadsworth, Belmont, Calif., 1995.

32. Roger Matthews, "Developing a Realist Approach to Prison Reform," pp. 71–87 in Lowman and MacLean, op. cit.

33. John Lowman, "Street Prostitution Control," pp. 1–17 and Roger Matthews, "Regulating Street Prostitution and Kerb-Crawling: A Reply to Lowman," pp. 18–22 in *British Journal of Criminology* 32, spring 1992. See also John Lowman, "The 'Left Regulation' of Prostitution," pp. 157–76 in Lowman and MacLean, op. cit.

34. Elliott Currie, "Retreatism, Minimalism, Realism: Three Styles of Reasoning on Crime and Drugs in the United States," pp. 88–97 in Lowman and MacLean, op. cit.

35. Anthony Borgman, *Crossing the Postmodern Divide*, University of Chicago Press, Chicago, 1992.

Postmodernism rejects the modernist or "naturalistic" approach by arguing that all thinking and all knowledge are mediated by language, and that language itself is never a neutral medium. Whether or not people are aware of it, language always privileges some points of view and disparages others. For example, modernism privileges "scientific" thinking, holding that it has special validity and objectivity in comparison to other types of thinking. Postmodernists, in contrast, do not give scientific thinking a special position, and describe it instead as being no more nor less valid than other types of thinking. To a certain extent, postmodernists even attack scientific thinking because they attempt to "deconstruct" privileged points of view—i.e., to identify implicit assumptions and unsupported assertions that underlie the ways in which its point of view are legitimized and other points of view are disparaged. At the same time, postmodernists tend to seek out the disparaged points of view to make them more explicit and legitimate.[36] The goal is not simply to tear down one and replace it with the other, but rather to come to a situation in which different grammars can be simultaneously held as legitimate, so that there is a sense of the diversity of points of view without assuming that one is superior and the others are inferior.

Schwartz and Friedrichs point out that postmodernism itself is difficult to summarize because "there seems to be an almost infinite number of postmodern perspectives."[37] In addition, Schwartz has pointed out the difficulty of the writing style of postmodernist writers, stating that even after reading them several times, "I really do not know what the hell they are talking about."[38] Both these problems are related to postmodernism itself since it holds that linear thought processes, statements about cause and effect, syllogistic reasoning, objective analyses, and other standards of scientific thinking are no more valid than other forms of thinking. Thus, to the extent that one tries to "summarize" postmodern thought in some logical, coherent, systematic fashion, one con-

---

36. Because of this tendency to attack privileged lines of thinking, postmodernism in general, and deconstruction in particular, has been criticized as being nihilistic and relativistic. See Einstadter and Henry, op. cit., p. 298.

37. Martin D. Schwartz and David O. Friedrichs, "Postmodern Thought and Criminological Discontent," *Criminology* 32(2): 221–46 (May 1994). In addition, Schwartz and Friedrichs mention the possibility that "much of what has been published is only a pretentious intellectual fad." A particularly embarrassing episode related to this was the publication in a leading journal, *Social Text*, of a parody of postmodern thought. The author later explained: "I structured the article around the silliest quotes about mathematics and physics from the most prominent academics, and I invented an argument praising them and linking them together. All of this was very easy to carry off because my argument wasn't obliged to respect any standards of evidence and logic." Quoted in Scott McConnell, "City and Nation," *New York Post*, May 22, 1996.

38. Martin D. Schwartz, "The Future of Criminology," pp. 119–24 in Brian MacLean and Dragan Milovanovic, *New Directions in Criminology*, Collective Press, Vancouver, 1991.

tradicts postmodern thought itself. Nevertheless, at least some post-modern theorists have attempted to make such summaries while acknowledging the self-contradictory nature of the effort.[39]

Central to postmodernism is the view that modernism in general, and science in particular, has led to increased oppression rather than to liberation[40]:

(Postmodernism) contends that modernity is no longer liberating, but rather has become a force for subjugation, oppression, and repression; this contention applies to social science itself, which is a product of modernity. Postmodernists are disillusioned with liberal notions of progress and radical expectations of emancipation. . . The forces of modernism (e.g., industrialism) have extended and amplified the scope of violence in the world. Even worse, according to the post-modern critique, the major form of response to this violence is through rational organizations (e.g., the court system and the regulatory bureaucracies) with great reliance on specialists and experts. Such a response simply reproduces domination, the critique suggests, in perhaps new but no less pernicious forms.

The postmodernist response is to expose the structures of domination in societies as a means of achieving greater liberation. The principal source of this domination, according to postmodernists, is in control of language systems.[41] This is because language structures thought—i.e., the words and phrases people use to convey meaning are not neutral endeavors but support dominant views of the world, whether the people who use those languages know it or not.[42]

Postmodernists therefore examine the relationship between human agency and language in the creation of meaning, identity, truth, justice, power, and knowledge.[43] This relationship is studied through *discourse*

39. Three of the most readable summaries of postmodernism and of its application to criminology are found in Arrigo, op. cit., Schwartz and Friedrichs, op. cit., and Einstadter and Henry, op. cit., ch. 12. Arrigo (op. cit., pp. 449–50) acknowledges the "delicious irony" involved in attempting to summarize this perspective: "If postmodernism signifies a perspective outside or apart from standard methods of knowing, experiencing, and living, how can one nevertheless invoke that traditional discourse, which itself is anathema to the postmodern enterprise in law and criminology, to explain that enterprise." Similarly, Schwartz and Friedrichs (op. cit., pp. 222–23) state that "it may well be a fundamental contradiction to attempt any coherent definition of postmodernism. . . ," and Einstadter and Henry comment that "classifying postmodernist criminology is contradictory to the postmodernist project" (p. 281).

40. Schwartz and Friedrichs, op. cit., p. 224.

41. The following discussion relies heavily on Bruce A. Arrigo and Thomas J. Bernard, "Postmodern Criminology in Relation to Radical and Conflict Theory," *Critical Criminologist*, forthcoming.

42. Dragan Milovanovic, *A Primer in the Sociology of Law*, Harrow and Heston, Albany, N.Y., 1994, pp. 143–45, 155–84; Bruce Arrigo, *Madness, Language, and the Law*, Harrow and Heston, Albany, N.Y., 1993, pp. 27–75.

43. Stuart Henry and Dragan Milovanovic, *Constitutive Criminology: Beyond Postmodernism*, Sage, London, 1996, pp. 8–11, 26–44.

analysis, which is a method of investigating how sense and meaning are constructed. Specific attention is paid to the values and assumptions implied in the language used by the author.[44] Discourse analysis considers the social position of the person who is speaking or writing to understand the meaning of what is said or written. For example, to understand fully what lawyers mean when they speak *as lawyers*, it is necessary to understand quite a bit about "lawyering" as a historically situated and structured position in society.[45] There are many other "discursive subject positions" in crime and criminal justice which come connected with their own language systems—e.g., police, juvenile gang members, drug dealers, corrections officers, organized crime figures, corporate and political offenders, court workers, shoplifters, armed robbers, and even criminologists.

Postmodernist criminologists point out that, once people assume one of these "discursive subject positions," then the words that they speak no longer fully express their realities, but to some extent express the realities of the larger institutions and organizations. Because people's language is somewhat removed from their reality, people are described as *decentered*—i.e., people are never quite what their words describe and always are somewhat tending to be what their language systems expect or demand.[46]

For example, women who have been raped must present their stories to prosecutors, who then reconstruct and repackage the stories into the language of the courts—i.e., "legal-ese."[47] The woman may testify at the trial, but her testimony may not deviate from the accepted language system without jeopardizing the chances that the defendant will be convicted.[48] Even when the defendant is convicted, the woman who has been raped may leave the court with a deep and dissatisfying sense that her story was never fully told, her reality never fully seen, her pain never fully acknowledged. The language of the court system expresses and institutionalizes a form of domination over the victim, and this is one reason that victims so often are dissatisfied with the courts.

44. For applications within criminology, see Peter K. Manning, *Symbolic Communication: Signifying Calls and the Police Response*, MIT Press, Cambridge, Mass., 1988; Dragan Milovanovic, *Postmodern Law and Disorder*, Deborah Charles, Liverpool, U.K., 1992; and Arrigo, op. cit.

45. Peter Goodrich, "Law and Language: An Historical and Critical Introduction," *Journal of Law and Society* 11: 173–206 (1984).

46. Henry and Milovanovic, op. cit., 1996, p. 27.

47. Milovanovic, op. cit., pp. 145–50.

48. Bruce A. Arrigo, "An Experientially-Informed Feminist Jurisprudence," *Humanity and Society* 17(1): 28–47 (1993).

A similar situation happens with defendants who are accused of crimes. Criminal defense lawyers routinely repackage and re-construct the defendant's story into "legal-ese" as part of constructing the defense. The lawyer does this because it is the only way to win the case, but the full meaning of the defendant's story is normally lost in the process. Less-experienced defendants may object because the story that is told in court has so little resemblance to what actually happened. But more sophisticated defendants know that this is how the game is played. Even if the defendant "wins" the case (i.e., is acquitted), there has still been a ritualistic ceremony in which the reality of the courts has dominated the reality of the defendant. Thus, independent of who "wins" the case, the language of the court expresses and institutionalizes the domination of the individual by social institutions.

Other postmodern analyses have demonstrated the way that official language dominates participants in the criminal justice process, so that the participants themselves experience the system as marginalizing, alienating, and oppressive. These include studies of jailhouse lawyers,[49] police officers responding to 911 calls,[50] and the experience of female lawyers in criminal courts.[51] In each case, one view of reality (i.e., that of the inmates, the police, and the female lawyers) is replaced by another (i.e., the language of the court or correctional system), thereby affirming and legitimizing the status quo.

Postmodernists describe the present situation as one in which discourses are either dominant (e.g., the language of medicine, law, and science) or oppositional (e.g., the language of prison inmates). The goal of postmodernism is to move to a situation where many different discourses are recognized as legitimate. One of the ways of doing that is to establish "replacement discourses" in which the language itself helps people speak with a more authentic voice and to remain continuously aware of the authentic voices of other people.[52] The goal is greater inclusivity, more diverse communication, and a pluralistic culture. To achieve these ends, postmodernists listen carefully to the otherwise excluded views in constituting the definition of criminal acts. They conclude that creating a society in which alternative discourses liberate citizens from prevailing speech patterns will also legitimate the role of all citizens in the project of reducing crime. The result will be greater re-

49. Dragan Milovanovic, "Jailhouse Lawyers and Jailhouse Lawyering," *International Journal of the Sociology of Law* 16: 455–75 (1988).

50. Manning, op. cit.

51. Arrigo, *Madness, Language, and the Law*, op. cit.

52. Henry and Milovanovic, op. cit., p. 204.

spect for the diversity of people in the entire society. Ultimately, this would include less victimizing of other people by criminals, and less official punishment of criminals by agents of the larger society.[53]

Postmodernism exposes a basis for power and domination in societies that has been ignored in earlier conflict and Marxist theories. However, it has tended toward an "appreciative relativism"[54] and "communal celebration,"[55] which resembles early simplistic Marxist views of crime, especially to the extent that it "appreciates" or "celebrates" the actions of criminals when they victimize other people. This contradicts the later "left realist" approach, which concludes that crime is a real social problem that needs to be addressed by real criminal justice policies. Pepinsky, however, argues that coercive social policies merely perpetuate the problem[56]:

Crime is violence. So is punishment, and so is war. People who go to war believe that violence works. So do criminals and people who want criminals punished. All these believe violence works because they also believe that domination is necessary. Someone who is closer to God, natural wisdom, or scientific truth has to keep wayward subordinates in line, or social order goes to hell.

Similarly, Quinney states[57]:

. . . the criminal justice system in this country is founded on violence. It is a system that assumes that violence can be overcome by violence, evil by evil. . . This principle sadly dominates much of our criminology. . . When we recognize that the criminal justice system is the moral equivalent of the war machine, we realize that resistance to one goes hand-in-hand with resistance to the other. This resistance must be in compassion and love, not in terms of the violence that is being resisted.

Ultimately, these criminologists have come to the conclusion that the violence of punishment can only perpetuate and increase the violence of crime. Only when criminologists and the public give up their belief in the effectiveness and appropriateness of violence can we reasonably expect criminals to do the same thing.

53. Arrigo and Bernard, op. cit.

54. Einstadter and Henry, op. cit., p. 289.

55. This term is used by Einstadter and Henry (ibid., p. 299, fn. 13) in reference to Borgman, op. cit.

56. Harold E. Pepinsky, "Peacemaking in Criminology and Criminal Justice," in Pepinsky and Richard Quinney, eds., *Criminology as Peacemaking*, Indiana University Press, Bloomington, 1991, p. 301. Einstadter and Schwartz (op. cit., pp. 295–97) describe peacemaking criminology as a "replacement discourse" within the context of postmodernism. It is derived largely from the Marxist tradition, but has a heavy emphasis on appreciative relativism as a conflict-reduction technique.

57. Richard Quinney, "The Way of Peace," in ibid., p. 12

FEMINISM AND FEMINIST CRIMINOLOGY

Like Marxism and postmodernism, feminism is an extremely broad area of social theorizing that has applications to the field of criminology, although this is by no means its major focus. Like postmodernism, there are numerous branches of feminism and feminist criminology, with numerous disagreements and shadings of meanings within those branches. What follows here is only a brief overview intended to give a sense of the area and to identify its major themes.

The initial feminist writings in criminology were critiques that argued that a number of topics related to women offenders had largely been ignored or heavily distorted within traditional criminology.[58] For example, traditional criminology theories largely failed to explain the criminal behavior of women. A few theories within traditional criminology had addressed the subject, but they were simplistic and relied on stereotypical images of women.[59] Most criminology theories simply did not address the subject in any way.[60] In addition, most traditional criminology theories were effectively gender-neutral—i.e., they applied to women as well as to men and therefore did not explain the differences between women and men in their participation in crime. When the gendered nature of crime was addressed (i.e., men commit the vast majority of crimes), the theories tended to focus on supposed characteristics that implied women's inferiority and tended to reinforce their subordination to men in the larger society.[61] Traditional criminology theories also failed to address the different ways women were treated by the criminal justice system.[62] For example, women accused of sexual crimes

---

58. Dorie Klein, "The Etiology of the Female Crime: A Review of the Literature," *Issues in Criminology* 8: 3–30 (1973); Carol Smart, *Women, Crime and Criminology: A Feminist Critique*, Routledge and Kegan Paul, Boston, 1976. These are briefly reviewed in Sally S. Simpson, "Feminist Theory, Crime, and Justice," *Criminology* 27(4): 605–31 (1989); and in Kathleen Daly and Meda Chesney-Lind, "Feminism and Criminology," *Justice Quarterly* 5(4): 497–538 (Dec. 1988).

59. Some of these theories are Cesare Lombroso and William Ferrero, *The Female Offender*, Appleton, New York, 1867; Bonger, op. cit.; and Otto Pollock, *The Criminality of Women*, University of Pennsylvania Press, Philadelphia, 1950. See the discussion of these theories in James W. Messerschmidt, *Masculinities and Crime*, Rowman & Littlefield, Lanham, Md., 1993, pp. 4–11.

60. Eileen B. Leonard, *Women, Crime and Society: A Critique of Criminology Theory*, Longman, New York, 1982; Ngaire Naffine, *Female Crime: The Construction of Women in Criminology*, Allen and Unwin, Boston, 1987.

61. Carol Smart, *Women, Crime and Criminology: A Feminist Critique*, Routledge & Kegan Paul, Boston, 1976; Frances Heidensohn, *Women and Crime*, New York University Press, New York, 1985. For a brief discussion with some examples, see Messerschmidt, op. cit., pp. 2–4; or James W. Messerschmidt, *Capitalism, Patriarchy and Crime: Toward a Socialist Feminist Criminology*, Rowman and Littlefield, Totowa, N.J., 1986, pp. 1–24.

62. Jane R. Chapman, *Economic Realities and the Female Offender*, Lexington Books, Lexington, Mass., 1980; Susan Datesman and Frank R. Scarpitti, *Women, Crime and Justice*, Oxford University Press, New York, 1980; Clarice Feinman, *Women in the Criminal Justice System*, Praeger, New York, 1986. Some of the differences are reviewed in Simpson, op. cit., pp. 612–17.

were often treated more harshly than men accused of the same crimes, but women accused of violent crimes were often treated more leniently than men. These differences in treatment led to differences in official crime rates (e.g., higher rates of sexual offenses but lower rates of violent offenses), which then affected the explanations of women's criminality by criminology theories. Finally, none of the existing criminology theories discussed the new roles that women were taking on in the larger society as part of what was then called "women's liberation," and how those new roles might impact women's participation in criminal activity.

The critiques that pointed out these many problems with traditional criminology were followed by two books on the subject of women and crime that appeared in 1975. In *Sisters in Crime: The Rise of the New Female Criminal*,[63] Freda Adler argued that women were becoming more aggressive and competitive as they moved out of the traditional home-bound social roles and into the previously largely male world of the competitive marketplace. Essentially, Adler believed that women were taking on what had been masculine qualities as they fought the same battles that men had always fought. She argued that a similar transformation was occurring among criminals, where "a similar number of determined women are forcing their way into the world of major crimes. . . ." Now, she argued, there were "increasing numbers of women who are using guns, knives, and wits to establish themselves as full human beings, as capable of violence and aggression as any man."

In that same year, Rita James Simon published *Women and Crime*.[64] Simon also described recent changes in the types and volume of crime committed by women, but argued that it was not because they were taking on formerly masculine characteristics. Rather, as they moved out of the traditional home-bound roles, women encountered a much wider variety of opportunities to commit crime. This was particularly true of opportunities to commit economic and white-collar crimes, which required access to other people's money in positions of trust.

Both Adler's and Simon's theories argued that liberation from traditional women's roles would result in increases in crime committed by women. The major difference between the two had to do with the prediction about the type of crime these new female criminals would commit: Adler's theory suggested a larger portion of this crime would be violent, whereas Simon's theory suggested it should be predominantly in the area of property and white-collar crime.[65] Later research suggested

---

63. McGraw Hill, New York, 1975.

64. *Women and Crime*, Lexington Books, Lexington, Mass., 1975. See also Simon and Jean Landis, *The Crimes Women Commit, the Punishments They Receive*, Lexington Books, Lexington, Mass., 1991.

that Simon's opportunity thesis had more validity, but on the whole there was little evidence that this "new female criminal" existed at all.[66] In addition, Simpson suggested that these theories generated enormous interest among nonfeminist criminologists, and in some ways set back the cause of a feminist criminology because it "diverted attention from the material and structural forces that shape women's lives and experiences," and ignored broader questions of how those forces shaped women's lives.[67] Because of this, other feminist criminologists argue that neither theory should be described as feminist criminology.[68]

After Adler's and Simon's contributions, criminological writings that focused on explaining women's participation in crime expanded dramatically.[69] Many of these writings could be described as a part of traditional criminology itself, filling in gaps and correcting the distortions of the past. As such, they were part of what came to be called *liberal feminism*.[70] This branch of feminism basically operated within the framework of existing social structures where it worked to direct attention to women's issues, promote women's rights, increase women's opportunities, and transform women's roles in society.

Soon, however, several strands of "critical" feminism arose, which directly challenged the social structures within which liberal feminism operated. These strands looked at the much more fundamental questions of how women had come to occupy subservient roles in society and how societies themselves might be transformed. The first such strand is known as *radical feminism*, and its central concept is that of "patriarchy." Originally a concept used by sociologists like Max Weber to describe social relations under feudalism, the term was resurrected by Kate Millett in 1970 to refer to a form of social organization in which men dominate women.[71] Millett argued that patriarchy is the most fundamental

65. Ted Alleman, "Varieties of Feminist Thought and Their Application to Crime and Criminal Justice," pp. 3–42 in Roslyn Muraskin and Ted Alleman, eds., *It's a Crime: Women and Justice*, Prentice Hall, Englewood Cliffs, N.J., 1993.

66. Simpson, op. cit., p. 610.

67. Simpson, op. cit., p. 611. Daly and Chesney-Lind (op. cit., p. 511) also point to the "limitations of the liberal feminist perspective on gender that informed their work."

68. Allison Morris, *Women, Crime and Criminal Justice*, Blackwell, New York, 1987, p. 16. Daly and Chesney-Lind (op. cit., p. 507) agree with her conclusion.

69. For a collection of readings on the subject, see Muraskin and Alleman, op. cit. See also brief summaries in Simpson, op. cit., and Daly and Chesney-Lind, op. cit.

70. Alison Jaggar, *Feminist Politics and Human Nature*, Roman and Allanheld, Totowa, N.J., 1983. For brief discussions of liberal, as well as radical, Marxist, and socialist feminism in criminology, see Simpson, op. cit., p. 607; Daly and Chesney-Lind, op. cit., p. 507, 537; Alleman, op. cit., pp. 9–11; Einstadter and Henry, op. cit., pp. 264, and Franklin P. Williams III and Marilyn D. McShane, *Criminological Theory*, 2nd ed., Prentice Hall, Englewood Cliffs, NJ, 1994.

71. Kate Millett, *Sexual Politics*, Doubleday, New York, 1970.

form of domination in every society. Patriarchy is established and maintained through sex role socialization and the creation of "core gender identities," through which both men and women come to believe that men are superior in a variety of ways. Based on these gender identities, men tend to dominate women in personal interactions, such as within the family. From there, male domination is extended to all the institutions and organizations of the larger society. Because male power is based on personal relationships, these feminists concluded that "the personal is political."

Where Millett had placed the root of the problem in socialization into gendered sex roles, *Marxist feminists* combined radical feminism with traditional Marxism to argue that the root of the problem of male dominance lay in the fact that men own and control the means of economic production. That is, Marxist feminism tied patriarchy to the economic structure of capitalism. This resulted in a "sexual division of labor" in which men control the economy and women serve them and their sexual needs.[72] As with Marxist criminology generally, Marxist feminists argue that the criminal justice system defines as crimes those actions that threaten this capitalist-patriarchal system. Thus, the actions by women that are defined as crimes primarily take the form of property crimes (when women threaten male economic dominance) and sexual offenses (when women threaten male control of women's bodies and sexuality). As with Marxists generally, some Marxist feminists take an "instrumental" view of the criminal law, in which law is described as a direct instrument of men's oppression, while others take a more complex "structural" view that looks to overall patterns through which law maintains the system of patriarchy in the long run.[73] An additional source of women's criminality in this perspective is found in the frustration and anger that women feel in being trapped in these limiting social roles.[74]

Finally, *socialist feminists* retained both the focus on social roles and economic production, but moved away from a more rigid Marxist framework. In particular, they added a strong element about natural reproductive differences between the sexes, which underlies male-female relationships in the larger society. Before birth control, women were much more at the mercy of their biology than men—menstruation, pregnancy,

---

72. Polly Radosh, "Woman and Crime in the United States: A Marxian Explanation," *Sociological Spectrum* 10:105–31 (1990).

73. Dawn Currie, "Women and the State: A Statement on Feminist Theory," *Critical Criminologist* 1(2): 4–5 (1989); Einstader and Henry, op. cit., pp. 267–68.

74. Radosh, op. cit.; Daly and Chesney-Lond, op. cit.

childbirth and nursing, menopause—all of which made them more dependent on men for physical survival. The biological role of women in being pregnant, giving birth, and nursing babies led to their taking major responsibility for raising children, who require extensive care for long periods of time. Ultimately, this led to a "sexual division of labor" in which men work outside the home and women work inside it, which then forms the basis for male domination and control over women.[75] Therefore, the key to an egalitarian society lay not in women taking ownership of the means of economic production, but in women taking control of their own bodies and their own reproductive functions. Once they have done that, then they can move on to taking their rightful place in the larger societies.

Messerschmidt makes an additional argument that radical and Marxist feminists tended over time to transform Millett's original argument about gendered sex roles into one that attributed the problem to the "essential" characteristics of men and masculinity.[76] That is, radical feminists argued that the problem is not that males are socialized into sex roles with certain characteristics, but that it is in men's nature to be dominating and violent. Thus, what started out as a socialization theory became an "essentialist" theory that pointed to biological differences between men and women as the foundation for patriarchy. This "essentialism" eventually led to a celebration of all characteristics that were said to be "essentially female" and a condemnation of all characteristics that were said to be "essentially male." Messerschmidt argues that the basic problem lies in socialization into sex roles and that biological arguments about male aggressiveness are simply false. He therefore developed a social structural theory, consistent with socialist feminism, of how males are socialized into roles that lead to violence and domination.

Liberal, radical, Marxist, and socialist feminisms are all widely recognized as separate strands of feminism, but several other "strands" also are sometimes mentioned.[77] One of these is "postmodern feminism." Smart, for example, discusses how discourse is used to set certain women

---

75. Shulamith Firestone, *The Dialectics of Sex: The Case for Feminist Revolution*, William Morrow, New York, 1970. For a brief discussion, see Alleman, op. cit., pp. 29–31.

76. Messerschmidt, op. cit, 1993, pp. 45–50. See also Messerschmidt, "From Patriarchy to Gender: Feminist Theory, Criminology and the Challenge of Diversity," ch. 9 in Nicole Hahn Rafter and Frances Heidensohn, *International Feminist Perspectives in Criminology*, Open University Press, Buckingham, U.K., 1995; and the discussion on "controlling men's violence toward women" in Daly and Chesney-Lind, op. cit., pp. 520–21.

77. See, for example, Daly and Chesney-Lind, op. cit., p. 501; and Simpson, p. 606.

apart as "criminal women."[78] Other feminists reject postmodernism, claiming that feminism should be seen as a modernist project adhering to standards of scientific objectivity.[79]

Whether or not they adhere to postmodernism as a whole, a large number of feminists now take an "appreciative relativism" stance within feminism that is similar to postmodernism. That is, they recognize and appreciate many different feminist voices as legitimate, and refrain from analyzing, classifying, and ultimately picking apart those different voices.[80] On the other hand, many feminists also claim that feminist thinking is superior to "male-dominated" thinking, which they describe as biased, distorted, and lacking objectivity due to its loyalty to male domination.[81] But because it neither privileges nor disparages particular points of view, postmodernism itself would seem to suggest that "male-dominated" thinking is as legitimate as feminist thinking. To that extent, postmodernism seems difficult to reconcile with feminism.[82]

Clearly, feminist criminology has filled in many gaps and corrected many distortions in traditional criminology. But in this role, it fits within the enterprise of traditional criminology itself. The larger question concerns whether there is some definable and separate "feminist thinking" that diverges from and is even incompatible with traditional criminology.[83] It is to this larger and much more complex issue that feminist criminologists are now turning.

Daly and Chesney-Lind make an argument that is related to this point: "The place of men and women in theories of crime cannot be separated from . . . the place of men and of women in constructing theory and conducting research."[84] That is, they argue that there are differences between men and women criminologists, and that these differences are

78. Carol Smart, *Feminism and the Power of Law*, Routledge, London, U.K., 1989; and "Feminist Approaches to Criminology or Postmodern Woman Meets Atavistic Man," pp. 70–84 in Loraine Gelshorpe and Allison Morris, eds., *Feminist Perspectives in Criminology*, Open University Press, Milton Keynes, U.K., 1990. For a different postmodernist feminist view, see Christine Garza, "Postmodern Paradigms and Chicana Feminist Thought: Creating a Space and Language," *Critical Criminologist* 4(3/4): 1–2, 11–13 (1992). These are reviewed in Einstadter and Henry, op. cit., pp. 285–86.

79. Einstadter and Henry, op. cit., p. 299.

80. On the other hand, such broad inclusion of diverse women's experience tends to weaken arguments about women's common experiences of oppression. See Dawn H. Currie, "Challenging Privilege: Feminist Struggles in the Canadian Context," *Critical Criminologist* 3(1): 1–2, 10–12 (1991).

81. Jagger, op. cit., p. 370. For a discussion of this view, see Daly and Chesney-Lind, op. cit., pp. 499–500.

82. Einstadter and Henry, op. cit., pp. 299–300.

83. Smart, 1990, op. cit., p. 261.

84. Daly and Chesney-Lind, op. cit., pp. 518–19.

associated with differences in the types of problems that they address, in the types of theories that they construct, and in the types of research that they conduct.

Daly and Chesney-Lind point out that the problem of gender and crime in criminology has taken one of two forms[85]: the *generalizability* problem, which focuses on whether traditional criminology theories, which explain male criminal behavior, can be generalized to explain female criminal behavior; and the *gender ratio* problem, which focuses on explaining why women are less likely, and men more likely, to engage in criminal behavior. The "generalizability" problem has been addressed primarily by male criminologists.[86] Daly and Chesney-Lind also suggest that this is the "safe" course of action, intellectually and professionally, for female criminologists who are just entering the field since it uses "a domesticated feminism to modify previous theory."[87] The problem with this approach, however, is that the research on generalizability is decidedly mixed, so that the traditional male-oriented criminology theories have limited value for explaining female criminality.[88] This may be because the theoretical concepts on which they are based "are inscribed so deeply by masculinist experience that this approach will prove too restrictive, or at least misleading" when applied to female crime.[89]

Almost all women criminologists who examine gender and crime have addressed the "gender ratio" problem, as opposed to the "generalizability" problem. In doing this, their research has been more likely to involve observations and interviews, and they "have displayed more tentativeness and a discomfort with making global claims" at the theoretical level. In contrast, the men criminologists who address the gender ratio problem have been more bold in making grand theoretical claims, and have tended to do empirical research that involved statistical analysis of quantitative data. Daly and Chesney-Lind state that the women criminologists[90]

are more interested in providing texture, social context, and case histories: in short, in presenting accurate portraits of how adolescent and adult women become involved in crime. This gender difference . . . (is related) to a felt need

85. Ibid., pp. 514–20.

86. See, for example, John Hagan's power-control theory, reviewed in Chapter 18, pp. 246–48.

87. Daly and Chesney-Lind, op. cit., p. 518.

88. Ibid., p. 514.

89. Ibid., p. 519.

90. Ibid., p. 518.

to comprehend women's crime on its own terms, just as criminologists of the past did for men's crime.

The problem for these women criminologists is that "global or grand theoretical arguments and high-tech statistical analyses are valued more highly by the profession."[91] The women criminologists therefore run the risk that their approaches "will be trivialized merely as case studies, or will be written off as not theoretical enough."[92]

ASSESSMENTS OF CRITICAL THEORIES

Most societies based on Marxism have now collapsed, which clearly suggests that economic systems based on Marxism have fatal flaws. However, the new nations that have emerged from the collapse of Marxist societies have experienced large increases in crime as they re-established capitalism.[93] This suggests that there may be some validity to the claim within Marxist criminology that there is a link between crime and capitalism. At a minimum, criminologists might examine recent developments in the former communist countries to determine whether capitalism is causally related to certain types and levels of crime. If a relationship between political economy and crime rates does exist, it may be because, as was suggested in Chapter 8, that capitalism tends to be associated with higher levels of economic inequality, and the inequality itself, rather than the capitalist economic system, causes crime.

Postmodernist criminology has many similarities to Marxist criminology, but shifts attention from economic production to linguistic production. Postmodernists draw attention to the uses of language in creating dominance relationships, which would seem to have a great deal of merit in general and in the study of crime in particular.[94] In addition, the development of "replacement discourses" that are inclusive and accepting, instead of exclusive and rejecting, could have consid-

91. Ibid., p. 518.

92. Ibid., pp. 519–20.

93. See, for example, Stephen Handelman, "The Russian 'Mafiya,' " *Foreign Affairs* 73(2): 83–92 (1994); Robert M. Lombardo, ed., "Organized Crime IV: The Russian Connection," *Journal of Contemporary Criminal Justice* 11(4): 213–97 (1995).

94. The use of language in creating dominance relationships was a major focus of Bernard, *The Consensus Conflict Debate*, op. cit. The book attempted to show how social theories use certain language systems (the "form" of the theory) to construct ideas about who and what is legitimate in the society (the "content" of the theory). These ideas about legitimacy are then used to privilege certain people and to repress others in the society. The book showed that these patterned ways of constructing legitimacy go back as far as Plato and Aristotle and are the actual point at issue in what is known more recently as "the consensus-conflict debate."

erable benefits for criminology and may well be a method to reduce crime.[95]

However, postmodernists take a position of "appreciative relativism" that privileges all points of view equally and treats scientific discourse as having no more validity than any other language. This may go too far for most criminologists, who hold to the validity of the basic scientific process despite all of its practical difficulties. Indeed, criminologists may look at postmodern criminology from a scientific perspective. One of its fundamental assertions is that violence begets violence, so that the violence of our present criminal justice policies will only increase the violence of criminals in our society. This, in the last analysis, is an empirical assertion that can be tested with scientific research—e.g., the violence of criminal justice policies in different states or nations could be compared to the crime rates of those states or nations. If the postmodernists are correct, there should be a clear relationship between violent criminal justice policies and violent crime.

Even if criminologists do not agree that all types of thinking have equal legitimacy with scientific thinking, they may want to consider that there is at least one alternate way of thinking that merits further exploration: feminine thinking.[96] Scientific thinking is typically masculine—linear, rational, quick, certain, objective. "Feminine" thinking tends to be slower, intuitive, more circular and iterative, more tentative, and in many ways similar to the way Daly and Chesney-Lind report women criminologists have approached the gender-ratio problem in criminology. Perhaps criminology needs to adopt enough "appreciative relativism" to encompass what has previously been a feminine approach to crime.

95. For example, Braithwaite's shaming theory, discussed in Chapter 18, pp. 303–4, makes some similar arguments about inclusive and exclusive uses of language in responding to deviance. However, he does so in the context of a traditional scientific approach, rather than a postmodern approach.

96. See, for example, Marion Woodman, *Leaving My Father's House: A Journey to Conscious Femininity*, Shambhala, Boston, 1993. Woodman argues that "masculine" and "feminine" are principles in every person, and that they are not confined to one gender or the other. Her use of these terms is similar to Thomas Moore's use of the terms "spirit" and "soul" in his books *Care of the Soul* and *Soul Mates* (HarperCollins, New York, 1992 and 1994).

CHAPTER 17

Developmental Criminology

Most theories in criminology focus on the relationship between crime and various biological, psychological or social factors, and they assume that these factors have the same effect on offenders regardless of their age. In contrast, developmental theories assume that different factors may have different effects on offenders of different ages. These developmental theories therefore explain crime in the context of the life course: i.e., the progression from childhood to adolescence to adulthood and ultimately to old age. For example, developmental theories may assert that some factors explain criminal behavior that starts in childhood or early adolescence, but other factors explain crime that starts in late adolescence or adulthood. Some factors explain the fact that a person begins to commit crime, while other factors explain whether the person continues to commit crime for a long time or quickly stops.

A substantial number of criminologists argue that these developmental theories do not contribute anything new to criminology, and that the standard theories that do not consider age and the life course are adequate to explain crime. A major debate about this issue was fully engaged by the mid-1980s. At its center was an argument about the relationship between age and crime. But the debate also was entangled in complicated arguments about criminal careers, since that concept refers to the development and progression of offending over time. The debate also involved a particularly fierce argument about the type of research needed to test criminology theories. We begin with a review of this debate and of some of the evidence that was marshalled to defend each side. We then discuss other developmental theories that have been recently proposed.

THE GREAT DEBATE: CRIMINAL CAREERS, LONGITUDINAL RESEARCH, AND THE RELATIONSHIP BETWEEN AGE AND CRIME

In 1986, the National Research Council's Panel on Research on Criminal Careers published a two-volume work entitled *Criminal Careers and "Career Criminals."*[1] The panel's research was based on ideas that had been brewing for some time. In 1958, a study in Philadelphia had concluded that 6 percent of juveniles accounted for 52 percent of all juvenile contacts with the police in the city and 70 percent of all juvenile contacts involving felony offenses.[2] This led to the idea that there was a small group of active "career criminals" who accounted for a very large portion of crime.[3] This in turn led to the idea that crime rates could be reduced dramatically by locking these chronic offenders up.[4] Subsequently, a great deal of money was poured into research that attempted to develop these ideas so they could form the basis for practical crime policies.

Although the distinction was unclear at first, the ideas of "career criminals" and "criminal careers" are very different. A *career criminal* is thought to be a chronic offender who commits frequent crimes over a long period of time. In contrast, the term *criminal career* does not imply anything about the frequency or seriousness of the offending. It simply suggests that involvement in criminal activity begins at some point in a person's life, continues for a certain length of time, and then ends. Many people have short and trivial "criminal careers"—they commit one or two minor offenses and then stop.

The Panel on Research on Criminal Careers introduced a new set of terms with which to describe criminal behavior in the context of a criminal career. *Participation* refers to whether a person has ever committed a crime—it can only be "yes" or "no." *Prevalence* is the fraction of a group of people (such as all those under 18 years of age) that has ever

---

1. Alfred Blumstein, Jacqueline Cohen, Jeffrey A. Roth, and Christy A. Visher, *Criminal Careers and "Career Criminals"*, National Academy Press, Washington, D.C., 1986.

2. Marvin Wolfgang, Robert Figlio, and Thorsten Sellin, *Delinquency in a Birth Cohort*, University of Chicago Press, Chicago, 1972.

3. The idea of a career offender dates much further back than the Wolfgang et al. study, but it was this study that spurred new enthusiasm in the area. See Michael Gottfredson and Travis Hirschi, "The True Value of Lambda Would Appear to Be Zero: An Essay on Career Criminals, Criminal Careers, Selective Incapacitation, Cohort Studies, and Related Topics," *Criminology* 24(2): 213–33 (1986).

4. In actual fact, the Philadelphia study did not support this conclusion. See Thomas J. Bernard and R. Richard Ritti, "Selective Incapacitation and the Philadelphia Birth Cohort Study," *Journal of Research in Crime and Delinquency* 28(1): 33–54 (1991).

participated in crime. *Frequency* (symbolized by the Greek letter lambda) refers to the rate of criminal activity of those who engage in crime, measured by the number of offenses over time. *Seriousness*, of course, concerns the severity of one's offenses. *Onset* and *desistance* refer to the beginning and end of a criminal career, while *duration* refers to the length of time between onset and desistance.

The first major use of this new language system was to interpret the aggregate relationship between age and crime, which set off the "Great Debate" mentioned above. It has long been known that crime rates rise rapidly throughout the adolescent years, peak in the late teens or early twenties, and steadily decline from then on. The traditional view has been that the decline in this curve after about age 20 is due primarily to changes in frequency—i.e., the number of offenders remains the same but each offender commits fewer offenses. In contrast, career criminal researchers suggest that the decline is caused by a change in participation—i.e., the number of offenders declines but each remaining offender still engages in a high rate of offending. If these researchers are right, then those offenders who continue to commit crimes at high levels after their early 20s are "career criminals" who need to be incapacitated. On the other hand, if all offenders gradually commit fewer crimes, then none of them are "career criminals" in the sense of being a more frequent and chronic offender than the others.

This interpretation of the age-crime relationship also has another implication. Because some offenders always participate whereas others end their careers early, it may be necessary to develop different models for predicting participation and frequency. It may be that one set of factors influences whether someone participates in crime, whereas another set of factors affects the frequency and duration of their criminal acts.

Essentially, this represents the central contentions of the two sides in the "great debate" mentioned above. On the one side were the career criminal researchers, notably Alfred Blumstein, Jacqueline Cohen, and David Farrington, while on the other side most notably were Michael Gottfredson and Travis Hirschi.[5] Gottfredson and Hirschi took

---

5. This debate can be reviewed in a series of articles: Alfred Blumstein and Jacqueline Cohen, "Estimation of Individual Crime Rates from Arrest Records," *Journal of Criminal Law and Criminology* 70: 561–85 (1979); Travis Hirschi and Michael Gottfredson, "Age and the Explanation of Crime," *American Journal of Sociology* 89: 552–84 (1983); David Greenberg, "Age, Crime, and Social Explanation," *American Journal of Sociology* 91(1): 1–21 (1985); Gottfredson and Hirschi, "The True Value of Lambda Would Appear to Be Zero: An Essay on Career Criminals, Criminal Careers, Selective Incapacitation, Cohort Studies, and Related Topics," *Criminology* 24(2): 213–33 (1986); Blumstein, Cohen, and David Farrington, "Criminal Career Research: Its Value for Criminology," *Criminology* 26(1): 1–35 (1988); Gottfredson and Hirschi, "Science, Public Policy, and the Career Paradigm," *Criminology* 26(1): 37–55 (1988); Blumstein, Cohen, and Farrington, "Longitudinal and Criminal Career Research: Further Clarifications," *Criminology* 26(1): 57–73 (1988).

the position that, independent of other sociological explanations, age simply matures people out of crime. The decline of crime with age therefore is due to the declining frequency of offenses among all active offenders, rather than declines in the number of active offenders. Because of this, Gottfredson and Hirschi argue that there is no reason to attempt to identify and selectively incapacitate "career criminals."

The debate on the relationship between age and crime led to a particularly ferocious dispute about the type of research that is required to test out these theories. Much prior research in criminology looked at aggregate crime rates—for example, burglary rates in a given city. But these aggregate rates say nothing about whether burglaries are committed by a small number of offenders who each commit a large number of burglaries or by a large number of offenders who each commit only a few. To answer this question, career criminal criminologists focused on the patterns of crimes committed by individual criminals over a period of time, rather than on aggregate crime rates within a particular location.[6] In particular, they tended to use "longitudinal research," which follows the same individuals over a long period of time. An early example of longitudinal research, as discussed in Chapter 4, was carried out by the Gluecks, who followed the lives of 500 delinquents and 500 nondelinquents over many years, attempting to assess why some juveniles become delinquent or criminal and others do not.[7]

In contrast, most other criminologists have used "cross sectional" research, which compares different individuals at the same time. For example, criminologists might examine a number of juveniles in a particular city, find out which juveniles commit the most offenses, and assess what types of factors are associated with those juveniles. Cross-sectional research is much cheaper than longitudinal research since it can be done at one time. Gottfredson and Hirschi argue that because the age-crime relationship is invariant, cross-sectional research is sufficient, and it is an unnecessary waste of resources to collect information about the same individuals over a long time period.[8] Other criminologists, however, believe that longitudinal data collection and analysis can be beneficial to

6. This was based on their view "that crime is committed by individuals, even when they organize into groups, and that individuals are the focus of criminal justice decisions" (Blumstein et al., op. cit., p. 12).

7. Sheldon Glueck and Eleanor Glueck, *500 Criminal Careers* (New York: Knopf, 1930); *Juvenile Delinquents Grown Up* (Commonwealth Fund, New York, 1940); *Unraveling Juvenile Delinquency* (Harvard University Press, Cambridge, 1950); and *Delinquents and Nondelinquents in Perspective* (Harvard University Press, Cambridge, 1968).

8. Michael Gottfredson and Travis Hirschi, "The Methodological Adequacy of Longitudinal Research on Crime," *Criminology* 25(3): 581–614 (1987).

the study of criminal behavior.[9] They argue that cross-sectional designs only allow the study of correlates of criminal behavior, whereas longitudinal designs allow for the study of causation because they can establish which factors came first. Longitudinal research also allows one to assess the extent to which prior behavior influences present and future behavior. Additionally, it allows assessment of whether different models are necessary to explain behavior at different points in the life course.

CRIMINAL PROPENSITY VS. CRIMINAL CAREER

After considerable thrashing about, the age-crime debate described previously boiled down to a debate between the "criminal propensity" and the "criminal career" positions. Gottfredson and Hirschi espouse the *criminal propensity* position. Essentially, they argue that some people are more prone to commit crime and other people are less prone, but everyone's propensity to commit crime is relatively stable over their life course after the age of about 4 or 5. That propensity might manifest itself in a variety of patterns of behavior, due to chance and circumstances, so that individuals with the same propensity might actually commit somewhat different amounts and types of crime. But because criminal propensity is essentially constant over the life course, it is unnecessary to explain such factors as age of onset of crime, duration of a criminal career, and frequency of offending. Actual variations in the amount of offending by given individuals then are explained primarily by their point on the age-crime curve. Everyone will follow the age-crime curve, in the sense that they all will have their greatest criminal involvement in their late teens and decline thereafter. But over the entire age curve, those with the lowest propensity always will have the lowest actual involvement with crime, while those with the highest propensity always will have the highest actual involvement. Thus, the age-crime curve, combined with variations in the propensity to commit crime, looks like Figure 17–1.

Gottfredson and Hirschi argue that the age-crime curve itself is invariant and does not require any explanation. Therefore, all that is required is to explain why different people have different criminal propensities.[10] And because criminal propensity does not vary over the life

9. See, for example, Scott Menard and Delbert Elliott, "Longitudinal and Cross-Sectional Data Collection and Analysis in the Study of Crime and Delinquency," *Justice Quarterly* 7(1): 11–55 (1990).

10. In *A General Theory of Crime* (Stanford: Stanford University Press, 1990) Gottfredson and Hirschi argue that the propensity toward crime is a product of low self-control, and allow for variation in the effect propensity has on actual behavior by introducing opportunity into their model. Low self-control only brings about criminal behavior when opportunities for such behavior are present. See Ch. 13, pp. 213–17.

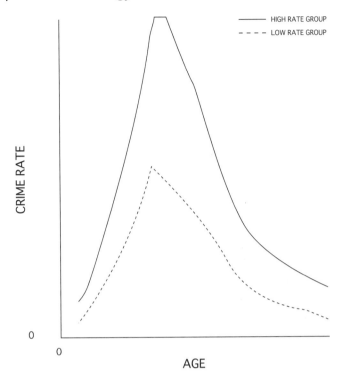

FIGURE 17–1 Hypothesized relation among age, propensity, and crime. (From Travis Hirschi and Michael Gottfredson, "Age and the Explanation of Crime," *American Journal of Sociology* 89[3]: 565 [1983]. Reprinted by permission.)

course, the explanation can be tested with cross-sectional research, and there is no need for the more expensive longitudinal designs. This is the context for their theory of low self-control, as presented in Chapter 13.

In contrast to the criminal propensity position is the *criminal career* position, which we have previously discussed. According to this position, different sets of variables may explain behavior at different points in the life course. Thus it is necessary to build separate models for age of onset, participation, frequency, duration, and desistance. To some extent, then, the debate focused on whether the entire "criminal career" could be explained with a single causal theory (the "criminal propensity" position) or whether different causal processes were at work at different points in the life span (the "criminal career" position). In particular, the debate took on the focus of whether it was necessary to have separate causal models for participation and frequency, since those were the two crucial factors in the two contrasting explanations of the age-crime curve.

Once the age-crime relationship debate was established as one that posed criminal propensity and criminal career positions against each other, researchers went to work attempting to garner support for one or the other position. Although the issue is not yet resolved,[11] there is some preliminary evidence supporting both positions.

Probably the strongest evidence for the criminal propensity position comes from Rowe, Osgood, and Nicewander, who fit a latent trait model to crime data.[12] A latent trait is a quality that is unobservable, but can be inferred through various measures. If it exists, then the inherent propensity to commit crime would be a latent trait because, for a given person, there is no way to directly observe it. The question, of course, is whether it exists at all. The way Rowe et al. decided to test this was to make certain assumptions about the latent "criminal propensity" trait and then use those assumptions to predict how criminal activity would be distributed among offenders if such a trait actually existed. They then compared those predictions with the actual distribution of offenses that had been found in four different cities. Rowe et al.'s model was basically atheoretical in that it did not discuss where this latent propensity toward criminal behavior comes from. Instead it was just a test to see if such a propensity may exist. According to the propensity position, such a trait should account for differences in both one's likelihood to participate in criminal behavior and one's frequency of participation, since both of these outcomes stem from the same source. Applying their models to four different sets of data on individual behavior, Rowe et al. found solid support for the propensity position.[13]

In contrast, researchers who examined the criminal career position attempted to determine whether the separate components of criminal careers required different causal explanations. Unlike the propensity po-

11. D. Wayne Osgood and David Rowe have recently attempted to lay out a detailed guide of how researchers may begin to competitively test the propensity and criminal career positions, in "Bridging Criminal Careers, Theory, and Policy Through Latent Variable Models of Individual Offending," *Criminology* 32(4) 517–54 (1994).

12. David Rowe, D. Wayne Osgood, and W. Alan Nicewander, "A Latent Trait Approach to Unifying Criminal Careers," *Criminology* 28(2): 237–70 (1990). These researchers define propensity in terms of the relative stability of causal factors (p. 241).

13. In each data set, there is a distribution of how many offenders committed zero, one, two, etc. offenses. For example, in Wolfgang's Philadelphia cohort, 65 percent of the cohort committed zero offenses, whereas 2.3 percent were responsible for nine or more. Rowe et al.'s study assumes that latent propensities are normally distributed, that the relationship between one's propensity to engage in crime and rate of offending (lambda) is exponential, and that the relationship between lambda and observed offending can be modeled with a Poisson distribution (a probabilistic distribution of relatively rare events occurring over a continuum of time). Combining these probabilistic relationships, the authors produced frequency distributions that were very similar to actual distributions of offenses in data sets from Philadelphia, London, Richmond (Calif.), and Racine (Wis.). While this represents strong support, it also should be noted that the validity of such modeling depends on the validity of the assumptions described above.

sition, these scholars usually tried to operate within at least some sort of theoretical framework. For example, Smith, Visher, and Jarjoura examined the influence that variables from labeling, control, and differential association theories had on the different components of the criminal career: participation, frequency, and persistence (continuation of offending beyond initiation).[14] According to the criminal career perspective, different causal processes should be responsible for these different components. These authors found that differential association variables applied in the same fashion to each of the indicators, but differences occurred in the other two theoretical arenas. For example, negative peer labeling was associated with persistence but not frequency of delinquent behavior. After demonstrating that "...at least three dimensions of delinquency . . . have some common and some unique correlates"[15] the authors were reluctant to make definitive statements about the accuracy of the criminal career position. A more recent empirical examination of initiation and continuation of delinquency resulted in the same conclusion, that there are some similarities and some differences across models of the different types of indicators of delinquency.[16]

Criminal career proponents also hypothesized that criminal careers may consist of variation in offense specialization and seriousness, such that some offenders may tend to progress toward the concentration on one or a few offense types, and may tend to escalate toward more serious offenses. Blumstein, Cohen, Das, and Moitra have demonstrated that adult offenders tend to specialize (especially with drug and fraud offenses) and for some crime types (such as assault) would escalate toward more serious behaviors.[17] These patterns only held for white offenders, however; as a possible explanation for the race difference, they speculated that blacks may specialize as juveniles, and their study only addressed adult offending.[18]

THE TRANSITION TO DEVELOPMENTAL CRIMINOLOGY

During the height of the debate over the age-crime relationship, Tittle called for an increased reliance on theory:

14. Douglas Smith, Christy Visher, and G. Roger Jarjoura, "Dimensions of Delinquency: Exploring the Correlates of Participation, Frequency, and Persistence of Delinquent Behavior," *Journal of Research in Crime and Delinquency* 28(2): 6–32 (1991).

15. *Ibid.*, p. 29.

16. Douglas Smith and Robert Brame, "On the Initiation and Continuation of Delinquency," *Criminology* 32(4): 607–29 (1994).

17. Alfred Blumstein, Jacqueline Cohen, Somnath Das, and Soumyo Moitra, "Specialization and Seriousness During Adult Criminal Careers", *Journal of Quantitative Criminology* 4(4): 303–45 (1988).

18. *Ibid.*, pp. 342–43.

Gottfredson and Hirschi assert that the criminal careers concept and, by implication, its associated research are without theoretical import. This is astonishing! . . . It is equally curious that Blumstein et al., contend that the criminal
careers concept and research are theoretically significant, but without showing
how . . . where is the actual theory? . . . We have theorists who refuse to theorize and we have researchers who acknowledge they should theorize but
don't. . . . It is clear enough to most of the rest of us that issues of age and
crime are amenable to social explanation and that such explanation ought to
be the main goal of criminological work bearing on the age/crime phenomenon.[19]

Tittle suggests that two theories may best be able to support the criminal career position: labeling and control (see Chapters 13 and 14 for a
description of these theories). Labeling theory implies that dynamic
processes are at work over one's life development, such that the longitudinal study of criminal careers would be necessary to explore it. Actions are met with reactions by one's referential groups (peers, society,
etc.). The informal and formal reactions subsequently affect one's future behavior. Such a theory inherently requires a longitudinal perspective. Labeling theory can explain both the drop-off in participation
in late adolescence and the existence of a chronic offender. In the first
case, those who commit crimes during adolescence but who are not
caught and labeled may end up with a noncriminal identity and eventually desist from such behavior. Those who are caught, sanctioned, and
labeled, on the other hand, may revert from primary to secondary deviance, as Lemert suggests, and become steady offenders.[20]

Tittle also argues that social control theory may be able to explain the
age-crime relationship from the criminal career perspective. Many people bond to their parents as a child and hence do not engage in criminal behavior, but as they enter adolescence these bonds are reduced.
In this period they cannot bond to conventional adult society, and their
weakened bonds with their parents allow the possibility for them to engage in delinquent behavior. As they leave adolescence, however, they
develop other kinds of bonds and once again become "straight." Those
individuals who were not well bonded as children may be unable to "re-
bond" after adolescence, and thus may represent chronic offenders.[21]
Tittle is careful to point out that both of these explanations (labeling

---

19. Charles Tittle, "Two Empirical Regularities (Maybe) in Search of an Explanation: Commentary on the Age/Crime Debate," *Criminology* 26(1): 78 (1988).

20. *Ibid.*, pp. 79–80.

21. *Ibid.*, pp. 81–82.

and control) are only possibilities, but at least they ground the age-crime relationship in a theoretical context.

More recently, Nagin and Land, in a piece of research that found support for both the criminal career and propensity positions, suggested that "a moratorium should be called on strong either-or theoretical positions on the nature of criminal careers and that theoretical and empirical efforts should be directed instead to new challenges."[22] And indeed, although some scholars are still attempting to compete the two positions against each other, there is clearly a developmental criminology forming, one which has strong roots in developmental psychology, and one which is oriented toward originating new theories that treat crimes as social events in the life course.[23] As new developmental theories are being built and evaluated, the criminal career-criminal propensity polarity is becoming less central to theorists.

This is not to say that the work on criminal careers is irrelevant to modern developmental criminologists. On the contrary, it is this debate that has brought about the new enthusiasm for a developmental criminology. The terminology of the criminal career paradigm has been directly adopted by those pursuing theory development from the developmental perspective. For example, in Rolf Loeber and Marc Le Blanc's comprehensive review of the developmental literature and argument for a developmental criminology, they organize their review around the following terms: activation, aggravation, and desistance.[24] These concepts are closely akin to the core concepts of the criminal career paradigm. Activation refers to the continuity, frequency, and diversity of criminal activities. It consists of acceleration (increased frequency), stabilization (continuity over time), and diversification (of criminal activities). Aggravation is a developmental sequence that escalates in seriousness over time. Desistance refers to a decrease in the frequency of offending, a

22. Daniel Nagin and Kenneth Land, "Age, Criminal Careers, and Population Heterogeneity: Specification and Estimation of a Nonparametric, Mixed Poisson Model," *Criminology* 32(3): 357 (1993).

23. One of the first attempts to direct research away from the criminal career debate was made by John Hagan and Alberto Palloni ("Crimes as Social Events in the Life Course: Reconceiving a Criminological Controversy," *Criminology* 26[1]: 87–100, [1988]). These authors suggest that the field of criminology substitute the idea of "social events" for "criminal careers," looking at the causes and consequences of behavior in the life course, either in the short or long run. This calls for the broadening of the foci of criminological theories from behaviors labeled criminal or delinquent to antisocial behaviors in general.

24. Rolf Loeber and Marc Le Blanc, "Toward a Developmental Criminology," in *Crime and Justice: A Review of Research*, eds. Michael Tonry and Norval Morris, vol. 12, University of Chicago Press, Chicago, 1990, pp. 375–473. The division of concepts into activation, aggravation, and desistance is attributed to Marc Le Blanc and M. Fréchette, *Male Criminality Activity from Childhood through Youth: Multilevel and Developmental Perspectives*, Springer-Verlag, New York, 1988.

reduction in its diversification (specialization), and a reduction in its seriousness.

In the following sections we review two developmental theories, which each contribute a different twist.[25] Thornberry's interactional theory explores the relationship between past and present criminal behavior, shows how causal processes of delinquent behavior are dynamic and different forces shape each other over time, and shows that causal influences may depend on the period of an individual's life. Sampson and Laub's longitudinal study pays special attention to the tension between stability and change perspectives in developmental psychology and criminology. They argue that although prior behavior is a strong determinant of present and future behavior, turning points in individuals' lives do exist, and change (both positive and negative) can occur at any point in a developmental sequence.

THORNBERRY'S INTERACTIONAL THEORY

Thornberry's interactional theory combines control and social learning theories (see Chapters 12 and 13), attempting to increase their collective ability to explain delinquent behavior.[26] To Thornberry, these theories are flawed by their reliance on unidirectional causal structures. He attempts to develop a model in which concepts from these theories affect each other over time, reciprocally, and in which actual delinquent behavior also reciprocally affects the theoretical concepts. Also, Thornberry believes that the contributing causes to delinquent behavior will change over an individual's life course.

Interactional theory is based mostly on control theory, viewing social constraints as the primary cause of delinquency. However, reduced social constraints may free up behavior but delinquency still "requires an interactive setting in which (it) is learned, performed, and reinforced."[27] The theory is comprised of six concepts from control and social learning theory: attachment to parents, commitment to school, belief in conventional values, association with delinquent peers, adopting delinquent values, and engagement in delinquent behavior. Three models are of-

25. Two other important developmental theories are by G. R. Patterson, Barbara DeBaryshe, and Elizabeth Ramsey, "A Developmental Perspective on Antisocial Behavior," *American Psychologist* 44(2): pp. 329–35 (1989); and Terrie Moffitt, "Adolescence-Limited and Life-Course-Persistent Antisocial Behavior: A Developmental Taxonomy," *Psychological Review* 100(4): 674–701 (1993). Moffitt's theory is briefly described in Chapter 7.

26. Terrence Thornberry, "Toward an Interactional Theory of Delinquency," *Criminology* 25(4): 863–87 (1987). An earlier version of this section is found in Thomas J. Bernard and Jeffrey Snipes, "Theoretical Integration in Criminology," in Michael Tonry, ed., *Crime and Justice: A Review of Research*, University of Chicago Press, Chicago, 1996, pp. 314–16.

27. Thornberry, op. cit., p. 865.

fered, for early adolescence (11–13), middle adolescence (15–16), and late adolescence (18–20). The division of a theory into different models for different phases in this manner is one of the distinguishing characteristics of developmental theory.

Thornberry's main goal in interactional theory is to sort out the debate between control and social learning theorists: the former argue that delinquent behavior affects the peers one attaches to; the latter argue that one's peer associations affect delinquent behavior. Thornberry argues that peer associations may affect behavior, but behavior in turn can influence one's selection of peers. In interactional theory concepts from control theory are the most important contributors, because delinquency will probably not occur unless social constraints are reduced. Thus, the greater one's attachment to parents and commitment to school, the less likely one is to engage in delinquent behavior. Belief in conventional values is influenced by both attachment and commitment, and it affects delinquent behavior indirectly, through its reciprocal influence on commitment to school. Delinquent behavior negatively influences attachment and commitment. It also influences belief in conventional values, indirectly through its influence on attachment. As Thornberry says, ". . . while the weakening of the bond to conventional society may be an initial cause of delinquency, delinquency eventually becomes its own indirect cause precisely because of its ability to weaken further the person's bonds to family, school, and conventional beliefs."[28]

Also included in Thornberry's interactional theory are hypotheses about how models of delinquency might vary over the adolescent time period. Generally, the models for early, middle, and late adolescence are not very different; however, he does note a few expected disparities.[29] In middle adolescence, attachment to parents is expected to play a smaller role, since the adolescent is more involved in activities outside the home. Also, delinquent values are expected to exert a more important influence on commitment, delinquent behavior, and association with delinquent peers than they do in early adolescence, since these values have had more time to solidify. In late adolescence, two variables are added to the model: commitment to conventional activities such as employment, college, and military service, and commitment to family, such as marriage and having children. These variables essentially supplant attachment to parents and commitment to school, since they are more relevant during this time period in an individual's life.

28. *Ibid.*, p. 876.
29. *Ibid.*, pp. 877–82.

Interactional theory has been partially tested: Although the full theoretical model has not yet been tested, Thornberry and his colleagues have published longitudinal tests of the relationships between the control theory concepts and delinquency and of the relationships between the learning theory concepts and delinquency.[30] They have reported general support for the reciprocal relationship between both control and learning concepts and delinquent behavior. One interesting finding is that past delinquent behavior influences present behavior in two ways. First, it has a direct effect, independent of any of the social variables in the model. Second, it has an indirect effect through the way it influences the control and learning variables, which in turn change behavior. The exact nature of the relationship between past and present (or present and future) delinquent or criminal behavior is of extreme interest to developmental criminologists.

SAMPSON AND LAUB'S AGE-GRADED THEORY OF INFORMAL SOCIAL CONTROL

In their study of 500 delinquents and 500 nondelinquents described previously, Sheldon and Eleanor Glueck gathered and analyzed one of the most comprehensive data sets of individuals available in the area of criminology, publishing findings from this data from the 1930s through the 1970s. Their primary goal was to assess the factors most related to juvenile delinquency. Even though the Gluecks had excellent data with which to work, their analyses have been criticized on methodological grounds. In 1985, John Laub located the original Glueck data, and he and Robert Sampson spent several years reconstructing and reanalyzing it, responding to many of the methodological criticisms. From their secondary analysis of these data came a major developmental study, in which the authors developed a longitudinal theory of delinquency and crime, and used both quantitative and qualitative methods to support their arguments.[31]

The theory has three components, relating to the life phases of the individual. The first component explains juvenile delinquency; the sec-

30. Terrence Thornberry, Alan Lizotte, Marvin Krohin, and S. J. Jang, "Testing Interactional Theory: An Examination of Reciprocal Causal Relationships among Family, School, and Delinquency," *Journal of Criminal Law and Criminology* 82: 3–35 (1991); and "Delinquent Peers, Beliefs, and Delinquent Behavior: A Longitudinal Test of Interactional Theory," *Criminology* 32(1): 47–83 (1994).

31. Robert Sampson and John Laub, *Crime in the Making: Pathways and Turning Points Through Life*, Cambridge: Harvard University Press, 1993. See also John Laub and Robert Sampson, "Turning Points in the Life Course: Why Change Matters to the Study of Crime," *Criminology* 31(3): 301–26 (1993); and Sampson and Laub, "Crime and Deviance in the Life Course," *Annual Review of Sociology* 18: 63–84 (1992).

ond explores behavioral transitions undergone as juveniles become adults; and the final component explains adult criminal behavior.

Juvenile delinquency, argue Sampson and Laub, is best explained by the individual's family context, and by his or her school, peers, and siblings. The most important family context factors influencing delinquency are erratic and harsh discipline by parents, mother's lack of supervision, parental rejection of child, and child's emotional rejection of his or her parents. These family factors may be influenced themselves by structural characteristics, such as a crowded household, low family SES, high residential mobility, parental criminality, family disruption, family size, foreign-born status of the family, and the mother's employment status. The effect of these structural variables on delinquency is indirect, as they are mediated by the process variables (such as harsh discipline).[32]

These structural factors are also expected to influence variables that relate to one's school, peers, and siblings. Disadvantaged structural conditions may result in weak attachment to school, poor performance in school, attachment to delinquent siblings, and attachment to delinquent peers. All these may in turn increase the likelihood of delinquent behavior.[33]

The remainder of Sampson and Laub's theory pertains to stability and change in the life course. They try to make sense of the apparent paradox that the best predictor of adult criminal behavior is childhood antisocial behavior and juvenile delinquency, but yet most delinquents do not become criminals as adults. For example, Robins has stated that "Adult antisocial behaviour virtually *requires* childhood antisocial behaviour [yet] most antisocial youths do *not* become antisocial adults."[34] Sampson and Laub argue that stability between adolescence and adulthood is a result of cumulative and interactional continuity, as delinquency "closes doors," reducing opportunities for positive life changes. They also state that childhood delinquency reduces the likelihood of positive adult social bonding, which in turn increases the potential for adult criminal behavior. This continuity, they argue, is independent of social class, background, family, and school factors.[35]

Despite the evidence of stability, Sampson and Laub also argue that change is common in the life course, that juvenile delinquents often do not turn out to be adult criminals, and that adult behavior can change

32. Sampson and Laub, *Crime in the Making*, pp. 65–71.

33. *Ibid.*, pp. 101–6.

34. Lee Robins, "Sturdy Childhood Predictors of Adult Antisocial Behaviour: Replications from Longitudinal Studies," *Psychological Medicine* 8: 611 (1978). See also Moffitt, op. cit., p. 676.

35. *Ibid.*, pp. 123–25. A similar argument is found in Moffitt, op. cit.

as well. As adults, the quality and strength of social ties is the strongest influence on whether one will engage in criminal behavior. Attachments to a spouse, job stability and commitment, dependence on an employer, and other such factors, will reduce the likelihood of criminal behavior. They refer to these social bonds as Coleman does,[36] calling them *social capital*, which pertains to relations among persons, and can be viewed as social investment. Even though juvenile delinquency negatively influences adult social capital, the development of social bonds as an adult can reduce the likelihood of crime, independent of one's childhood experiences. Thus, while one may be disadvantaged by one's past, he or she is not totally constrained by it.

Sampson and Laub's empirical analysis of the Gluecks' data found general support for their developmental theory.[37] The strongest effects on delinquency were family, school, and peer factors, which were influenced somewhat by structural variables. Structural variables did not have much of a direct effect on delinquency, instead influencing delinquency through their effect on these informal social control variables. As expected, childhood delinquency was an important predictor of adult criminal behavior. Independent of one's past, the development of strong social bonds as an adult reduced the likelihood of crime and deviance.

CONCLUSION

Although developmental psychology has been around for a long time, developmental criminology is fairly new and it will take some time to assess how much support for it is garnered within the criminological community. Despite the tentative status of developmental theories within criminology, these theories are the basis for enormous funding by agencies that sponsor criminology research. In particular, the Project on Human Development in Chicago Neighborhoods, funded jointly by the MacArthur Foundation and the National Institute of Justice,[38] is eventually expected to cost around $80 million. This project attempts to look not only at community contextual influences on individuals, but also individual change over time, examining multiple pathways that peo-

---

36. James Coleman, "Social Capital in the Creation of Human Capital," *American Journal of Sociology* 94: 95–120 (1988). See the discussion in Ch. 10, p. 151.

37. Sampson and Laub, op. cit., pp. 247–49.

38. For a description of this project, see "Massive Study Will Trace Developmental Factors That Cause or Prevent Criminality," *NIJ Reports*, 220 2–4: (May–June 1990); David L. Wheeler, "Looking Beyond the Causes of Violence, Researchers Investigate Ways to Prevent It," *Chronicle of Higher Education*, Nov. 4, 1992, pp. A7–A9; and Ellen K. Coughlin, "Pathways to Crime," *Chronicle of Higher Education*, April 27, 1994, pp. A6–A7. In the Coughlin article, Michael H. Tonry is quoted as saying: "By a factor of 10, maybe by a factor of 20, it's the largest social-science research project ever undertaken in this country concerning crime and delinquency."

ple can take into and out of antisocial, delinquent, and criminal behavior. The study is unique in that it will look at how the changing relationship between an individual's development and his or her community's development may affect one's likelihood to engage in delinquency or crime. It is not expected to be completed until 2003.

Developmental theories of crime attempt to demonstrate that a single theory does not work well when explaining crime, because those factors that influence criminal behavior depend on what phase of the life course an individual is in. Thus, either multiple theories are necessary, or at the minimum, developmental characteristics need to be taken into account by any theory that attempts to explain crime at the individual level. The ultimate goal is to increase the power of criminology theories to explain crime. The other way to incorporate multiple theories in an effort to increase explanatory power is simply to integrate them with each other. This is the subject of the next chapter.

CHAPTER 18

Integrated Theories

As the preceding chapters amply demonstrate, there are a very large number of theories in criminology.[1] Most criminologists believe that the way to reduce the number of theories is by falsifying some of them. According to this view, different theories make contradictory predictions. These contradictory predictions can be tested against each other by research, by determining which predictions are consistent with the data and which are not. Theories whose predictions are inconsistent with the data are falsified and can be discarded, reducing the total number of theories. This is the "falsification" process.

Other criminologists, however, believe that, for a variety of practical reasons, the falsification process has failed to work. These criminologists turn to integration as a way to reduce the number of theories. They argue that the different theories do not contradict each other, but focus on different aspects of the same phenomenon and therefore make different predictions about it. The different theories therefore can be combined through integration into a smaller number of "larger" theories. These criminologists also argue that, by combining theories, the resulting theories will be more "powerful" in the sense that they can explain more of the variation in crime. Integration then is an alternative to falsification as a way to reduce the number of theories in criminology.

Most theories "integrate" at least some previously existing material in their arguments, so there is no firm and fast line between integrated theories and other theories. But we present here several different the-

---

1. Earlier versions of several of the sections in this chapter are found in Thomas J. Bernard and Jeffrey B. Snipes, "Theoretical Integration in Criminology," in Michael Tonry, ed., *Crime and Justice: A Review of Research*, University of Chicago Press, Chicago, 1996, pp. 301–48. This article also includes a more extensive history of the integration debate.

ories that reasonably can be described as integrated theories, in order to facilitate further discussion of integration in general.

ELLIOTT ET AL.'S INTEGRATED THEORY

Elliott and his colleagues opened the current round of debate on integration by publishing an article that explicitly attempted to combine strain, control, and social learning perspectives to explain delinquency and drug use with greater power.[2] They accomplish this by first integrating strain with social control theories, then by integrating social learning theories with control theory, and finally by combining all three.

The first step involved integrating strain and control theories. Elliott et al. described strain theories as making the argument "that delinquency is a response to actual or anticipated failure to achieve socially induced needs or goals (status, wealth, power, social acceptance, etc.)." Control theory, in contrast, holds that the strength of an individual's conventional social bonds is inversely related to the probability that the individual will engage in delinquent behavior. Thus, control theory assumes constant motivation to commit crime and focuses on the strength of bonding to conventional others, while strain theory assumes constant bonding to conventional others and focuses on the strength of the motivation to commit crime.

Elliott et al. integrate these two arguments in several ways. They argue that delinquency should be highest when an individual experiences strong strain *and* weak control. They also assert that strain is one of the sources of weak social controls—i.e., strain weakens a person's bonds to conventional others. They agree that other sources of weak social controls include inadequate socialization and social disorganization, an argument that is found in control theories. But Elliott et al. add that social disorganization also increases the likelihood of strain.

The second step involved integrating social learning theories and control theories. Where control theory focuses on the strength of conventional bonds, social learning theory is interested in the relative balance between conventional and deviant bonds. It suggests that delinquency is affected by the balance between the rewards and punishments associated with both conforming and deviant patterns of behavior. Adolescents receive rewards and punishments for their behavior primarily from

2. Delbert S. Elliott, Suzanne S. Ageton, and Rachelle J. Cantor, "An Integrated Theoretical Perspective on Delinquent Behavior," *Journal of Research in Crime and Delinquency* 16: 3–27 (1979); Elliott, David Huizinga, and Ageton, *Explaining Delinquency and Drug Use*, Sage, Beverly Hills, Calif., 1985; Elliott, "The Assumption That Theories Can Be Combined with Increased Explanatory Power," pp. 123–49 in Robert F. Meier, ed., *Theoretical Methods in Criminology*, Sage, Beverly Hills, Calif., 1985.

families, schools, and peers. While families and schools generally reinforce conventional behavior, peer groups are more likely to reinforce deviant behavior.

Elliott et al. integrate social control and social learning theories by arguing that an individual can form strong or weak bonds to conventional or deviant groups. Deviant behavior, they argue, is most likely when the individual has strong bonds to deviant groups and weak bonds to conventional groups, while it is least likely when the individual has strong bonds to conventional groups and weak bonds to deviant groups.

The third step in integrating strain, control, and social learning theories is to propose a single line of causation that includes variables from all three theories (see Figure 18–1). Strain, inadequate socialization, and social disorganization are all said to lead to weak conventional bonding. This then leads to strong delinquent bonding, which, in turn, leads to delinquent behavior. Strain can also directly affect strong delinquent bonding, as at least some strain theories argue, but Elliott et al. argued that most of the effect of strain operates through the weak conventional bonding. In addition, weak conventional bonding can directly affect delinquent behavior, as control theories argue, but Elliott et al. argued that most of its effect operates through the strong delinquent bonding.

The authors identify the integrated model with the social control rather than the social learning perspective, reasoning that the control perspective is more general and can explain deviance across levels of explanation, and that it is more sociological in that it places great importance on the role of institutional structures in controlling deviant behavior. They then supported their model with longitudinal data from the National Youth Survey. They found *no* direct effects of strain and social control concepts on delinquent behavior. Instead, most of the variance in delinquent behavior was explained by bonding to delinquent peers.

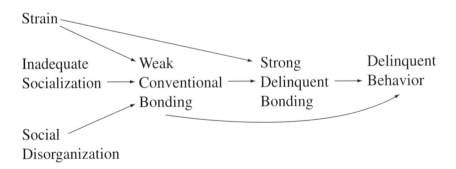

FIGURE 18–1   From Delbert S. Elliott, David Huizinga, and Suzanne S. Ageton, *Explaining Delinquency and Drug Use*, Sage, Beverly Hills, CA, 1985, p. 66.

Much of the debate about the usefulness of integrating criminology theories has swirled around Elliott et al.'s initial effort. The most prominent critic has been Hirschi, who argued that strain, control, and social learning theories fundamentally contradict each other and therefore cannot be integrated without fundamentally distorting one or more of the theories.[3] Hirschi particularly was concerned that Elliott et al. had distorted control theory. This theory includes a fundamental argument that the motivation to crime is rooted in human nature and therefore does not vary from person to person. In Hirschi's view, Elliott et al. could falsify this assertion by demonstrating that the motivation to crime does vary, but they cannot simply "integrate" control theory with strain theories, which explains crime in terms of variations in the motivation to commit it. Similarly, if the motivation to commit crime does not vary, then the bonding to deviant others will have no effect on the likelihood of committing crime. Elliott et al. can falsify control theory by demonstrating that deviant bonding does affect delinquency (a finding that they report), but they cannot simply "integrate" control theories with a theory that makes the opposite assertion. While Elliott et al.'s integration attempt has been the subject of extensive debate, the other integrated theories described below are much more recent and not subject to such analysis.

BRAITHWAITE'S THEORY OF REINTEGRATIVE SHAMING

A second example of an integrative theory is Braithwaite's theory of reintegrative shaming, which draws on labeling, subcultural, opportunity, control, differential association, and social learning theories. Rather than simply combining concepts from earlier theories, as Elliott and his colleagues did, Braithwaite creates a new theoretical concept—reintegrative shaming—and shows how it fits into a web of other theoretical concepts.

Braithwaite describes shaming as "all social processes of expressing disapproval which have the intention or effect of invoking remorse in the person being shamed and/or condemnation by others who become aware of the shaming."[4] He then divides shaming into two types: stigmatization (when the shaming brings about a feeling of deviancy in the shamed) and reintegration (when the shamers ensure that they maintain bonds with the shamed). Reintegrative shaming occurs when the violator is shamed into knowing what he or she did is wrong but is also

3. Travis Hirschi, "Separate but Unequal is Better," *Journal of Research in Crime and Delinquency* 16: 34–38, 1979.

4. John Braithwaite, *Crime, Shame, and Reintegration*, Cambridge University Press, Cambridge, U.K., 1989, p. 100.

allowed reentry into the conforming group. The core argument of the theory is that reintegrative shaming leads to lower crime rates, whereas stigmatizing shaming leads to higher crime rates. Braithwaite uses this argument to explain many different types of crimes involving the victimization of some individuals by others, but he does not use it to explain "victimless" crimes.

Braithwaite then describes how other criminology theories are related to this core argument. Individuals with more social bonding are more likely to receive reintegrative shaming and thus less likely to commit crime. Labeling theory is drawn on to explain stigmatization, and once an individual is stigmatized, he or she is more likely to participate in a deviant subculture, and thus more likely to commit crime. The theory also acts on a structural level. Greater urbanization and mobility (from social disorganization theory) lessen the chance that "societal communitarianism" will exist. Communitarianism, or interdependency among individuals in a culture, tends to be associated with reintegration, while the lack of it leads to stigmatization. This in turn results in blocked legitimate opportunities, formation of subcultures, presence of illegitimate opportunities, and higher crime rates.

Because Braithwaite's theory is fairly recent, it has not yet received much discussion in the literature, nor has it been subjected to much empirical testing. Several criticisms have been offered, sparking some exploration of potential problems with the theory.[5] The first test of integrative theory finds support for the relationship between reintegrative shaming and criminal behavior (in this case, nursing home compliance with the law).[6] However, this is the only link it examines, and so the relationship between shaming and concepts from other theories remains unexplored.

TITTLE'S CONTROL BALANCE THEORY

Charles Tittle proposes a general theory of deviance that integrates essential elements from differential association, Merton's anomie, Marxian conflict, social control, labeling, deterrence, and routine activities theories.[7] He first argues that each of these theories is defensible in its own terms, but each is incomplete in that it does not answer questions

---

5. See Christopher Uggen, "Reintegrating Braithwaite: Shame and Consensus in Criminological Theory," *Law & Social Inquiry* 18: 481–500 (1993). Braithwaite's comment and a response by Uggen follows.

6. Toni Makkai and John Braithwaite, "The Dialectics of Corporate Deterrence," *Journal of Research in Crime and Delinquency*, 31(4): 347–73, 1994.

7. Charles R. Tittle, *Control Balance: Toward a General Theory of Deviance*, Westview Press, Boulder, Colo., 1995.

the other theories are designed to answer.[8] He then argues that an adequate theory must be able to explain a broad range of deviant behaviors, must fully account for those behaviors, must be precise in its causal arguments (e.g., including statements about when those processes operate with greater or lesser force and the time intervals between causes and effects), and must explain the entire causal chain and not simply start with preexisting causes that themselves are not explained.[9]

Like Braithwaite, Tittle then proposes a new concept around which to integrate the propositions from earlier, simpler theories: control balance. His central assertion is that "the amount of control to which an individual is subject, relative to the amount of control he or she can exercise, determines the probability of deviance occurring as well as the type of deviance likely to occur."[10] This accepts the premise of traditional control theories (like Hirschi's) that controls are the central concept in explaining conformity.[11] However, it contradicts those theories by asserting that control also is a central motivating factor that explains deviance: people who are controlled by others tend to engage in deviance to escape that control, while people who exercise control over others tend to engage in deviance in order to extend that control.[12] In this theory, then, conformity is associated with "control balance" rather than with control itself. That is, people are likely to engage in conforming behavior when the control they exert over others is approximately equal to the control that others exert over them. This results in a U-shaped curve with the most deviance being committed by those who have the greatest control and those who have the least.[13]

Tittle defines deviance as "any behavior that the majority of a given group regards as unacceptable or that typically evokes a collective response of a negative type."[14] But rather than explaining deviance as a single construct, he divides it into six types: predation, exploitation, defiance, plunder, decadence, and submission.[15]

8. Ibid., pp. 1–16.

9. Ibid., pp. 17–53.

10. Ibid., p. 135.

11. Ibid., p. 142.

12. Ibid., p. 143. Tittle defines "being controlled" as "a continuous variable conveying the extent to which expression of one's desires or impulses is potentially *limited* by other people's abilities (whether actually exercised or not) to help, or reward, or hinder, or punish, or by the physical and social arrangements of the world." He defines "exercising control" as "a continuous variable reflecting the degree to which one can limit other people's realization of their goals or can escape limitations on one's own behavioral motivations that stem from the actions of others or from physical or social arrangements."

13. Ibid., p. 183.

14. Ibid., p. 124.

15. Ibid., pp. 137–41.

Predation involves direct physical violence or manipulation to take property, and includes such behaviors as theft, rape, robbery, fraud, and homicide. Exploitation is indirect predation, where the exploiter uses others to do the "dirty work." Examples are contract killings, price-fixing, and political corruption. Defiance occurs when individuals revolt against norms or values, by engaging in such acts as violating curfews, vandalism, political protests, and "sullenness by a marital partner." Acts of plunder are typically undertaken by people without much of a social conscience, are considered to be particularly heinous, and include such behaviors as destroying fields to hunt for foxes, pollution by oil companies, and unrealistic taxes imposed by occupying armies. Decadence refers to behavior that is unpredictable and viewed by most as irrational; examples are group sex with children and sadistic torture. Acts of submission involve "passive, unthinking, slavish obedience to the expectations, commands, or anticipated desires of others."[16] Examples are eating slop on command or allowing one's self to be sexually degraded. One may question whether several of the acts described in these categories are deviant (such as eating slop on command). According to Tittle, the theory explains more than deviance: It explains submission, decadence, and the other categories. Thus, an act may be submissive and not necessarily deviant but still be explained by the theory.[17]

There are four primary concepts employed in control balance theory: predisposition, provocation, opportunity, and constraint. Predisposition toward deviant motivation includes one's desire for autonomy and his or her control ratio, which is the "amount of control to which the person is subject relative to the amount that he or she can exercise."[18] Tittle deems one's desire for autonomy as relevant to predisposition, but notes it varies very little across individuals. Varying more dramatically across individuals is the control ratio. Within each individual, it may be fairly stable overall, but can also vary from situation to situation, since different contextual circumstances may arise, affecting the balance of control.

Provocations are "contextual features that cause people to become more keenly cognizant of their control ratios and the possibilities of altering them through deviant behavior..."[19] Examples include verbal insults or challenges. Constraint refers to the likelihood that potential control will actually be exercised (compared to the control ratio, which

16. Ibid., p. 139.
17. Ibid., p. 140.
18. Ibid., p. 145.
19. Ibid., p. 163.

refers to potential control and not actual control). Finally, opportunity is defined in the traditional manner, relating to the circumstances under which it is feasible to commit a given act. For example, it is difficult to rape if there are no people present, or it is difficult to burglarize with no dwellings around.

The causal processes comprising control balance theory are fairly complex, so we shall limit this discussion to the core theoretical mechanisms. Deviant behavior occurs when one attempts to alter his or her control ratio, whether temporarily or permanently. Thus, deviance serves a purpose for the person committing it. When the amount of control exercised is roughly the same as the amount of control one is subjected to, control balance occurs, and the probability of deviance is low. But when the ratio is not balanced (in either direction), the likelihood of deviance increases at a rate proportional to the degree of imbalance. Motivation drives the likelihood of deviant behavior, and motivation is influenced strongly by the control balance ratio. Other variables, such as provocations, constraint, and opportunity also converge in influencing the actual probability of deviance occurring, but one's motivation (and predisposition toward motivation) are the most important contributing factors to deviance.

Control balance theory explains type of deviance in addition to likelihood of deviance. Those with a balanced ratio are likely to conform. Those who have a higher ratio of autonomy to repression (are more likely to exercise control than to be controlled) are likely to engage in exploitation (minimal imbalance), plunder (medium imbalance), or decadence (maximum imbalance). Those who have a lower ratio of autonomy to repression (are more likely to be controlled than to exercise control) are likely to engage in predation (marginal imbalance), defiance (moderate imbalance), and submission (extreme imbalance). A question that immediately comes to mind is why the most serious forms of deviance (such as predation) are coupled with the slightest imbalances. Tittle explains this by saying that when control deficits are small, people will be able to commit more serious acts of deviance without as much fear of controlling response than if they had larger control deficits. People with marginal control deficits will usually be deterred from deviant acts, but when they do commit them, according to Tittle, they will be more serious in nature. People with more extreme control deficits will be "less able to imagine that such behavior will escape controlling responses from others,"[20] and thus their deviance will take less serious forms (such as submission and defiance). Similarly, people with control

20. Ibid., p. 187.

surplus (more autonomy than repression) will commit acts of deviance with seriousness that is in proportion to how controlled they are. Individuals with only a slight advantage will feel more limited in the extent to which they can exercise control, and will commit less serious acts (exploitation, compared to plunder and decadence).

Tittle's theory is too recent to have been subject to criticism or testing. Our brief summary of it masks its complexity as well as Tittle's exertion in building a neatly structured theory. Much of his book is devoted to detailing the requisites of a good theory and showing how most criminological theories lack some of the features of solid theory. He then builds control balance theory with these features in mind (breadth, comprehensiveness, precision, and depth) and provides an important chapter that discusses the contingencies of control balance theory (under what conditions might certain causal mechanisms not work). Tittle's theory does a nice job of explaining deviance committed by several segments of society, including both skid-row bums and political and corporate criminals.

VILA'S GENERAL PARADIGM

One of the broadest and most complex approaches to integration is taken by Brian Vila.[21] According to Vila, if a theory is to be general enough to explain all criminal behavior, it must be ecological, integrative, developmental, and must include both micro-level and macro-level explanations. An ecological theory considers the interconnection of individuals and their physical environment. A developmental theory allows for changes in the causes of crime as well as changes in crime itself over time, particularly as related to the age of the individual. Integrative theories allow for the inclusion of factors from multiple disciplines and from multiple theories. Finally, theories that use concepts at more than one level of explanation recognize that within-person variation, variation in social structure, and variation in the person-structure interaction all can affect individual behavior. Vila reviews a number of theories that meet at least two of these conditions, but shows that no theory to date meets all of them. Therefore, he calls existing criminology theories "partial theories."

21. Brian Vila, "A General Paradigm for Understanding Criminal Behavior: Extending Evolutionary Ecological Theory," *Criminology* 32(3): 311–60 (1994). Vila's theory is an extension of Lawrence E. Cohen and Richard Machalek, "A General Theory of Expropriative Crime," *American Journal of Sociology* 94: 465–501 (1988). Cohen and Machalek only attempted to explain expropriative crimes, such as theft and embezzlement, whereas Vila tries to explain all crime. Vila does not describe his approach as a theory; rather, he describes it as a paradigmatic model from which theory should develop.

Vila argues that biological factors must be included in any theory[22] so he criticizes developmental theories such as Sampson and Laub's[23] for ignoring their role. Not only must individual genetic traits be considered in a general theory, but intergenerational transmission of these traits must be considered as well. For this reason, the effect of biological factors may be lagged over lengthy periods.

Vila also criticizes existing theories for not allowing macro-level correlates of crime (such as social disorganization) to vary over time. Because macro-level contributors are dynamic, an individual's position in society is in flux. Ecological contributors to crime, such as opportunities provided by one's physical environment, also have the potential to change over an individual's lifetime.

Vila stresses the *interaction* of ecological, micro, and macro causal factors. For example, macro and micro factors might interact in the effect of cultural beliefs on parental style; macro and ecological factors might interact in the effect of sociocultural heterogeneity on opportunities for crime; and micro and ecological factors might interact in an individual attempting to modify his or her local environment. When allowing for both causal directions to occur across the three types of factors, the result is six types of two-way interaction terms.

A central assumption of the model is that all crime involves the seeking of resources. Expropriative crimes (such as theft and fraud) are aimed at acquiring material resources. Expressive crimes (such as sexual assault and drug use) are aimed at obtaining hedonistic resources. Economic crimes (such as illegal gambling and narcotics trafficking) are aimed at obtaining monetary resources. Political crimes (such as terrorism) are aimed at obtaining political resources. All crimes are committed with one or more of the following strategic styles: force, stealth, and fraud. The extent to which a person develops these styles depends on the interaction between biological, sociocultural, and developmental factors. All these affect the motivation toward crime, which is determined by how much resources a person has and how much that person desires. But only when an opportunity also exists to commit crime will the motivated individual commit a crime.

An interesting aspect of Vila's paradigm consists of its choice of an empirical method to assess theories that develop from the paradigm. Mathematical chaos theory, rather than traditional linear models, ac-

---

22. Ibid., pp. 328–30.

23. Robert J. Sampson and John H. Laub, *Crime in the Making: Pathways and Turning Points Through Life*, Harvard University Press, Cambridge, Mass., 1993. See the discussion of this theory in Chapter 17, pp. 296–98.

cording to Vila, will best predict the development of criminality over an individual's life. Chaos theory is appropriate because initial conditions (such as early childhood experiences with parental style) set off trajectories of behavior. Thus, initial conditions are more important than most subsequent events in influencing long-term behavior. General linear models cannot appropriately model this pattern.

On one hand, Vila's paradigm is frustratingly general. The sense one gets is that everything affects everything and that these effects are continuously changing over time. On the other hand, it is intuitively appealing, because criminality is so much more complex than any of the major criminological theories allow for. The evolutionary ecological paradigm incorporates the complexity of human behavior, but a question we must answer is: Are social scientists capable of testing theories that are as complex as required by this paradigm?

BERNARD AND SNIPES'S INTEGRATED MODEL

Bernard and Snipes chart a middle course between Hirschi's stance against integration and integrated theories like Vila's, which seem too complex to test.[24] Their goal is to interpret criminology theories in a way that allows them to be both broadly integrated and readily tested.

Hirschi argued that theories which contradict each other cannot be integrated with each other. He also argued that most criminology theories contradict each other, basing that argument on an interpretation of criminology theories that classifies them into three mutually exclusive categories: strain, control, or cultural deviance.[25] Bernard and Snipes agree that theories that contradict each other cannot be integrated, but they disagree with Hirschi's argument that most criminology theories contradict each other. In their view, the problem lies with Hirschi's interpretation and classification of criminology theories, not with the theories themselves.

According to Hirschi's interpretation, "strain" theories are social psychological theories in which frustration functions as an independent variable at the individual level. But Bernard and Snipes argue that most so-called "strain" theories make a macro-level social structural argument linking rates and distributions of crime to socially structured contexts. In general, these theories argue that social structures shape people's self-interests and that people tend to follow their self-interests, but most of these theories make no causal argument about frustration and crime at the individual level. Hirschi also describes "cultural deviance" theo-

24. Bernard and Snipes, op. cit.
25. Ibid., pp. 324–30.

ries as social psychological theories in which culture operates as an independent variable at the individual level. In contrast, Bernard and Snipes describe these theories as using shared cognitions as an intervening variable between social structural conditions and criminal behavior. Based on their interpretation of criminology theories, Bernard and Snipes conclude that these theories make different but not incompatible arguments, and therefore they can be broadly integrated with each other.

Bernard and Snipes also argue that criminologists should shift their focus from theories to variables. Hirschi had criticized criminologists for frequently treating different variables as if they were "owned" by different theories. For example, attachment is often treated as if it were "owned" by Hirschi's control theory. Researchers who find that attachment is related to crime in the way that Hirschi's theory describes often then conclude that Hirschi's theory has been validated. Bernard and Snipes agree with Hirschi's point but go even further. They argue that the only important question is: What variables are related to crime, and in what ways? For example, they would focus solely on whether attachment is related to criminal behavior, and in what way it is related. They therefore view the question of whether Hirschi's theory is valid or not as not particularly important. In fact, they view the question about Hirschi's theory as being counter-productive to the extent that it draws criminologists into endless and meaningless debates that waste everyone's time.

This approach places theory in its proper role in the scientific process. Theory interprets the results of past research by explaining why certain variables are related to other variables. More important, it charts the course of future research by hypothesizing about possible relationships among variables that research has not yet observed. In contrast, criminologists sometimes have treated theories as stable entities, meaningful and important in themselves. Depending on their point of view, they either validate or falsify them, but they do not see them as flexible tools, essential to the scientific process, but subject to revision and reinterpretation with each iteration of that process.

Bernard and Snipes propose a new interpretation of criminological theories to replace the strain/control/cultural deviance interpretation. Their new interpretation is based on the location of independent variation in the theory.[26] Criminology theories may contain independent variables that exist along a continuum from those that focus on indi-

---

26. They also discuss the direction of causality, since theories that argue different causal directions may be incompatible (p. 330).

vidual differences to those that focus on social structural characteristics. Despite the continuous nature of the variables themselves, the level of data used to test criminology theories is more clearly bifurcated: Most theories are tested using either individual-level data (such as self-report surveys) or aggregate-level data (such as official crime rates). Bernard and Snipes believe that levels of explanation are best interpreted in terms of the level of the data used to test the dependent and independent variables.[27] Most criminology theories require the same level of data for both the independent and dependent variables; thus, there are two main types of criminology theories: those using aggregate-level data and those using individual-level data. Societal-level theories link social structural characteristics to variations in the rates and distributions of crime and thus require aggregate-level data both in dependent and independent variables. Individual-level theories, in contrast, link individual characteristics to the probability that an individual will engage in criminal behaviors, and thus use individual-level data for both the dependent and independent variables.

Based on this argument, Bernard and Snipes argue that there are two categories of criminology theories: structure/process and individual difference theories. Structure/process theories explain variations in criminal behavior by variations in social structural characteristics, as manifested in the structured environment to which the individual responds.[28] Structural arguments link structural conditions to the rates and distributions of criminal behavior within a society, while process arguments explain why normal individuals who experience those structural conditions are more likely to engage in that behavior. This type of theory is based on three implicit assertions. First, crime is a response of individuals who are freely choosing and whose choices are constrained by the immediate environment. Second, the immediate environment is structured, in that its characteristics are causally related to the broader structural features of social organization. And third, criminals are "normal" in that they are similar to noncriminals in the processes by which they interact with the immediate environment and in the motives that direct their responses to the environment. Structure/process theories include those theories classified as "strain" and "cultural deviance," structural level control theories, and classical and rational choice theories, among others. They are theories that are at the aggregate level and use aggregate-level data.

27. Ibid., p. 332.

28. This definition is close to that of Ronald Akers, in *Deviant Behavior: A Social Learning Approach*, Wadsworth, Belmont, Calif. 1985. See Ch. 12, p. 197. See also structure/process arguments in the "Unified conflict theory of crime" (Ch. 15, p. 254) and in Sampson and Laub, op. cit. (Ch. 17, p. 297).

Individual difference theories, in contrast, are theories that use variations in characteristics of individuals to predict probabilities that the individual will commit crime. This type of theory is based on three implicit assertions. First, differences in the probability of engaging in crime are explained by differences that are uniquely attributed to the individual. Second, the individual characteristics may be explained by interactions with others within the environment, but the environment itself is not explained by social structural characteristics but by the characteristics of the persons within it. Third, since crime is explained by individual characteristics, criminals themselves are assumed to be different from noncriminals in some measurable ways. Examples of individual difference theories are biological and psychological theories of crime, Gottfredson and Hirschi's theory of low self-control, and to some extent, Hirschi's original control theory.

Structure/process and individual difference theories are not mutually exclusive. Individual difference theories generally do not argue that independent variation cannot be explained by structural characteristics. And structural variation theories generally do not argue that independent variation cannot be explained by individual differences. The appropriate relation between individual difference and structure/process theories is modeled by the relation between the theories of low self-control and routine activities. Routine activities theorists control for individual differences but do not deny their existence or their relation to the likelihood of engaging in crime. Rather, they assume that there is a "constant supply of motivated offenders" and that variations in the rates and distributions of crime can be explained solely by changes in the structured situation. In contrast, self-control theorists control for variations in the structure of the situation, but they do not deny the existence of such variations or their relationship to the rates and distributions of crime. Rather, they maintain that, within any given situation, people with certain characteristics are more likely to engage in crime than people with other characteristics.

Bernard and Snipes emphasize that the level of data analysis must correspond to the level of the theoretical argument in the theories. Individual-level theories cannot be tested with aggregate-level data, and structure/process theories cannot be tested with individual-level data. The first mistake is almost always avoided, but the second mistake is frequently made, in part because the strain/control/cultural deviance interpretation describes structure/process theories as making individual-level arguments.

Based on their interpretation of theories as being either individual difference or structure/process, Bernard and Snipes argue that competitive testing of criminology theories, in which two or more theories are tested against each other with the goal of falsifying one or more of them—is almost always inappropriate.[29] Structure/process theories cannot be tested against individual difference theories, since the level of data analysis must correspond to the level of the theoretical argument. Competitive testing of two or more individual difference theories seems inappropriate, because different theories make different but not necessarily contradictory predictions, since criminal behavior is explained by multiple factors. Competitive testing of two or more structure/process theories may also be inappropriate, for the same reason: There is "multiple-factor causation" for rates and distributions of crime, just as with individual criminal behavior. Because one theory is supported does not mean that other theories cannot be supported.

While competitive testing of theories within and between categories is almost always inappropriate, Bernard and Snipes argue that integration of theories, both within and between categories, is almost always possible.[30] Theories almost always control for variation explained by other types of theories rather than denying it. Structural arguments can be integrated with other structural arguments and individual difference theories with other individual difference theories, since the competition among these is empirical rather than theoretical. The question should be the extent to which each theory contributes to explaining criminal behavior or rates of crime, relative to the other theories. It is possible (and even likely) that many theories are all supported by the data, but some are more powerful than others in explaining the outcomes. The only theories that may contradict each other are processual theories, since it is possible to explain the same relationship with more than one process, or causal explanation. In this instance, competitive testing may be useful.

Although it seems theoretically possible to create a single theory of crime that incorporates structural conditions, processes, and individual characteristics, Bernard and Snipes do not argue that we should construct such a broad integration. Theories such as Vila's, discussed above, seem too broad to be subject to formal testing. Although individual difference and structure/process theories are not inherently contradictory, since they refer to different types of outcomes and different levels of data, integrating across these types raises an enormous set of complex-

29. Bernard and Snipes, pp. 338–41.
30. Ibid., pp. 341–43.

ities, and may be unwise at this point.[31] That is not to say that new theories (rather than integrations of old theories) that incorporate arguments at both levels of explanation should not be developed. In fact, multilevel theories will probably be the most useful explanations of criminal behavior.

CONCLUSION

Some criminologists may argue that focusing on variables rather than on theories will turn criminology into an atheoretical enterprise. Our view, in contrast, is that this is a practical approach in which theory assumes its proper role in the scientific process. It will allow criminology to increase the explanatory power of its theories and to identify practical policy implications of theories that ultimately might reduce crime.

In the next chapter, we present an overall assessment of criminology theories based on our integration model. That chapter therefore serves two purposes. First, it provides a conclusion to the entire book by presenting an interpretive overview of all the different theories in the book. Second, it provides a concrete illustration of our approach to interpreting and integrating criminology theories.

31. Ibid., pp. 342–43. On the other hand, for an example of scholarly work that includes both individual difference and structure/process theories in the context of a risk factor approach, see Robert J. Sampson and Janet L. Lauritsen, "Violent Victimization and Offending: Individual-, Situational-, and Community-Level Risk Factors," pp. 1–114 in Albert J. Reiss, Jr., and Jeffrey A. Roth, eds., *Understanding and Preventing Violence*, vol. 3, National Academy Press, Washington, D.C., 1994. For a similar approach, see the "Task Force Reports from the ASC to Attorney General Janet Reno," *The Criminologist* 20(6): 3–16 (Nov.–Dec. 1995).

CHAPTER 19

Assessing Criminology Theories

The different chapters in this book presented and discussed many different types of theories in criminology. At the end of each chapter, there was a brief assessment of the extent to which the theories in that chapter contributed to our understanding of crime. In this chapter, we present an overall assessment of the extent to which criminology theory, taken as a whole, contributes to our understanding of crime.

The basis for this assessment is our own model for interpreting and integrating criminology theories, as presented at the end of the last chapter.[1] This model includes a classification system that focuses on the sources of independent variation within the theory, rather than on the theoretical arguments per se. It described two types of theories: individual difference theories assert a relationship between the characteristics of individuals and the probabilities that those individuals will engage in criminal behavior, and structure/process theories assert a relationship between the characteristics of societal units and the rates and distributions of crime within those units. In this conclusion, we add a third type: theories of the behavior of criminal law. These theories seek to explain why some people and behaviors, and not others, are defined and processed as criminal.[2]

---

1. Thomas J. Bernard and Jeffrey B. Snipes, "Theoretical Integration in Criminology," *Crime and Justice: A Review of Research* 20:301–48 (1996).

2. Theories of the behavior of criminal law were not discussed in the Bernard and Snipes article due to space considerations (ibid., p. 343). However, integrating these theories with the other was discussed in Thomas J. Bernard, "A Theoretical Approach to Integration," pp. 137–59 in Steven F. Messner, Marvin D. Krohn, and Allen E. Liska, eds., *Theoretical Integration in the Study of Deviance and Crime*, State University of New York Press, Albany, N.Y., 1989.

SCIENCE, THEORY, RESEARCH, AND POLICY

As described in the first chapter of this book, the theories assessed here all take a naturalistic and scientific approach to the problem of crime. This approach describes relations among observable phenomena, so that the resulting theories can be falsified. We therefore do not consider in this chapter those theories which take a spiritualistic approach to the problem of crime, nor do we consider those postmodern and feminist theories that are nonscientific in their approach. This does necessarily mean we think these theories are invalid. Indeed, criminology and the larger society may benefit from the replacement discourses and the types of feminine thinking that stand in opposition to the scientific approach which we take here. But our overall goal in this chapter, and in this book in general, is to advance criminology as a science.

Our approach is also decidedly policy relevant. By interpreting theories in terms of their sources of independent variation and directions of causation, the policy options that might reduce crime become apparent. This has not always been the case in the past. Criminology theories, particularly of the structure/process type, often describe crime in terms that are intuitively appealing but which are not particularly clear in terms of what they are actually saying from a scientific or policy point of view.[3] The policy implications of the theory draw one's attention directly to the sources of independent variation within the theory. This focus on policy implications also is consistent with good theorizing since, as Lewin pointed out in his famous aphorism, there is nothing as practical as a good theory. In the context of this aphorism, this chapter could be interpreted as assessing the extent to which criminology theories are "good theories" in the sense of being practical.[4]

In this chapter, we do not make the traditional distinction between classical and positivist theories in criminology. In the first three chapters of this book, we initially made that distinction since it is deeply embedded in current views of the field. But we argued in Chapters 2 and 3 that classical theories really are scientific theories, focusing on the effects of punishment policies on crime rates. Therefore, this distinction between classical and positivist theories is artificial.

A more fundamental distinction is found in the two different approaches initially taken by Quetelet and Lombroso, as described in

---

3. See Jack Gibbs, "The Methodology of Theory Construction in Criminology," pp. 23–50 in Robert F. Meier, ed., *Theoretical Methods in Criminology*, Sage, Beverly Hills, Calif., 1985.

4. For an example of crime policies that are informed by criminology research, see "Critical Criminal Justice Issues: Task Force Reports for the ASC to Attorney General Janet Reno," *The Criminologist* 20(6): 3–16 (Nov./Dec. 1995).

Chapter 3. Quetelet initially looked at different areas of France and tried to determine which social characteristics were associated with higher or lower crime rates in those areas. Lombroso initially looked at criminals and tried to determine which individual characteristics were associated with more or less criminal behavior. By the end of their careers, both theorists had incorporated elements of the other's approach in their explanations of crime, which clearly indicates that these two approaches are not incompatible. Rather, they are entirely separate questions: Why are some people more or less likely to engage in crime than others, and why do some social units have higher or lower crime rates than others? These separate questions are the basis for what we call individual difference theories and structure/process theories.

In examining both types of theories, it is important to distinguish between *correlation* and *causation*. For example, in Lombroso's time, the crime problem in Italy was concentrated in the southern part of the country, where people had somewhat different physical features than the people who lived in the north. Lombroso therefore found a correlation between crime and certain physical features. He then went on to argue, based on Darwin's theory of evolution, that those physical characteristics were causally related to crime. It is now clear that Lombroso was right (at that particular time and place) to assert that there was a correlation between crime and physical features, but he was completely wrong to argue that those physical features were causally related to crime.

Our focus is always on causation rather than correlation. Individual difference theories assume that some people are more likely than others to engage in crime, regardless of the situation they are in. These theories therefore attempt to identify the individual characteristics that cause these differences in behavior. Structure/process theories assume that there are certain types of social situations that have higher crime rates regardless of the characteristics of the people who are in them. These theories therefore attempt to identify the social characteristics that cause these differences in crime rates. There is no contradiction between these two types of theories—they simply are separate scientific problems.[5]

---

5. This is roughly comparable to the approach taken in Albert J. Reiss and Jeffrey A. Roth, eds. *Understanding and Preventing Violence*, vol. 1, National Academy Press, Washington, D.C., 1993, ch. 3. See also Robert J. Sampson and Janet L. Lauritsen, "Violent Victimization and Offending: Individual-, Situational-, and Community-Level Risk Factors," pp. 1–114 in Reiss and Roth, eds., *Understanding and Preventing Violence*, vol. 3, National Academy Press, Washington, D.C., 1994.

INDIVIDUAL DIFFERENCE THEORIES

Many of the theories we have reviewed, particularly in the early chapters of this book, focused on characteristics of individuals which are thought to increase or decrease the probabilities that that individual will engage in crime. In reviewing these characteristics, it is important to keep in mind two points. First, none of these characteristics absolutely determines that the person will engage in crime. Most people with these characteristics do not engage in crime at all—it is just that people with these characteristics are somewhat more likely than other people to engage in crimes.[6] Second, while these characteristics may increase the probability a particular individual will engage in crime, they may have no effect on overall crime rates. This is similar to the situation with unemployment.[7] Certain factors may increase the probability an individual will be unemployed—e.g., poor education, motivation, and job skills. Most often, however, increases in unemployment rates are not caused by increases in the number of people with these characteristics. Instead, they are caused by societal characteristics that have nothing to do with the characteristics of individuals—e.g., interest rates, budget deficits, trade deficits, stock market prices. Similarly, increases in crime rates normally are not caused by increases in the number of people who have these characteristics. Factors associated with increases and decreases in crime rates are reviewed in the next section. With these two points in mind, we now review the individual difference theories discussed in the various chapters in this book.

While Lombroso's theories connecting crime to physical appearance are clearly false, the "body type" theories of Sheldon and Cortés are more difficult to assess. There seems to be some correlation between body type and likelihood of engaging in criminal behavior. However, we believe that this correlation probably is mediated by some other variables, such as personality or motivation. We conclude that physical appearance, in itself, is never actually a cause of crime, and therefore we suggest that theories focusing on physical appearance be abandoned.

Similar issues, although in a more complex form, arise with theories about intelligence. There are clear correlations between lower IQ scores and an increased likelihood of committing crime. The question is whether there is some sense in which low intelligence itself causes crime. This question is complicated by several empirical issues, which are re-

---

6. See, for example, David P. Farrington, "Early Predictors of Adolescent Aggression and Adult Violence," *Violence and Victims* 4: 79–100 (1989). This article gives percentages for a very large number of characteristics of those who engage in adolescent aggression, teenage violence, adult violence, and who have been convicted of a violent crime.

7. This analogy was presented in Chapter 3, pp. 36–37.

viewed in Chapter 6. For example, intelligence itself cannot be directly measured, and the principle measure of intelligence—IQ scores—may instead measure reading ability or the motivation to succeed at academic tasks. It is also complicated because the suggested causal paths between low intelligence and crime imply that low intelligence itself is not the causal factor. For example, one such causal path is through school failure. If this is the case, then school failure rather than low intelligence is the actual cause of crime. Given appropriate teaching techniques, children with low intelligence could succeed in school and would be no more likely to engage in crime than other children. At the same time, children with high intelligence can experience school failure for a variety of reasons, and then would be more likely to commit crime. Similarly, it has been suggested that low intelligence affects crime through the failure to learn higher cognitive skills, such as moral reasoning, empathy, or problem solving. But high intelligence children can fail to learn these cognitive skills for a variety of reasons, in which case they would be more likely to engage in crime. And delinquent children, who on the average score only eight IQ points lower than nondelinquent children, could be taught these cognitive skills with a little extra effort, much as children with learning disabilities are taught reading and math. If this were done, then low intelligence children would be no more likely to commit crime than other children. Again, the source of independent variation does not seem to lie in low intelligence itself, but in other factors. For these empirical and theoretical reasons, at this point we tentatively conclude that intelligence itself has no independent causal impact on crime.

A different situation exists with certain biological variables. In general, twin and adoption studies support the notion of a biological and hereditary impact on human behavior. But aside from these narrowly focused research designs, we are unable to measure the effect of hereditary factors on the probability of engaging in criminal behavior. If genetic research examining specific identifiable risk factors continues to develop at its current rate, it is possible that it may eventually contribute to an overall theory of individual differences.

Other studies of specific biological characteristics suggest some modest causal impacts on the likelihood of committing crime, including neurotransmitter imbalances such as low serotonin, hormone imbalances such as extra testosterone, central nervous system deficiencies such as frontal or temporal lobe dysfunction, and autonomic nervous system variations such as unusual reactions to anxiety. In addition, alcohol intake at least temporarily increases the likelihood of engaging in crime, as do many illegal drugs. Other biological factors seem to have long-term effects on the likelihood of criminal behavior, including ingesting some toxins such as lead, suffering certain types of head injuries, and pregnancy or birth complications.

All these have been linked—at least tenuously—to antisocial, deviant, or criminal behavior. However, the processes by which these variables are linked to criminal behavior are not well understood. One major problem lies in determining the direction of causation. For example, high testosterone levels may increase the likelihood of participating in crime, but it is also possible that participation in crime increases testosterone. In addition, testosterone may act on some third variable, such as social integration, which then causes crime. Thus, it is unclear whether high testosterone itself has a causal impact on crime.

Despite these many questions, it seems reasonable at this point to conclude that causal relationships exist between these biological characteristics and the probability of engaging in criminal behavior. If this is the case, then there are a variety of policy interventions that could reduce crime—e.g., prescribing lithium carbonate to increase serotonin levels. The major danger with these policy interventions is that they could be applied to offenders who have normal biology. For example, a very small portion of offenders may have low serotonin levels but, given the political nature of public policies, a very large portion of offenders could end up receiving lithium carbonate.

Psychoanalytic theories of criminal behavior may or may not have some validity, but they seem almost impossible to test. In addition, the sources of independent variation that they identify are not susceptible to practical interventions through crime policies. Thus, even if these theories are true, they are not useful. If "nothing is as useful as a good theory," these cannot be described as good theories, at least as they apply to crime.

In the past, results from personality tests have suggested that certain "personality types" are associated with an increased likelihood of committing criminal and delinquent behavior. But much of the time, these results seem to consist of applying fancy psychological labels to criminals. These fancy labels add nothing to our knowledge about the person or to our ability to do anything to reduce the criminal behavior. There may be some personality characteristics associated with an increased risk of engaging in criminal behavior, but research to date has not clearly determined what those are. At present, the best candidate may be impulsivity, which recent research consistently links to antisocial or criminal behavior. Impulsivity may be linked to other individual characteristics—e.g., Gottfredson and Hirschi argue that people who are impulsive, insensitive, physical (as opposed to mental), risk-taking, short-sighted, and nonverbal will have higher probabilities of committing crimes, while Moffitt pointed to impulsivity combined with "negative emotionality," in which people experience emotions such as anger and anxiety in a wider range of situations than other people. In addition, Walters described eight specific thinking patterns characterized by "a global sense of irresponsibility, self-indulgent interests, (and) an intrusive approach to interpersonal relationships."

At this point, we conclude that all these characteristics are at least somewhat linked to increased tendencies to commit crime. If this is the case, then various cognitive or cognitive-behavioral therapies might be able to change these patterns of responses, thus reducing the tendency to commit crime. Psychologists have also generally concluded that earlier childhood problem behaviors and poor parental child management techniques, such as harsh and inconsistent discipline, are both associated with increased likelihood of later criminal and delinquent behavior. If this is the case, then policy implications would focus on training parents in effective child-rearing techniques, and early cognitive-behavioral interventions with problem children.[8]

The above individual differences are derived from biological and psychological theories in criminology, but implications about individual differences can also be found in some sociological theories. For example, Akers's and Sutherland's theories suggest that people who associate with others who are engaged in and approve of criminal behavior are more likely to engage in it themselves. Agnew's strain theory suggests that people are more likely to engage in crime when they experience negative emotions, such as disappointment, depression, fear, and anger, because they are unable to escape from relationships and situations in which they are not treated the way they want. Various cultural theories suggest that certain shared cognitions may be associated with increased likelihood of committing crimes—e.g., the lower class "focal concerns" of trouble, toughness, smartness, excitement, fate, and autonomy; the exaggerated sense of "manliness" found in subcultures of violence; or the tendency to see threats everywhere and feel justified in responding to threats with extreme violence, as found in subcultures of angry aggression. Hirschi's control theory suggests that people who are more attached to others, more involved in conventional activities, have more to lose from committing crime, and have stronger beliefs in the moral validity of the law, are less likely to engage in criminal and delinquent behavior. These can be phrased in the reverse to indicate characteristics

---

8. See, for example, Peter W. Greenwood, Karyn E. Model, C. Peter Rydell, and James Chiesa, "Diverting Children from a Life of Crime," Rand Corporation, Santa Monica, Calif., 1996.

that increase the probability of committing crime. Finally, "lifestyle" theories suggest that certain characteristics increase the likelihood that a person will be a victim of crime: frequently being away from home, especially at night; engaging in public activities while away from home; and associating with people who are likely to commit crime.

To summarize, the following individual differences seem to be associated with increases in the probability of committing criminal behavior:

1. A history of early childhood problem behaviors and of being subjected to poor parental child-rearing techniques, such as harsh and inconsistent discipline; school failure and the failure to learn higher cognitive skills such as moral reasoning, empathy, and problem solving.
2. Certain neurotransmitter imbalances such as low serotonin, certain hormone imbalances such as high testosterone, central nervous system deficiencies such as frontal or temporal lobe dysfunction, and autonomic nervous system variations such as unusual reactions to anxiety.
3. Ingesting alcohol, many illegal drugs, and some toxins such as lead; head injuries, and pregnancy or birth complications.
4. Personality characteristics such as impulsivity, insensitivity, a physical and nonverbal orientation, and a tendency to take risks.
5. Thinking patterns that focus on trouble, toughness, smartness, excitement, fate, and autonomy; an exaggerated sense of "manliness"; a tendency to think in terms of short-term rather than long-term consequences; a tendency to see threats everywhere and to believe that it is appropriate to respond to threats with extreme violence.
6. Chronic physiological arousal and frequent experience of negative emotions, either because of an inability to escape from negative situations or because of a tendency to experience negative emotions in a wider range of situations than other people.
7. Association with others who are engaged in and approve of criminal behavior.
8. Weaker attachments to other people, less involvement in conventional activities, less to lose from committing crime, and weaker beliefs in the moral validity of the law.

Finally, the following individual differences seem to increase the probability that a person will be a victim of crime.

9. Frequently being away from home, especially at night; engaging in public activities while away from home; and associating with people who are likely to commit crime.

The competition among all these different theories is largely empirical, over which factors explain more and which explain less of the variation in crime. The relative contribution of each characteristic can be, and certainly is, often debated. As in some recent integrated theories, it is important to recognize both multiple causes (independent contributions from different theories) as well as interactive causes (synergistic contributions from different theories) in explaining crime. One particularly important area of interaction may be in the area of biosocial theory. This recognizes the independent impact of biological and social variables, as well as the interaction between them. The point is that certain biological characteristics may have a large impact on crime under some social circumstances, but little or no impact under others.

Integrating the various individual difference theories must be done with careful attention to the way in which the theories may fit together, especially with respect to causal order. The point is to clearly identify the sources of independent variation, and to eliminate other variables. The actual sources of independent variation become clear when thinking about policy recommendations derived from these theories. For example, as mentioned above, high testosterone levels may not actually increase criminal behavior, but instead may reduce social integration, which then increases criminal behavior. If this is true, then administering drugs to reduce testosterone will not reduce crime unless steps also are taken to increase social integration. At the same time, increasing social integration may reduce crime whether or not testosterone levels are reduced. In addition, certain subcultural beliefs may be causally related to crime, but those beliefs may themselves be caused by structural conditions. If that is true, then policies directed at changing the beliefs will be ineffective, since the beliefs will be continually regenerated by the structural conditions that generated them in the first place. Policies therefore must be directed instead at changing the structural conditions that generate those beliefs.

STRUCTURE/PROCESS THEORIES

In contrast to individual difference theories, we have also discussed a wide range of structure/process theories, especially in the later chapters of this book. These theories assume that there are some situations that are associated with higher crime rates, regardless of the characteristics of the individuals who are within them. The theories therefore attempt to identify variables in the situation itself that are associated with higher crime rates.

In discussing these theories, it is important to keep several points in mind. First, these theories tend to be more complex and descriptive, and it is sometimes hard to determine the location of independent variation. To the extent that is true, the policy recommendations of the theory will be vague. Second, these theories often have been interpreted and tested at the individual level. This necessarily involves some variation of the "ecological fallacy,"[9] and it has led to considerable confusion about the theories themselves. Third, situations with high crime rates often have a large number of variables, all of which are correlated with each other and all of which are correlated with crime—e.g., poverty, inequality, high residential mobility, single parent families, unemployment, poor and dense housing, the presence of gangs and illegal criminal opportunities, inadequate schools, and a lack of social services. It can be extremely difficult to determine which (if any) of these variables is causally related to high crime rates, and which have no causal impact on crime at all.[10] Finally, the number and complexity of these theories means that many are left out or shortchanged in the following discussion. For all these reasons, our summary of structure/process theories may evoke more disagreement and dissatisfaction than the summary of individual difference theories we just presented.

In spite of these daunting problems, we offer the following interpretation and assessment. In each case, we first assert that some structural characteristic is associated with some rate or distribution of crime. This is the "structure" portion of a structure/process theory. We then provide a brief description of the supposed reasons why normal people in this structural situation might have a greater probability of engaging in crime than people in other situations. This is the "process" portion of a structure/process theory.

Economic modernization and development are associated with higher property crime rates. Originally, Durkheim argued that the process by which normal people within this structural situation would engage in higher rates of crime involved normlessness associated with rapid social change, but now that argument appears to be incorrect. Rather, the process probably involves changes in the routine activities in which people engage, and in the wider range of opportunities for crime that exist in a developed society. In particular, as societies develop, people spend more time away from their homes, which exposes both them and their homes to victimization. In addition, people own much more property that is both valuable and portable and therefore can be stolen. Property crimes tend to increase until the society is quite highly developed, and then to hold steady at that very high level. The process involved in

9. W.S. Robinson, "Ecological Correlations and the Behavior of Individuals," *American Sociological Review* 15: 351–57 (June, 1950).

10. See the discussion of multicollinearity in Chapter 8.

stabilizing those crime rates probably involves the increasing effectiveness of counter-measures, such as target hardening, surveillance, alarm systems, and neighborhood watches. Since modernization probably is not a reversible process, these counter-measures are the only policy implications associated with this line of theory.

Economic modernization and development is not strongly associated with higher rates of violence. Many undeveloped societies are extremely violent and at least some developed societies have little violence. However, at least in its initial stages, economic development tends to be associated with a great deal of economic inequality, and economic inequality is associated with higher rates of violence. Thus, usually there is at least an initial burst of violent crime at the beginnings of economic development. Societies that retain a great deal of economic inequality after they are developed also tend to retain high rates of violent crime.

The association between economic inequality and high violent crime is sometimes asserted as a structural argument without any discussion of the process by which people who live in situations with high economic inequality come to commit high levels of violence. Other times, process arguments involving feelings of frustration or relative deprivation are presented. The policy implications of this structural argument involve reducing economic inequality to decrease the levels of violence in the society as a whole. Of course, this policy could also reduce the overall rate of economic growth in the society. If that is the case, it would be necessary to balance the gains associated with violence reduction against the losses associated with slower economic growth before implementing this policy.

In addition, societies whose cultures have a strong emphasis on the goal of material success while only a weak emphasis on adhering to the legitimate means will tend to have higher rates of instrumental crime than other societies. This is particularly true if the noneconomic institutions in the society (families, schools, jobs, and even politics) are all strongly affected by and even subservient to the needs of the economic system. If those societies also have social structures that unequally distribute the legitimate means among social groups, then the rates of instrumental crime will be distributed inversely to the distribution of the legitimate means. Finally, illegitimate means of achieving material success often develop in situations with few legitimate means. This includes delinquent and criminal gangs comprised of youths who aspire to make lots of money but have little expectation of being able to do so by legitimate means. Once illegitimate means develop, then rates of instrumental crime in those situations further increase. However, in areas where there are neither legitimate nor illegitimate means to achieve material success, there may be higher rates of violent crime.

On a separate but comparable matter, people in general and adolescents in particular seek to gain social status among their peers. People who are unable to achieve status according to conventional criteria tend to band together, create new criteria for distributing status, and then distribute status to themselves according to those new criteria. This may take different forms (e.g., computer nerds), but in high-crime neighborhoods with a strong cultural demand for material success but no legitimate opportunities to achieve that success, there may be a tendency to give status on the basis of the commission of criminal acts.

There has been a controversy about the processes by which these structural situations generate higher crime rates. The traditional view has been that people in these situations feel high frustration, and that the frustration itself generates higher crime rates. A more recent view is that people simply have a tendency to act in ways that are consistent with their self-interests, and that they therefore pursue material success or status by whatever means are available. In this second view, it does not matter whether people in these situations feel frustrated or not.

Policy implications of these theoretical arguments include changing the culture by reducing the emphasis on achieving material success and increasing the emphasis on adhering to the legitimate means. One way to do this would involve strengthening noneconomic institutions (families, schools, jobs, and politics), so that they are not so strongly influenced by the needs of the economic system. Another way is to attempt to arrange things so that social status is achieved by following the legitimate means. This, of course, would be quite tricky. In addition, policy implications involve changing social structures by equalizing the distribution of legitimate opportunities to achieve material success. This also can be quite tricky, as illustrated in the failures of the War on Poverty. Attempts to deal directly with illegitimate opportunity structures (e.g., illegal drug networks) will probably fail without first dealing with the larger culture and structure.

At the neighborhood level, particularly under conditions of economic development and economic inequality, with cultures emphasizing economic success and structures limiting access to it, crime is associated with social disorganization. High crime neighborhoods tend to have three structural characteristics: poverty, frequent residential mobility, and high family disruption. The process by which these structural characteristics result in high crime rates involves anonymity, lack of relationships among neighbors, and low participation in community organizations. Ultimately, this means that the neighbors are unable to achieve their own common values and goals—a condition described as social disorganization. The neighborhood then spirals into decay and crime. Policy implications of this theory include a variety of measures directed at changing the structural conditions giving rise to this situation. It would also be possible to directly address the neighborhood anonymity, but without addressing the structural conditions that generate this anonymity in the first place, such policies are unlikely to reduce crime.

Other shared cultural ideas, besides those involving the value of material success, can also be causally related to crime. In particular, when cultures and subcultures include ideas that justify the use of violence in a wide variety of situations, then one can expect higher rates of violent crime. Some of these cultural or subcultural ideas may be structurally generated. For example, the structural conditions of poverty, inner-city environments, racial discrimination, and social isolation may generate, in a process involving chronic high physiological arousal, the subcultural ideas that it is appropriate to become angry in a very wide variety of situations and that, once angry, it is appropriate to use extreme violence as retribution. If the subcultural ideas are structurally generated, then policy responses that attempt to deal directly with the ideas will fail. Instead, policy must address the structural conditions that generate these ideas in the first place. Other cultural or subcultural ideas may be unrelated to current structural conditions. For example, the exaggerated sense of "manliness" among Southern white males seems unrelated to any current structural conditions. Policy responses may directly address these ideas, for example, through the media.

The media, of course, may also serve to disseminate cultural ideas that are favorable to law violation. Both the techniques and rationalizations to commit crime can be repeatedly presented in a favorable light. This is particularly true for violent crime. In addition, media can create the impression that violence, even when it is legal, is the primary method for resolving interpersonal conflicts. When the media and other cultural institutions engage in these practices, one can expect higher rates of violence and crime in the society. The process by which this takes place involves social learning, which includes direct learning of the techniques and rationalizations, and indirect learning by observing the consequences of these behaviors when others commit them. Policy implications include encouraging or requiring the media to more consistently present images favorable to obeying the law and favorable to nonviolent methods of resolving interpersonal conflicts.

Finally, societies that rely on stigmatizing shaming, in which the bonds to the shamed person are permanently broken, will tend to have higher crime rates than those that rely on reintegrative shaming, in which the bonds to the shamed person are maintained and they are welcomed back into the societal community. The process involves the limitation of legitimate opportunities and the establishment of subcultures. And societies with a control balance (i.e., where people exert approximately as much control over others as is exerted over themselves) will tend to have less crime than those with a control imbalance (i.e., where some people exert a great deal of control over others while other people have little or no control over anything). The process here involves a natural tendency for people to extend their control over others. Whether societies engage in stigmatizing or reintegrative shaming, and whether or not they have a control balance, may be affected by a variety of other societal characteristics, such as economic inequality.

Marxist criminologists have argued that capitalism itself is a cause of crime. While the explosion of crime in the new nations of the former Soviet Union seem to support this notion, we tentatively conclude that this is not the case. Rather, crime probably is caused by the other above-described conditions, all of which may be associated with capitalism: economic development, economic inequality, a cultural emphasis on material success combined with structural limitations on access to legitimate means of achieving that success, neighborhood social disorganization, the dissemination of cultural values that approve of the use of violence in a wide variety of situations, the use of stigmatizing shaming, and the presence of control imbalances.

To summarize, the following structural arguments describe societal characteristics that seem to be associated with higher crime rates. Each structural argument is followed by a brief description of the processes that are said to operate in those structural situations that result in people in those situations, regardless of their individual characteristics, having an increased tendency to commit crime.

1. Economic modernization and development is associated with higher property crime rates. Property crime tends to increase until the society is quite highly developed, and then to hold steady at a high level. The processes that result in this pattern of crime involve changes in routine activities and in criminal opportunities, which eventually are balanced by the increasing effectiveness of countermeasures.

2. Economic inequality is associated with higher rates of violence. The process may involve feelings of frustration and relative deprivation.

3. Cultures that emphasize the goal of material success at the expense of adhering to legitimate means are associated with high rates of utilitarian crime; an unequal distribution of legitimate means is associated with an inverse dis-

tribution of utilitarian crime; in situations without legitimate means to economic success, the development of illegitimate means is associated with increased utilitarian crime while the lack of such development is associated with increased violent crime; in these structural situations, the inability to achieve status by conventional criteria is associated with status inversion and higher rates of nonutilitarian criminal behavior. The processes involved in these structural patterns either involve frustration or the simple tendency to engage in self-interested behavior.

4. Neighborhoods with poverty, frequent residential mobility, and family disruption have high crime rates. The processes involve neighborhood anonymity resulting in social disorganization.

5. Poverty, urban environments, racial discrimination, and social isolation are associated with high rates of extreme violence associated with trivial conflicts and insults. The process involves chronic physiological arousal, which generates cognitions about when it is appropriate to become angry and the extent of violence that is appropriately used when angry.

6. Media dissemination of techniques and rationalizations that are favorable to law violation are associated with increased rates of law violation. The process involves direct learning of techniques and rationalizations, and indirect learning by observing the consequences criminal behaviors have for others.

7. Societies that stigmatize deviants have higher crime rates than those that reintegrate them. The process involves blocked legitimate opportunities and the formation of subcultures.

8. Societies in which some people control others have higher crime rates than societies in which people control and are controlled by others in approximately equal amounts. The process involves people's natural tendency to expand their control.

Phrased in this way, the various structure/process theories do not seem to be incompatible with each other. It certainly may be true, and it is even quite likely, that some of the above arguments are false. But that is an empirical question about each particular assertion. Empirical support for one of these arguments would not imply a lack of support for any other argument. To that extent, depending on their empirical support, all these structural arguments can be "integrated" into a single theory that describes the characteristics of societies with higher or lower crime rates.

While many of the process arguments are similarly independent of each other, there is at least some tendency for them to actually contradict each other. The major example of such a contradiction is found in the traditional description of strain, control, and cultural deviance theories. These describe three different social psychological processes associated with criminal behavior. All these cannot be true at the same time, although it is possible that one or another is involved with specific subsets of the criminal population. At any rate, there is at least some role for competitive testing for process arguments, whereas there appears to be none whatsoever for the structural arguments.

Finally, there is no contradiction between these structure/process theories and the individual difference theories reviewed above. Nothing in the structure/process theories contradicts the assertion that there are some people who are more likely to engage in crime regardless of their situation. Similarly, nothing in the individual difference theories contradicts the assertion that there are some situations in which people, regardless of their individual characteristics, are more likely to engage in crime. These are separate assertions, so that both types of theories can be "integrated" in a larger theory of criminal behavior.

THEORIES OF THE BEHAVIOR OF CRIMINAL LAW

A number of arguments are made in various chapters of this book that have implications about how the criminal law itself behaves. These arguments are quite separate from arguments about the types of people who are more likely to commit crime, or the types of situations that are likely to have higher crime rates.

For example, Durkheim and Erikson argued that, in mechanical societies, law defines the moral boundaries of the society by excluding and punishing criminals and other deviants. In normal times, societies need a relatively constant level of punishment to maintain social solidarity. But when social solidarity is threatened, the punishment function can be expected to expand, regardless of the level of crime. This particular theory could be used to explain the fact that, in the last twenty years or so, crime rates in the United States have remained relatively constant but incarceration rates have increased sixfold. Durkheim's theory would suggest that this great expansion of incarceration is motivated by a threatened sense of social solidarity in the larger society, rather than by the perceived threat of crime itself.

Sutherland argued that the state responded to the victimizing behaviors of lower-class people with criminal sanctions, but responded to the victimizing behaviors of white-collar people with regulations and civil violations. The theory focused on the ability of white-collar groups to define the norms about what constitutes crime. Therefore, variation in the enactment and enforcement of criminal laws, rather than variations in victimizing behavior, explained the class distribution of official crime rates.

Non-Marxist conflict theories make a similar argument, but focus on interests rather than values or norms. According to this theory, people in both legislatures and criminal justice agencies act in ways that are consistent with their interests, where those interests are shaped by social structure. Evaluative ideas (including values and norms) also are shaped by interests, so that ultimately they influence what people think is right and wrong, good and bad, just and unjust, criminal and legal. Because of these interests, legislators and criminal justice agents are more likely to define the behaviors typical of low power groups as criminal, and the behaviors typical of high power groups as legal, independent of the actual harm the behaviors cause to life or property.

Conflict theory argues that the enactment and enforcement of criminal law is shaped by the distribution of political power. This is one element—stratification—in Black's much broader theory of the behavior of law. Black also argues that law is shaped by four other factors: morphology, organization, culture, and social control. Essentially, these characteristics define what is seen as "more serious" or "less serious" crimes. For example, Black would argue that crimes committed by an individual against an organization are seen as "more serious," and thus as deserving greater punishment, than comparable crimes committed by an organization against an individual. Similarly, crimes committed by a person without culture against a person who is highly cultured are generally seen as more serious, and thus deserving greater punishment, than comparable crimes committed by a person with high culture against a person who entirely lacks culture.

Finally, Marxist theories argue that, regardless of what other interests are served by the criminal law, it must serve the economic interests of the owners of the means of economic production. If the criminal law harms their economic interests, then the owners can simply move the means of production to a jurisdiction where their interests will be served. Thus, people who enact or enforce criminal laws that harm the economic interests of the owners of the means of production will find that they have impoverished themselves. This effectively gives the owners of the means of production veto power over the content of criminal law.

In addition to these explicit theories, many theories of criminal behavior contain implicit theories about the behavior of criminal law. For example, Gottfredson and Hirschi[11] describe "the nature of crime" as acts that involve simple and immediate gratification of desires but few long-term benefits, are exciting and risky but require little skill or planning, and generally produce few benefits for the offender while caus-

---

11. Michael Gottfredson and Travis Hirschi, *A General Theory of Crime*, Stanford University Press, Stanford, Calif., 1990, pp. 15–44, 89–91.

ing pain and suffering to the victim. They derive this "natural definition" from an analysis of the characteristics of ordinary crime. While this argument is phrased in terms of a natural law philosophy, it actually makes an implicit assertion about the behavior of criminal law enactment and enforcement agencies. Specifically, if Gottfredson and Hirschi are right, then legislators and criminal justice agents must generally define and process "low self-control" acts as criminal, but not "high self-control" acts. This is no longer a philosophical statement, but instead an empirical assertion.

From the point of view of a scientific criminology, there are advantages to translating Gottfredson and Hirschi's philosophical statement about the "nature of crime" into an empirical assertion about the behavior of criminal law: Empirical assertions can be tested with research. For example, it is clear that at least some actions that are "high self-control" are defined and processed as criminal. Reversing Gottfredson and Hirschi's statements, "high self-control" actions would be complex and involve delayed gratification of desires and few short-term benefits, are dull and safe while requiring considerable skill and planning, and generally produce large benefits for the offender while causing little pain and suffering to the victim. These are the characteristics of several types of white-collar crimes. If we are making empirical assertions about the behavior of criminal law, then we can examine why some "low self-control" actions are not defined and processed as criminal, while some "high self-control" actions are. It is more difficult to do that in the context of philosophical arguments about "the nature of crime." Like the rest of criminology, theories of the behavior of criminal law must move beyond philosophical statements and become scientific, so that its assertions are subject to empirical testing.

Summing up, the following are some assertions about the behavior of criminal law:

1. When social solidarity of a society is threatened, criminal punishment increases independent of whether crime increases.

2. The enactment and enforcement of criminal laws reflect the values and interests of individuals and groups in proportion to their political and economic power.

3. In addition to stratification, the quantity of law that is applied in particular cases is influenced by morphology, culture, organization, and the extent of other forms of social control.

4. Regardless of what other interests are served by the criminal law, it must serve the economic interests of the owners of the means of economic production.

5. Actions that involve simple and immediate gratification of desires but few long-term benefits, are exciting and risky but require little skill or planning, and generally produce few benefits for the offender while causing pain and suffering to the victim are more likely to be defined and processed as criminal than other actions.

These assertions about the behavior of criminal law are not necessarily incompatible with each other. If some of these assertions are supported by empirical research, it would not necessarily imply lack of support for other assertions. For example, it may be true that "low self-control" behaviors are more likely to be defined and processed as criminal, but it also may be true that people who lack political and economic power are more likely to be defined and processed as criminal. If both were true at the same time, then low self-control people who have very little power would have higher official crime rates than low self-control people who have a lot of power.

Theories of the behavior of criminal law do not contradict theories of criminal behavior. More than anything else, they ask a different question: Why are some behaviors and people, and not others, defined and processed as criminal? However, that separate question has implications for theories that address the causes of the behaviors that are officially defined and processed as criminal. For example, Gottfredson and Hirschi's theory of criminal behavior (criminals have low self-control) implies a theory of the behavior of criminal law (law enactment and enforcement officials define and process low self-control actions as criminal, but not high self-control actions). To the extent that their theory of the behavior of criminal law is wrong, then their theory of criminal behavior is also wrong because low self-control behavior would not be the same as criminal behavior.

Ultimately, criminologists must come up with theories that simultaneously explain the behavior of criminal law and the behavior of individual criminals. This could be described as a "unified theory of crime."[12] If Gottfredson and Hirschi's implicit theory of the behavior of criminal law is made explicit, then theirs is a unified theory of crime, since it includes coordinated explanations of why certain behaviors are defined and processed as criminal and why certain people engage in those behaviors. The relevant question then becomes the empirical adequacy of the theory: both their theory of how criminal law behaves and their theory of why individual criminals behave the way they do must be consistent with the observed data.

---

12. See Bernard, "A Theoretical Approach to Integration," op. cit. See also the "unified conflict theory of crime" in Chapter 15, pp. 253–55.

CONCLUSION

As the authors of this textbook, we believe that it is time to stop the widespread competitive testing of criminology theories, and to focus instead on integration by looking at theories in terms of their variables and the relations among them. The essential question should be: Which variables are related to crime, and in which ways? Once that question is identified, then theories of criminal behavior break out into two broad categories: individual difference and structure/process. Between categories, criminology theories are complementary and do not compete with each other at all. Within categories, most of the competition among the theories is empirical rather than theoretical. Thus, competitive testing of criminology theories is almost always inappropriate, and integration among theories is almost always possible.

Theories of the behavior of criminal law address an entirely separate question: why some people and behaviors, and not others, are defined and processed as criminal. Some explicit theories of the behavior of criminal law have been offered, but they are few and relatively undeveloped in comparison to theories of criminal behavior. In addition, theories of criminal behavior often contain implications that amount to implicit theories of the behavior of criminal law. All these theories tend to be relatively simplistic conceptions of how the criminal law enactment and enforcement process actually works. In the future, these theories must be based more closely on empirical research on the actual behavior of legislators and criminal justice agents. This will introduce a great deal of complexity into these theories that is not presently there. The theories themselves should then be empirically tested, as part of a scientific criminology.

Ultimately, theories of the behavior of criminal law must be integrated with theories of criminal behavior to produce unified theories of crime. These theories would offer coordinated and consistent explanations of why certain behaviors are defined and processed as criminal and why certain people engage in those behaviors. This would result in a more complex, empirically adequate, and policy-relevant understanding of the phenomenon of crime.

Subject Index

Name Index